From Lathes to Looms

*China's Industrial Policy in
Comparative Perspective, 1979-1982*

From Lathes to Looms

China's Industrial Policy in Comparative Perspective, 1979-1982

DOROTHY J. SOLINGER

Stanford University Press, Stanford, California

1991

Stanford University Press
Stanford, California
© 1991 by the Board of Trustees of the
Leland Stanford Junior University
Printed in the United States of America

CIP data appear at the end of the book

Preface

THIS BOOK WAS CONCEIVED and written in that heady, hopeful decade for China scholars of the 1980's. Access to policymakers, to local economic bureaucrats, and to intellectuals was unprecedented and exhilarating. All of this had several consequences for this project. Most basically, it meant that many interviewees were frank, patient, and exceedingly helpful, generous with their data and their time, and open in their explanations.

Their openness spurred me to want to show comparativists how in certain respects the workings of the Chinese political economy, as it struggled toward reform, could be understood along lines similar to those that provided insights about political economies in some noncommunist nations. I even imagined that the Chinese case might set a worthy example for handling certain problems in some noncommunist states.

Indeed, my first urge to write this book grew out of musing about the simultaneous but very dissimilar efforts to handle the burden of obsolete heavy industrial plant and facilities in Pittsburgh, where I then lived, and in China. The state-managed Chinese experience, with its bureaucratically guided mergers and conversions and the resulting apparently negligible unemployment, seemed to me the superior one. Starting from that vantage point, I elected to adopt a framework that eschewed the usual "communist studies" approach and to write in a very broadly cross-systemic vocabulary. Some of my chief findings emerged out of reading about France and Japan.

At the turn of the decade, however, the study has ironically proven to bear more messages for other now formerly socialist states than for the democracies. For with the fall of the old regimes, the experiment described here—of shifting investment toward consumer goods production—is one their lopsided economies must now confront as they plunge into their own restructuring processes.

The research this project involved reflects my association with a number of institutions. In the early 1980's, when I first got the inspiration to carry it out, I was working at the University of Pittsburgh in the University Center for International Studies. There I participated in its program on Regional Structural Change in International Perspective, arguing for the inclusion of China when everyone else was discussing Western Europe and Japan. The center's Contemporary China Program and its Asian Studies Program and the university's Research Development Fund awarded me grants for the summers of 1983 and 1984 to go to China to interview on this theme. Around that time Pittsburgh had established "sister city" ties with Wuhan in China, so I chose Wuhan, a large industrial center not unlike Pittsburgh, for my research site.

In the autumn of 1984, and again more briefly in the spring of 1985, I continued this work in Wuhan. A grant from the Committee on Scholarly Communication with the People's Republic of China enabled me to build on the contacts in the city's economic bureaucracy I had established with the generous assistance of the Wuhan Foreign Affairs Bureau to pursue my interviews in more depth. I also had excellent access then, before, and since to the Wuhan University Library. I am happy to have this chance to thank all the people who spoke with me, introduced me to others with useful information, and provided me with materials while I was in China during these four trips. They brought this project to life for me in a way that no other research experience I have had has done.

During the first nine months of 1985, as a Fellow at the Woodrow Wilson International Center for Scholars, I had the leisure to read comparatively on the politics of industrial policy and on the experiences with it in France and Japan. At the end of 1985, as a Visiting Research Associate at the University of Michigan's Center for Chinese Studies, I had the opportunity to test out my ideas with—and receive critical response from—that center's large and helpful group of China scholars.

Preface vii

The following summer, 1986, was spent at the London School of Economics, where as a Visiting Fellow I again had a chance to talk with a wide range of scholars working on similar themes. Most of my writing was done at the University of California at Irvine, where I received a Faculty Career Development Program grant that allowed me time off to write in the autumn of 1987. I am thankful for all this support, and I only hope this volume shows the effect of my associations with these many institutions.

Over several years of writing drafts I have built up a debt to many colleagues and friends who talked over my ideas with me, read a chapter, or worked through an entire draft. Douglas Ashford in Pittsburgh first suggested that I look at France and Japan when I told him of my plan to study China in conjunction with some capitalist countries. Ronald Brickman, David Easton, Harry Eckstein, Bernard Grofman, Seth Masters, Barry Naughton, and T. J. Pempel all helped me structure my thoughts at various points thereafter.

Edward Lincoln commented on my first effort at setting forth my comparative perspective for the research seminar in which I presented my work at the Wilson Center. Then, at the University of Michigan, Lenore Barkan, Robert Dernberger, Albert Feuerwerker, Kenneth Lieberthal, Donald Munro, Michel Oksenberg, Martin Whyte, and Michael Yahuda read this same paper and, in a seminar, questioned and challenged my early thinking. Michael Yahuda read versions and gave me criticisms of several of the early chapters while I was in London. Joyce Kallgren, Susan Shirk, Christine Wong, and John Zysman have all commented on individual chapters. Kenneth Lieberthal and Andrew G. Walder provided me with useful critiques of initial versions of the entire text.

I am also grateful to those who were present at sessions of the Southern California China Colloquium (May 1987), Susan Shirk's panel on the politics of finance at the annual meeting of the Association for Asian Studies (March 1988), the UC Irvine State Study Group (October 1988), and the UC Berkeley Comparative Communism Seminar (November 1989) who joined in the discussion of individual chapters that I presented at those meetings.

It is for those who read through the entire manuscript in its penultimate—and nearly penultimate—forms that I feel a special appreciation. Chalmers Johnson, John Wilson Lewis, Steven Topik, and R. Bin Wong all took the time to do this, and I greatly value their good suggestions, both large and small, as well as their encouragement.

Crafting the framework for this study and trying to get my data to fit into it has been a sometimes stimulating, sometimes frustrating enterprise. Thomas Bernstein's steady involvement, good spirits and intellectual companionship, and willingness to read more than just one draft lightened my burden enormously. A suggestion from him also inspired the title of this volume. And besides these more global contributions, the careful reader will note small attributions to Tom for some of the footnotes. For all these gifts, I thank him most of all.

As authors often do, I admit here my determination to retain my basic approach despite the occasional contrary reactions of others. Thus this set of acknowledgments simply expresses gratitude for the time and efforts of these people and is not a statement of anyone's responsibility for any portion of the final product but my own.

Today, on the anniversary of the 1989 Tiananmen massacre, with memories of this volume's germination but with a vastly altered spirit, I close these pages nostalgically. May we see another day when China's evolution can again inspire the optimism about that country that first sparked this project years ago.

D.J.S.
June 4, 1990

Contents

Introduction   1

PART ONE: FRAMEWORK

1. China's Economic Readjustment in Comparative Perspective   9
2. Conditions for Industrial Restructuring: Crisis and the Foundations for State Power   26

PART TWO: CRISIS AND DECISION

3. Crisis and the Economic Threat   47
4. Political Opportunity   70
5. The Politics of Readjustment at the Top   84

PART THREE: IMPLEMENTATION

6. Priority for Light Industry: Bureaucracy and Modes of Compliance   123
7. Abandoning Heavy Industry: Insulation and Forms of Resistance   163

8. Rationalization: The Limits of
   Verticalism and Unitism   194

   Conclusion: Cross-Systemic
   Implications of the Chinese Case   221

   Abbreviations   253
   Notes   254
   Bibliography   301
   Index   323

Tables

1. Composition of Gross Industrial Output　10
2. Indexes of Gross Output Value of Industry by Sector　10
3. Investment in Capital Construction by Branch of Industry　53
4. Newly Increased Fixed Assets in Capital Construction by Branch of Industry　53
5. Ratio of Investment in Light Industry to Total State Investment　54
6. Investment in Capital Construction for Light and Heavy Industry, Wuhan and National　62
7. Wuhan City Investment by Industrial Sector, 1979–1983　62
8. Principal Financial Items of State-Owned Industrial Enterprises by Sector, 1982　91
9. Difference in Investment and Performance on the Eve of Readjustment by Industrial Sector　91

10. Total Revenue by Industrial Sector 92
11. Quarterly Change in Gross Industrial Output Value in the First Three Quarters of 1981 107
12. Capital Construction Investment by Industrial Sector 136
13. Investment in Capital Construction by Industrial Sector as Percent of Total Investment 136
14. Gross Output Value of Industry by Sector 156
15. Indexes of Output Value by Branch, 1952, 1978, 1982 157
16. Sources of Investment in Wuhan City Metallurgy Bureau, 1979–1982 190

From Lathes to Looms

*China's Industrial Policy in
Comparative Perspective, 1979-1982*

Introduction

FOR MORE THAN THREE DECADES at various times all manner of critics of actually existing socialist states—from domestic dissidents, establishment economists, and other intellectuals to politicians and outside commentators—have aimed their fire at one of the most unfortunate consequences of the Stalinist-style command economy: its unerring proclivity for privileging heavy industry over other economic sectors.

The obvious consequence has been that, ironically, these systems set up in the name of "the people's" interest have shortchanged their constituents' livelihood. State plans ordered factories and foundries to spew out an endless stream of machinery and metals but far fewer consumer items and general daily necessities than the populace would have demanded, had it been allowed to make its pressure felt in a functioning marketplace.

In the late 1970's the Chinese leadership was able openly and soberly to scrutinize its system. Such an examination became possible, finally, only with the passing of the nearly all-mighty Mao Zedong, and soon thereafter with the drastic undermining of the radical thrust his approaches legitimized, through the canny politicking of Deng Xiaoping. By late 1978 the political elite planning economic policy was able to reach a consensus to make a radical, strategic switch.

The ability of this elite to turn around the proportions of industrial output with remarkable rapidity to favor consumers was bolstered not only by the demise of this one terribly powerful personage. Under the brief and ineffectual reign of Mao's immediate successor, Hua Guofeng, there had been a shortsighted and mismanaged effort to right the economic disorders that had

2   *Introduction*

attended the just terminated ten-year-long Cultural Revolution. But the program that Hua and his colleagues promoted only heightened the already grossly imbalanced sectoral proportions.

Their attempt at economic recovery, by continuing to downgrade the production of light industrial products, when added to the whole panoply of political and social disasters that had accompanied the societal-wide chaos of the Cultural Revolution, contributed to a severe alienation among the masses. This first post-Mao program also threatened to deplete the vital stocks of crucial national resources, particularly petroleum. For China had begun in the 1970's and at an accelerated rate under this transitional and temporary rule to export raw materials in exchange for modern equipment and technology from abroad, as its backward economy struggled to enter the modern world.

At the end of this interregnum a group of rehabilitated, reinstalled leaders, fresh from a long stretch of victimization during the Cultural Revolution, surveyed the nation's economic plight along with its many other troubles and settled on an admittedly quick-fix solution. This remedy was one their reconstituted regime, despite a fair degree of debilitation over the previous decade, was capable of carrying off.

Though there is no evidence of conscious borrowing, in its vision and in its tactics the agenda they chose was notably resonant with what is elsewhere labeled "industrial policy."* China's program, like ones enforced by certain other governments, notably France and Japan, amazingly swiftly transferred investment and other factors of production away from previously favored sectors to trades in need of a massive infusion of inputs.

The chief economic goals were two: quickly to increase the financial returns to the central government and to lay a foundation for a reoriented future pattern of national growth that would make a mark on world markets. Socially, the new leaders hoped to open up new employment channels and to meet mass needs for consumer goods. This study shows why and how these goals were chosen at this juncture and spells out how they were realized.

*Later, in 1988 and 1989, Chinese documents and media did begin to use the term "industrial policy" (*chanye zhengce*). By that time, however, the state was arguably no longer equipped to carry out such a policy. I discuss this issue in the concluding chapter.

The striking similarity between China's plan and what had worked in France and Japan after World War II led me to literature on those countries in my effort to identify broad systemic factors that permitted and facilitated such a shift. My reading repeatedly highlighted a set of categories of two types that these three countries shared, both at the level of elite perception and in societal, behavioral terms. It is these similar conditions that provided the framework of analysis for this project.

Leaders in all three countries believed they confronted a crisis, a time at once of political opportunity as they replaced a group of deeply discredited predecessors, but also one of economic threat as they coped with variously damaged economies. At the societal level all three governments nonetheless were capable of concentrating resources at the national center, a capability buttressed in each by traditions of bureaucracy, state involvement in industrial ventures, and an organic ideology of the state.

They were assisted in addition by interpersonal societal patterns according to which members of encapsulated social units were practiced in obeying superiors (verticalism) and were less inclined to form horizontal bonds across units (unitism). This latter inclination served to insulate politicians and planners, thus assisting them in their objective of pushing through policy while largely avoiding crippling or coordinated resistance from affected parties. Focusing on elite perceptions and on patterns in state-societal relations, I emphasize behavioral dimensions of the formation and execution of industrial policy more than other studies of such policy do.

This story of China's bout with industrial policy takes a particular tack. Instead of—as is usually the case—comparing this nation with other socialist states, it aims to keep the emphasis on broadly comparative categories. These categories—crisis, resource concentration, and political insulation—enable the analyst to make statements about state decisional and implementational capabilities and mechanisms that cut across the typical system divide. Thus I talk about China and its program of economic readjustment from 1979 to 1982 within a framework of variables that could be applied to capitalist democracies as well as to more authoritarian socialist planning systems.

The plan of the book follows this format. In the first chapter I make the case for using the concept of "industrial policy" to discuss China's restructuring and for drawing on language that grows out of an implicit cross-systemic comparison. In the second chapter I allude to the presence in China of an elite perception of crisis and of long-standing behavioral patterns that allowed this elite to resolve its crisis through an economic readjustment. Chapters 3 and 4 develop in some depth the nature of the crisis that China's leaders confronted, first the economic threat, at several levels, then the sudden political opportunity that arose in 1978 and its background.

These first four chapters present the context for the economic readjustment in China—the social structural factors that facilitated structural transformation and the economic and political environment in which those factors were activated. Chapters 5 through 8 use these factors as a framework to examine the politics involved in this new Chinese industrial policy. They are premised on the assumption that a given policy, rooted in a specific set of capabilities, creates particular political conditions.

Chapter 5, about policy making, looks at the politics of agenda setting and decision about this redeployment in China. It shows how the crisis identified in Chapters 3 and 4 heightened decision makers' concerns about resource concentration and popular stability. It also recounts how these concerns, in turn, fashioned the decisional discourse in the leadership's debates over economic readjustment over the years 1979–82, as these concerns constrained the manner in which affected parties presented their claims. The chapter reveals that these same concerns accounted both for the shift to light industry in 1979 and for the turn back toward heavy industry just a few years later. This focus on elite concerns as the core consideration in decision making takes issue with analyses that emphasize the lobbying of interest groups as decisive in policy change.

Surprisingly, in some ways the politics surrounding this policy in socialist China were even more competitive than in democratic France and Japan. Most fundamentally, since the bulk of national resources in China flowed from a central budget as of the early 1980's, and since the state owned virtually the entire industrial stock, the zero-sum trade-off between winners and losers that marks industrial policy anywhere took on an urgency even more intense, if more subtly expressed, than in a market system.

For all the contention—between the representatives of the two

Introduction 5

large industrial sectors and between the regions in which they are based, and between levels in the administrative hierarchy—became focused on just one pot of funding. Thus this industrial policy with its reallocation set up its own brand of politics, with its particular competitive dynamic. Chapter 5 develops this theme.

The political questions addressed in Chapters 6 through 8 are these: How did the social structural features described in Chapter 2 that shored up the readjustment (specifically, verticalism and unitism) combine with the policy dynamics set in motion by readjustment to shape the execution of decision? Here the focus is on policy implementation: the manner of eliciting compliance and the modes and management of resistance.

Each of these last three chapters deals with the politics of one of the three principal dimensions that have been identified in the comparative literature on industrial policy. All three of these dimensions were present in the Chinese policy, just as they were in Japanese and Western conceptions—first, prioritizing the allocation of investment and other resources for the winners (in this case, light industry); second, in some sense abandoning the losers (here, heavy industry) to a market of sorts; and third, finding ways to rationalize the arrangement of the assets of individual firms.

Whereas the material for Chapter 5 is drawn from the national press and media, the data on implementation come largely from the local Wuhan city press, from journals from that area, and from 100 hours of interviews I held with economic bureaucrats and factory managers in that city in 1984 and 1985. Wuhan made a good case for study of this policy because it is a large industrial center housing substantial concentrations of both heavy and light industry.

It is not until the final chapter, when I bring together my findings and their implications, that I explicitly point to elements in the French and Japanese situations—at both contextual and behavioral levels—that were in gross terms roughly comparable to those faced by Chinese politicians in 1978. Nonetheless, throughout the study I have used brief comparisons from the French and Japanese experiences to underline the similarities of response that conduct of industrial policy can elicit in countries across the systemic spectrum.

PART ONE

Framework

ONE

China's Economic Readjustment in Comparative Perspective

FROM 1979 TO 1982, China's leaders finally achieved an objective that had been on their agenda more than once in the past: the shift of investment and other productive resources from heavy to light industry. Enmeshed for decades in the nets of the Stalinist-style command economy, which decrees that development must proceed on the foundation of heavy industry,[1] the nation's budgets had repeatedly—indeed, it seemed, automatically—favored the metallurgical and producer goods sectors, neglecting the output of commodities for daily use, despite periodic efforts to redress the balance.

Accordingly, after three decades of nearly uninterrupted priority allocation following the communist takeover in 1949, the output value of heavy industry had increased 90.6-fold, while light had grown only 19.8-fold.[2] Looking at representative trades, economists calculated that the output value of machine building had jumped up 53-fold, but that of textiles had expanded a mere 3.5-fold between 1953 and 1980.[3] Under these conditions, social and political interests tied to heavy industry were consistently dominant over the years.

But despite this long-term hegemony of the heavy industry sector, a policy called "economic readjustment" (*jingji tiaozheng*) introduced in early 1979 managed to make a significant change in the respective proportions the two branches represented in the gross value of industrial output in a remarkably brief span of time: whereas heavy industry accounted for 56.9 percent and light for 43.1 in 1978, light industry rose to a share of 51.5 per-

TABLE 1
Composition of Gross Industrial Output
(Percent)

Year	Light industry	Heavy industry	Year	Light industry	Heavy industry
1949	73.6%	26.4%	1978	43.1%	56.9%
1952	64.5	35.5	1979	43.7	56.3
1957	55.0	45.0	1980	47.2	52.8
1960	33.4	66.6	1981	51.5	48.5
1965	51.6	48.4	1982	50.2	49.8
1971	43.0	57.0	1983	48.5	51.5
1975	44.1	55.9			

SOURCE: State Statistical Bureau 1986: 34.

TABLE 2
Indexes of Gross Output Value of Industry by Sector
(The preceding year = 100)

Year	Light industry	Heavy industry	Year	Light industry	Heavy industry
1950	130.1	154.1	1978	110.8	115.6
1952	123.5	143.5	1979	109.6	107.7
1957	105.7	118.4	1980	118.4	101.4
1960	90.2	125.9	1981	114.1	95.3
1965	147.7	110.2	1982	105.7	109.8
1971	106.5	121.4	1983	108.7	112.4
1975	113.0	116.8			

SOURCE: State Statistical Bureau 1986: 33.

cent, with heavy standing at only 48.5 percent at the peak of the policy in 1981 (see Table 1).[4]

Another way of telling the tale is to point to the drop in heavy's share of industrial investment during these years. In the crucial three-year period of the readjustment, 1979 to 1981, its proportion fell from the 90 percent it had occupied over the years 1966 to 1975 to only 80 percent.[5] Another set of indicators shows that from 1978 to 1982 the average annual increase in the output value of light industry jumped as high as 11.7 percent. At the same time, heavy increased by just 5.9 percent (see Table 2).[6]

In brief, this was a massive switch of resources between industrial sectors, the results of which have held over time. Writing in 1984, a prominent Western economist remarked, "The Chinese have achieved a remarkable change in the composition of output in the past five years."[7] As late as 1985, the effects were still visible: taking 1978 as a base of 100, as of 1985 the index of heavy's output was just 175, as against light's, which had escalated to 227.[8] And in mid-1988, over half a decade after the policy had been terminated, the Chinese themselves announced:

> After more than 30 years of construction and reform, and particularly during the past 10 years, our production structure has been markedly improved. A "one-third each" ratio between agriculture, light industry and heavy industry has been established. Light and heavy industry in the main contribute a 50-50 proportion of total output value, and a better balance has been achieved between major sectors of the economy.[9]

How did this happen, and how can we best understand the process? What does such a major, rapid reorganization show us about the potential in the system for change, both political and economic? What do we learn from it about the boundaries and modes of political-economic experimentation in the People's Republic under particular conditions? What are its political implications for decision making and for the response of affected parties?

This book borrows from several bodies of comparative politics literature to address these questions. The simple answer those literatures suggest is that three factors were crucial: a moment of *crisis* that promoted elite consensus, a relatively responsive *bureaucracy* to allocate resources in new ways in accord with elite designs, and *insulating tactics* that neutralized or appeased the losing social forces—affected workers, managers, and local industrial firms.

These factors enabled a dominant group of politicians at the central level to push this program through and made it possible for top leaders to override expressions of opposition by the heavy industrial interests that were disadvantaged by the policy. These heavy industrial interests would in normal times have stymied and undercut the program.

ECONOMIC READJUSTMENT, INDUSTRIAL POLICY, AND STRATEGY-LED DEVELOPMENT

In both its conception and its operation this program of economic restructuring resembled what students of advanced industrial democracies label "industrial policy." The basic idea behind the policy was to raise the productivity of the recipient industry—in this case, light industry—as a way of enhancing national wealth overall. Operationally, China's economic readjustment involved transferring production factors—funds, raw materials, fuel and energy, transport capacity, labor, and foreign exchange—from one industrial branch, the heavy industries, to another, light industry, with its consumer goods and textiles.

Organizationally, as in advanced industrial countries executing industrial policy, the state bureaucratic apparatus was crucial. Those setting policy in 1979 bolstered the power of an existing organ, the State Economic Commission, to channel resources to the new priority sectors. Also, as elsewhere, the banking system played a key role; the state bank significantly redirected its credit toward firms in these two trades. Centralized resource control, shored up by elite consensus in a time of crisis, here as in other places executing industrial policy made possible the use of these policy instruments.

At the same time, organizational control permitted the State Council to issue commands to enforce the program, commands that would largely be honored. Its directives ordered both central government departments and local administrations to give priority in supplying fuel, power, raw materials, and transport to the favored branches, as well as to afford these branches new investment, loans, and foreign exchange.[10]

Overall, readjustment entailed five components: reversing the traditional order of priority given to heavy industry, light industry, and agriculture; increasing the share of consumption in national income; reducing the consumption of energy; increasing exports, especially of manufactured goods; and emphasizing plant modernization and improved efficiency in existing enterprises. The authors of a binational study of the program adjudged that "China fulfilled the[se] main objectives of adjustment during 1979–81."[11] Thus the policy enjoyed "success" in the sense that it fulfilled the leadership's intention in effecting industrial readjustment, that is, in shifting investment and abruptly restructuring the course of national economic growth.*

*In using the word "success," I am not attempting to assess whether the program promoted a more rapid achievement of national economic modernization, accel-

Because of the conceptual and operational parallels between China's readjustment and restructuring policies elsewhere, this study borrows concepts and perspectives from the literature on industrial policy in advanced capitalist democracies and in newly industrializing countries (NICs). This literature is helpful in elucidating special dynamics in the state-society relationship that industrial policy entails and in identifying state capacities and social requisites that make such policy possible.

In its broadest formulation, according to one specialist on the subject, "Industrial policy means initiating and coordinating *governmental activities* to lift the productivity and competitiveness of a whole economy and of particular industries in it. . . . Above all it means the infusion of *goal-oriented, strategic* thinking into public economic policy"[12] (emphasis added). Here the emphasis is on *state-centeredness* and purposiveness. In effect, the state intervention into the economy that industrial policy necessarily involves essentially substitutes political decisions for the market mechanism.[13] It does this through an explicit, coherent, coordinated, and typically short-term macro structural transformation of the national economy. Intentionality is also a requisite of industrial policy, properly understood: "Public policies that have unintended consequences for industrial competitiveness and exclusively private sector competitive strategies would not be considered industrial policies."[14]

Thus the capacity to carry out industrial policy presupposes a state in which a group of key central leaders are in command of the bulk of the nation's resources and, because they have agreed among themselves over economic policy, are capable of acting decisively. Phrased a bit differently, the state is most effective when consensus and control of resources are present at the top of the political system.

Times of crisis can often heighten these powers; as one study of French industrial choices points out, "Changes occur most often at moments of crisis which require speedy adjustment of one kind or another."[15] Another, on Japan's economic policy, states, "In general, the role of the government and its degree of

erated growth, enhanced participation in the world economy, stimulated a higher overall national gross value of industrial output, or increased per capita income, although all of these are usually subsidiary goals of a readjustment.

reliance on authoritarian intervention are enlarged by actual or anticipated crisis conditions in the environment."[16]

But more is entailed than unified intent at the apex; there must also be a way to deliver the goods to the new recipients and to neutralize opposition from concerned social forces. This social dimension is brought out in the Japanese use of the word "targeting" to isolate what they consider the core hallmark of such policy. Programs that target are ones "aimed at a particular industry or firm, singling it out for expansion relative to others."[17]

Yet one more delineation of this concept calls it "government policy undertaken to *change the allocation of resources* among industries, or the levels of certain productive activities . . . from what they would be in the absence of such a policy. An industrial policy is concerned with *encouraging* production, investment, research and development, modernization and reorganization in certain industries, and *discouraging* such activities in others"[18] (emphasis added). Similarly, another analyst defined this type of policy as referring to "the efforts of governments to influence the allocation of resources among or within industrial sectors."[19]

These formulations bring to the fore the *reallocative* character of industrial policy. Politically, what happens under its regimen is that the industries that make up a national economy are separated *in a new way* into winners and losers.* As some branch or branches are privileged, primed to expand, others (previously but no longer favored, or perhaps simply temporarily diminished by a short-term redivision of limited resources) are in some sense abandoned, most generally to the play of market forces. This was no small task in the Chinese case because a way needed to be found to redirect large amounts of state resources rapidly across vast geographical space; moreover, the losers had for decades been the chief recipients of state largesse.

A related body of comparative literature, that on the political economy of growth and the state's role in it in the NICs, suggests mechanisms that made this change possible. Authors writing on

---

*Chalmers Johnson has alerted me to the fact that the term "picking winners" was invented and used by neoclassical economists as an attack on the idea of industrial policy. Despite his advice, I adopt it in this work to highlight the way the policy suddenly slices up the industrial world into the recipients and the deprived.

this subject speak of state-centered, "strategy-led development," obviously growth whose requisites would be similar to those for industrial policy. One volume in particular that concentrates specifically on the East Asian variety of NIC is especially useful, for Taiwan, Hong Kong, Singapore, and, to some extent, South Korea, are all places whose population also experienced the Mainland Chinese's Confucian past with its authoritarian paternalism; they too have partaken of China's tradition of bureaucratic rule.

Frederic C. Deyo's conclusion to this study of the East Asian NICs posits two preconditions for this type of statist development: "economic institutional consolidation" and "political closure."[20] The first of these focuses on implementation: "The institutional configuration most conducive to the effective implementation of strategy characteristically centers on a few powerful state agencies that closely link decisional and operational authority in strategy-relevant policy issues. Such agencies perform essential functions," among them, political control. A strong, at least relatively responsive state bureaucracy would be the minimal means of satisfying this condition. Only a hierarchically structured and centrally coordinated, state-controlled agency could manage the transferal of resources readjustment requires. Indeed, recent writers on the state have stressed the importance of effective bureaucratic machinery for state intervention in the economy.[21]

Political closure, the other precondition, refers [among other things] to the confining of strategy determination to a manageably narrow political coalition of dominant groups—a coalition able to deny domestic political opponents a voice in economic decision making and thus to effect rapid and coherent strategy shifts in response to changing economic circumstances. . . . [It also] specifies the need for broader exclusion of (or restricted access of) popular-sector groups from strategy to *insulate* technocratic economic planning from the vagaries of populist politics. [Emphasis added.]

At the elite level, it was the sense of crisis that forged the mandatory consensus and thereby excluded opponents of the policy, along with their claims, from the decision-making arena. At lower administrative levels, strategies of insulating and sheltering the policy against negative responses were critical in depriving losers who had once been clients. Absolute closure would, certainly, have vastly expedited policy execution. But just finding means of silencing—even for a time—once powerful forces that stood in opposition would be a big step in that direction. For our purposes, the key notion here is the ability of leaders to insulate a policy, by whatever means, even if not entirely to close out its opponents.

This book considers China's economic readjustment from 1979 to 1982 in light of insights derived from these two bodies of comparative literature. From definitions and relationships presented in these sets of material it is possible—by considering the nature of the policy itself—to deduce the specific requisites for selecting and executing that policy, as well as the organizational and political dynamics associated with these requisites.[22]

Thus these comparative policy concepts—industrial policy and strategy-led development—together highlight three critical features of the policy process: any government policy must elicit sufficient agreement at the top that *resolution* can be reached among central politicians; it must be bolstered by the availability of *organizational forms* that can push the policy through the system; and there must be some mode of *sustaining* the policy *against opposition*. In the case of major, controversial shifts in resource distribution, all of these criteria must be present in a particularly heightened fashion.

In adopting this perspective, my framework calls into question the value for a study of industrial policy of simply relying on the more typically used frameworks for studying China comparatively, namely the authoritarian model of politics and the socialist model of political economy. I contend that using asystemic categories for analysis can provide fresh interpretations for understanding the success or failure of this policy, whether the policy is undertaken in a socialist or a capitalist context.

SUSPENSION OF THE AUTHORITARIAN-CUM-SOCIALISM MODELS

Most typically, comparative studies of post-1949 China seek to understand its policy by reference to other socialist states. This is in line with popular conventional wisdom and with typical social science policy analysis. Such analyses tend to approach the interpretation of a piece of political behavior—such as the selection and implementation of industrial policy—in terms of dichotomous systems: democracies versus authoritarian polities, capitalist or socialist economies.

In this approach, the most common method used in analyzing the experience of any given set of states is to compare countries in which either the political or the economic system (or, most characteristically, both) are the same.[23] This purportedly comparative practice actually may lead analysts to assume that the difficulty or ease of carrying out the policies in question is tied simply to the system they are investigating. Thus the explanatory variables used in reaching conclusions in such research are often systemic ones: the role of the communist party or of the state plan in socialist states; the federal system, the electoral system, checks and balances, interest group pluralism in democracies.

But the obstacles or facility uncovered may in fact have at least as much to do with the nature of the policy itself and its own requisites and dynamics, with the moment of policy choice and the larger political-economic context, or with facets of the states in question other than their formal economic or political system. Timeless comparisons undertaken among a group of democratic, capitalist societies, for example, may sometimes not take us substantially further in understanding the workings of a policy under review than a single-society study written without reference to a comparative dimension.

Therefore, the task is to find categories that transcend the single case and its system and take note of outstanding contextual conditions that states of any sort might encounter. Such categories can then explain similarities of behavior across different kinds of systems, as well as different forms of behavior occurring in same-type systems.

Democracy-Authoritarianism

Lester Thurow's book *The Zero-Sum Society* addresses what he sees as the impediments the democratic American system poses for the redistribution that accompanies economic change. Thurow blames our political system and its interest groups for a national inability to "disinvest." "The need to cut consumption creates strains in a democracy that do not exist in a dictatorship," he claims. The problem he sees is principally the presence of too many interest groups voicing claims. Each group, he maintains, appeals to government for protection and for aid in stopping or retarding the process of reallocation as it tries to make others perform what it itself seeks to escape: action in the "general interest." Thurow closes with a query that his method cannot permit him to address: "Does our inability to act reflect fundamental irreconcilable divisions that no political process could overcome, or is there something wrong with our political system?"[24]

Thurow is certainly accurate in pointing to the barrier against policy change raised by the resistance of groups affected by cutbacks. But he is wrong in believing that only democracies suffer from such an affliction and, indeed, that the democratic system itself is the problem. For, as Josef Brada and John Montias have shown in their study of Eastern European industrial policy, in socialist Czechoslovakia and Poland enterprises supported by the ministries in charge of them managed to divert resources to meet their targets instead of obeying commands for structural change. In addition, some powerful but initially excluded enterprises were able to bargain successfully to get on the list of beneficiaries. This was especially the case for firms doing machine building, which for over two decades had been a top-priority sector.[25]

Thus Thurow misses the simple fact that democracy itself is not necessarily the obstacle. In any state a fundamentally redistributive program such as industrial policy will always and everywhere have winners and losers. When the losers include groups long favored by the state, they are bound to have clout that must be handled and connections that can continue to work on their behalf.

The crucial question becomes, then, not whether a state is democratic or authoritarian, but whether its leaders are able to use existing—or to devise new—insulating strategies that will appease and thereby silence the losers. Put into the language used above, what methods have they employed to effect political closure such that crucial economic institutions are sufficiently responsive? Political leaders can, theoretically, design and deploy such methods in both democratic and authoritarian states, and they may be more able to do so at some times than at others.

Other authors who have written in a more explicitly comparative mode than Thurow nevertheless start from similar premises. Mancur Olson, for one, pinpoints "special-interest organizations" or what he calls "distributional coalitions," such as those found historically in Great Britain, which he views as brakes on a society's capacity to reallocate resources and so to adapt to changing conditions in a manner that makes for economic growth.

But he speaks only of democracies in his book on economic growth and social rigidities and draws his conclusions in a way that applies only to places where such coalitions are openly active and legitimated. By contrast, Alec Nove's study of the politics of socialism reminds us that in socialist states everyone from managers of individual firms to party secretaries in command of specific regions or localities to ministers in the capital identifies with his or her realm of responsibility and presses for allocations, authorizations, and credits whenever allotments are being made.[26] Again, one must inquire about how—using what mechanisms of control and incentives and under what particular circumstances—a given system (democratic or authoritarian) can circumvent or redirect such pressures.

Like the works of Olson and Thurow cited above, the volumes edited by Peter Evans et al. and Peter Katzenstein trace these problems with interest groups to the nature of the political system in which they are embedded. Thus when Theda Skocpol analyzes the democratic United States, she emphasizes its federal system and division of sovereignty among branches. These institutions, she believes, result in a form of state power that is "fragmented, dispersed, and everywhere permeated by organized societal interests."[27] But the political institutions in a democracy may not be the most important factor.

Others of Skocpol's variables are closer to the mark. Two of these are the national government's lack of a powerful career civil service and of an authoritative planning system. Both, if present, would help satisfy Deyo's call for "economic institutional consolidation."[28] Also, the absence that she notes of a central bank under direct executive control and of public ownership of key parts of the economy—both of which indicate a lack of central resource control—may be of more significance for the execution of certain economic policies than is the form of the political system or the fragmentation of power among diverse interests.[29]

An indication that this is the case comes from considering democratic states such as France and Japan. Both, like China in 1979, have strong, relatively compliant bureaucracies and means of controlling national investment resources from the center, and both were able, despite their democratic institutions, to restructure their economies from the national center in the aftermath of World War II.

Katzenstein's introduction to his edited work on comparative foreign economic policy in advanced industrial states falls into this same general category of work that attributes problems in policy implementation specifically to system type. He does recognize that bureaucracies can contain their own internal brand of politics, but he attributes the resulting difficulties in a smooth execution of policy in the United States to the bureaucracy's autonomy from the executive, which he says derives from the rule of law in democratic systems.

He then speculates that such bureaucratic politics may simply reflect a "particular American syndrome, the internal fragmentation of the American state." Reminiscent of Thurow's musing noted above, Katzenstein goes on to wonder whether this syndrome might be instead a function of the "push and pull which accompany policy making in all advanced industrial states."[30] Phrasing his question in this fashion, but making no judgment, eliminates from consideration the possibility that pluralism and federalism, found in many advanced democracies, are not the only breeding grounds for bureaucratic battles and the lack of control that is their counterpart. But it also obscures the possibility that there are ways of overcoming bureaucratic fissures even in some democracies—as well as in authoritarian states, under certain conditions—so that economic restructuring can be carried through.

Capitalism-Socialism

The overwhelming bulk of the analysis of socialist societies similarly looks at them all as variations within a common category and usually compares them only with each other. A seminal work that distinguishes the market- or exchange-based mode of social control from the command- or authority-type mode is Charles Lindblom's *Politics and Markets*. The former mode organizes capitalist societies while the latter predominates under socialist systems.

Lindblom does show that there are variants of communism; he is also careful to state at the outset that "for capitalists and communists alike, the fundamental alternatives are the same, though they may choose to combine them in different ways." Furthermore, he finds "striking similarities between state-directed systems and market systems [which] confuse any simple distinction between the two." Still, his guiding purpose is to describe what he lays out as two contrasting "politico-economic systems"—one democratic, one communist—*qua* systems, and not to assess their similar or different ways of handling like policies.[31] Thus his analysis continually returns to the theme of differentiating the two modal systems.

And yet, as this study of China's economic readjustment will show, the measure of success that policy enjoyed derived in large part from the mix of market and command-style mechanisms used in its conduct, just as, for example, French and Japanese industrial policy also did in the early postwar era.* In China, as economic reform got under way coterminously with readjustment, the abandoned losers were placated by the presence of the market, which provided an additional arena for their economic activity and a new source for the supplies denied them under the old state plan. In this case, then, similarities in policy style can cut across the politico-economic system and so may yield more insights than a simple focus on system type would do.

Another book that speaks of categories of states, if not alluding to the more formalized concept of "system," is Chalmers Johnson's *MITI and the Japanese Miracle*. This study presents a distinction that might be viewed as a refinement of Lindblom's dichotomy, although Johnson does not refer to Lindblom directly. He first proposes a division between what he calls "plan rational" and "plan ideological" economies, thereby collapsing the usual

---

*The concluding chapter of this volume will treat parallels with the French and Japanese cases.

demarcation between societies that are planned (or, in Lindblom's terms, rely principally on authority or command) and those that are market-centered.[32]

He uses this distinction between ideologically guided and nonideological planning to separate behavior under the command (read communist or socialist) economies from Japanese practice, where planning is rational. In the former, he maintains, "state ownership of the means of production, state planning and bureaucratic goal-setting are not rational means to a developmental goal" (though he implies that they might once have been) but "are fundamental values in themselves." Johnson then distinguishes regulatory or market-rational states, which are concerned with economic competition, from developmental or plan-rational states, which set substantive social and economic goals. This distinction basically rests upon whether the state industrialized early or late, with regulatory states being those that did so first.

Although Johnson's mode of categorization steers clear of the usual capitalism/socialism labels, he is still essentially stating that there are two "rational" forms of state, neither of which is socialist, and one irrational, or "ideological," form of state, which is socialist. This method of analysis will not help to reveal the factors that helped China readjust its economy, nor will it assist us to discover the ways in which China's approach had some key features in common with industrial policy in certain nonsocialist states.

Specifically, Johnson's framework slights the extent to which bureaucracy—sometimes precisely because it is ideologically guided—in a socialist setting might be an extremely efficacious policy tool. Nor does this model provide for what some might term the "irrationality" of co-opting, shielding, and placating losers. These are all modes of effecting political insulation which worked well in China and which often help industrial restructuring to succeed. Indeed, they are strategies in which even the "rational" Japanese state indulges, as Johnson notes elsewhere in his study.

Thus using form of state or mode of production categorizations as gross explanatory factors can obfuscate rather than expose crucial dynamics of the operation of policies. To avoid this pitfall,

I borrow instead from John Zysman the idea that the policy problem itself may structure the operational methods used to solve it, just as the policy also molds the behavioral responses of target groups.[33]

Soviet-Style Economies

Over the several decades preceding the collapse of the Eastern European regimes in late 1989, other socialist states made efforts to readjust their economies away from the bias toward heavy industry that marked them all. For the most part, they failed in these attempts. The same asystemic explanatory vocabulary laid out above can also account for the experiences of other socialist states. Thus one needs to inquire in each case whether there was sufficient leadership consensus for effecting, in Deyo's words, "rapid and coherent strategy shifts," whether the leadership had managed to install insulation against resistance, and whether there were means of ensuring a relatively responsive bureaucracy throughout the system.

Dating from the 1950's, certain leaders in the Soviet Union and in several of the Eastern European states at least advanced proposals for sectoral shifts in investment and even tampered with their budgets a bit in line with these proposals. Malenkov and later Khrushchev in the Soviet Union, Nagy in Hungary, and a group of politicians in Poland all contributed to this effort.[34] Later reform attempts occurred periodically in succeeding decades, notably in these same countries and in Czechoslovakia.[35]

But one or more of the conditions addressed above was always lacking. First, the economies of the East European states were generally subject to a dependence in the past that has not applied in the Chinese case, certainly since the 1950's. Both their reform efforts and the shapes of their economies were hostage to varying degrees to their subservience to the Soviet Union: at any moment initiatives could be canceled, and economic restructuring often had to be fitted into the division of labor in COMECON (Council for Mutual Economic Assistance).[36]

Proponents of reform in that period generally had to contend with domestic opponents who could rely on or at least appeal to applies in the bloc for support. Thus until recently Eastern European countries have lacked two of the key conditions for Deyo's "political closure": "It refers in part," he holds, "to the external autonomy that permits domestic developmental coalitions in formulating strategy to assert national over foreign interests in cases where these diverge."[37]

Those favoring change also were unable to fulfill another of his conditions for closure: they could not deny domestic political opponents a voice in decision making. Thus reform efforts frequently foundered on lack of leadership unity in Eastern Europe, which, unfortunately, usually coincided with periods of proposals for change. For instance, Kazimierz Poznanski found in Poland in the past "an exceptional lack of unity and/or division within the leadership which tends to intensify during periods of economic difficulty and/or political challenges to the regime."[38] But of course it is in such periods of difficulty that reform gets onto the agenda. The resulting political splits obviously limited the chances for restructuring to succeed.

Additionally, bureaucratic subversion of these programs repeatedly stuck reform at an impasse.[39] With few exceptions, political struggle and blockage by bureaucrats most typically halted reforms before they took effect and carried these economies back along a path of recentralization. Here, then, though bureaucracies were present, they were insufficiently responsive to policy change, perhaps because they were inadequately placated and compensated for potential losses.

Yet another issue, as Morris Bornstein notes, is that when investment transfers occurred among industrial sectors, they usually accompanied attempts to modify the structure of the economic system.[40] But apparently the latter sort of reform, which is market-oriented, held more fascination for analysts, who filled the literature with studies of movements to introduce "economic pragmatism"—the devolution of decision making to enterprises, the shift from commands and directives to indirect economic levers, wage and price reforms, attention to consumer demand. So scholars have paid far less attention to allocatory alterations.

A last problem is that by and large changes in intersectoral funding which deprived the heavy industries in socialist states' industries typically were either minuscule or terribly short-lived. Philip Hanson, for instance, shows how very little the shares of the different sectors changed in the proportion of total gross investment in the Soviet Union from 1937 to 1964, despite battles over and rhetoric about paying more heed to consumption.[41] The Chinese case before us, then, is distinctive.

At this stage of the analysis, I have simply asserted that, since industrial policy emphasizes the role of the state and political will in redirecting economic resources, and since it carves up the political economy into winners and losers in new ways, successful conduct of this policy will need to satisfy certain political and organizational requisites. But the categories—substantial elite consensus, modes of political closure and insulation, and economic institutional consolidation—still remain broad and abstract. The following chapter will flesh out these factors by specifying more concretely what they entailed in the Chinese case at the juncture in question.

TWO

Conditions for Industrial Restructuring
Crisis and the Foundations for State Power

THE LAST CHAPTER asserted that crisis, bureaucracy, and political insulation provide a political foundation for major economic restructuring, for these factors respectively lay the grounding for elite consensus, for effective policy implementation, and for shielding the policy against opposition. The argument was developed from literature that defines the nature of industrial policy in generic terms—its state-centeredness and its divisiveness. Here I will examine more specifically the properties of these three factors and the character of the particular crisis that spurred politicians in China to action in the late 1970's.

The behavioral patterns that buttressed bureaucratic arrangements and that disposed—and enabled—political elites to insulate their policies from the affected publics also must be more concretely defined. The analysis that follows builds on concepts that eschew the usual systemic labels but that capture instead traditions in state-society relations that transcend these labels. It is grounded in an assumption that there are often significant continuities between relevant traditions and current social practices. In the case of post-1949 China in particular, the traditions I will refer to carried special weight because they were specifically selected from the repertoire of past mass behaviors and emphasized by the communist leaders in order to shore up their own power.

CRISIS AND CONSENSUS

The perception of a crisis goads to action. Such moments are especially pregnant with political possibility. In the words of one author writing comparatively on the politics of economic policy making: "Prosperity blurs a truth that hard times make clearer: the choice made among conflicting policy proposals emerges out of politics. The victorious interpretation will be the one whose adherents have the power to translate their opinion into the force of law. . . . Economic crisis leads to policy debate and political controversy; out of conflict, policies emerge."[1]

Even a subjective feeling of crisis among a political elite can serve to mobilize and unify individuals who might otherwise have been at odds. Indeed, crisis is often ultimately a matter of perception, defined by the parties involved. The authors of a study of industrial crisis in various Western European countries observe that times of crisis carry an air of ambivalence, at once suggesting threat and offering opportunity.[2] Interestingly, this definition of the notion of crisis matches exactly with the Chinese term for crisis, *weiji*, whose two component characters mean, respectively, peril and opportunity.

In China, the recently concluded Cultural Revolution played such a mobilizing role in the late 1970's, through its massive destruction and its dislocation meted out by domestic strife. That widely recognized fiasco not only pushed aside key factions in the leadership who had sponsored the movement and who represented old avenues to economic growth, but it also legitimated the rejection of past strategies, admission of their failure, and a search for something novel.

The opportunity and the threat of the crisis can be broken down into four components in this case, two of them tied to threat, two to opportunity. These components created an unusual convergence of circumstances in which a set of factors empowered the state and its dominant leaders to move in an unusual way, for they so jolted the leadership that a thorough switch in the economy seemed indicated, one that would require purposive, centralized, bureaucratic direction.

The two-part threat was economic. It derived in the first instance from what an almost panicked political elite suddenly acknowledged to be *a backward and imbalanced industrial structure*. Most Chinese leaders had by 1979 become convinced that further pursuit of the Stalinist-style pro–heavy industry model of growth was spelling disaster for China.

Along with this recognition came a challenge, linked to *a new relationship with the international economy*. The China of 1979 had long been estranged from the world market, but at that point the leadership suddenly determined to build up its backward economy in order to confront, connect with, and eventually catch up with the more advanced countries. The sudden intensification of interaction with the world economy thus issued from a searching reevaluation of old economic strategies and their justifications; that interaction itself then went on to force further shifts in domestic economic strategy.

Political factors offered the obverse side of crisis, opportunity. Changed political alignments and redefinitions issued from what had been over the previous decade a politically induced crisis. This opportunity resided in a *leadership switch* in which the newly installed (actually, a recently rehabilitated, former) elite guided a sudden national *consensus over economic growth* as the overwhelming priority. Thus a political opportunity was created for the ways of discredited, past leaders to be set aside and a new beginning broached.

Not just a turnover of leaders, but the passing of power to a group with shared objectives and a joint commitment to abandon past methods, formed the opening for doing something novel that Peter Gourevitch ties to crisis. "Crisis," he found for his cases, "opened the system of relationships, making politics and policy more fluid."[3] It is just this sense of crisis—perceived or otherwise—which often forges consensus among groups that previously had quibbled or quarreled.

The crisis was manifested in macro terms by the burdens of bottlenecks, capital shortage, backwardness and stagnation, even obsolescence. Chinese economists calculated that annual growth rates in industrial output value had fallen from 17.9 percent in the period 1963–65 to 9.1 percent by 1971–75 and that profits realized per 100 *yuan* of fixed assets had dropped from 23.6 *yuan* in 1957 to only 12.1 *yuan* by 1976.

Moreover, the long-term backwardness in light industry had

created serious tensions in market supplies, as investments in heavy industry shot up from 38.7 percent of total investment in the First Five-Year Plan period (1952–57) to 52.8 percent by 1978.[4] Micro-level management was characterized by a prevalence of more or less self-sufficient firms or other economic units unconcerned with specialization or larger-scale cooperation.

Decision makers judged that only by restructuring could the nation hope first to catch up and eventually to compete with the technologically more developed countries. The long period of near autarky served to fuel a "quest for rank" and an "urge to catch up." Certainly, one incentive to become linked into the world economy was a new consciousness of the backwardness of China's economy in international terms.[5]

Industrial policy, with its priority allocations, was well fitted for this moment of crisis, which introduced new economic concerns at the same time that the politics of the period facilitated coping with them. Domestic concerns centered around the job of laying an infrastructural foundation for future development. This could be accomplished by targeting and fostering new growth industries. Targeting, in turn, would require investing in selected key sectors for high returns.

Internationally, the consciousness of crisis demanded a focus on exports for earning foreign exchange, along with an openness to new technology that could be purchased with the earnings from exports. This demand for purchases and assistance from the world market, like the long-term growth goals at home, also required identifying and promoting a few specific sectors of national comparative advantage. At the same time, despair over the past along with political and attitudinal changes in the national mood legitimated experimentation and so bolstered this search for a new strategy.

Beginning in 1977, China's leaders undertook a major transformation in the country's involvement with the world economy, including a huge boost in trade with the United States and its Western allies. By the early 1980's the United States and Europe together were supplying more than a third of China's import needs. China also became engaged for the first time in a wide range of new economic dealings with the West that went far beyond simple exchange. These connections included joint ventures with foreign investors, management consulting contracts and licensing agreements with foreign firms, technical aid from international organizations, and loans from commercial banks, foreign governments, and international financial institutions.[6]

Opportunity beckoned as China experienced a time of political possibility, in which the immediately past elites were discredited so that others could wash the slate clean of past policy. For the groups that had dominated the economy in the recent past—the proponents both of Maoist campaign-style development and of the heavy industry–biased planned economy—had been associated with the perpetration of damaging internal struggles. Meanwhile, the economic bureaucracy and its officials provided continuity.

Opting for a major economic transformation was the product of a reevaluation of past strategy, spurred by a generalized national consensus in favor of economic growth and modernization as the overriding goal. Growth was to be achieved through an entirely new start, beginning with recovery, driven forward by a concentrated push, and within only a few years setting the foundation for an even larger-scale takeoff. The Chinese were able to work with the already long-in-place apparatus for planning, even as they loosened its hold in simultaneous experiments with market reform.

In sum, the basis for the elite consensus that underwrote restructuring lay in a crisis—in a sense of economic threat based on international isolation and backwardness and a more or less urgent cry for rebuilding; and in political opportunity, whch appeared with a leadership succession, accompanied by a mass consensus focused on a new national goal. This set of circumstances permitted—indeed, one could say even pressed—political elites to unify around a new policy, a major economic shift.

FOUNDATIONS FOR STATE POWER: BUREAUCRACY AND INSULATION

An important foundation for China's ability to conduct readjustment lay in its traditions of state-societal interaction. China has in its historical repertoire of behaviors both a mode of state control over the people and a collection of passive, dependent, self-protective mass sociocultural orientations to the state.[7] This particular mode of control and these mass orientations were bolstered by the communists upon their ascent to power in 1949, and they remained available for decades thereafter. The presence of these patterns significantly strengthened the hand of the central government in shifting investment and resources among industrial sectors when its leaders set out to execute industrial policy. When joined to the relative centralization of national monies that the state enjoyed then, these supports made redeployment of resources a genuine possibility.

Continuities in these crucial supports, plus the Communist Party's promotion of them over the years, gave the state the capabilities for effecting structural change. The supports can be grouped around two central factors: first, a pattern of political-economic arrangements (not necessarily socialist, not always authoritarian) that includes a central government capable—under certain circumstances—of disposing of the bulk of societal resources, that is, a government that can concentrate resources. For this, Deyo's economic institutional consolidation, in short, a reliable bureaucratic apparatus, was crucial.

Second, the culture possesses forms of sociopolitical organization that enabled the political elite to repress and/or appease the losers among the population, even if only for a time. Such repression/appeasement might be done through the nurturing of paternalistic-dependency relations, as with subsidies to preserve groups in danger; by forcibly putting down resistance; by excluding potentially disruptive influences from the policy process; or by providing alternative channels for the disadvantaged to use in satisfying needs the state will not meet. All of these methods stymie the inevitable opposition by affected groups that attends redistribution anywhere, even if open and legitimate interest groups are not a part of the state.

These forms of sociopolitical organization made possible the political insulation of decision makers and thereby allowed their policy to go forward. For such measures preserve the necessary modicum of stability and, perhaps most important for the course of industrial policy, shield decisions and bureaucracies so that politicians ultimately need cope only with their own internal politics but not with undue social pressures.

The Chinese population, of course, has not always been quiescent. But when transferring resources at crucial moments, the post-1949 state has been inclined to handle recalcitrance by insulating itself, and it has been assisted by certain customary patterns of social interaction. The next section examines the sociopolitical supports that combined to form these two central capabilities, one shoring up state action, the other limiting social response.

Concentrating Resources

In China after 1949 centralized concentration of resources, in particular, the state's mobilization of capital and credit for officially decreed goals, was accomplished in two stages, first by expropriation of the holdings of the major, Kuomintang (KMT)-connected bourgeoisie just after Communist Party takeover, and then through the "socialist transformation" of the rest of industry and commerce in the mid-1950's.[8] The entire process of transferring the nonagricultural assets of the private sector to state hands was thus actually spread out over a seven-year stretch, from 1949 to 1956.

Once that prolonged episode of nationalization was finished, the government could determine the macro direction of industrial development at any juncture, subject only to the political condition that a relative consensus first be reached within elite policy councils. This ability to chart national economic policy and the broad uses to which national assets should be put held, more or less, at least until the fiscal decentralization measures that came with economic reforms in the years after 1980.[9] Implementation always rested on a generally responsive state bureaucracy.

Three elements in Chinese society's historical cultural repertoire were activated by the crisis in 1979, as well as by the heightened sense of legitimacy engendered by a rehabilitated leadership renouncing past errors. These traditions bolstered the ability of the state to act forcefully in the economic realm on the basis of the concentration of resources it commanded. The elements were, first, a tradition of state economic activism and state involvement in the economy (for short, statism); second, an official belief system that legitimated such statist dominance; and third, a strong bureaucracy fairly well insulated from popular pressures.

Statism

Chinese economic statism historically tended to be predatory. Its common mode was to force businessmen into collaboration with the state. Merchants in China frequently must not have appreciated the interference of the state in their affairs and the preying on their profits that accompanied this philosophy. But they were certainly well schooled in an age-old pattern whereby their business was entangled in elaborate nets of private-public partnership.[10]

Industrial modernization, after all, had begun with government as opposed to private initiative in the official self-strengthening movement that got under way during the Tongzhi Restoration (1862–74). At that time, in another period of crisis, a perceived imminent threat from the West, the central government set up arsenals and dockyards to produce armaments.

In the succeeding two decades, a system with its origins in the traditional imperial salt monopoly,[11] known as *guandu shangban* (official supervision and merchant management), developed, which underwrote the initiation of modern civilian industry.[12] Under this arrangement, the state appointed official supervisors. Private merchants and gentry then put up share capital, in return for which they received official protection and monopoly rights but also fell subject to sometimes heavy state exactions. The ventures involved ranged from cotton spinning and weaving to mining, railways, and modern banks.[13] Though many of these ventures ultimately foundered, often enough because of too much state interference, they fell into a very old pattern of state intervention into the economy and actually revivified that tradition.

In the twentieth century, while business support was essential to the rise of the Nationalist regime of 1927–37, once the regime was in power businessmen found they had little influence. Instead, the government regularly extorted funds from them for purposes of its own.[14] This background provided a firm precedent for communist organization of the national economy after 1949 and, specifically, for periodic state-sponsored reorganizations at leadership discretion, such as the economic readjustment of 1979–82.

A Legitimating Belief System

Contemporary Chinese political philosophy harks back to an ideological heritage that stresses the organic nature of the state. That ideology, though not always capable of guiding practice, nevertheless stands in reserve, as it were, to be called upon to legitimate state initiatives in times of perceived national crisis.

Andrew J. Nathan and Donald Munro trace this Chinese ideal of an organic, harmonious state to Confucian thinkers, Nathan discussing the reformer Liang Qichao in the late nineteenth century and Munro speaking of the famous neo-Confucian Zhu Xi of the Song dynasty. Liang, for instance, carried forward a long-held doctrine that insisted that harmony was essential to the strength of any social organism, particularly the state, and that private interests had to be suppressed to ensure that harmony. Similarly, Zhu believed that "the ideal political relationship is the harmonious interaction of the occupants of different but mutually dependent roles within a unified state."[15]

Squarely within this tradition, communist politicians after 1949 drew on a concept of "the people" in whose name alone the country's resources were to be concentrated and expended and of a "national chessboard" atop which local and departmental pawns were, supposedly, to be placed solely by the central-level political elite. Frequent calls have filled the media over the years enjoining local administrations to eschew partial interests for the sake of the welfare of the country as a whole. When the policy of economic readjustment was enunciated in 1979, it was justified in the name of an overriding national purpose for which it was proper to reorder national resources.

Strong Bureaucracy

The seminal study of the historical Chinese bureaucracy, by Etienne Balazs, examines the institutional and philosophical dimensions of the more than two-millennial bureaucratic tradition in this state, which was actually the originator of the modern bureaucracy. Entrenched bureaucratic traditions shored up imperial power over centuries, as the common training of its officials ensured the application of relatively uniform policy—if adapted to local variations—throughout the empire. An elaborate, finely regulated hierarchy of command and obedience tied basic-level bureaucrats to superiors held responsible for their every performance.[16]

Probably it makes sense, following Alfred G. Meyer and Jerry Hough, to view the present-day party-led state as a whole as a giant bureaucratic system, "something like a modern corporation."[17] That bureaucracy operates analogously in many ways to its imperial predecessor, with lower-echelon administrators closely supervised by higher-ranking officials and with policy execution guaranteed through requirements of approval for the performance of the most picayune actions.

This is a bureaucracy whose hierarchical rankings, status system, and officials' appointment procedures are structured meticulously from the State Council with its dozens of ministries and commissions down to the provincial and then urban subordinate offices of these agencies. Cadres at each level in the hierarchy, as historically was the case, continue to be held responsible for the appointment and the behavior of those at the level below within their areas of functional and geographic jurisdiction.[18] This bureaucracy perhaps more than most is threaded together by ubiquitous formal processes guided by rules that dictate the specific units to be consulted and the often myriad steps to be pursued in any undertaking.

But all this formalism, though not unimportant, chiefly provides the outer shape of the system. Informal networks fashioned by the mutual obligations, bargains among, and negotiations within sets of well-acquainted cadres supplement and sometimes may actually override the formal system.[19] The centrality of personal ties provides continuity under communism with traditional Chinese society and its organizational style. I observed one indication of this personalism in my own interviews within the urban economic bureaucracy of the city of Wuhan, where I frequently encountered personnel serving as bureau chiefs and deputy chiefs who had worked together in the same general area or even in the same work unit throughout their careers.

Another prominent feature of the administrative organization in China as in other countries dominated by a communist party is the pervasive presence of the party leaders at each level in choosing, transferring, and removing from office the cadres in all positions of any significance at the next lower level. What are called party core groups in the offices of provincial economic, planning, industrial, and indeed all other functional "systems" at this echelon have the authority to recruit those working in the subordinate bureaus beneath them at the city level.[20]

Certainly in the recent reform era, the Chinese themselves have lamented over and labored to undo the corporatelike fusion of party and government and the interference of party bureaucrats in economic affairs that accompanies it. Despite persistent party domination, however, and the heavy infusion of ideology that has informed the work of this bureaucracy since 1949, through the early 1980's this was an administrative organ that was primed to effect developmental goals. The national-scale coordination readjustment called for came from the bond established between policy and detailed bureaucratic regulations, as Chapter 6 will show.

Thus historical legacies of an interventionist state and a belief system that supported it formed a foundation for modern-day massive bureaucracy. This amalgam of traits, more or less continuous despite regime change, made industrial policy, which is best enforced bureaucratically from a national center through state action, a real possibility.

Political Insulation

Successful economic readjustment requires a certain kind of link that joins the state to the social forces it governs. The dynamics of this union must somehow neutralize opposition from affected groups whose members might perceive important state policy initiatives as inimical to their interests. Policy must be able to go forward while those it touches remain suitably silent. This might be done through any number of forms of repression or cooptation. Johnson and Zysman, writing on Japan and France respectively, have said that this insulation of decision makers is essential to the success of the redistributive measures that were at the heart of industrial policy in those countries; they also generalize about the significance of this capability in any state embarking on restructuring policies.[21]

Indeed, there is evidence that China's political elites in the late 1970's were extremely sensitive to the potential for social instability as they carried out economic readjustment and so were careful to find ways to placate and to appease those social forces that would be adversely affected.[22] What features present in the social structure and in the cultural orientations of the population played into these plans?

Three patterns of social behavior drawn from China's historical behavioral repertoire[23] were reinforced after 1949, and they buttressed bureaucratic policy implementation in the post–Cultural Revolution crisis era. In the discussion that follows they will be referred to as unitism, weak horizontalism, and verticalism.

Unitism

Unitism designates the tendency for small social units to draw boundaries around themselves, to encyst against cooperation with outsiders. The self-enclosed family unit, the basis of this pattern, has served as a model that has had a strong influence on many other organizational formations in Chinese society.[24] Attached to this orientation has been a sense of suspicious inwardness, a cell-like encapsulation, that affects industrial behavior to this day.

This inclination, greatly intensified by the communist organization of society, is named, literally, unitism (*danweizhuyi*).[25] Though such powerful attachment to individual groups poses difficulties for overall societal integration, the main problem is horizontal, not vertical, integration. For the disjointedness among peer groups that has been the result has typically made for weak horizontal ties in China. Thus, ironically, this trait facilitates state efforts to penetrate society, as the state faces disgruntled isolated units but not organized groups of discontented.

Linked to this tendency toward inwardness, enterprises are often comprehensive functionally, which greatly limits their dependence on outside entities. The Chinese themselves refer to the "small [or large] but complete" firm, a term that suggests a mode of reducing the risk of relying on outsiders by practicing internal diversification.[26] One writer, talking about this characteristic, refers to "a cultural tendency of Chinese organizations that begin with one function to proliferate into others," which he terms "gigantism." He found a symbol of this "tight communal organization" in "the physical wall surrounding any large factory, university, hospital."[27]

Closely related to unitism is an intense attachment to locality. Historically, the organization of craftsmen into guilds, with their strong provincial character, smacked of this same local particularism.[28] The citywide guild alliances of the late nineteenth century give additional evidence of this pattern.[29] Vivienne Shue's recent volume on the relationship between Chinese state and society speaks of an age-old localism, insularity, and lack of lateral intercourse in the countryside as well.[30]

Localism continues in China today in the commercial blockades erected to hoard regional resources, thereby obstructing the market reforms instituted in and after 1979.[31] And it finds perhaps its most prevalent manifestation in the *kuai* (literally, lump, referring to a clod of earth or, in a larger sense, a geographical region) axis of the crisscrossing *tiaotiao kuaikuai* pattern that structures the national bureaucratic decision-making and responsibility system.* Local loyalties give only a slightly larger form to the unitism that lies at their root, and, like unitism, they add to a tendency toward weak horizontal ties throughout society as a whole.

Chie Nakane, writing on a similar proclivity in Japanese society, makes the very interesting point that the hostility between unconnected groups that is part of unitism in that country has reduced the collective power of society against state historically present there. This orientation then facilitates the vertical transmission of commands from government, such as those that drove the readjustment effort, even as it obstructs horizontal combinations in opposition.[32]

Kuai stands for the horizontal, regional dimension of the bureaucracy, the localities, in which party committees and ultimately party secretaries must reach local consensuses, "balance" local resources, coordinate plans, and meet production and financial targets designated by upper levels. The *tiao* axis refers to the vertically ordered functional systems stretching down to the localities in parallel fashion and capped at the top by ministries and commissions in Beijing which bear national-scale accountability for all work units engaged in the field of activity over which they have charge.

Weak Horizontalism

Because of this generalized tendency toward atomization of society, horizontal groupings have generally been fragile historically in China. True, unions of various sorts were prevalent enough. Guilds, clans, and all sorts of same-status groups (same county, same school, same province) did exist. But these were generally ascriptive collectivities, and the cooperation they furthered was geared in most cases to the performance of mundane, daily joint activities rather than to changing the behavior of politicians. Guilds, for example, had little traffic with the state, not seeking its support or even recognizing the civil law.[33]

In any event, such bodies resisted blending with others beyond their own borders. For example, fears of loss of autonomy for constituent units could easily discourage combinations that attempted to transcend the bounds of the single guild.[34] In the realm of worker politics, the trade unions of the 1920's and 1930's were formed of preexisting clusters—native place assemblages, gangs, and guilds—and the ongoing tensions below the surface in the unions persistently reflected these lines of fission.[35] This disinclination to merge into large clusters had its analogue at the official level: dynastic Chinese law banned private associations, viewing them as potentially subversive;[36] and even horizontal elite associations that could serve political functions were prohibited by the imperial Qing state.[37]

Under the People's Republic, the promotion of "weak horizontalism" has been an explicit objective of the state. Regime-sponsored "mass organizations" have had no autonomy, there have been generally weak horizontal ties between units,[38] and movements of protest (with the exception of the state-initiated Cultural Revolution) have inevitably been short-lived because the state quickly steps in to repress and halt them. To the extent that ties were formed across units (until the Tiananmen demonstrations of mid-1989), this was typically done more on person-to-person or small group-to-group grounds, on the basis of *guanxi*, or connections, and was usually for individual advantage via barter or the exchange of favors rather than for creating building blocks that would lead to larger-scale and permanent issue-oriented bodies.[39] As a prominent Chinese political scientist put it, "In China, the behavior of one person is determined by the 'orders' of another person while the behavior of one institution is determined by the 'orders' of another institution. The 'administrative orders' are always 'vertical orders.' China lacks 'lateral associations' and 'lateral flow of information.'"[40]

Andrew G. Walder presents a good case for the dependency of the workers in Chinese enterprises in the People's Republic, which, he notes, made organization outside the scope of the party a near impossibility,[41] at least through the late 1980's. This view of the customary crippled state of pressure groups shores up Nakane's reflection on the potential for state penetration.[42] In Chapter 7 we will see that this system forced dissatisfied heavy industrial firms and their workers into passive and atomized modes of resistance during the readjustment.

Verticalism

The engineered dependency Walder points to in China under the People's Republic is part and parcel of the industrial paternalism that has marked Chinese firms historically.[43] Gail E. Henderson and Myron S. Cohen pinpoint Confucianism, with its stress on obedience and dependence on authority, as its source.[44] David Strand writes of the "protective and predatory powers held by patrons and bosses" in labor affairs in Beijing during the 1920's;[45] and Gail Hershatter's study of labor in Tianjin holds that the power of guilds lay in their ability to give and receive patronage, "the coin of the realm in pre-Liberation Tianjin."[46]

Such paternalism, which still typifies Chinese industrial relations, finds larger expression in vertical chains of command generally. Here again is a basis for state power. Writing on Japan, Johnson considers the vertical bureaus that manage each separate industry in that country to be a prerequisite for successful guidance and control of industrial policy.[47] Laurence Wylie's similar point about France is particularly pertinent to the reorganization of industrial policy. He observes that a vertical form of organization—often viewed by some analysts as a foundation in other contexts for bureaucratic rigidity and inflexibility—can actually serve as a force for change in a society accustomed to obeying commands when hierarchical authorities send down orders mandating changes.[48]

Potentially a form of repression[49] or, at best, co-optation, paternalism works well in societies where units have only weak horizontal bonds with peer groups. Obviously, it is also a compatible social formation where the family model organizes much of society. Thus verticalism, like unitism, grows out of the paternalistic family patterns characteristic of Chinese society and is present in the whole range of social groups, from school to workplace, to company, to ministry. The search for security that throws little units back on themselves also leads them to look above for protection when their own limited power fails to fill their needs.[50]

Besides this submissiveness in the behavior of lower-order units toward their higher-ups in work hierarchies, Chinese government has also historically institutionalized such reliance on and cultivation of superiors through unitary, centralized political arrangements. Accordingly, officials in lower-level government administrations to this day must appeal above for funds, appointments, and approval of their decisions. Indeed, *pizhun*, or approval, is the taken-for-granted roadblock to be navigated in any official transaction.[51] Such vertical relations are the hallmark of the *tiao* dimension of the *tiaotiao kuaikuai* pattern noted above.

But, though often maligned for preventing autonomy at lower levels, verticalism can also be comforting, especially in the case of large-scale industrial transformation. As Jesse R. Pitts sagely put it in discussing the role of the French trade association, "The doctrinaire-hierarchical tradition of French culture . . . links industrial activity to the state in a manner which reassures the French because the unknowns of movement seem to be neutralized. . . . Change is accepted because it is clear that change is unlikely to threaten social status or to conflict with order."[52] Along the same line, Stanley Hoffmann notes that the French "people trust the state to subsidize change."[53]

As a socialist country with its "soft budget"[54] system that—with only a handful of exceptions—has not allowed even the most inefficient firms to go bankrupt,[55] China has been criticized (not least of all by its own economists in recent years) for overprotectiveness.[56] In fact, even the effort at structural transformation has been characterized as a form of caretaking (*zhaogu*), helping to set failing enterprises on their feet.[57]

But both French and Japanese industrial society have long been shot through with just such care, with the protectors and preservers being French cartels that "shelter the inefficient"; employers that make provision for their workers; municipal authorities; and ministries.[58] Such vertically structured, paternalistic protection generally serves to check aberrant behavior on the part of excluded groups or units, either through repressing or appeasing the potential perpetrators. The upshot is that unpopular state policies, thus insulated, can proceed.

Thus, coddling as well as commands—both of which are tied to verticalism—can serve as key components in macro readjustment programs. As Zysman put it writing on industrial policy in France, such policy by its very nature necessarily involves the "politics of protection and subsidy." Elsewhere, he aptly observes: "Industrial policy has many nuances. It is not simply a long-term strategy to renovate and rebuild, but in some sectors a social policy to preserve."[59] Others have made similar points about Japan, showing that state subsidies and protection, properly applied, can act as incentives,[60] or that there can be a symbiosis between policies of protection and compensation on the one hand and aggressive industrial modernization on the other.[61]

Thus in capitalist as well as in socialist societies, government can be a patron whose aid is expected; subsidies and bailouts and the promise of them can eliminate the fear of risk in a way that Janos Kornai and many other commentators have typically associated only with centrally planned economies and in a negative vein.[62] Here, then, is yet another justification for drawing on literature written about a type of policy, regardless of systemic disparities between the various governments or economies that handled that policy.

This chapter takes one step further the analysis of the three factors described in Chapter 1 that enabled China's politicians to push through their economic readjustment. First, it begins to describe the nature of the political-economic crisis that these leaders believed they confronted after the Cultural Revolution. And second, it suggests historical sociopolitical foundations for a bureaucratic concentration of resources at the national level and for a tradition of societal weakness. In the case of industrial policy, this weakness contributed to insulating the agency executing the policy (whether through repression or through appeasement) and thereby promoted social stability at the same time that state purposes that were unpopular in some quarters were being met.

The result of these factors that unified decision makers and bolstered their power was that the political elite in China in the late 1970's was in a position to command and to coddle—in short, to institute industrial policy—when crisis beckoned, without encountering crippling checks from below.

PART TWO

Crisis and Decision

THREE

Crisis and the Economic Threat

POLITICIANS TAKING STOCK of the state of the national economy in early 1979 identified two separate strands of the crisis it faced. One of these was new: the recently greatly intensified "opening to the world" which China had launched in 1978 posed novel challenges, both developmental and budgetary. The other one was older: a systemic crisis that could be traced back to the installation of the Soviet-style growth model in the 1950's, combined with troubles from the ten-year Cultural Revolution, which exaggerated features of that Soviet model.

These two sources of crisis parallel the two factors of threat in the crisis syndrome identified in the last chapter: a new relationship with the international economy and a backward and imbalanced industrial structure. This chapter will discuss how these two factors influenced the decision to readjust the structure of investment in China. The chapter closes by introducing the city of Wuhan to illustrate the systemic issues more concretely.

OPENING TO THE WORLD

Chinese trade began to expand with the initiation of détente with the United States in 1971. But a major qualitative shift occurred around the time of the normalization of diplomatic relations and the implementation of a domestic program entitled the Four Modernizations in 1978.[1] The change, by contrast with everything that had gone before, was such that one observer could refer to "China's almost continuous isolation from the mainstream of the world economy and S & T [science and technology] system during the last three decades" [i.e., before 1979].[2]

Almost as soon as this more serious integration took off, the major issue rapidly became how to finance the exchange.

As early as 1975, the question of incorporation into the world economy and the problem of paying for it had entered the political agenda. The answer at first was to use China's raw materials, in particular petroleum, as the primary export. This idea was suggested in 1975 in a document sponsored by Deng Xiaoping.[3] But opposition from the radical Gang of Four, whose adherents seconded and even exaggerated Mao's autarkic approach to development,[4] forced that solution aside until after they were deposed in late 1976. By late 1977, though, an alteration began, when Deng's 1975 designs came back onto the agenda.

The first public mention of the intention to switch China's stance in the world economy came in Premier Hua Guofeng's address to the First Session of the Fifth National People's Congress (NPC) in February 1978, when he declared, "There should be a big increase in foreign trade." But Hua mentioned only the export of agricultural and sideline products and of industrial and mineral products (in that order), saying nothing specifically about themes that were to become central not long after: light industrial products as export commodities and massive technology import.[5]

By the time of the Second Session of that NPC in summer 1979, big changes had occurred even in rhetoric. On that occasion Hua was much more emphatic and explicit than he had been sixteen months before. At this second meeting he stated:

Economic exchanges between countries and the import of technology are indispensable, major means by which countries develop their economy and technology. It is all the more necessary for developing countries to import advanced technology . . . to *catch up* with those economically developed, in order to accelerate the four modernizations . . . we shall be taking energetic steps to develop foreign trade.[6] [Emphasis added.]

This statement, however, served more as a justification for steps that had been taken overenthusiastically the previous year and already curtailed by mid-1979 than as a harbinger of something as yet untried. For in the sixteen months intervening between the two sessions those in command of the economy had leaped beyond what the resources of the country could support, purchasing plant and initialing contracts for raw material export. As economist Xue Muqiao later mused, "After 1976 . . . everyone recognized . . . that the national economy was already on the edge of collapse. . . . Because we opened to the world market, many countries competed to invest in China. We got excited and sought to go too fast."[7]

That excitement plunged China into unexpected difficulties. When oil production reached a plateau by the end of 1978,[8] the leadership found itself overcommitted in its agreements to import foreign factories, technology, and expert aid. Two-way foreign trade doubled between 1977 and 1979, but there was suddenly a deficit in trade amounting to U.S. $2.1 billion, and a sizable dip into foreign currency reserves had to be made as well.[9]

At this point the idea of turning to the light and textile sectors as the source of foreign exchange caught on. Chen Yun, at a 1979 report meeting of the newly created Finance and Economics Committee that he chaired, listed the export of textiles, light industrial products, and handicrafts, as well as of heavy industrial products, as the fastest of four possible ways to earn foreign exchange.

Notably, Chen ranked heavy industrial products after light industrial products and textiles; the other three foreign exchange–earning possibilities he cited were the export of petroleum and coal (apparently now considered a growth point for the long term rather than a ready source of funds), tourism, and development in the special economic zones and in Guangdong and Fujian provinces.[10]

With this decision to use the light industrial and textile trades to generate the capital critically necessary for China's new international stance, the backwardness of the domestic economy came full circle to the fore again. This backwardness had fueled the choice for foreign involvement in the first place, and it now returned to haunt the leadership.

Thus opening to the world was paradoxical. It was necessary to help China out of the perceived economic crisis that was frustrating the post-Mao leadership, but it forced further exposure and testing of the vulnerable and noncompetitive domestic economy with its many weaknesses.[11] As a foreign trade official put it in 1980:

> The readjustment of the national economy and the development of foreign trade are interrelated and interdependent. The development of production through readjustment will make possible the promotion of exports. . . . It will also be viable to improve the quality of exports and the quantity of imports, which in turn will raise the capacity for imports of advanced technology and equipment as well as other commodities that China needs, thereby ensuring speedy growth and a strengthening of the economy.[12]

Thus, the reasoning went, readjustment should yield an enhanced level of productivity, which would create more and better exports. The foreign exchange these exports would bring in would be used for imports, which, in turn, would spur further growth. Success, however, rested on the reorganization of the domestic economy to set these forces in motion.

The problem was the seemingly intractable tie between backwardness and the need to export.[13] That is, from the perspective of the elite then in control, backwardness made foreign input mandatory in the form of imports, funding, technology, and advice.[14] But China needed to give something in exchange. And as of 1977–78, when the choice to turn outward was made, China's economy was still skewed toward heavy industry and was laboring under the guidance of the Petroleum Group, the members of which wished to continue to bolster and rely upon that sector.

Unfortunately, the products of the industrial departments in this sector were sadly lacking. As Zhao Ming from the State Planning Commission candidly admitted at an early 1988 forum held by the *People's Daily*'s economic department, "Heavy industry started very early in the country but has been unable to enter the international market."[15] Probably this sector's unsuitability for foreign competition grew out of its favored and protected place in the domestic economy over three decades. As Dwight H. Perkins put it in discussing manufactures as a whole, "The bureaucratic command system is also an obstacle to the expansion of exports of manufactures. It is difficult for enterprises used to supplying goods of poor quality to a captive market to convert to meeting the constantly shifting demands for high-quality stylish products required by export markets in the West and Japan."[16]

Even in Shanghai, where the proportion of machine-building products roughly at the current world-class level was twice as high as it was nationally, only 10 percent of total output could meet that standard.[17] As one analysis of that city's machinery trade put it, "the quality [of various parts of our machines] is too low, which influences the whole machine, and so [our machines] lack competitive ability and can't be exported."[18] Renovating the products of light industry, it seemed, would be comparatively both cheaper and faster.[19]

Thus there was a double edge to thinking about the world economy and China's potential place in it: Chinese leaders were now interested in inputs for their modernization program, and they had to export something in return. But at the same time, they reexamined every facet of their own domestic economy comparatively with that of nations far more developed and found themselves nearly hopelessly behind. Here, then, was one part of the threat, the aspect of the economic crisis that was new as of the 1979 readjustment.

SYSTEMIC CRISIS

But the threat caused by indulging in massive foreign purchases and in confronting the challenges of competing internationally was a corollary to a set of more rudimentary macro-level malfunctions in China's socialist system.* According to the post-Mao elite, those more basic blights on the national economy had been taking shape over several decades. Among the symptoms that analysts sought to explain were drops in the speed of development and in the gross value of industrial output over a twenty-year period.[20]

Economist Ma Hong targeted the imbalance in the proportions between agriculture, light industry, and heavy industry, or, as he

---

*Critics also reassessed the micro properties of firm management and of the cumbersome vertical bureaucracies that mediated firm management. But readjustment was not aimed at these features of the system so they will not be discussed here. Those more micro properties are the subject of discussions of reform of the economic structure, on which a vast literature exists in both Chinese and secondary sources.

put it, "in essence, the relationship between the means of production and the means of consumption" as the "most crucial" source of such failings. Accordingly, he advocated that "solving the contradictions in this relationship should be our point of departure in solving the series of problems relating to the economic structure."[21]

Foreign economists by and large agreed with the Chinese appraisal. A few took a more short-range view: one spoke of the recent "serious impact of the Cultural Revolution"; another termed the economy "profoundly disrupted in the decade of political upheaval and economic mismanagement" (again, meaning between 1966 and 1976, the Cultural Revolution period). This second analyst found the manifestations in structural imbalances, depressed standards of living, and gross inefficiencies.[22]

Other outsiders have stressed more basic strains such as "allocative inefficiencies that had accumulated to serious levels by the end of the 1970's" and were "even more serious" than in other socialist countries, or the "extensive" form of growth, based on adding inputs to increase reproduction rather than on enhancing the productivity of existent stock. These properties of the socialist economic system, they held, had led to inefficiencies and to declines in long-term growth rates.[23]

Chinese assessments of the macroeconomy's failures clustered around three themes: sectoral imbalance and the corresponding disproportion between accumulation and consumption; what was viewed as an undue emphasis on high output targets and speedy growth; and the slicing of the economy into vertical and horizontal command structures (*tiaotiao kuaikuai*) that often threw individual units back on their own self-protective devices, curtailing cooperation and specialization throughout the economy as a whole.

Disproportions and Sectoral Imbalance

Many statistics were marshaled after 1978 to illustrate the point that heavy industry had received excessively preferential treatment over the years. For instance, in 1949, heavy industry had represented just 26.4 percent of the total gross value of industrial output; after three decades of skewed investment, the figure had climbed to 57.3 percent. The outcome, as noted in Chapter 1,

TABLE 3
Investment in Capital Construction by Branch of Industry
(Yuan 1 billion)

Year	Machine building	Metallurgy	Textiles
1978	4.08	4.69	1.39
1979	3.62	3.47	1.41
1980	3.78	3.25	2.33
1981	2.44	2.74	1.97
1982	2.71	4.30	2.12
1983	2.68	4.25	1.71

SOURCE: State Statistical Bureau 1986: 202.

TABLE 4
Newly Increased Fixed Assets in Capital Construction
by Branch of Industry
(Yuan 1 billion)

Year	Machine building	Metallurgy	Textiles
1978	3.39	2.75	.78
1979	3.18	6.22	1.23
1980	3.32	3.13	1.70
1981	2.26	1.41	2.14
1982	2.73	1.86	1.65
1983	2.40	1.33	1.11

SOURCE: State Statistical Bureau 1986: 203.

was that heavy industry increased 90.6-fold, while light grew only 19.8-fold (see Tables 3 and 4).[24]

As of 1979, the investment ratio of light to heavy industry was one to eight. But the imbalance had been even more drastic in the past: the ratio had gone as high as one to ten and even up to one to fifteen in earlier decades.[25] The light sector had been granted only about 5 percent of total national capital construction investment annually, on the average, over the years 1952–78. Its share within overall industrial investment amounted to a mere 9 percent, again as an annual average, during that period.[26] And for 30 years, the ratio of investment in light industry to total state investment had always hovered around 2 percent. The percentages in the various five-year plan periods are shown in Table 5.

The most obvious consequence of the tilt toward heavy industry from the viewpoint of the readjustment was that the light and

TABLE 5
Ratio of Investment in Light Industry to Total State Investment

Plan period	Years	Percentage
First	1952–57	2.5%
Second	1958–62	2.4
Third	1966–70	1.8
Fourth	1970–75	1.9
Fifth (first 3 years)	1975–78	1.9

SOURCE: *FBIS*, Dec. 5, 1979, p. L7 (translation of a report from Xinhua [New China News Agency], Nov. 29, 1979).

textile trades were shortchanged. The share of heavy industry in the gross value of agricultural and industrial output varied over the years. It sometimes reached as high as 52.1 percent (in 1960) and was up to 41.1 percent in 1978, when the post-Mao critique began. In that year, agriculture's proportion stood at 27.8 percent, while light industry accounted for 31.1 percent.[27]

Neglect of the light and textile industries reflected a generalized disdain for the market and a consequent ignoring of its signals in the regulation of economic activity.[28] An overall shortage of consumer goods, as well as a deficiency in the range of goods offered, resulted.[29]

The effect of these policies was severe tension between market supplies and purchasing power. In 1978 and 1979, for instance, the difference between supplies and purchasing power had amounted to several billion *yuan*.[30] Analysts also directed attention to the backwardness of light industry, an outcome in part of the obsolescent state of the technology used in its factories. Much of the equipment matched international levels of the 1940's and 1950's, with a not insignificant proportion dating back to models from the 1920's and 1930's.[31]

The great bulk of the light industrial sector was managed by local governments, whereas the major heavy industrial plants were under the supervision of central-level ministries, which intensified the problem of light industry's insufficient clout.[32] This lack of power was evident in many ways, for example, the relative paucity of materials distributed to this sector. Factories in the light sector often were "squeezed" in energy allocation as well because they had to cede to heavy industry in times of tension and shortage. In Shanghai, from 1974 to 1978, the electrical switch for light and textiles (L&T) was reportedly often turned off; in Hubei, "whenever a proposal was made to reduce the power supply, it always affected the light and textile industries and the households."[33]

A telling illustration of the equipment problem in this sector appeared in the journal *Economic Management* in early 1983. According to its data, as of 1979 just 1.3 percent of the output value of the machine-building industry was used in producing equipment needed for the technical transformation of the L&T industries and for daily-use electrical and machinery products combined.[34] Even in the major industrial center of Shanghai, textile equipment dated mainly from the 1950's. Yet other problems were crowded floor space and dangerous working conditions in light industrial factories.[35] Indeed, cramped quarters for light industry was an irritant on a national scale.[36]

Policy during the Cultural Revolution period, with its stronger than usual denigration of the market and of living standards, aggravated an already very strained situation. Over the ten-year period from 1966 to 1976, more than 20,000 collective enterprises and over a million workers were transferred out of the second light industrial system (which mainly produces clothing), and a billion *yuan* of its assets were shifted to other ministries.[37]

As of 1978, the investment for the state-owned enterprises in this trade accounted for a mere 0.27 percent of the national budget's total investment, and the collectives in that sector received no investment from the national budget. These firms also suffered from a high taxation rate, and some 60 percent of the trade's output value was not provided for (in investment or supplies) in either the national or the provincial plans.[38]

These imbalances had an especially adverse effect on consumption. According to Nicholas Lardy, from 1957 to 1977 consumption grew at only 1.3 percent in real terms, while per capita output increased at the rate of 3.4 percent a year. He concludes that this was largely the result of the rising share of national output that was allocated to investment.[39]

But the L&T industries were not the only ones that encountered tensions in this economic system. Skewing funding and other resources toward heavy industry had a negative effect on heavy industry itself, which became imbalanced internally, resulting in "weak links" in the national economy. Because of the concentration on metallurgy and machine building, other branches of heavy industry were slighted.

One manifestation of the internal maladjustment within heavy industry was a mismatch between the processing capacity that had been built up and the amount of raw materials available to put that capacity to use. In the machine-building trade, the processing ability of the extant machine tools surpassed the supply of steel materials by three- to fourfold.[40] Hubei province, typical in this regard, provides an example of this skewing, with heavy industry as a whole accounting for 84 percent of the province's fixed assets in 1980, and the fixed assets in its metallurgical and machine-building industries representing nearly two-thirds of the fixed assets within the entire industrial sector.[41]

This tilt toward heavy industry was exacerbated in the decade of the 1970's, when the number of enterprises doubled under implementation of the program of promoting "five small industries" in every locality. But many of these operated under capacity or could not even begin operation because of an inadequate supply of materials and energy.[42] According to economist Liu Guoguang, writing in early 1980, more than a quarter of industrial production capacity could not be fully put into use for want of the requisite electricity.[43]

Shortfalls in energy, along with transport, were still another consequence of placing an overwhelming priority on machinery and metals. Energy and transport thus became bottlenecks both because they suffered from a lack of investment and because the favored departments consumed so much of the available energy and communications facilities.[44] These bottlenecks plagued the entire national economy. Solving all these problems would have to entail shifting resources to the neglected sectors. Chapter 6 examines how this was done for the light industrial sector.

High Targets and Speed

The Stalinist-style command economy in China as elsewhere was driven by an "extensive" approach to growth. Such growth was the natural concomitant of high output targets to be met under pressure of speed. Firms striving to reach these objectives in this hectic process naturally neglected economic results and the quality of the product. They relied on new capital construction for promoting development and ignored the technical transformation of existing plant. Ma Hong characterized the total effect as "an unsound cycle of 'high speed, high accumulation, low efficiency and low consumption.'"[45]

Resultant poor quality affected not only the final products but the producer goods themselves. Since so much effort was always directed at simply turning out more and more, there was no time either for proper maintenance or for creating sophisticated tools. A great deal of equipment went for years without adequate renovation, in the interest of simply meeting quantity targets.[46] The machine tools that issued from this system were inefficient and lacked precision, and quick-fix repairs substituted for serious overhauling. The progressively more and more worthless machinery called for nearly constant tinkering, which meant time wasted in factory shutdowns while patchwork mending went on.[47]

Excess capacity became the rule for ordinary, simple tools that were fabricated in bulk, but there were serious shortages of more modern equipment and processes.[48] The sorry result was that the huge output in the machine-building trade often amounted to "empty financial income" because much of it sat in warehouses, unused.[49]

The stagnation and backwardness that were the consequences of this set of practices left their ugly mark even on the privileged First Ministry of Machine Building: of its more than 26,000 products, a shocking 60 percent matched the international level of the 1950's or before. Those equivalent to world-class products of the 1970's constituted only a tiny 5 percent of the output.[50]

Overall, then, not just the light and textile sectors suffered under the regimen of the high-target, quantity-centered, rapid growth that readjustment was meant to curtail and turn around. Machine building, too, despite its priority treatment and political clout, was set back by having to perform in accord with the behavior this system rewarded.

Tiaotiao-kuaikuai

The third feature of the macroeconomy of the socialist planning system that readjustment aimed to reorganize was the combination of verticalism and unitism the Chinese call *tiaotiao ku-*

aikuai. This system, which, as of the late 1970's and early 1980's required double permission for virtually all of any given unit's decisions and behavior, takes its title from its two strands of oversight: the vertical (*tiao*, or strip) and horizontal (*kuai*, or chunk, lump) leadership under which bureaucratic organs and units labored in China.

This arrangement served to carve the national economy into a kind of checkerboard.* On that board each economic unit, whether it was an industrial firm, a shop, a bureaucratic department, or a locality—at any level of the administrative hierarchy up to the State Council—constituted its own self-enclosed sphere.

Each such unit had to answer to and seek approval for its activities and its expenditures from two different overseers. The first of these was the superior-level organ in its functional hierarchy (the *tiao*) charged with its management. In addition, each such unit fell under the supervision of a territorial coordinator (the *kuai*). Thus the urban industrial bureaus were subordinate not just to provincial bureaus and central-level ministries above them in their line of specialization, but also were obligated to reach consensus with organs in the territory in which they were located.

To cope with the pressures resulting from this set of double demands, each unit sought to draw boundaries around itself, to ensure its ability to meet its planned commitments, to enhance its security, and to guarantee its possession of an adequate supply of the requisite inputs for doing its job or for bartering purposes. As Xue Muqiao once explained, "Many of our factories, large and small, tend to be all-inclusive because the present system of management compels them to rely on no one but themselves."[51] The protective self-encapsulation that repeated itself throughout the system led to many economic features that the readjustment critics found irrational.

As this system of dual pressures steered firms (as well as larger units such as cities) toward realizing the maximum degree of both vertical integration and self-reliance of which they were capable, they prided themselves on being "small [or large, as the

---

*Despite the use of the past tense here, for the most part this framework, in its major outlines, still held in mid-1990.

case may be] yet complete" (*xiao* [or *da*] *er quan*). Along with this went a pattern of striving to "do 10,000 things without seeking anyone else['s aid]" (*wan shi bu qiu ren*).

This system had several interrelated unhappy effects. One was duplication of equipment and processes throughout the system. Neither specialization nor cooperation could emerge within such a framework, and much slack and wasted capacity built up. The parts and equipment produced often did not match together or form a complete set (*bupeitao, buchengtao*): the majority of the plants could make some spare parts with some degree of effectiveness but lacked the skill to manufacture a complete piece of complicated equipment.[52]

The *tiaotiao* aspect of this syndrome was especially pronounced in the field of machinery production. During the Cultural Revolution, the various ministries asserted their independence even more forcefully than usual. As each bolstered its own system (*xitong*) of control, almost every ministry set up the capacity for manufacturing machinery. By 1977, 41 different central-level departments were running machine-building enterprises.

The First Ministry of Machine Building, which ought to have unified and coordinated the management of such firms, supervised only about one-tenth of them, representing a mere one-third of the output value of such enterprises nationwide.[53] As one commentator put it, every level in the economic system—whether province, city, district, county, commune, or even brigade—had its own machine-building industry, each surrounded by protective, exclusive boundaries.[54]

At the micro level, the average tractor, machine tool, and diesel engine factory each had its own foundry, forge, and repair works, plus a workshop for manufacturing tools, instead of there being specialized citywide centers to perform each of these functions.[55] Some 80 percent of the factories under the First Ministry of Machine Building were said to be all-around factories (*quanneng*), which meant that enterprises usually did about 80 percent of their own casting and 90 percent of their own forging.[56]

The inefficiency of such a mode of organization became obvious when statistics gatherers found, for example, that nationally the utilization rate of metal-cutting machine tools in 1977 was a mere 54.6 percent.[57] Critics described this most prized department, on which the entire national economy depended for its equipment, as characterized by imperfections, shortages, and slipshod workmanship, turning out products in small batches and at high costs. Chinese analysts judged that many of the flaws derived from what they considered irrational command and organizational systems in the national macroeconomic structure. Chapter 8 will discuss how an effort at rationalization attempted to deal with these problems.

Thus the uncoordinated showering of benefits on the branches of heavy industry, which were then charged with turning out very high quantities of equipment and material at any level of quality consistent with high speed, and the need to respond to orders from superiors as well as from territorial overseers, all combined to construct an industrial system in urgent need of restructuring. A look at the industrial economy in one particular city will illustrate this overview.

WUHAN: A BACKWARD BUT PROMINENT INDUSTRIAL BASE

Chapters 6 and 7, which detail the local politics of implementing the economic readjustment, are based on data from the major central China city of Wuhan.[58] I chose this city as my case study in large part because it presented in very sharp outlines the issues that the readjustment program was to address.

History and Industrial Structure

An inland port city, Wuhan is composed of three towns, Hankow, Wuchang, and Hanyang. The city is the capital of Hubei province, and its location along the Yangtze, and in recent decades on the trunk line Beijing-Guangzhou rail line, has long made it a critical communications and transport hub. Also for locational reasons Wuhan historically served as a crucial commercial entrepôt. It became a treaty port in 1861.*

Industry in the city began with the growth of the iron and steel

---

*Wuhan is situated in the center of Hubei province and of central China and lies on the middle reaches of the Yangtze River, about 700 miles downriver to the west of Shanghai and 850 miles to the east of the city of Chongqing. On the north-south axis, Beijing is a bit over 800 miles to the north and Guangzhou about 685 miles southward.

and textile trades in the late 1800's under the viceroyship of Zhang Zhidong. By the mid-1920's, Wuhan had achieved "a fairly balanced and integrated pattern of industrialization." In the next decade, however, natural and political disasters, along with a loss of overseas markets, led to tens of thousands of business failures and retrenchments.[59] During World War II, when the Kuomintang government moved some 450 industrial enterprises to the interior, about half of them were placed in Wuhan. But after Japan occupied Wuhan, it sacked the city's material equipment. According to recent Chinese sources, the destruction was so complete that by the end of the war, Wuhan's industry was "on the verge of death."[60]

Once the national economy was rehabilitated in 1952, the central government set out to fashion a number of inland industrial bases in an effort to redistribute industry throughout the country, away from its prior concentration on the coast and in Manchuria. Wuhan was a major beneficiary of this policy. During the First Five-Year Plan, 7 of the 156 key-point construction projects undertaken throughout the country were centered in this city, including a huge iron and steel plant (the Wuhan Iron and Steel Works), a heavy machinery factory, a boiler factory, and a meat processing plant.

For several years following the start of construction on these projects in 1957, Wuhan and Hubei enjoyed a share of national investment resources well above their proportion of the national population. Then, after 1975, when industrial investment moved away from the more mountainous, inaccessible regions where the "Third Front" strategy had based it during the Cultural Revolution, Wuhan again received a most generous donation of funds from the central government. In 1976–77, investment in the city amounted to as much as 5.3 percent of total national investment.[61]

Despite the largesse that the central government bestowed on the city over the years, Wuhan's economic decline matched that at the national level. In mid-1979, Mayor Li Renzhi announced that Wuhan's rate of growth had dropped from the average of 17.8 percent per year maintained during the seventeen years before the Cultural Revolution to 7.7 in the thirteen years since 1966. He also revealed that state-owned industrial enterprises in

TABLE 6
Investment in Capital Construction for Light and Heavy
Industry, Wuhan and National
(Percentage of total investment)

Plan period	Wuhan		National	
	Light	Heavy	Light	Heavy
First	6.1%	29.5%	6.8%	38.7%
Second	5.2	66.4	Not given	
Third	5.5	55.2	4.7	54.5
Fourth	5.5	52.5	6.1	52.1

SOURCES: For Wuhan, interview with the Municipal Planning Commission, May 28, 1984; for the national figures, *HQ*, no. 17 (1983), p. 41.

TABLE 7
Wuhan City Investment by Industrial Sector, 1979–1983
(*Yuan* 1 million)

Year	Heavy	Light	Total investment	Percent light
1979	364	83.79	447.79	18.71
1980	364	99.12	463.12	21.40
1981	311	111.00	422.00	26.30
1982	302	149.80	451.80	33.16
1983	333	110.20	443.20	24.86

SOURCE: Interview, Wuhan City Municipal Planning Commission, Nov. 13, 1984.

the city had experienced a decline in labor productivity of 13.2 percent between 1966 and 1978.[62] Wuhan's investment in capital construction for light and heavy industry as a percentage of total investment has historically been close to the national ratios, as shown in Tables 6 and 7. As one source pointed out, the structure of fixed assets in Hubei's light and heavy industrial sectors stood in a ratio of 1 to 4.5, whereas in Shanghai the figure was 1 to 1.92; in Jiangsu it was 1 to 2.35; and in Guangdong, 1 to 2.02.[63]

It was not just that light industry suffered in Wuhan, for it suffered in China as a whole before 1978. This city's consumer goods sector was also weaker than those of its competitors in the same trade. Even the local paper admitted that its products were low in quality and few in color. Besides, they had experienced slow upgrading in comparison with those in other places.[64] This inferiority reflected a generalized problem in Wuhan's industry: throughout both light and heavy industry, equipment lacked matching parts, and many products tended to be made in a single variety, which had been turned out continuously over ten to twenty years.[65]

Mayor Li admitted that development of the city's light industry had been retarded, the victim of insufficient allocations of electricity, fuel, and important raw materials.[66] Electricity in particular was a special problem in this municipality because of the giant appetite of the Iron and Steel Works. Additionally, two researchers discovered that in 1980 of Wuhan's 783 machine-building enterprises, only 53 served light industry. The output value of those 53 accounted for a mere 2.5 percent of the total output value of all the local machinery plants in Wuhan that year.[67]

Perhaps the substandard quality of goods produced in Wuhan can be partly explained by comparing the equipment in its factories with that in the plants of Shanghai. In Wuhan about 40 percent of the machinery in operation as of the early 1980's entered into use in the 1950's and 1960's. Even machines that came into use in the 1970's were mostly crudely made with low precision and backward performance.

In Shanghai, by contrast, over a period of twenty years some renovation had been done. Besides, each 100 *yuan* of fixed assets there produced an output value 2.9-fold higher than that in Wuhan and supplied 5.1-fold higher profits than did the same amount of investment in Wuhan.[68]

Particular Trades

Textiles. Wuhan is one of the five large textile bases in the nation. Its cotton yarn output ranked second in 1979, its cotton cloth third.[69] In its favor, it boasted a "rather complete system" as of mid-1979.* But as a provincial spokesman admitted at that time, though the textile stock across Hubei as a whole was sizable, its quality was poor and the skills of its managers low.[70]

Frequent denial of adequate electricity to the enterprises in this branch went a long way toward explaining its problems. As of 1978, the electricity supplied to the textile firms satisfied less than half of their need. According to the city paper, before the read-

---

*At that time, Wuhan had 97 textile enterprises, housing altogether 520,000 spindles, 13,000 looms and 12 printing and dyeing lines, and employing 72,000 staff members and workers.

justment policy was put into effect, the special line reserved for the light and textile trades was encroached upon by other users and sometimes was casually (*suibian*) turned off.[71] In periods of most serious strain, the textile trade as a whole received enough power to operate only two to three days a week, but even under ordinary conditions it could count on running just four or five days out of seven.[72]

The equipment in the textile plants was also a major obstacle to quality production. Much of it was old in 1979, of mixed styles and patterns. Since most of the machinery parts could not be used interchangeably, repair and maintenance were difficult when they were done at all. But two sources claim that there was virtually no investment for renovating old textile enterprises in the city before readjustment.[73]

In the 1950's and early 1960's, some of the old textile enterprises were permitted to renovate a batch of ancient equipment. But the work done was mostly tinkering and partial. In the Wuhan No. 5 Cotton Mill, for instance, of the 160 spinning frames, 69 (43 percent) were in the style of the 1930's, 63 were from the 1950's (but equivalent to the international 1940's level), and the 28 from the 1960's made up only 17 percent of the total.[74]

Crowded buildings and scarce raw materials constituted two more impediments to this trade's work. To take just one case, the Wuhan Cotton Factory, a twenty-year producer of bedsheets, had a purportedly high reputation both domestically and abroad. But because it was situated in the downtown area, with miserably limited quarters, it was unable to expand its production to meet the demand.[75] City bureau officials reported a lack of coal in their plan and insufficient transport capacity, especially for the movement of coal.

Two other outstanding problems plagued the Wuhan textile trade in the late 1970's. First was its pitifully weak capacity in printing and dyeing. The capacity for finishing could handle only some 54 percent of the textiles turned out (as against 103 percent in Tianjin, for example). It was bemoaned that Wuhan's spinning capacity outran its weaving ability, and weaving capabilities outpaced dyeing. Reports in the local press, expressing a desire that the city should sport a total textile system, complained that city plants had to send hankies to Hunan to be finished and to ship some wool products to Shanghai for dyeing and processing.

These transfers created management confusion as well as raising costs.

Second, there were serious gaps in the more sophisticated lines of textiles: production of wool, hemp, and silk was practically nonexistent in the city when readjustment began. Only 14 colors in these lines were put on the market in 1978, though within two years this number was increased to 802 through the aid of readjustment policies.[76] These deficient production conditions resulted in obsolescent product structure, compared to international standards and to more progressive centers within the country. As of 1978, chemical fibers and blended yarn amounted to only 14.33 percent of total output, while the figure for Shanghai was twice that; in Shanghai, polyester blended cloth represented 27 percent of the gross value of output of all cloth, while in Wuhan it was only 16 percent. Knitted products were also in short supply.[77]

In spite of these difficulties and shortcomings, this city, which was known as a heavy industrial base, depended a great deal on its textile trade for generation of revenue and for exports. The system supplied 35 percent of the capital accumulation for the city and accounted for one-fifth of its industry's gross value of output in 1979. At that time the profits from textiles represented nearly half those of the city's entire industry (46 percent), as against 29 percent nationally.[78] And textile exports amounted to a full one-half of the value of all exports from the city in this period,[79] as against one-fifth nationally.

Overall, Wuhan's textile trade did a middling job in a city where industrial products as a whole were second-rate. But this branch here as elsewhere in China obviously struggled under a set of additional burdens cast upon it by the priorities of the typical Soviet-style economy. In this system supplies served the producer goods industries, and the maintenance and upgrading of textile machines were largely ignored.

Light industry. Wuhan is a city with two light industry bureaus, a feature of the industrial bureaucracy in many of the larger cities. The first bureau manages a total of ten trades;* the

---

*According to an interview with bureau officials on November 17, 1984, these ten are food products, wine and brewing, daily-use chemical products (such as soap), cigarettes, packaging materials, daily-use machinery (watches, bikes, sewing machines), paper, glass, enamel, and pens.

second specializes in things to wear, including clothes, hats, and shoes. Here as throughout the country, light industry was at a disadvantage. But as with textiles, local officials lamented the lack of high-class products in Wuhan relative to other major municipalities.

Their explanation echoed the account offered by city textile officials. They too pointed to old equipment, backward technology and design, late establishment of the trade,* and lack of investment, the latter a problem until the 1960's. Before 1979 the equipment was mostly self-produced or obtained in pieces from Tianjin and Shanghai. Nothing seemed to match together or to form complete sets. Equipment from the 1930's and 1940's accounted for 2.4 percent of the stock; another 16.8 percent came from the 1950's; and an additional 28.11 percent dated from the decade of the 1960's. Reportedly, as much as 47.3 percent had been around from (or was in the style of) the 1920's. Without the requisite capital, there was no way to renovate this ancient machinery.[80]

Another source of difficulty was the meager supply of raw materials. As of 1980 in Hubei only 5.6 percent of the steel metals produced in the province was used in light industry; the amounts of pig iron, timber, and machine-building equipment devoted to that sector were similarly minuscule: 6.7, 7.4, and 17.6 percent, respectively.[81]

The effect of this neglect showed up in the products manufactured in the city. Of the many products made in plants controlled by the First Bureau, only 23 were important enough to be listed in state, ministry, provincial, or city plans. Of those, more than half (14) were in such short supply that the bureau could satisfy only 40 percent of the city's needs for paper, sewing machines, thermoses, and soap powder, for example. An important cause, said the newspaper, was low investment.[82]

A telling indication of the problems in Wuhan's light industry was that during the readjustment the Second Bureau had to halt production of 45 different products it had been manufacturing

---

*Historically, Wuhan specialized in cotton so that both knitting and wool developed late. In addition, the renovation of its equipment was retarded relative to other places, and its share of imported equipment was smaller than elsewhere. This information was supplied by the officials from the Wuhan Textile Bureau, November 14, 1984.

because all of them were finally acknowledged to be unsalable. The bureau also decided to cut back on the output of another 95 that "lacked competitive ability." That system had been exploited during the Cultural Revolution years, when the percent of products serving livelihood needs dropped from 70.4 percent in 1965 to a mere 44.9 percent in 1978.[83] Wuhan's light industry, like its textiles, had a double cross to bear.

Machine building and metallurgy. By the early 1980's Wuhan's machine-building industry boasted as many as 23 different trades, turning out somewhere between 4,000 and 5,000 kinds of products. But only 3.5 percent met international standards of the 1970's, and the ones at the standards of the 1940's and 1950's made up 43.2 percent of the total.[84]

Like textiles, Hubei's machinery industry presented a paradox. The province stood fourth nationally in output value in this branch of industry, but some of its large, backbone enterprises had undergone no large-scale renovation since 1949. In fact, almost half of the 5,000 pieces of equipment in nine key-point enterprises sampled had been in use continuously for more than twenty years.[85] Moreover, the utilization rate of the province's machine-building equipment was as low as 45 percent.[86]

One significant source of the backwardness was the *tiaotiao-kuaikuai* system that chopped up the management of the trade, especially at the 1,181 sites where machine-building activities occurred in Wuhan. These multitudinous workshops were governed by more than 40 different management systems and individual departments, and the result was a utilization rate that generally reached only 30 percent. Naturally, specialization and division of labor were pitifully scarce in this system, where even separate workshops were "small yet complete."[87]

This problem was particularly evident in the casting trade, where many factories had each set up a casting workshop to create their own little systems. Some such factories opened their blast furnaces only twice a month, and each oven could not handle even ten tons of molten iron, though usually an oven can consume thirty tons. Such operations wasted the city's supply of pitch coke.

The Shanghai Machine Tools Casting Factory employed only about 500 workers, and its products had a rejection rate of less than 5 percent; furthermore, production costs there were only 360 *yuan* per ton. But in Wuhan's dozen or so machine tool factories, each with its own casting section, more than 1,090 people did casting at a cost of 650 *yuan* per ton and a rejection rate of 15 percent.[88]

Much the same situation marked the metallurgy trade. This branch of industry was spoiled, especially during the Cultural Revolution, when its only charge was to produce in quantity and when customers, because of their "hunger" for the metals the bureau had to offer, were not selective but "blindly purchased" whatever was available. One newspaper story likened the city's metallurgy bureau of that era to the "emperor's daughter" who "needn't worry" about suitors.[89]

But as in the case of machine building, beneath the surface of a surfeit of riches lay a spate of serious flaws. Here too the equipment in use before 1979 was old and unmatching. And this local trade even by 1982 (when its iron production capacity and output stood second or third nationally) suffered from "two bigs" and "two fews." The big things were iron smelting and rolled steel; the few were mining and smelting steel. This meant that the ability to smelt ore surpassed the amount of ore and pitch coke available, and the capacity for rolling steel outran the ability to smelt steel. The result was that in 1981 the utilization rate for the province's steel rolling equipment was only 48.9 percent.[90]

This detailed picture of the economic structure in Hubei and Wuhan makes more vivid the maladjustments the command economy had created. It is too simple just to stress that heavy industry had been favored and light industry consequently damaged in a sort of zero-sum game. In fact, none of the investment had been used in the most efficacious fashion. Rectifying the wrongs would certainly call for some shift in investment and a transferal in allocation patterns. But it was apparent that success in that endeavor could hardly solve all the problems.

CONCLUSION

No three-year policy could fix the host of systemic and structural weaknesses, nor, for that matter, could it begin to address them all. But at least the conjuncture of factors that composed a crisis syndrome did make it possible for the rehabilitated political elite under Deng Xiaoping to chart a different course in the country's ongoing search for amassing funds, for social stability, and for genuine, world-class modernization. With the shift in investment priorities in favor of more light industry, a start in tackling these weaknesses was to be set into motion. Light industry, whose receipts were to lay the foundation for future takeoff, would lead an export-oriented excursion into development.

Whether China should expand economically had never been at issue. But the string of corollaries to this particular strategy one by one contravened just about every tenet of the old, discredited radical Maoist approach to expansion. Rather than austerity and plain living, consumption was to pacify the populace. Not self-reliance but integration into the world order would promote technical advance. And whereas the state of yore had amassed its wealth by rapid and often rupturing surges, now a stable balance was to bolster the budget. Seeking sectoral proportion and satisfying the people's livelihood became the modes of meeting the long-held goal of economic growth.

Crisis had carved out a space for choice. Into that space had to be fitted answers to pressing issues: deficits in foreign trade that would surely mount as oil stocks drained off if the imports of technology from abroad, vital to upgrading the obsolescent national economy, were to continue; and, as we will see in the next chapter, at home, disgruntled consumers and restive, unemployed youths whose will to play a positive role in a quietly productive social order was in question.

It required a reconstituted elite—one alienated from the solutions of the past by the Cultural Revolution and by the doctrinaire developmental approaches of its designers and more or less consensually committed to revamping old strategies—to choose a fresh answer. The next chapter, on the political opportunity in the crisis, shows how such an elite came to that consensus.

FOUR

Political Opportunity

CRISIS IN THE AFTERMATH of the Cultural Revolution was in part a matter of possibility. The perpetrators of that egregious episode had discredited themselves politically, clearing the way for other politicians to push entirely different policies, of which the economic ones were most prominent. There were still small battles to be fought between the survivors and the rehabilitated, but the cause of readjustment came into its own finally after the survivors—who still favored heavy industry if not Maoist radical campaign-style approaches—undermined their credibility by some massive mistakes.

This chapter starts this story by pointing out that by late 1978 most Chinese politicians believed that the country had reached a socioeconomic crisis. Not only was generation of resources threatened, but social stability was at stake as well.

CRISIS PERCEPTION

In early 1979, several top Chinese leaders painted the country's predicament in crisis proportions. Chen Yun, newly named a vice chairman of the Party Central Committee and made a member of its Politburo Standing Committee at a landmark December 1978 meeting (a stature he had enjoyed in the days before the Cultural Revolution, when he had masterminded a major economic readjustment and recovery program following the Great Leap Forward), was the man mainly responsible for this critique.[1] Chen later elaborated his criticisms in a series of party meetings in the succeeding months.

On one such occasion, in March 1979, Chen proclaimed that "today's proportional maladjustment is much more serious" than the post–Great Leap Forward crisis of 1961 and 1962 and that its resolution would require two to three years of readjustment, at best three.² The next month, party vice chairman Li Xiannian presented the overall rationale of the readjustment policy and underlined the perceived gravity of the situation. He spoke of the "very serious results" that had come about as the national economy suffered longtime interference and destruction at the hands of the perpetrators of the Cultural Revolution. As he put it, "The national economy fell into collapse; this really is a kind of economic crisis."³

This anxious mood was shared among the reconstituted post-Mao elite. Reference to such a consensus appears in an assessment by party economist Xue Muqiao, whose words evince a sense of the threat that was part of the crisis: "After 1976 everyone recognized that there had been 10 years of catastrophe, that the national economy was already on the edge of collapse."⁴

The threat, however, was joined by opportunity. A. Doak Barnett speaks of "systemic problems which had accumulated over more than two decades [and] required major innovations in policies." He goes on to explain: "It was the recognition of the seriousness of these problems, as well as the traumatic effects of the Cultural Revolution, that created a sense of major crisis in China after Mao's death, and it was this sense of crisis that predisposed many Chinese leaders to consider major policy changes."⁵ In a positive vein, then, consensus centered on economic rehabilitation and rebirth as Mao's successors rejected the aims of class struggle and revolutionary transformation that had shaped or at least informed past policies in China most of the time for decades.

LIGHT INDUSTRY FOR RESOURCE GENERATION AND SOCIAL STABILITY

The program these new leaders proposed was enmeshed in a tangled web of cause and effect, which grew out of the interaction of the four elements of the crisis syndrome. At its core lay a new model for economic development, with light industry as its springboard. This sector was to lead the way to overall national economic growth while at the same time satisfying the regime's constant goals of resource generation and social stability. Readjustment was to draw upon but also to further the state's ability to concentrate resources and to restrain resistance.

Light industry could furnish capital by providing foreign exchange.[6] Receipts from its exports, added to the benefits that a more balanced economy should bring, were then to lay a foundation for future growth and modernization. As early as February 1979, just two months after the Third Plenum, arguments were rife in the press pointing to the benefits of directing resources toward light industry. These included its need for only relatively small amounts of investment, its quick results, its provision of much revenue and foreign exchange for the state,* its ability to satisfy the people's needs, and its service to other sectors.[7]

Besides, light industry could contribute to stability in two ways: by courting consumers long suffering from lean markets of low-quality daily-use commodities, scantily stocked,[8] and by supplying jobs as its labor-intensive productive processes absorbed millions of urban unemployed.[9]

Politicians, worried about potential unrest, hoped to channel popular reactions in positive directions. After all, economists were arriving at calculations that showed that from 1971 to 1978 "nonproductive accumulation" (roughly two-thirds of which is housing) had continuously fallen below 25 percent of total investment and had dropped in 1976 as low as 18 percent. The gap in this funding "directly affected the people's standard of living," in Dong Furen's estimation, when he compared these figures to the 40.2 percent spent in this way during the First Five-Year Plan of the 1950's.[10]

One article admitted that "the question of living standards affects the stability of the country."[11] This concern is also clear in a June 1979 *People's Daily* editorial. "If we don't change," it warned, "we can't have high-speed, planned, proportionate development, and the masses won't forgive us."[12] Similarly, sometime later, Vice Premier Gu Mu told a visiting Japanese economic delegation that there was an urgent problem of restoring the confi-

*RMRB's editorial of February 20, 1979, stated that light industry supplied 20.1 percent of the national financial income and 21.2 percent of the foreign exchange in 1977.

dence of the Chinese people, "for without economic readjustment their livelihood would be in jeopardy."[13]

Thus readjustment amounted to a new approach to capital accumulation and stability, aimed at rectifying two of the wrongs identified at the hallmark December 1978 Party Third Plenum:[14] imbalance among industrial sectors and the slighting of livelihood, both of which had been present since the 1950's. Usually the Third Plenum is identified as the progenitor of the decentralizing and marketizing "reform" program that got under way at roughly the same time readjustment did.

But the plenum's communiqué, besides instigating economic reform to "transform the system and methods of management" and to dilute the Stalinist-style economic structure's "overconcentration of authority," also drew attention to the issues involved in readjustment. It noted "quite a few problems in the national economy, [and] some major imbalances [that] have not been completely changed." The document also pointed to "a series of problems left hanging for years as regards the people's livelihood in town and country [that] must be appropriately solved." The text set as a critical goal for the next few years the achievement of a comprehensive balance so as to lay a solid foundation for rapid development. And it held it "imperative to improve the livelihood of the people."[15]

In all, readjustment was conceived as an expedient measure, an interlude during which wrenching shifts would be set in motion. These changes were to turn economic activity from the direction it had pursued for more than a quarter of a century and to set a foundation for future development. The alterations were also to provide what were seen as the requisite conditions for the more thorough reform planned for the total economic structure.[16] As Chen Yun saw it, the "main goal" of readjustment was to set the economy in gear for rapid growth. For, as he put it, "developing according to proportions is the quickest kind of speed . . . the aim is to go forward according to proportions."[17]

OPPORTUNITY: POLITICAL POSSIBILITY
A History of Failed Efforts

The "crisis syndrome" outlined above formed the backdrop in China for a dramatic yet largely untold story: the rapid righting of a decades-old disproportion between light and heavy industry in the total economic structure. Major and lasting readjustment of the Chinese economy's investment structure—away from its preponderant skew toward heavy industry and, by favoring light, toward greater balance—was toyed with, talked about, and briefly tried out on and off for over twenty years. Then suddenly this feat became a possibility in a context of crisis in early 1979.

This was by no means the first post-1949 Chinese effort at reorientation of the structure of national investment.[18] As Lin points out, the leadership's push to put in motion a new developmental strategy was one long attended by "frustrated ambitions" and a sense of "lost opportunities."[19] Debates had commenced during the 1956 Eighth Party Congress, when proposals were made to bring an end to the First Five-Year Plan's sectoral disproportions, material bottlenecks, and malcoordination in the course of preparing for the Second Plan.[20]

The critics identified ills typically associated with the centrally planned, heavy-industry-centered Soviet-style growth mode. In the mid-1950's critics were already arguing for readjustment in the ratio of investment going to consumption as against accumulation (meaning investment, usually in capital goods and minerals) and for realigning the sectoral distribution of funding (more for consumer than for producer goods), similar to the readjustment proposals of the late 1970's.

Even Mao himself is on record as championing an increase in funding for light industry (and agriculture) in early 1957. In the original version of his speech on the handling of contradictions among the people, he advocated that

the ratio of investments in heavy industry, light industry and agriculture should be substantially adjusted in comparison with the past . . . I think [we should give] further consideration to this ratio in the Second FYP. In sum [we] should help light industry [and] agriculture develop. . . . Heavy industry still takes precedence. But by taking the new road, will the rate of industrial [development] be quicker than the Soviet Union's or not? It may look a little slower, [but will be] a little faster. . . . [If] the peasants increase [their] purchasing power, [then] light industry will have both materials and a market [and] heavy industry will have a market, too.[21]

But little came of these intentions. As two Chinese analysts explained it: "Why have Mao's guidelines on simultaneously developing heavy, light, and agriculture not been followed? The trouble is that giving undue prominence to heavy industry has become a habit, a habit far stronger than the Party's guidelines and policies."[22]

Moreover, these issues raised in 1956 and 1957 remained unresolved. For the discussions that brought them to the fore were followed quickly by the antirightist campaign, which first quashed that debate and then led headlong into the full-scale disequilibrium of the Great Leap Forward. For some twenty years a continuing, if often interrupted, conflict over this issue simmered and sometimes boiled.

Those favoring an imbalanced emphasis on heavy industry claimed that faster growth was possible. They were countered, usually without effect, by those preferring balance, who charged that imbalance wasted resources, led to inflationary pressures, had negative incentive effects, and increased social instability.[23] The ongoing interplay was one between radicals' ambitious economic surges on one side versus the academic plaints offered by economists (along with a group of "haste makes waste" politicians—principally Chen Yun[24] and Bo Yibo) on the other.

In the wake of the Leap's disastrous denouement, Mao again seemed to favor some righting of proportions and stable strategies, at least at first. At the Ninth Plenum of the party's Eighth Central Committee held in January 1961, Mao spoke of jointly pursuing agriculture and light and heavy industry, a plan he claimed had been under discussion then for five years but had yet to find fruition.[25]

The early 1960's saw another effort by economists and their political allies to stress balance over speed (at times expressed as "speed through balance") and to find other sources for growth besides increased accumulation. Chen Yun, supported by Liu Shaoqi and Zhou Enlai, argued for a focus on the market, agriculture, and the production of more manufactured goods for daily use, and for drastic reductions in the targets for heavy industry and capital construction.

By 1962, however, this was a dead issue for Mao, who, supported by officials in the heavy industrial sector, insisted that China was already recovering from the Leap sufficiently that no extraordinary measures were required.[26] He even attacked the readjusters of that era at the summer 1962 meeting at Beidaihe, charging them with being overly pessimistic. Despite Mao's opposition, though, Chen Yun's design was implemented over the years 1963–65 so that the economy finally recovered.[27]

Even in the midst of that rehabilitation, though, an outline for the 1966–70 Five-Year Plan aimed at extending its measures was scuttled when Mao intervened in the planning process in May 1964. The proposed plan had envisioned a major concentration on restoring living standards, developing agriculture, and expanding the production of consumer goods. But Mao decreed that there must be a new program of building basic industry in the hinterland, known as the Third Front strategy.[28]

The early 1960's round closed with the Cultural Revolution and its terroristic ban on all discussion of economics and market-prone approaches. Even Zhou Enlai's moves in the early 1970's to restore stability to planning became embroiled in the ultraleftist attacks and intraparty struggles that did not die down until Mao's demise in late 1976.

Ideological Obstacles

In all these debates over the decades of Mao's rule the academic economists and their haste-hating confreres confronted a fearsome ideological obstacle that accounted for their repeated defeats. That hurdle had two roots: the Soviet developmental strategy with its doctrinal underpinning and Mao's own philosophical stance in regard to growth.

The Soviet strategy for economic development drew on ideas derived from Marx's discussions of simple and expanded reproduction. The first to advance this formula was the Soviet economist G. A. Fel'dman in the 1920's; soon after, the Soviet politician E. A. Preobrazhensky popularized it.[29] This strategy was premised on the notion that any economic system can be divided into two departments, one for producer goods and the other for consumer goods.

The theory behind this approach held that accelerated growth depends on annual increments in the percentage of investment allocated to producer goods. As critical Chinese commentators noted in the early 1980's, their country had drawn this credo from the Stalin period, a time when the Soviet Union had been surrounded by imperialists. The Chinese had then erroneously made it into an inviolable universal law, aping its arrangement of production.[30]

The other impediment the Adjusters[31] faced, and of course the more vivid of the two, was Mao, along with those who supported him and those who took their cue from his ideas and then carried them further than he himself did. Some have tried to cite Mao's Eighth Party Congress–era speech "The Ten Great Relations" of April 1956 as evidence that he favored expanding the portion of investment going into agriculture and light industry.[32] It is true that he said, "Our present problem is that we must appropriately readjust the investment proportions between heavy and light industry and agriculture, developing light industry and agriculture more."[33] But Mao had quickly explained that his motive in this proposal was to strengthen the previously neglected sectors for specific ulterior purposes. In fact, his primary aim was to invigorate those branches so they could increase the funds for capital accumulation going to the producer goods departments. Moreover, Mao openly announced in this same address that he fully backed the Soviet system's priority allotment to heavy industry.

Mao's philosophical conception of economic development rested on a view that imbalance was a kind of "natural law." In his opinion, development had a "wave-like" pattern as a matter of "inevitable regularity." Furthermore, he held, "balance is nothing but a temporary, relative unity of opposites"; in short, "economic development . . . [was] not a balanced and consistent progress."[34]

To say that the hegemony of these ideas about heavy industry and imbalance, enforced by Soviet precedents and Mao's power, had a chilling effect on economic discourse would be understating the case. Once debate opened in the late 1970's many of those

78   CRISIS AND DECISION

who had earlier been forced into silence described the climate they had passed through. As one commentator noted:

> For a long time some theories have fettered our thinking. For instance, in the relations between production and the people's livelihood, giving all-round attention to the former is Marxist while paying attention to the latter is revisionist. Within production, promoting heavy industry is regarded as Marxist while engaging in light industry is revisionist. Within heavy industry, "taking steel as the key link" is considered to be Marxist, not taking it as the key link is regarded as revisionist. In the relationship between accumulation and consumption, the more that is accumulated, the more Marxist it is while paying attention to consumption is revisionist.[35]

In this vision revolution entailed an "attack," high targets, and speed. Balance was pejoratively labeled "right conservatism," and taking practical limits into account was "negative balance" and castigated as "the theory of conditions." In contrast, gaps in planning, equated with "revolutionary spirit," were considered a favorable factor, and relying on subjective initiative was called "positive balance."

Since in this environment it was "better to be left than right," some, who "with fear in their hearts" saw "the necessity of readjustment . . . dared only to think, not to speak or to act, or found it sufficient to speak but hesitated to advance, and spoke but only haltingly." Others, overcome by an "illness" of "fearing rightism," subscribed to "leftist planning," which, as one economist delineated it, "can only add, but not subtract, and can only set up, but not close down enterprises."[36]

By late 1978, then, readjustment and its advocates had passed through a long history of thwarted efforts. And yet these proponents had not been totally cowed into submission. As the coast gradually became clearer, they were ready to launch their program once again.

Collegial Succession and Consensus

The inclination for change. A link between leadership succession and policy innovation is the subject of a much-cited work.[37] Its author posits their connection in an undifferentiated, broadbrushed fashion, simply asserting that "new leaders advocate new priorities in socialist nations." According to this study, the most important factors that determine the extent to which they will do so are the presence of new people and the duration of the previous regime.[38]

Yet compared with successions in other socialist states in the past, the Chinese outcome has been somewhat distinctive.[39] As Tang Tsou stresses, it was the Cultural Revolution that made the difference.[40] The horrors of that rampage stigmatized the entire program and the procedures of its proponents, ushering in, as Tsou says, a "sweeping historical reexamination" by the leaders who followed.

By late 1978, Deng Xiaoping had consolidated his leadership role by engineering a succession of gentle ousters of people progressively more and more distant from, but still ideologically loyal to, Mao and his more radical strain.[41] An important part of the victory for a new economic policy was the fiasco of efforts by pro–heavy industry politicians—most of whom had been relatively closer to Mao and some of his ideas than to reformers—in the immediate post–Cultural Revolution period. The result of Deng's maneuvers was that, on the eve of the 1979 readjustment decision, past radical ignominy and more recent masterful politicking had restructured the agenda.

Those remaining at and returned to the helm of power by the end of 1978 were thus at once scarred personally (many of them having been victims of the radicals) and aghast at what the nation had suffered under the former radical regime. This mood enabled decision makers with a range of inclinations to cohere around concepts of reform, modernization, and development.

These men were concerned with pushing Mao's divisive tactics of class polarization and ideological purification from the policy platform. Thus they united collegially both around what they favored—growth—and against what they were ready to disown—movements and struggle. And because the big pushes of the radical purists had historically been tied to the pro–heavy industry strategy, it became possible suddenly to promote a new investment program.

The gradual buildup of support for readjustment. This consensus was not at first total, however.[42] As Xue Muqiao later told it, after the Gang of Four's fall in October 1976, the leftover leadership by and large subscribed to a general indictment of the state of the economy.⁴³ And yet this consensus by no means heralded smooth sailing for policy makers wanting a shift in course. Instead of being able quickly to institute a program of intersectoral proportion and balance, pro-readjustment partisans met obstructions to their plans, both at first and remittingly even after readjustment became policy.⁴⁴ A deepening of the generalized, systemic crisis in the national economy caused in part by the dominance of the pro–heavy industry group just after 1976 had to be supplemented by mounting deficit, depleting oil stocks, and rising urban unemployment before these basic changes were more roundly endorsed.

Readjustment aimed to reduce heavy industry, and so a major source of its opposition came from the members of the so-called Petroleum Faction, a group of politicians and economic bureaucrats based in the oil and heavy industrial departments who were in charge of the economy from 1976 through 1978.⁴⁵ Their return in force to the commanding posts of the economic bureaucracy took place at the end of 1976, with State Planning Commission chief Yu Qiuli and Vice Premier Li Xiannian in top control.

This group controlled the chairmanships of the State Planning, Economic, and Capital Construction Commissions and the Ministries of Petroleum, Metallurgy, and Chemical Industry. Its members continued to support the faster growth strategies and the bias toward capital construction and heavy industry that the Stalinist-style economic model entailed. These officials were also responsible for what Chae-jin Lee has termed the "frenzied spree of foreign plant purchasing" that went on in 1978.⁴⁶ As the funds and resources for financing their schemes ran down, and as economic problems accordingly intensified, the door to readjustment opened up.

At the Third Plenum of the party's Eleventh Central Committee, Chen Yun characterized the years 1977–78 as having been marked by serious errors. Continued excessive concentration on steel, he believed, had created more imbalances and unemployment, further deterioration of light industry and agriculture, and neglect of consumers. At that plenum, attacks on some of Mao's close associates and the reinstatement into key Politburo posts of Chen Yun and others who had been targets of the Cultural Revolution laid a foundation for more sweeping critiques of recent economic strategy and, by implication, of the whole thrust of the old developmental approach.

This set of critiques began with a censure of the Ten-Year Development Plan (1975–85) that had been put together by the Petroleum Faction. Reportedly, capital construction expenditures had come to 47.9 billion *yuan* in 1978, a 50.2 percent increase over 1977, causing the rate of accumulation to shoot up to 36.5 percent (only 2.5 percentage points lower than the 1958 Great Leap Forward's 39 percent, Xue Muqiao noted).[47] In addition, U.S. $7.8 billion had been committed in contracts to import foreign plants.[48]

Once these extravagances came to light, readjustment-oriented leaders began to call for revisions in the draft economic plans for the next two years.[49] A reduction in the number of planned construction projects and the termination (only temporary in some cases) of imports of foreign plants and of contracts for foreign-aided projects followed.[50]

These events quickly culminated in a stock-taking involving both scapegoating and self-criticizing at the April 1979 Party Central Work Conference, where the policy of readjustment was formally adopted. Here Vice Premier Gu Mu blamed ongoing problems of imbalance in 1976–78 on Cultural Revolution–era disruption initiated by Lin Biao and the Gang of Four. Gu thus attributed the situation confronting the leadership in 1979 to the period when they had held sway, even after Lin had died and the Gang had gone.[51]

Apparently these two post-Gang years had been a controversial time, with those in charge proud of their accomplishments in restoring production, but with others becoming increasingly dissatisfied.[52] Deng later referred to "two years of confusion following the smashing of the Gang, which developed into even greater imbalances."[53] And Xue Muqiao, speaking in late 1980, labeled the growth that was achieved in 1977 and 1978 as merely a matter of recovery that included a big element of "sham" because quality was down and costs were up, while much of the output, unusable, had ended up in warehouses.[54]

In distinction to Gu, party Vice Chairman and Vice Premier Li Xiannian took on a large part of the blame for recent economic failures. Li, representing the party center and the State Council in introducing the policy of readjustment at the April 1979 party meeting, must have been atoning for his own errors of the previous two years, when he had been in charge of the economy, and so was implicitly criticizing himself: "The basic cause of the malproportions is Lin Biao and the Gang of Four's destruction. But after shattering them, we didn't recognize enough the seriousness of the proportional maladjustment. We were too rash in regard to economic development, and our steps were too unstable. This also was an important cause."[55]

Ma Hong later asserted that following the decision for readjustment, consensus obtained by the summer of 1979. According to him, this time leaders were in agreement in their opposition to the economic structure that had been formed over many years of focusing on steel output, putting heavy industry ahead of light and of agriculture, and being closed to the world.[56] But even then all conflicting voices had not been silenced. Xue Muqiao later revealed: "Some comrades who had long done economic work, in the wake of early 1979 decisions, said that, 'accumulation is the only source of expanded reproduction,' and claimed that lowering the accumulation rate would lower the speed of the development of production, which ultimately would make it impossible to improve the standard of living."[57]

And indeed, the Second Session of the First National People's Congress, which met in June and July of that year, gave intimations of persisting differences among top leaders, evident in the way the main speakers characterized the previous two years and in the tone in which they talked about readjustment. Premier Hua Guofeng said nothing about enforcing the decrease in the tempo of development that the April meeting had called for or about that convention's commitment to reductions in heavy industry.

In fact, Hua continued to encourage "high-speed development" and the expansion of all branches of the economy, including heavy industry. State Planning Commission Chairman Yu Qiuli agreed that "high-speed development" was an ongoing priority. And both Hua and Yu presented positive accounts of accomplishments they considered worthy of the prior two years, referring to "solid achievements in economic recovery and growth."[58]

Nonetheless, the patent failure of their years at the helm greatly weakened their clout in policy councils, and readjustment was put into effect.

By the spring of 1979 the political climate in China was conducive for making major economic changes. The analysis here has directed attention toward issues of succession, discrediting of the past, and a pro-growth consensus, all of which combined to fashion a moment of political possibility. A substantial portion of the post-Mao successor elite was agreed that an economic crisis existed. Moreover, these men were bent on adopting a new strategy of growth to cope with the ills that the methods of the past had fostered. True, the continuance of varying perspectives among Chinese leaders meant that the path of this program would be littered with a certain amount of recalcitrance and infractions. Still, the larger picture was that consensus on generalities had given opportunity its opening.

FIVE

The Politics of Readjustment at the Top

THE CRISIS THAT PRESENTED both an economic threat and a political opportunity called on state capabilities for resource concentration and relied on passivity among the people; it also heightened the elite's usual concerns about control over resources and over social stability. Although China's socialist economy puts its own stamp on those concerns even in normal times, crisis brought the concerns to the fore with particular force.

Indeed, in both the 1979 decision to increase investment for light industry at the expense of heavy and in the 1981–82 return to an emphasis on the heavy sector, a sense of crisis made these two rather ordinary state goals (or elite values) take on a particular urgency: revenue generation-cum-resource concentration and the social stability that comes from political insulation. These goals, I will argue, became the critical criteria in the policy formation of the period, and so accounted for both of these sectoral choices. Moreover, in this context of crisis it was these elite values or concerns, and not the preferences and power of petitioners, that determined the policy outcome twice in these years.

Scholars have begun to interpret Chinese decision-making processes in terms of either two-way bargains or one-way lobbying initiated by those demanding favors. Analysts have used these models to explain resource transfers in China today, for example, in accounting for the central government's disbursal of investment to the regions and to functional bureaucracies. Each of these models conceives of the representatives of special interests as coming to the central government armed with a certain degree of clout. If that clout is sufficient, it will enable these delegates somehow to trade on their power or to lobby for their claims.

The result, then, will be that petitioners with power resources get what they want; alternatively, the conferral of privilege issues from a bargain between two parties. In the case of policy making, the bargain is one between the central government and party organs and a functional or geographical interest, which, to succeed, must possess a pack of benefits it can barter.[1]

Both models take as a premise the centrality of power resources in the hands of the claimants, which, in these analyses, determine the outcome of policy conflict. Additionally, these two explanations share an assumption that the status quo is being maintained and that allocatory commitments will remain within a framework of immobility or, at best, marginal change. D. Michael Lampton, who has argued for the bargaining model, says of this stasis of allocations: "Within systems and individual bureaucracies resources are treated as a 'lump' to be carved up among subordinate entities according to the percentages previously applicable."[2] He states elsewhere that "budget shares among systems tend to remain relatively stable over time, reflecting an incremental budgetary process," and that "the competition is for marginal increments."[3]

Similarly, Kenneth Lieberthal and Michel Oksenberg, speaking of regional funding in China, highlight this same continuity of funding over time as applied to subsidizing geographical units:

> In effect, the leaders of each province have struck their deal with the Center. A package has been worked out concerning the revenue flow between the two, the amount the Center will invest in the province, the amount of foreign currency at the disposal of the province, the amount of scarce centrally-controlled material resources (such as electricity) the Center will allocate to the province, and so on. This package is subject to an annual review and *marginal adjustment*. (Emphasis added.)[4]

Susan Shirk used the concept of lobbying in a 1985 publication to explain the favoritism bestowed on the heavy industrial sector before the 1978 reforms. She does admit that light industry benefited more from the reforms than heavy did, at least at first.

Still, she considered "the opposition of heavy industry a serious threat to the future of the economic reforms," even after the reforms had been under way for some time. This, in her view, is "because heavy industrial systems exercise considerable influence over policy decisions in a socialist political economy."[5]

But bargains and lobbying as modes of interaction best describe marginal adjustments in normal times, not the more massive and exceptional transfers that characterize crises or the sudden departures in resource disbursal that issue from industrial policy. Thus the emphasis these authors have put on stable, typical times precludes reaching an understanding of policies such as the 1979–82 readjustment, which jarred that equilibrium. Certainly if only the resources already and repeatedly granted to heavy industry defined all decisional outcomes, heavy industry could never have been deprived as it was in the years between 1979 and 1982.

In the crisis of the readjustment period, major shifts in investment among sectors occurred in which special interest bureaucratic pleaders were passive and reactive, not provocative or powerful. Moreover, in demonstrating that heavy industry has not consistently been stronger in the post-Mao era, the argument will point to the limits on interest-oriented bureaucratic power in this socialist state. Instead, it will posit that the heavy industrial sector in recent years has been able to exercise clout only when its development appeared to the members of the central elite to fit into their preferences and to match their perceptions of the current imperatives of the economic environment.

ANALYTIC FRAMEWORK

Economic Readjustment, Redistributive Policy, and Agenda Formation

Two concepts from the American literature on politics, redistribution and agenda setting, delineate the dynamics of China's 1979–82 disinvestment and redeployment of resources better than the concepts of bargaining and lobbying do. Both of the former concepts emphasize the centrality of power at the top of the political system and underline the passivity of petitioners in the process of seeking funding at such times of readjustment.

Economic readjustment, a policy of disinvestment, reallocated investment among industrial sectors. By transferring resources, it shared structural features with the policy type that Theodore Lowi long ago labeled "redistribution." Although the term "redistribution" generally refers to social policy, like China's industrial readjustment it involves a shift of goods—wealth, property rights, or any other valued benefit—among groups in society (in the case of readjustment, this was a shift among industrial sectors). Such shifts are unfailingly conflictual because they are bound to result in a new division of beneficiaries into winners and losers.

The hallmark of redistribution is that relatively disadvantaged groups become the recipients of some value that theretofore had been in the grip of the previously more privileged. The short-changed party(ies) typically relates to the rearrangement in zero-sum terms[6] as it grabs desperately for the favors lost.[7] Chinese readjustment of the late 1970's and early 1980's fits this pattern. For, unlike the contemporaneous decentralizing and distributive reform policies, the choice to reallocate defined the political competition in its broadest terms as one between two sides. Since the overwhelming bulk of investment capital was state-owned and centrally distributed at that point, the competition in China was even more pronounced than it would have been in a capitalist setting (contrary to the presumptions of writers on capitalist distributive policies discussed in Chapter 1), directed as it was at just one pie.

Analyses of redistributive politics in democracies provide further insights about the dynamics of readjustment. First, successful redistribution requires a much more thorough command of national resources at the apex of the system than do Lowi's other modes of politics; here is the theme of resource concentration introduced in Chapter 2. Second, elites must possess sufficient autonomy to take such decisions in isolation from outside pressures.[8] This entails the exclusion of disfavored social groups from the policy process and the insulation of decision makers, the social patterns for which were also laid out in the second chapter. Both for redistributive policy in general and for the Chinese readjustment in particular these two factors highlight the essential part played by the top political leadership in initiating action on the issue at hand and in settling the inevitable ensuing contention among affected groups.

The literature on redistribution also talks about the centrality of the "relative strength of competing ideologies" at the moment of resolving conflict. And it directs attention to the importance of petitioners' "packaging" their programs in a way that fits the current "political climate" in order to obtain a hearing.[9] Contending groups in China did indeed enter the policy-making arena touting their own respective ideologies of economic growth to bolster their claims; and their pleas succeeded only to the extent that they resonated with the climate in the air.

A study of agenda formation in the U.S. Congress focuses in greater depth on some of these same themes.[10] It emphasizes the role of feedback in reorienting perceptions within leadership ranks. In turn, new perceptions produce changed policy climates, thereby opening "windows" for policy alteration. This study too makes the point that the demands of special interests are accepted only if they fit into that new climate. That these two bodies of literature—whose insights in both cases are drawn from studies of democratic polities—have application to the Chinese case shores up this study's asystemic approach to policy analysis.

Application to China and the Readjustment

Certain contextual and systemic factors in the Chinese case add weight to these borrowed bits of analysis because they reinforce the significance of both centrally managed resource accumulation and decision making at the apex of the polity. In the post-Mao era (especially in the decade beginning with the watershed Third Party Plenum of December 1978), a new priority was placed on economic modernization (elite consensus on growth as the overriding priority) and whatever served it, along with a rejection of the previous norm of political and class struggle as the chief criterion for judging policy.

Consequently, the political elite repeatedly evaluated feedback from past policy principally by asking whether prior policies had contributed to generation of state revenue and popular stability. At crucial junctures, such as 1979 and 1981, feedback indicating threats to these two conditions opened a window for a radical shift in political climate and thereby triggered major policy and investment switches.

Petitioners had no part in initiating these shifts. Instead, they were captives of an alternation of growth models that was mediated by feedback interpreted solely in terms of revenue growth and stability. Thus interest group spokespersons were repeatedly compelled to "package" their requests in accord with the prevailing climate. That is, those seeking financing had to couch their demands in the language and according to the policy context set by elite concerns and decisional biases. Occasionally pleaders failed to do this. But when a particular claimant presented its demands without reference to policy climate but instead using the same arguments at both of the two very disparate decision points (1979, 1981), its identical arguments had opposite effects at the two times because of the differing climate that prevailed at each juncture.

The preeminence of the goal of economic modernization after 1978 supplemented older concerns that had always marked China as a socialist state. State ownership of the overwhelming bulk of productive assets in China had long since put its stamp on the policy process: at least since the mid-1950's it had made for an emphasis on capital accumulation at the apex of the system. More than usually, though, in this time of perceived crisis, state ownership of national assets focused both policy makers and claimants on the centrality of building up national wealth. This focus oriented the policy debate at each round toward the contribution to state-controlled funds that each sector could make. Because the Chinese economy is state-owned, the preponderance of the capital returns generated by each sector at the time of the readjustment policy still redounded to the state, that is, to the central treasury. Therefore, proponents of each sector routinely argued that the receipts to the state from their favored sector could, with sufficient support, be larger than those of the other.*

In this spirit, representatives of the two sectors put forth contending ideologies in regard to readjustment. Each rested on an alternative model of resource generation and accumulation. One

---

*Despite the growth of funds under local control after the early 1980's, contention for investment between sectors is still couched in the same language.

90 CRISIS AND DECISION

emphasized light industry as the primary engine for engendering the creation of national riches; the other, in accord with the usual stance of Stalinist-style economic thinking, put its faith in heavy industry as the only dependable source of state wealth. The principal claims advanced by the supporters of each model were the superior capability of their respective sector to accumulate funds for the state and to satisfy mass needs (and thereby to promote popular stability).

The dominant philosophy for most of the first three decades under the People's Republic had championed heavy industry's superior ability to foster growth. But in early 1979 proponents of light industry were able suddenly to push their proposals through an open "policy window."[11] At the next key juncture, in 1981, however, doubts about the light-industrial model pried open a new window. By then developments in the economy had prepared the overwhelming majority of the elite to be persuaded that a downswing in heavy industry, unless checked, spelled financial disaster for the state.

The brief on behalf of light industry begins by stating that popular purchase of its consumer goods sops up currency which is then deposited in the state bank. Also, exports of such goods earn foreign exchange for the state; and the possibility of producing these goods in relatively short time spans means that the profits from that sector bring the quickest returns to the state accumulation effort.[12]

But China, like all socialist states, put a vastly greater initial investment into the producer goods or heavy industrial sector. Therefore, though profit and taxation rates are lower in this sector, they are assessed on a much larger base. For this reason, advocates of heavy as well as of light industry had grounds for alleging that their favored sector performs crucial fiscal functions for the state and so could potentially be the more valuable one. And in fact, data from the *Statistical Yearbook of China* for 1983 show that these claims could genuinely be matters for debate: in 1982, when investment for heavy industry had already picked up again, the comparative figures were as shown in Table 8.

One can get a rough idea of the respective foundation from which the two sides placed their pleas during the readjustment period by considering the following figures: during the Fourth Five-Year Plan (from 1970 to 1975), heavy industry received just

TABLE 8
Principal Financial Items of State-Owned Industrial
Enterprises by Sector, 1982
(*Yuan* 1 billion)

Category	Light industry	Heavy industry
Year-end fixed assets, original value	76.84	360.66
Year-end fixed assets, net value	53.51	237.89
Profits and taxes	43.44	53.78

SOURCE: State Statistical Bureau 1983: 293.

TABLE 9
Difference in Investment and Performance on the Eve
of Readjustment by Industrial Sector

Category	Light industry	Heavy industry
State capital construction investment, Fourth 5-Year Plan, 1970–75 (billion *yuan*)[a]	10.30	87.49
Output value supplied per 100 *yuan* of fixed assets, 1975 only[b]	388.11 *yuan*	88.24 *yuan*
Taxes and profits supplied per 100 *yuan* of fixed assets, 1975 only[b]	62.69 *yuan*	17.29 *yuan*

SOURCES: (*a*) Guojia Tongjiju bian 1985: 72; (*b*) Ma and Sun 2: 745.

under 87.5 billion *yuan* in investment, while light got a mere 10.3 billion.[13] But in 1975 each 100 *yuan* of fixed assets in the average state-owned light industrial enterprise supplied 388.11 *yuan* in output value and 62.69 *yuan* in taxes and profits for the state. In that same year heavy industry yielded only 88.24 *yuan* in output value and 17.29 *yuan* in taxes and profits per 100 *yuan* of fixed assets (see Table 9).[14] This ability of light industry to more or less hold its own over the years in the face of grossly less state investment is evident in the figures in Table 10.

The numbers in Table 9 indicate that in the plan period that immediately preceded the decision to readjust, heavy industry

TABLE 10
Total Revenue by Industrial Sector
(Yuan 1 billion)

Year	Light industry	Heavy industry	Year	Light industry	Heavy industry
1950	1.46	.55	1978	33.62	50.89
1952	4.24	1.99	1979	34.42	52.52
1957	8.30	6.96	1980	37.58	52.16
1960	14.11	22.19	1981	41.26	47.98
1965	14.25	20.49	1982	42.43	51.99
1971	20.78	34.52	1983	42.63	64.83
1975	26.01	36.66			

SOURCE: State Statistical Bureau 1986: 513.

was receiving over eight times the investment that light industry was, while light industry was contributing 4.4 times the output value per *yuan* of fixed assets and 3.63 times the taxes and profits. Thus each side had a reasonable foundation on which to base its claim of serving state accumulation efforts: the returns on heavy industry were necessarily far weightier, given the greater stock of investment with which it had to work; but light industry arguably had the potential, once supported, to make an even greater donation.*

Indeed, documents from the period demonstrate that at each instance when the elite altered the focus of allocations, leaders made their decision on the basis of the financial losses and benefits that had just accrued to the state as an outcome of the last set of measures adopted. Thus when it was evident that a current distribution was threatening state accumulation, leaders criticized and reversed the decision to so distribute. Petitioners were forced to recognize this decisional dynamic which made their pleas its captive, not its instigator.

Effects of the Socialist Planned Political Economy: State-Led Demand and Interdependence of the Economy

State ownership of the nation's productive assets, along with the effort at running a planned economy[15] from the national cap-

---
*In 1977 light industry supplied 29.46 billion *yuan* in revenue to the state; heavy turned over 37.35 billion, not a great difference. These figures are in State Statistical Bureau 1986: 513.

ital in China during the readjustment period, were additional aspects of the socialist system that affected the policy process in the same direction as the factors addressed above. These features of the political economy created an interdependence fueled by political will among the several sectors in the national economy. This interdependence, like the dominant focus on state capital accumulation, was yet one more circumstance that promoted passivity among pleaders during the readjustment. I call this form of interdependence state-led demand.

State-centralized resource concentration made possible central elite domination of the economic policy-making process at this juncture, if not complete control over policy consequences.* Since the overwhelming bulk of productive assets had long been collected into state coffers in China, the interdependence among sectors and branches that obtains in all national economies was triggered by political will there, as expressed in the national plan. Under such conditions, state-led demand (set in motion by investment decisions made in the capital) first drove economic change in any favored sector.

Further demand on other sectors then was generated through the effects of the prior state economic decision, rather than being sparked—as it would be in a private, unplanned, more marketized economy—by the preferences and choices of an array of autonomous economic agents. Petitioners, obviously, fell subject to this pattern.

There are several examples of the effects of this state-led demand during the years under examination. For instance, when the agricultural responsibility system, which, in essence, broke up the huge communes into family farms, was first implemented

---

*It is well known that as the coterminous reform program progressed, the grip of the central government over revenues and materials steadily waned as lower levels of administration and enterprises derived new autonomy and powers of control with the program's various decentralization, marketing, and profit retention schemes. But the center did manage to shift the direction of *planned* state budgetary investment away from its long-term skew toward heavy industry and to create a far more balanced industrial structure in the period under question. Even through 1986, the light and heavy industrial sectors remained roughly balanced in output value. For instance, *BR*, no. 39 (1987), p. 5, states: "Economists in Beijing say the most significant achievement of the recent period [1979–86] has been the establishment of correct ratios among the different kinds of investment and investment in various sectors and areas."

in late 1979 and for about two years thereafter, the agricultural tool-making departments within the machine-building trade were plunged into a serious, if temporary, depression.

That depression occurred because the tiny new farms had neither a use nor, at first, provided the funds for the large-scale implements and equipment that had worked the soil under the communes' management. The machinery bureaus throughout the country thus had to convert their output to meet the changed demands of the farm sector caused by the political decision to dismantle communes.[16]

Changes in the countryside as a result of this and other reforms that greatly raised peasant incomes also affected the light industrial branch. For the first time in post-1949 China, the more affluent rural residents had the purchasing power to be selective in their shopping. The light industrial firms were consequently forced to upgrade the quality and increase the varieties of their products to meet this shift in demand. Both of these examples illustrate the principle of state-led demand in that the demand on the individual sectors was a direct outcome of state policy toward other sectors in the state-owned economy rather than being primarily or initially market-induced.

These various forms of interdependence and mutual interaction within the Chinese state-owned economy, once set in motion, had their own inexorable logic and dynamic of development. As a result, state-led demand as an independent force in its own right, and not just state investment in response to any special pleading, contributed to the growth of any sector that happened for a time to be its beneficiary.

Spokespersons for the individual sectors were keenly aware of this interdependence of economic departments within the state-run economy, and this consciousness influenced the form and the rhetoric of competition among sectors. When delegates of each major trade and sector stated their own requests, they very frequently sought to legitimate these requests by explaining how their trade's growth (which would of course take off only with new state investment, resources, and other advantages) would have special payoffs for the state's economy as a whole.

But these would be payoffs not just for state accumulation in general. Their sector's development, they claimed, would also produce yields for whatever other sector was then being favored by state policy. Here once again, then, was a case—and a cause—of the essential passivity of the petitioners in this state-run economy in the readjustment era.

The main consequence of state ownership and planning for the present discussion is that the state-owned and managed economy added to the usual obstacles that in any political system keep forces out of favor (even ones that were once treated preferentially) from reorienting major, redistributive investment decisions detrimental to their interests at times of change in the agenda. That is, these factors added to the passivity of pleaders in a situation of reallocation. At the same time these factors enhanced the obsessions with state economic growth and popular acquiescence that the crisis thrust to the top of the agenda.

In sum, the very framework and organization of the state-owned and directed political economy of China refashioned but did not eliminate the larger pattern of a two-sided rivalry for favors, or the zero-sum, competitive claims that exist in any context in which redistribution is occurring or threatening to occur. But this framework, in particular the concentration of resources in state hands (which marks socialist economies but which at particular times has marked some capitalist ones as well[17]), kept that rivalry from significantly obstructing this redistributive policy. It did so in part through political insulation—by restricting decision making over and hence access to the wherewithal for growth.

The organization of state ownership and planning also overruled intersectoral rivalry by disposing decision makers at this time of perceived crisis to consider and accept only claims that coincided with the capital accumulation model current at any time. And third, the socialist economy's framework kept reallocation on course by setting up a state-directed interdependent economy which threw claimants into an essentially reactive stance.

The state-owned and planned economic structure and its dynamics thus acted, in conjunction with crisis, to repress group claims. This process amounted to a political imperative of the state-owned economy, which governed the politics of readjustment in China at least as much as did the authoritarian form of

96 CRISIS AND DECISION

the political system in the readjustment period. The state's economic structure and dynamics were able to create a barrier, limiting—but by no means eliminating—that ubiquitous scramble among affected groups that marks the politics of pleading everywhere in times of redeployment.

Though political conflict certainly ensued in reaction to readjustment policies, and though affected groups attempted to press for their interests, such conflict and pressure neither drove policy change nor created a major obstacle to such change at this time of macro reorganization of resource allocation. In short, the concepts of lobbying and bargaining fail to provide adequate descriptions of the policy process during readjustment.

Instead of bargaining, opponents of the policy had to couch their complaints in the language and according to the policy context set by elite decision makers and within the constraints of state-led demand and the interdependence of the state-run economy. Redistributive policy, a sense of crisis among the elite, and the socialist economic system reinforced each other to produce this result. The discussion that follows will illustrate this argument by presenting the factors that created the policy climate at the two key junctures of the readjustment period: early 1979, when the decision was reached to favor light industry, and 1981, when a conjunction of forces led the elite once again to emphasize heavy industry.

1979: THE DECISION TO READJUST

Policy Climate

The decision in early 1979 to readjust the proportions of investment between the two industrial branches was a watershed turn away from the excessive emphasis on heavy industry that had been in effect for the better part of the preceding three decades. It came about when a shared sense of crisis facilitated the ascendancy of particular leaders and created a new climate for policy making. These men set about to shape the economic agenda in light of their own understanding—in some cases, their long-standing biases—of what at that juncture would best fulfill the goals of state resource concentration, while at the same time ensuring peace among the affected sections of the populace.

The foreign trade component of the decision was spelled out in Chapter 3. In addition, investing in light industry was to be a means of generating returns domestically. In secret party meetings held just before the Third Plenum convened in December 1978, some leaders had demanded revisions of ambitious draft plans for 1979 and 1980 that had been written and approved in the State Council only a few months before.[18] Immediately after the plenum concluded, Chen Yun, mastermind of a successful similar readjustment effort in the early 1960's, criticized those plans, urging that targets be reduced and the number of construction projects proposed be cut back.

Following Chen's cue and placing his faith in Chen's proven experience and economic expertise, Deng Xiaoping immediately suggested: "We must do an all-around readjustment, first by promoting some projects that will be easy to do and will quickly earn money, and by curtailing some iron and steel factories and some large projects. The keypoint in importing must be put onto those projects that see results fast and make a lot of money." The consequences of this new outlook emerged very rapidly. In the first few days of January, the Ministry of Light Industry held a conference at which participants were instructed to expand exports and earn more foreign exchange. And on the basis of Chen and Deng's instructions, the State Planning Commission began to revise the national economic plan for 1979.[19]

Despite some continuing disagreement over the program,[20] when the national plan was consolidated later in the year, it contained the stipulation that for the three years of readjustment beginning in 1979 light industry's development was to be faster than that of heavy industry. And at the November 1979 State Planning Conference, it was decided that the "six priorities" should be promised to light industry: namely, raw materials, fuel, and electrical power; measures for tapping potential, renovating and transforming enterprises; capital construction; bank loans; the use of foreign exchange and the importing of new technology; and transport capacity.[21] Seconding this policy, in early December the State Economic Commission also put its weight behind light industry.[22]

Thus a switch had taken place in the long-typical habit of accumulating capital for the state mainly from the heavy industrial sector; now a different group within the leadership sought to try to base growth on an alternative strategy—one that produced funds quickly with a lesser investment. This meant a boost for light industry because it was capable of concentrating resources for the state more rapidly.

Proponents of the light industrial model of capital accumulation continued to champion what they viewed as successes of the readjustment program on such grounds for over a year. Thus, in mid-1980, after about a year of pro–light industrial policies, the press announced that in the first half of 1980 industrial profits turned over to the state had increased by 1.9 billion *yuan*, thereby proving the accuracy of the preferential measures then being accorded the light industrial sector.[23]

Besides light industry's purported value for amassing foreign exchange and for boosting the domestic economy, a third factor in the decision to bolster this sector was the deep concern among the leadership about a potential for social instability in the cities. Several leaders made the case that the promotion of light industry, with its labor intensity and its large number of collective-ownership-sector firms, could go a long way toward dealing with the massive urban unemployment crisis that was then facing the regime.[24]

As Li Xiannian put it in his April speech introducing the policy of readjustment at a party work conference, "Stability and solidarity is the basic condition for realizing the Four Modernizations." He spoke as well of the "very sharp contradiction" between the need to cut back enterprises in the readjustment on the one hand but also to arrange for the employment of a large amount of labor power on the other.

Addressing the urban unemployment problem, which he termed "very serious," he noted that 20 million people needed jobs. He warned, ominously, "If the idle urban labor force is not handled appropriately, it [an upset] could be triggered at any moment, which would seriously influence social stability." Furthermore, Li, along with Chen Yun and others, expressly argued against sinking more investment into capital-intensive industry, in view of this unemployment crisis. As Li reasoned, "If we invest a large amount of capital and equipment, we will only have to reduce the labor power . . . and then the labor power that is saved would have no way to be arranged, and that would only give ourselves new difficulties."[25]

Overall, then, readjustment amounted to a new approach to both capital accumulation and social stability. It was clearly a decision taken by the top elite acting autonomously, in light of the then-current version of how best to cope with financial issues and with presumed popular responses. Because it deprived heavy industry, despite its representatives' possession of impressive resources and their long history of political clout and connections, the decision cannot be viewed as an outcome of lobbying by concerned special interests. Obviously, any bargaining chips heavy-sector petitioners possessed were insufficient to turn the course of resource disposal back in their own direction.

Demands and Debate

The decision to favor light industry sparked a set of troubled responses. Central leaders anticipated such reactions from concerned interests and hoped to address them. Li Xiannian, for one, framed the issue as follows:

> Ideological unification is necessary for this [readjustment] work. The national economy must be readjusted, and the entire economic livelihood must undergo many changes; some need to develop quicker, some slower; some will be raised up [shang ma], some pulled down [xia ma]. This will have implications for various localities, departments, enterprises and individuals' interests. In the developed and raised up [units], everyone will be happy, and it will naturally be easy to accept the direction of readjustment. Those to be pulled down and eliminated and with many real problems to be solved possibly won't be able to accept it.[26]

Chen Yun put the matter as an issue of dividing up finite funds: "If too much investment is used in one place, what will the others do? They [those demanding excessive investment] suggest that they won't hinder other people, but that really is not possible."[27] And economist Ma Hong described the ongoing disagreements and debates that accompanied this scrambling for benefits:

> What to readjust? What should be used as a standard in readjusting proportions? Each has his own standard; everyone says he himself is a short-line [a department producing a product in short supply]. So everyone demands investment from the State Planning Commission, no one

says he is a long line. With everyone bickering, the departments remain long lines as before.[28]

More often than not, the claims for redress were carefully conceived in the rhetoric and in terms of the same goals the elite had espoused. For everyone knew that those goals would serve as the criteria for the elite's accepting or rejecting pleaders' requests. In advancing their demands, deputies of the major industrial sectors nearly invariably did so in accord with one of three lines of argument. Each of these represents a rhetorical style that demonstrates the essentially reactive nature of their speakers' interest articulation.

One line of attack was to assert that one's industry could do a superior job in accumulating resources for the state; another was to state that one's own particular trade could make a great contribution to the then-current state goal of the Four Modernizations. And a third tactic was to claim that one's branch or department could assist in the growth of the light industrial sector in China's interdependent economy now that this sector had been designated as the favored one.

Such sectoral justifications for investment requests in terms of national priorities obviously took their cue from official propaganda of that period. At first, in the spring of 1979, when heavy industry had just been bested, it still maintained its aura of legitimacy. Therefore, official propaganda had to build support for the shift in priorities by stating that funding bestowed on light industry would ultimately also promote heavy industry. Thus a *People's Daily* editorial in late February called for "using light industry to nourish heavy."[29]

At the same time the media made a similar point from another angle, advancing the argument that this nurturing was inevitable because the two sectors were linked in an interdependent whole:

> Industry is a unified entity made up of many areas. Industrial departments coexist together. They not only compete against each other but cooperate together and there is a certain proportionate relationship between them. . . . We cannot look on any department in terms of an absolute. The one-sided grasping of steel not only couldn't promote industry and the national economy, but also couldn't promote the initial and final processes of the iron and steel industry . . . because steel production must have the support of other industries. . . . Only with the

advance of agriculture and light industry can there be a faster development in heavy industry, including the iron and steel industry.[30]

But the heavy industrial firms were thrown on the defensive when the decision at the top came out clearly for giving preference in funding to light industry. As the loss to come closed in on them, the newly apologetic heavy industrial departments had to struggle to justify their suddenly futile requests in accord with this changed priority. Just before the April Party Work Conference that put the final stamp on the readjustment policy, a heated debate around the issue of investment priorities appeared in the press.

A late March *People's Daily* editorial, obviously placed in the paper by proponents of heavy industry, called for building a number of key projects producing coal, electricity, oil, and construction materials and providing for the communications and transportation necessary for the Four Modernizations. It rested its case on a new claim—that, with proper investment, heavy could benefit the light sector: "We must *create conditions for* building light industrial plants, textile plants, housing projects and municipal public utilities"[31] (emphasis added). The terms of the debate had clearly shifted: now the idea was to request more direct investment for heavy, on the pretext that this would eventually be useful for light and consumer construction.

The economist Liu Guoguang chided such advocates of heavy industry. First, he noted, these people were claiming that the accumulation (or investment) rate (whose increase always brought along a rise in heavy industry) was not too high. According to them, Liu quoted, "there's a lot of things to arrange for the Four Modernizations, [so] much accumulation is necessary." He could see that spokespersons for heavy industry were trying to hold onto their privileged place by underlining their sector's potential contribution to the changed national priority. Another way advocates of the heavy industrial departments tried to promote their interests, according to Liu, was to push the point that "all three sectors are backward" because available "steel, cement, lumber, chemical raw materials, fuel, motive power, machinery for agriculture, and supplies and technical equipment for light industry are still insufficient." This inadequacy, heavy's patrons reasoned, meant that "China must first speed up the development of heavy industry, in order to strengthen its support of the other two sectors."[32] Thus, at this point, when the weight of elite opinion had shifted toward righting the long-term neglect of light industry, heavy's deputies had to paint their own demands in colors consonant with this decision.

Some plants were also put forward in the name of particular trades within the heavy industrial sector. For instance, one article disapprovingly quoted those who still tried to claim that the proportions between sectors were really not maladjusted or inappropriate because the steel smelted by the metallurgy departments and the caustic soda and soda ash produced by the chemical industry were produced for the purpose of serving light industry. Therefore, such advocates suggested, more investment for these departments should replace funding targeted for light industry directly.[33]

When the machine-building trade's advocates vainly sought to advance what they viewed as this trade's urgent need for funding for new equipment, they placed this desire within the context of the needs of the Four Modernizations, as in a piece in the journal *Economic Management* from early 1980:

In order that the machine-building industry can supply more and better technical equipment for realizing the Four Modernizations, it itself must have good quality, technically progressive machinery and equipment. But, at present, the majority of our machinery manufacturing enterprises have equipment that is old and backward, which influences product quality. This is not appropriate for meeting the demands of the Four Modernizations.[34]

Ironically, this argument, useless at the beginning stage of the readjustment, did convince people in the changed policy climate not much more than one year later. But in this context that privileged light industry, its proponents had an easy answer to these pleas: that equipping the machinery plants required a material base, which only the easy-to-start, quickly completed, and foreign-exchange-earning light industrial projects could properly provide.[35]

Thus the decision of the readjusting national elite clearly set up a contest for funding in 1979, when the leadership came to a consensus on switching the proportions of investment going to the various sectors and their subordinate trades. This was much the same result that a redistributive policy in a democracy would call forth, though among different contenders—industrial sectors in China, social groups in a democracy. But the state-led interdependent economy and the constant elite drive to concentrate state-owned resources in socialist China, heightened by crisis, dictated to the claimants the legitimate form that the rhetoric of their rivalry must take. These forces also predetermined the winners of the contest.

THE 1981 REVIVAL OF HEAVY INDUSTRY

John W. Kingdon's work on agenda formation contains insights about how American politicians pick new agendas in response to the feedback from monitoring existing programs. Changes in widely respected indicators and unanticipated consequences flowing from earlier policy decisions are two critical forms of feedback that, in the American context, initiate alterations in leaders' plans and foster new interpretations of reality. When a sufficiently large number of top policy makers admit the drawbacks of prior approaches, a window opens for proposals and conceptions pushed aside previously; in the process, a fresh policy climate is fashioned.[36]

In that transformed climate old alliances may well come unstuck as onetime partners split apart into different coalitions. The 1981 shift in the Chinese economic policy agenda fit this pattern. Change in climate led ministers and their minions to modify their perceptions as to how their particular mission could best be met. Such perceptions, then, made for a fluidity among alliance partners over a relatively brief time span. As new alliances formed around newly presented data from ongoing operations, there was obviously more force to pry open the window and to let in the altered climate.

A First Change in Climate, Late 1980

By 1980 the new policy of favoring light industry had already significantly affected the course of industrial growth on a nationwide scale. Not only was light industry increasing at a rapid tempo, but heavy industry was beginning to fall back rather drastically. Already in 1979 the growth rate of light industry had been 9.6 percent, while that of heavy was only 7.7.[37] The next year the results were more dramatic. The output value of light industry rose from 1979's 198.0 billion *yuan* to 234.4 billion, while heavy's went up a mere 3.7 billion *yuan*, from 261.1 billion up to only 264.8 billion.[38] In 1980, too, revenue derived from the light industrial sector expanded from 1979's 34.42 billion *yuan* to 37.58 billion, while returns from heavy actually dropped a bit, from the previous year's 52.52 billion to 52.16 billion.[39]

Clearly, the objectives of the readjustment program, which had aimed at enlarging the output of consumer goods at the expense of heavy industrial growth, were being fulfilled. At the same time, the coterminous market reform program seemed to be progressing smoothly. At the September 1980 Third Session of the Fifth National People's Congress, most of the principal speakers offered an optimistic outlook on the economy. Those who had been promoting reform (the Reformers) were still dominant over two other groups: those I have labeled Adjusters, the advocates of readjustment (with its demand for more central control and national-level resource concentration), and those I call Conservers, the supporters of heavy industry.[40]

But at this same meeting, Yao Yilin, just named chairman of the State Planning Commission, announced that coal and oil production had slowed down and that machine building was operating below capacity.[41] Still, at that time, except for complaints from the deputies from some of the provinces where heavy industry is based, such as Jilin and Liaoning, and where coal is mined, such as Shanxi, Henan, and Anhui—who asked for more investment and more work—there was no indication that these conditions should be a cause for worry. Accordingly, no new investment was granted for heavy industry, despite this lobbying by its advocates—areas and trades usually presumed to possess great clout. The publication of these pleas in the public press did nothing to alter the picture.

Beneath these successes of readjustment and this sanguine outlook on reform, however, lurked difficulties caused by the reform program's decentralization of funding and resource management. These problems were threatening the central government's revenue collection, just as the payoffs from heavy industry, for decades the regime's prime source of funds, had begun to decline. And at the same time, increased state outlays for consumption—hiked-up state purchase prices for agricultural products, subsidies for urban consumers that had already more than tripled since 1978,[42] industrial wage reforms, and the reinstitution of bonuses for workers—were all combining to produce large state budget deficits in 1979 and 1980, along with the issuing of excess currency and inflation.[43]

Feedback from these two aspects of reform—devolution and increased consumption costs—converged in late 1980 to produce a new policy climate. In that changed atmosphere the positions of politicians and the alliances among factions began to flex. For months before, readjustment advocates (Adjusters), based in the Ministry of Finance and in the People's Bank, had tried in vain to curtail local construction against the wishes of the supporters of heavy industry (Conservers). They had also been fighting fruitlessly against enterprise autonomy experiments throughout 1979 and 1980, in opposition to Reformers. But the severe deficits that economists at the Ministry of Finance uncovered late in 1980 turned the tide in the Adjusters' favor.[44]

Here was Kingdon's telling indicator: the research results of these economists showed that the reform program was overtaxing the state budget to an extent roundly perceived as alarming. The Finance Ministry, charged with ensuring a balanced national budget, was finally able to command support for its position when it pointed to a clear and imminent danger to the state's effort at amassing funds. Anxiety about budgetary shortfalls diverted leadership attention to what this time around became labeled a "latent" crisis. Everyone, or nearly everyone, had to admit that decentralization experiments and unchecked capital construction were wrecking national finances.

As a result, on the heels of the September 1980 Third NPC Session, the State Council, presumably using the new Ministry of Finance data, adjudged that a major deflationary policy was in order.[45] Consciousness of a new crisis induced the State Council to agree on a set of draconian measures in early 1981, which aimed at curtailing the excessive capital construction and extra-budgetary spending at local levels that were draining the central government's treasury.

A Second Change in Climate, Mid-1981

When the measures took effect, they aggravated the already considerable slowdown that readjustment policies had engineered in the rate of expansion of planned heavy industry. The decisions included a 21 percent cutback in budgetary appropriations for capital construction investment, a program of involuntary loans (in the amount of 8 billion *yuan*) for the localities, and treasury bond sales imposed on the localities and firms. Planned budgetary investment as a whole was slashed by 40 percent, enterprise bank deposits were frozen, and a new set of bank loans that had been earmarked for fixed investment was held back.[46] Moreover, large and medium projects in the 1981 plan were fewer by 28 percent than those in the 1980 plan.

These various recisions quickly led to a further and precipitous plunge in the growth rate of industry generally.[47] But the effect on heavy industry was certainly the most startling dimension of this drop. Speaking in December, economist Xue Muqiao revealed that from January through October, the large fall in heavy industry was primarily the result of coal's decline by 0.8 percent and of petroleum's decrease by 4.9 percent. But the decrease in machine building was the most significant factor. Since its output value accounted for one-quarter of all of industry's output value, when its production declined by about 15 percent in the first half of the year, the entire industrial growth speed dropped by 3.75 percent (see Table 11).[48]

Thus, once again, a revealing indicator was jolting the elite to revamp its strategy. As these unsettling data became clear to the leadership, its concern for the effects on state revenue began to tilt the force of opinion toward those who had argued before for a higher rate of accumulation and for keeping up the tempo of growth in heavy industry. For a second time, alliance partners shifted.

The switch in outlook becomes evident when one compares economist Xue Muqiao's statements from two periods. At the

TABLE 11
*Quarterly Change in Gross Industrial Output Value
in the First Three Quarters of 1981*

Quarter	Light industry	Heavy industry	Overall
First	9.9	−8.7	−.2
Second	13.1	−7.8	1.7
Third	14.0	−6.4	3.0
TOTAL	12.4	−7.6	1.5

SOURCE: Xue 1982b: 5.

end of 1980, when Xue was championing the readjustment, he had quoted critically certain "comrades who had been engaged in economic work for a long time," with whom he obviously disagreed at that point. He chastised them for reasoning that "'accumulation is the only source of expanded reproduction,' and that lowering the accumulation rate will lower the speed of development of production and then it will not be possible to improve the level of livelihood. . . . This intimidated many comrades," he noted disapprovingly. And, he went on, "These comrades said, 'We advocate lowering the scale of capital construction, but if we pull down projects already begun, this will create a great loss.' This is true, [he agreed] but how can we not [pull them down]? Disaster would come from going ahead."[49]

But within a year, in the wake of heavy's severe losses, Xue, and presumably other original Adjusters as well, had changed his mind. After some three years of arguing for light industry's growth and heavy industry's slowdown, Xue now threw in his lot with heavy's proponents. By mid-1981 he was conceding that "readjustment should make the development speed of light industry quicker than heavy's within a certain period, but it should not make heavy's growth appear as a negative number." At this point Xue was prepared to argue for the recovery of heavy industry, which would have to mean reinvestment in that sector: "In the next few years," he warned, "heavy must stop falling and must gradually rise."[50]

According to Xue Muqiao, the State Council recognized the deleterious effects on the economy of the harsh measures of the early months of the year almost immediately. It rapidly became evident to decision makers that, because capital construction had been cut back, demand for machinery went down, and the need for steel, machines, coal, and oil correspondingly declined. The conclusion drawn was that the reduction in investment for industry and the "slamming on the brakes" in issuing bank credit of early 1981 may have been necessary in the first quarter of the year but that their effect on overall production had been too severe.

Out of this changed policy context came the decision implemented in early autumn 1981 to resuscitate heavy industry. The Adjusters, convinced by then of the damage to state revenue that cutbacks were causing, were obviously willing at this point to make common cause with the supporters of heavy industry on behalf of rescuing the state's depleting funds from further decline.[51] Thus many of the same men who had only two years before wholeheartedly promoted light industry, and who less than a year earlier had scaled back heavy even more, were ready at last to heed heavy industry's pleas.

Already by the second quarter of 1981 the enterprises' capital, which had been frozen at first, was released; at the same time, bank loans were relaxed a bit, so that heavy industry's production slowly climbed back up.[52] By the fourth quarter, the heavy industrial firms had vigorously returned to their pursuit of output.[53] By September and October triumphant reports from individual localities as well as on a national scale were pouring in to proclaim that heavy industry's decline had finally been turned around.[54]

The irony is that the content of the pleas from heavy industry to which some observers have attributed the turnaround remained largely unchanged from 1979. Though futile in that earlier policy context, they now found a hearing. Yet the claimants' clout, bargaining chips, and connections could not have increased much in the few intervening years. Feedback, which formed this new policy climate, then, and not lobbying, bargaining, or permanent alliances made the difference in the elite's receptivity. The top decision makers, whatever their initial commitment to readjustment had been, were now willing to shift some funding back toward that sector and to accept the arguments of those areas suffering from the cutbacks, which they had not been willing to do heretofore.*

Another operative factor was that by the middle of 1981, the situation regarding the state's other crucial objective had worsened. Not only was the elite faced with a threat to the state's generation and concentration of resources; its politicians' confidence in being able to count on a quiescent population was also being shaken as workers idled by the cutbacks (both because of the initial reductions in funding for heavy industry and from the newer retrenchment) became mildly restive. Following in the wake of the rise of Poland's Solidarity movement just a few months before, which had drawn fearful attention from Chinese leaders, such dissatisfaction had to prove troubling.

Now leaders began again, as they had in early 1979, to speak of the danger of social instability. Concern over the forced inactivity and redundancy of labor power that would issue from the plant closings, suspensions, mergers, and conversions (*guanting bingzhuan*) that made up the readjustment effort had been present from the start. But discussion of problems that were actually occurring, rather than speculation about the probable outcome of projected policies, began to find its way into the press in greater force by spring 1981. For instance, an article published in the fall of 1981 noted:

> Now we still issue wages to enterprises closed, suspended, merged, and converted and don't reduce the workers in the factories. And if we issue fewer bonuses, there are [negative] opinions. And we still have the problem of those waiting for jobs. We shouldn't have high speed growth under these conditions, *but we need some speed* [a code word for increased growth in heavy industry] *or we won't be able to guarantee economic stability*. . . . Those involved say that our present concern is how to enliven the economy and make finance throw off its difficulties. . . . Grasping some consumer goods production [meaning the readjustment policy] has led to some results, but the heavy industrial departments have a large amount of workers with nothing to do . . . equipment is idle; in the capital construction ranks there are very many people in

---

*Delegates to NPC meetings from provinces strong in heavy industry in both 1980 and 1981 had put forward claims for their firms. But apparently a turn in state financial fortunes was needed before what have been termed "lobbyists" for heavy industry could make an impact on policy.

enforced idleness. There is equipment in the warehouses, and materials piled up. We are still paying wages, safekeeping fees, maintenance fees. All this is only consuming but not creating new wealth.[55] (Emphasis added.)

As a *Red Flag* commentator's article decried openly, "There are issues of political stability and unity involved in the staff and workers awaiting new assignments after *guanting bingzhuan*."[56] Such fears and injunctions must have been tied to the swelling of the ranks of the unemployed as readjustment wore on and to attendant demonstrations and isolated violent protests from redundant workers in spring 1981.[57]

The press did not really begin to make clear the argument for increasing the investment for heavy industry until after the decision to execute that increase had already been taken in September.[58] But when it did reveal the altered thinking of the elite, financial considerations clearly had played the largest role. One article from mid-October recited the many difficulties that heavy industry had suffered in the first half of the year and then explained, "We need to take measures to enliven it or it will bring much negative influence on the national economy."[59] Besides citing heavy's importance for energy, communications, transportation, and the renewal of equipment, this piece's central point was clear: heavy industry affected the state's financial income. Thus new economic feedback had switched the policy climate and an alternate model of capital generation and accumulation was now governing the politics of the readjustment.

On the same theme, an article in the September issue of *Economic Management* listed among the major problems in the national economy the "widespread losses and a considerable drop in profits handed to the state by the enterprises." Profits from the heavy industrial sector alone had fallen by 2.7 billion *yuan* because of the "insufficient production tasks and other factors" associated with the readjustment.[60] Premier Zhao Ziyang announced in December 1982 that state revenues had declined for three years in a row beginning in 1979 as a result of economic readjustment, combined with the efforts to solve "long-accumulated [consumption-related] problems" from the Cultural Revolution decade.[61]

And an economist writing from Shanghai opined that economic readjustment was forcing the state to make very expensive outlays, straining a budget already suffering from shortfalls in the revenues coming from heavy industry:

> The financial burden can't be dropped, price subsidies for the enterprises and fees for equipment maintenance and staff and worker payments each year were coming to some 450 billion *yuan*. If the speed of increase of the economy is slowed, or if no speed occurs or there is a loss of speed, this will increase our economic and financial problems, which will be bad both for the stability of domestic economic livelihood and for the political situation of stability and unity.[62]

And so the state's financial difficulties gave pro-heavy-industry advocates the entrée, or in Kingdon's terms the window they required for winning back lost funding. Once it opened, they could finally attract support for their case by convincing leaders worried about the state treasury that new monies for firms in this sector would fix the crisis. By contrast, identical fighting for their interests had been ineffectual in the earlier policy climate.

Thus the drain on the state treasury created by massive losses in heavy industry and the restiveness among inactive laborers prompted policy makers to reshape decisions and recast alliances. As the *People's Daily* summed matters up in early 1982, "Growth speed is necessary to satisfy the people's needs and to solve the state's financial difficulties."[63]

Of course, it is possible that other factors, not publicly enunciated, were at work as well. But the actors and the assets they commanded remained constant, and we must conclude that the elite in the economic policy realm reached its judgments at least in part in light of the centrality to the state of resource concentration and social stability and on the basis of its own perception of what at that point would serve these objectives, rather than in response to lobbyists' clamor.

Demands and Debate in 1981

Nonetheless, the allocation was not settled so simply in favor of more funding for heavy industry. Even after the September 1981 injection of new investment funding into that sector, arguing continued. Xue Muqiao presented the disagreements: "The abnormal situation in 1981 led to much debate in early 1982. Some thought that readjustment was too extreme, and that the country's economic future would be affected."[64] Several other sources also make reference to this debate, in which heavy industry's proponents put forward the selfsame arguments that had been rejected two years before.

The dialogue included a set of disagreements, centering on speed ("Some sang the tune of high targets, high speed"); the question of whether heavy industry should not again receive priority treatment, as in the past; and the rate of investment ("Some want to raise [it], as they see too few orders [for work to be done by heavy industrial firms], and productive capacity sitting idle").[65] Another reference from late 1981 says that an issue then under discussion was that, if the readjustment period did not see a certain speed (meaning in heavy industry's growth), the whole economy might atrophy.[66]

Opinions clearly varied, at least at first, as to how to deal with the effects of industrial slowdown. There were still advocates in high places for the light-industry-based model of capital accumulation. These people had already spoken out in the midst of the retrenchment of early 1981. Beginning in February and then at several later junctures during the year Premier Zhao Ziyang tried to convince other leaders that they must continue to expand the production of consumer goods.[67]

The April issue of *Economic Management* picked up the plaint, listing all the usual advantages of the light industrial accumulation model: consumer goods could satisfy the people's livelihood needs and in addition return money to the bank.[68] In April *Red Flag* joined that camp, speaking out on the capacity of consumer goods to increase the state's income.[69] This argument had carried the day in the climate of 1979, but pursuing its program had disappointed enough of the elite by 1981 that it no longer commanded the same attention.

Along with his now explicit but apparently unsuccessful promotion of consumer goods, Zhao had to find another way to present his preference for the light industry model. His strategy in the new climate was to try to show that its successful application would benefit heavy industry. This, of course, was the same line of argumentation that pro-readjustment forces had had to adopt in the early part of 1979, before the heavy sector had totally lost the floor; but then they had advanced it successfully.

Both in an April 1981 speech to a State Council plenary meeting and in his work report to the Fourth Session of the Fifth NPC in December that year Zhao suggested that heavy industry turn around its basic service orientation so that its main objective would become to support light industry and not just to meet its own needs. In December, struggling to legitimize his case, he claimed that there had been an improvement in the condition of heavy industry in the second half of the year in part because of just such efforts.[70]

The continuing push for consumer goods that Zhao's speeches and these journal articles evidenced forced the promoters of heavy industry in the fall of 1981 to enter the fray as well. In doing so, they too brought out their own timeworn logic, lecturing on the place of heavy industry within the interdependent national economy. Thus they made the brief once again that without the work of the heavy industrial plants there would be no technological equipment, power, or raw and other materials for the production of consumer goods, indeed, that light industry needed heavy industry if it were to develop.[71] Now that the weight of elite opinion had turned in its favor and the climate had altered, heavy's advocates were able to gain a hearing for words that had fallen on deaf ears only a short time past.

Added to these redundant recitations, something novel now entered the public discourse. When the new funding for heavy industry reached its destination, the press presented the reading public with brand-new interpretations of heavy industry and of the readjustment policy itself. Suddenly, spokespersons for that sector no longer had to justify their claims in terms of benefits for light industry, as they had been compelled to do for more than two years.

In fact, at this point the understanding of the needs and workings of the entire national economy—the understanding, that is, which had informed and indeed dominated economic policy two years earlier—underwent a shift. An article in the authoritative Shanghai paper *World Economic Digest* in September 1981 exemplified this switch when it announced, "Heavy industry's proportion in the economy should not fall any more. . . . We cannot deny that the high speed development of light industry over the past few years was facilitated by the sound heavy industrial basis built in the earlier period. We must never forget the important role heavy industry plays in the process of industrialization." Now "the purpose of readjustment" took on a new color: it was to "better coordinate the development of both sectors, not just to reduce the proportion of heavy while raising that of light."[72]

One more article offers yet another example of this altered analysis of the role of heavy industry in the state-led interdependent economy. This one treats the decline of heavy industry as a condition that, surprisingly enough to recent readers of the national press, might itself upset proportionate development. Such an argument stood in sharp contrast to the line in essays printed in 1979, according to which the turn of investment away from heavy industry was the very way to right imbalances. But now the logic was completely reversed: "If heavy industry atrophies, this will lead to maladjustment, affecting light industry and agriculture," which depended on it for their technical transformation, equipment renewal, energy and transport, and raw materials. "To make heavy industry have a certain speed of development," it recommended, "we first must enliven heavy itself." The final suggestion in the article indicates the extent to which the readjustment policy had become legitimate and suggests that its assumptions might even have begun to replace much older ones favoring heavy industry. This impression comes across in its use of words that would have been patently superfluous in the period before readjustment and unimaginable only two years earlier: "We need to recognize the importance of the development of heavy industry."[73] The article also makes plain that reinvestment in heavy industry had become policy once again. As one peruses such pieces from late 1981, it is clear that the readjustment had come full circle and that heavy industry's growth was now being validated for its contribution to other sectors in the national economy, rather than light being boosted for its financial benefits to accumulation or its provision of funding for the heavy sector.

The return in 1981 to the financing of heavy industry, if one can judge from published materials, was a response to three considerations—an understanding that increasing the financing for that sector would actually save the state from further economic loss (even if it would not, like investing in light industry, lead to rapid returns to the state treasury); that its recovery would provide places and activity for the laborers idled by the shutdowns of the readjustment program; and that the economy as a whole was ultimately interdependent so that a severe atrophy of any one sector—especially of heavy, still viewed by many as the foundation for the other sectors' work—would limit future economic growth in those other sectors and spell serious present decline for the economy overall.

AFTERMATH: MODERNIZATION AND NEW EMPHASES FOR INVESTMENT, 1982

Sometime around the middle of 1982 the central leadership announced that the goals of at least the first stage of readjustment had been achieved: a foundation had been laid for further development, and a balance between industrial sectors had been engineered.[74] Presumably, with the decision to revive heavy industry, such a public proclamation (or, perhaps, pretext) was in order.

Naturally, it is necessary in assessing such claims, as it always is at times of policy change in China, to ask whether the goals of readjustment had genuinely been met. Or, alternatively, was it simply that the enthusiasm for modern growth, coupled with the long-ingrained belief that only heavy industry could ultimately lead to long-term capital accumulation, had tried the patience of a leadership no longer so interested in promoting light industry alone?

But even if this were the case, the economic-cum-developmental arguments for pressing forward as they did at this point were persuasive in themselves. The point here is that one can adequately explain the return to a priority for heavy industry on such grounds as these without appealing to the argument that heavy's proponents had finally successfully lobbied for their sector's comeback.

For by then the problem was that, given the relative inactivity into which much of heavy industry had been thrown by the readjustment and by the "brake-slamming" of early 1981, a significant portion of the national economy was at a standstill as far as further modernization was concerned. Energy and transport bottlenecks were still strangling economic growth;[75] old equipment was hampering the factories' efforts to turn out high-quality machinery and merchandise; and the priorities set by the 1979 readjustment—to expand the output of the light and textile trades—no longer fit the needs of the next phase of development.

At this stage the leadership once again began to direct attention simply to "socialist modernization" and to ignore the more indirect objective of a modernization spurred by sectoral restructuring. This was a theme that had been in a prominent position on the policy agenda on and off ever since the December 1978 Third Plenum had first removed class struggle from top priority and substituted economic concerns in its stead. It was now possible wholeheartedly to resume the growth of basic industry and infrastructural development at least in part precisely because of the new returns that had been promised and indeed delivered to the state treasury as a result of the previous few years of input into the light and textile sectors.[76]

Once made the central focus of economic policy, modernization took off with an inexorable momentum. The elite now designed a switch in strategy, as its members built on the dynamic of development they had set in motion in strengthening light industry and agriculture in the previous two or three years. At the center of this strategy were two features: a return to a focus on the machine-building industry—for renovating old plant, easing bottlenecks through constructing "key projects," and supplying improved equipment for the other, now more developed sectors; and the more selective use of limited resources—for major cities, for what were called "key enterprises," and for quality products, rather than for sparking a greater quantity of output by any and all producers of light industrial goods.

Both of these shifts were a logical outcome of a State Council pronouncement from the second half of 1981. This directive commanded changing the old practice of emphasizing expanded reproduction by "extension" to a form of reproduction that would take place by means of "intension." That is, from then on, the plan was to abandon growth that aimed solely at increasing output and was achieved simply through increasing the inputs of factors of production.

In its place, a new form of growth was to occur by means of more efficient productive methods and a more judicious use of resources. The emphasis now was to entail upgrading old plant by what the Chinese term "technical transformation," a strategy that would involve using more modern equipment and relying more than previously on science and technology.[77]

This switch in approach was gradually etched out beginning in the second half of 1981 and continuing up until the fall of 1982. Parts of it were present in Zhao Ziyang's work report at the December 1981 NPC Session, and it also found expression in the Sixth Five-Year Plan (designed to cover the years 1981–85, but not published until late 1982). The economic component of party General Secretary Hu Yaobang's address to the Twelfth Party Congress in September 1982 also carried this line.

After that meeting, a set of new priorities explicitly replaced the light and textile trades as key points for investment. In a sense this could be counted as a defeat for light industry. But from another angle, the very successes in boosting the output of consumer goods and textiles and in agriculture had brought these sectors to a point at which their further progress would be checked unless heavy industry were churned up once again. Press analyses of the day took pains to point this out.

Thus, early in the year the *People's Daily* explained, "With the rather rapid development of agriculture and light industry, more and greater demands are being made on the metallurgy, machine-building and other sectors of heavy industry."[78] And as a later explication indicated, faith in heavy industry as the base of the national economy still ran deep: a 1985 issue of the *Beijing Review* reported that the products of heavy industry were "essential to developing the national economy in the long run" and to the improvement in living standards.[79] In 1982, definite measures to accelerate the growth of this sector began to appear.

Given the state-managed interdependence of the three primary sectors of the economy, this elite choice made sound developmental sense. Thus here was another component of the changed policy climate after mid-1981 that permitted the representatives of heavy industry to find a hearing and then to make a comeback: the interdependence of the planned, state-led economy could help to open windows for a given sector even as it had closed them under other circumstances.

For once heavy industry, in particular machine building, was given a green light, there were obvious spillover effects for other individual trades. That is, the machine-building trade needed the output of the iron and steel plants, which called on other branches of the metallurgical trade, which in turn required the work of the mining industry, the fuel industry, and the accessory parts producers. As a Hubei academic journal expressed the relationship, "Equipment renovation is a motive force, with a series of chain effects."[80]

The steady growth in the machine-building industry that took off in 1982 began in part from an urgent sense that orders had to be increased for that department, that it had to be given something to do. This was no doubt in part tied to concerns about restlessness among workers in that sector. It was also related to the new view that investment needed to be made selectively.[81]

In line with the new emphasis on intensive production and on "technical transformation"* of existing plant, the press began to discuss how the renovation of backward equipment could create wealth for the state to an extent not possible without such upgrading.[82] Again, capital accumulation, social stability, and a vision of how to achieve them were being used to justify a new strategy.

As one indication of the shift in priorities, production quotas for the enterprises under the First Ministry of Machine Building rose in 1982.[83] By midyear, voices in the media seemed mightily relieved to announce that this trade had "come out of the bottom of the valley"; it had been experiencing a steady upward trend since the beginning of the year, along with a "marked increase" in the profits it was delivering to the state. Its production level by then had already neared that of the same period in 1977, proclaimed another article.[84] And for the year as a whole, the

---

*The term "technological transformation" stood for the renewal of worn-out and obsolete equipment, the adoption of new technology, shifting production in accord with current technical demands, and the repair of dangerous factory buildings. See *FBIS*, Jan. 5, 1982, p. K5.

value of output in machinery making increased by 16.2 percent over 1981, when its value had fallen by 14.1 percent.[85] Suddenly, journalists were writing as if heavy's fall—in fact, as we have seen, chosen purposively in 1979—had actually been the result of a bad mistake, or at best, an accident.

CONCLUSION

This study of two key investment decisions over the years 1979 to 1982 challenges stalemate-politics models of the impact of interests on the Chinese policy process, at least for times of crisis. In their place, with the aid of some comparative literature drawn from work on the American system, it accounts for disinvestment and reinvestment programs by identifying structural features of the policy process particular to redistributive policies and to times of agenda shift.

An inexorable push for revenue generation and resource concentration at the top of the system and for a modicum of popular quiescence—conditions necessary for redistribution and highly prized in contexts of crisis generally, but especially valued in state-owned and run economies—forced contenders for funding to present their requests as if money for their sector's needs would serve those elite objectives. And that reactive stance was furthered as claimants found themselves caught up in a chain of economic causes and effects ultimately controlled by political will. Rival sectors' responses to the 1979 switch of priorities illustrates this pattern.

Two years later, the central government's revival of budgeted heavy industry on a national scale was the outcome of a deliberate elite decision, one taken in an altered policy climate and driven by specific feedback—the appearance of threatening indicators. It did not come about just because the heavy industrial ministries had constant clout within the policy process, or because of a fixed pattern of power among claimants or between petitioners and the policy elite. It was in addition more than just a function of ministries maneuvering to meet their missions in routine ways, with their usual allies.

Thus theories about marginal changes in normal times built on assumptions of immobility and stasis become irrelevant in interpreting situations of major disinvestment and reallocation. What this case shows is that in the post-Mao era bargains, lobbying, and alliance formation may have a role in the policy process, but it is essentially a subordinate one. Given an openness since the late 1970's to not just one but two alternative models of capital accumulation, bargains and the like take place within and are subject to a shifting context.

In the early 1980's it was the state-owned and still significantly planned economy that generated in its masters continual concerns for public resource concentration and mass quietude, along with the dynamic of mutual interaction among economic sectors that was charged by these leaders' decisions, that repeatedly refashioned that context. Times of crisis and macro readjustment bring this pattern to light.

PART THREE

Implementation

SIX

Priority for Light Industry
Bureaucracy and Modes of Compliance

CHAPTER 1 MADE THE POINT that China's readjustment, like industrial policy in democracies, involved picking winners—the sector or sectors that are encouraged to expand—and abandoning other trades to the play of market forces. Chapter 3 identified three malfunctions in Chinese assessments of the domestic economic system; the first and most prominent of these was sectoral imbalance and a corresponding disproportion between accumulation and consumption.

This chapter stresses the state-led strategic aspect of readjustment, that is, the measures and methods the central government used to enforce this policy. My approach is different from other analyses of readjustment that assume that its success was the result of decentralization and attendant new local powers, or that a sudden burst of market activity by itself made the difference.*

The chapter examines the process by which central bureaucracies rechanneled investment capital and other resources to the light industrial sector, the winner picked by the pro-readjustment leadership, in the period 1979 through 1981. By so reorienting

---

*The market incentives—prices, profit rates—that enhanced the output of light industry and sparked a dynamism that continued even after the formal termination of readjustment as a centrally designated policy in 1982 were first installed by central governmental decisions rather than being purely market-driven. Accordingly, heightened output of consumer goods even after 1982 was the product of local bureaucracies' responses to the central government's administrative initiatives. In brief, local governments had a new incentive to promote the output of the firms they owned (most of which were in the light sector) after reforms of 1980 entitled these governments for the first time to the bulk of the profits from their own firms.

priorities in these years, this leadership intended that the primary macro failure, sectoral imbalance, would be redressed. Chapters 7 and 8 will deal with the execution of two other key dimensions of readjustment as industrial policy, abandonment of losers and rationalization of the arrangement of the assets of individual firms. These chapters will also show how these dimensions corresponded to the other two systemic weaknesses analyzed in Chapter 3.

The material that follows is linked to earlier chapters in another way. The argument below emphasizes the extent to which readjustment was implemented at the local level through relying on the social structural behavioral traits I called verticalism and localism (the latter a form of unitism) in the second chapter. These traits, as they were manifested within the local industrial process, worked in tandem to inform the operational mechanisms by which resources that had been concentrated in Beijing were funneled downward to localities. Once the resources arrived at the lower administrative levels, officials in the localities relied on these forces to ensure that the resources were properly directed to centrally set targets.

Scholarship on China has tended to emphasize the negative, stultifying effects of bureaucratic paternalism (essentially, my verticalism). Other studies have also denigrated localism and its accompanying constant need for consensus building in industrial decision making at every level. These behavioral patterns, various scholars hold, are generically opposed to each other and so have one of two contradictory effects: either the force of localism strengthens localities and thereby stymies the enforcement of central policy, or encrusted vertical arrangements perpetuate the status quo and so leave lower levels strapped in a state of impotent limbo. Either way, it is difficult to reconcile such characterizations of these forces with any outcome of positive change.

Literature about China after the beginning of the post-1980 reforms details the effects of the decentralization of finances and supplies at that time.[1] Commentators point to an intensification of localism to which new powers over the purse pushed politicians at the grass roots as they took advantage of extra revenues to build expanded resource bases in their areas.

Christine Wong, for instance, maintains that these revenue-sharing schemes, which let most provinces retain all or a fixed portion of profits from local enterprises, exacerbated a remarkable encystment of local economies present even before the reforms began.[2] Describing the situation that issued from Cultural Revolution policies, she concludes, "By 1978, having given up the major portion of material and financial resources to local control, the central government's options for reforming the economy were limited to programs acceptable to the local government."[3] Reforms provided these already powerful players with the wherewithal for additional muscle.

This situation is quite different from what usually happens in socialist bureaucracies. For, as Kornai shows, these bureaucracies contain dysfunctional behavioral regularities growing out of their hierarchical power relationships that, through repetition over time, lock these political economies into a stalemate so that no real change can occur at any level. His work designates logjam as the more typical pattern in resource management in socialist economies.[4] A question I will address here is the extent to which the post-1980 reforms overrode the standard weakness and incapacity at local levels.

Paternalism and consensus building within localities have each been said to contribute to the stagnation found in socialist systems, especially at lower levels. Discussing the individual firm, Walder and Wong castigate industrial paternalism particularly for the obstacle they see it throwing up to reform efforts. Their charge is that the caretaking it entails absolves enterprise managers from having to solve their own production and marketing problems, leaving them dependent on bureaucratic superiors and so stuck in a "behavioral inertia."[5] The result is to keep the old, prereform system intact.

Arguing in a related vein, Lampton stresses that consensual decision formation can inhibit action for years because each affected party and office must be consulted and then finally consent before closure is proclaimed.[6] But, as I will demonstrate, although *systemic reorganization* may be obstructed by these features, change of another sort—shifts in resource allocation—need not be.

In a departure from the older, totalitarian visions of socialist systems, in which bureaucracies are nearly omnipotent, recent literature on China has discounted the capabilities of the planned, bureaucratic economy. And because many of the massive ventures of the past in China leaped ahead unlimited by economic concerns, there has come to be an equation of irrationality with socialist hierarchies of command.[7]

The 1979–82 economic readjustment did achieve the goal of sectoral reorganization set by its designers, so understanding that success will entail reconsidering the positive capacities of a vertically structured bureaucracy, with its base in largely consensually run localities, which were neither totally impotent nor excessively unruly. To undertake this reconsideration, it is useful to turn away from those who write on socialist states, many of whom may overemphasize the blockages they say bureaucracies invariably build to reform.[8]

In contrast, students of France and Japan think positively about bureaucratic arrangements, pointing to their contributions to macro readjustment. These two cases direct us to the efficacy—rather than to the obstructiveness—that a bureaucracy can exhibit under particular circumstances and for specific functions.

For instance, Johnson's study of MITI and Japanese industrial policy shows that the vertically ordered bureaus that manage each separate industry there are essential to the successful guidance and control that lies at the heart of managing sectoral policy.[9] This is an approach, like China's readjustment, that involves periodic alterations in the beneficiaries of state favors. Wylie, writing about France, notes that a vertical form of organization can act as a force for change when hierarchical authorities send down orders to bring about shifts.[10]

Several of the features that make those systems work can be found in the Chinese one as well. These include the "paternalism" of the French ministries,[11] procedures that guarantee the state's authority through the local government's continuing dependence on fiscal subsidies from central ministries,[12] and mayors' need for approval for their activities and financing for their projects from the top.[13] Writers on France and Japan see such elements of centralized systems as conducive to policy implementation.

In China similar vertical, bureaucratic arrangements helped to ensure the successes of the readjustment program. Several economic officials in Wuhan confirmed that this program operated as a planned, bureaucratic exercise, one that worked through administrative orders (*mingling*),* rather than being a product of market competition among sectors.

Obviously, the selective targeting of resources that is crucial to such a process had to depend on their centralized concentration and on a modicum of control over them at the apex of the system. And this had to be coupled with enough clout in the capital to ensure that these resources, once sent downward, would be used in the manner desired by top-level leaders.[14]

Not just the verticalism of bureaucracy but localism as well has been a part of the French and Japanese sociocultural heritage. Specialists on those societies offer insights into the connections between that trait and the success of restructuring efforts. Localism, which finds one form of expression in China in the complex consultative, consensual corporatism criticized above for causing stalemate, finds a parallel in Nakane's view of Japanese society. She believes that this orientation serves the emotional need for security of the individual member or group.[15] Similarly, in his 1967 study Mark Kesselman speaks of an "ambiguous consensus" against outsiders which bolstered the political maneuverings of French mayors.[16]

In each case collusive turning inward seems actually to have shored up the state's policy enforcement to the extent that localities as well as vertical hierarchies were charged with specific tasks, for which their centrally appointed officials were held responsible, in the course of policy implementation. The self-protective encapsulation of individual localities that accompanied the effort to attain these ends also worked to reduce the aggregate power of society against the state. As Nakane reasons with regard to Japan, such social atomization in that country eases the vertical transmission of government directives while obstructing horizontal combinations in opposition.[17]

These findings can be applied to the readjustment in China.

*As I was told by the officials from the Municipal Economic Commission (MEC), November 12, 1984, no economic incentives were used to carry out the readjustment; rather, "we used the plan to readjust."

128 IMPLEMENTATION

Organizational capabilities, fashioned from tried modes of collaboration and connections within cities, brought to fruition the central government's commands at lower levels. At the same time, the measures contained in the policy set up new incentives that called into play altered responses from and forged new relationships among affected agents as the program reallocated rewards in changed ways.

This chapter will illuminate the workings of those capabilities and responses by examining how the program's "six priorities" were applied in Wuhan. The data here, like that to be drawn on in Chapters 7 and 8, come mainly from the city's press, city and regional journals, and interviews with local bureaucrats from fourteen economic offices over the years 1983 through 1985.

THE SIX PRIORITIES: PRINCIPLES OF OPERATION

At the center of the readjustment policy was a program of according six priorities to factories in the light and textile sectors to ensure their faster development. This label was coined in the late fall of 1979 and proclaimed by the State Council in December. These two sectors were to receive guaranteed shares and preferred treatment in the distribution of raw materials, fuel, and electrical power; in technological transformation of equipment and plants; in capital construction; in bank loans; in foreign exchange and importing technology; and in transportation during the period that the policy was in effect.[18] Simply put, the delivery of these priority supplies, funds, and services accounted for the success of the readjustment.

Some analysts have attributed that success to local initiative in response to "economic levers." "The proportion of investment going to light industry has expanded rapidly since 1978," Naughton noted in 1983, but, he went on, "most of this increase has been implemented through the medium of a decentralization in investment control, through an expanded program of bank lending."[19] Elsewhere he remarks, "Local investment concentrated on consumer goods which yield high rates of return in terms of profit and taxes."[20]

It is true that documents from the period make it appear that the readjustment program was consigned to the localities to manage and that bank loans and other financial incentives played a prominent role in its implementation. From the start and repeatedly at intervals thereafter, national directives called on local authorities to give priority to providing the light and textile sector firms with the fuels, power, raw materials, and means of transportation they needed.

When this system worked, light's quick development was credited to party committees at various levels having strengthened and improved their leadership over that sector and to provinces and cities having organized the concerned departments in their areas to research and solve problems in light industrial production. Or, some media releases said, the top leadership in the localities had grasped the six priorities in the production of consumer goods by arranging increases in production plans and allocating additional raw materials or by providing local financial support.[21]

Banks seemed to have acquired expanded and, for China, unprecedented roles in this period, at least on paper.[22] For example, then Hubei province party secretary Chen Pixian announced at one point that the financial departments and the banks in the province should use the circulating funds under their control to help produce goods that cost little, saw quick results, and netted large profits and large amounts of foreign exchange.[23]

In reality, the scope for truly independent judgment and action both in the localities and for banks was quite limited at this stage. As one bureaucrat from the Wuhan Municipal Planning Commission (MPC) put it, "The center gave us an objective [*mubiao*]; [and] it was up to the city [only] to decide on the details of readjustment." The bureaucrats who managed this city economy were, after all, men who for decades had been accustomed to being evaluated on the basis of their locality's fulfillment of a centrally assigned mission.

They continued to be tightly constrained by bureaucratic bonds with their evaluator, their superior in their functional hierarchies.[24] In interviews municipal economic officials made it plain that, despite new local funding opportunities, they continued to be charged with, and to take very seriously, their job in fulfilling their unchanged responsibility for regional development in accord with national priorities. At this point that meant ensuring delivery of the six priorities to light industrial firms, to the extent possible.

An investigation of how these inputs were allocated and delivered in one major industrial city, Wuhan, will illustrate the very limited extent to which localities and banks actually acted on their own in this period. Interviews and press reports from that city suggest four principles about the operation of this process. Overall, they reveal that verticalism, rooted in a yet significant measure of the central government's ability to allocate resources (despite some leakages in lines of hierarchical authority and regardless of the mounting growth of extrabudgetary funds under local control as the 1980's progressed), combined with a localistic cooperation among the city's bureaucracies, remained the driving force of the implementation process.

First, bureaucratic delivery persisted in accounting for the major portion of the transfer of materials in this period. One study has found that as late as 1984, the proportion of planned supply of materials in relation to gross materials consumption still accounted for 73.16 percent.[25] Nevertheless, there is an important distinction to be made between the different directions in which things flowed. Materials and monies moved down the hierarchy much more effortlessly than requests—of which there were still plenty in this time—moved upward.[26] Thus the politics of donation—by which central-level offices gave supplies and funds to local governments and their enterprises (even if some strings were attached)—placed local actors in an entirely different stance from the politics of supplication.

Second, the donation process was a differential one depending on the item in question. Some things simply moved downward—reached their destination—much more easily, without getting stuck or diverted, as it were, than others, as if their slide through the funnel feeding them to the lower levels were freer. In fact, there were several processes of delivering the various priorities.

A third principle is that the central government had two ways of influencing the behavior of local economic officials and managers, one direct, the other more indirect. The distinction mainly rested on whether the particular project at hand was a "key-point" (*zhongdian*) one, for such projects elicited much more local compliance with Beijing's guidelines. In these cases, to the extent that the funnel from the center delivered inputs, central-level concern that the project be completed could secure local cooperation—both with the central order and among local departments—much more readily.

It was as though a bargain had been struck: when the local commissions, bureaus, and managers received the wherewithal for such projects, they understood that they had to "pay up."[27] This notion of compliance as a bargain between administrative echelons also appears in the literature on industrial policy in France and Japan.[28] In the Chinese case, local offices made good on their side of the deal by activating localism. In effect, cost sharing occurred, whereby the center contributed resources it commanded while the locality in turn was much more able than usual to marshal the consensus among departments that is crucial to carrying out any project in China.

Such formation of consensus among local offices on specific key-point projects could lead to unwonted efficiency in producing a workshop or a renovated piece of equipment. In these cases the press would report about how these projects "saw results," that is, went into operation on or even ahead of schedule and rapidly began to generate income. For, once inputs were designated and allocated, there was little left for the concerned departments in the city to haggle over. Moreover, since central-level monitors paid more attention to these projects than to others for which their contributions were less direct, they took care to verify local fulfillment of the bargain.

And fourth, the bureaucratic bodies that had held sway in the days of the prereform economy—namely, the municipal planning and economic commissions and the city finance bureau—continued to claim their old clout in the locality, regardless of the supposed new role for banks. The power in the readjustment program still rested with planners, who were answerable to their higher-level bosses. The bank became merely the agent of these time-tested corporate officials and coordinators.

A corollary of this power system was that there were no permanent alliances restraining the planners. Instead, planners simply sided with whatever functional bureaus they needed to in order to enforce the plan and thereby to appear compliant so as to continue to obtain resources from the top. At this time, therefore, local planners made common cause with representatives from the sectors newly designated by the priority program and did not automatically honor old loyalties to the once powerful heavy industrial bureaus and their plants. Here is a local version of that variability in the power of heavy industry stressed in Chapter 5, once again in accord with policy changes at the top.

All four of these principles—about the nature of resource flows, the varying delivery processes for different resources, central-local bargains, and intralocality alliances and power—illustrate the continuing relevance in the period of reform of the traits of vertical control and local corporatism.

MONEY, ELECTRICITY, AND MATERIALS

The six priorities are best discussed in three different sets, according to the ease of their delivery. The variation among them derived from the extent to which the central government was able to monitor their delivery, the facility of bartering the resource, its perishability, its possibilities for being used in alternative ways other than those intended, and, ultimately, the relative quantity of the item in question under central versus local control.

The first set of priorities concerned financial allocations. These included bank loans and investment;* funds for technology, equipment, and capital construction; and foreign exchange for importing. Rather than localities simply being able to respond to economic levers on their own in this period, as Barry Naughton's analysis suggests, monies directed downward were still subject to central control; indeed, financial disbursements were the

---

*Although investment was not cited among the six priorities, local bureaucrats still talked about it, and the press often made reference to projects, enterprises, and departments receiving "investment" in this period. What was called investment (in the prereform sense, of gratis appropriations), however, came to represent generally as little as 8 to 10 percent of a given sector's financial receipts from the state, with the remainder termed bank loans. Probably local bureaucrats by custom referred to funds issued from the state to the firms as investment, even though such funds were turned into loans (with low rates of interest and many opportunities for very favorable repayment terms) after 1980. For instance, officials from the Textile Bureau of Wuhan told me on November 14, 1984, that during the three years of readjustment (1979–81), 90 percent of their funding had come in the form of loans and only 10 percent in direct investment.

priorities that most successfully reached their destination. Zysman hypothesizes, generalizing from the French case, "Perhaps the easiest thing to coordinate in a centralized bureaucratic state is the allocation of capital because such decisions do not require the reorganization or agreement of lower level bureaucracies."[29] In the Chinese case, the efficacy of the monitoring procedures and the still far larger quantities of funds under central as opposed to local control appear to be the chief explanatory factors. Effective monitoring precluded diversion of funds for alternative uses.

Electrical power was not as tightly controlled by the center but was subject to a sufficient degree of upper-level supervision that it largely flowed in accord with policy. It was raw materials, the items most easily diverted from course, that posed the greatest problems.

Money: Loans, Investment, and Foreign Exchange

Amounts and sources. Funding was indisputably the most crucial of the priorities.[30] Once the readjustment policy was publicly enunciated, central decision makers rapidly directed large sums into the targeted sectors by allocating capital to the localities in the form of bank loans. By late summer 1980, just a little more than a year after readjustment was first implemented, the Wuhan city paper announced that in the previous year, the central government, Hubei province, and the city had together issued loans totaling more than 87 million *yuan* for 158 projects in Wuhan.[31]

According to the report, concerned departments in the city were responsible for selecting the superior units to support, seeing that the funds were targeted on marketable products, that they were used for raising quality and filling gaps in the production structure, and that they went for producing goods for which the work period was short and the financial results apparent quickly.

The article does not show the breakdown of the loan total coming from each of the three levels. But other sources suggest that it was clearly the central government that took the lead. One press release notes that in January 1980 the State Council endorsed a recommendation on funding for the country as a whole that had been jointly authored by the State Economic Commission, the People's Bank, and other units in the capital. The decision was to set aside 2 billion *yuan* worth of loan capital for mid- and short-term special project loans.

These loans, when combined with U.S.$300 million in buyers' foreign exchange loans, were specifically aimed at speeding up the production of light industry. By year's end, the amount actually spent on loans for light industry had shot up even higher: in 1980 1.63 billion *yuan* in special project loans were combined with another 990 million *yuan* in ordinary equipment loans for a total of 2.62 billion *yuan* of funds in loans nationwide.[32]

The People's Bank continued to inject huge infusions of capital into these sectors on a national basis in succeeding months. By early 1981, a staggering 80 percent of the People's Bank's 3.56 billion *yuan* in medium- and short-term loans for revamping equipment and introducing technical innovations had gone to the light and textile sectors. These monies funded the production of one-half to three-quarters of a million new bicycles, watches, and sewing machines for the consumers of the country.[33]

Even in 1982, when the readjustment program had begun to wind down and heavy industry was being revived, the People's Bank announced plans to contribute over half of 4 billion *yuan* worth of equipment to the light and textile sectors, and the Bank of China promised U.S.$1.5 billion in foreign exchange loans to aid in the manufacture of export commodities, most of which must have been light industrial goods.[34]

But what about the issue of decentralization? Lending that originated at the provincial and urban levels was exactly in step with this direction driven from the top. Immediately upon the promulgation of the readjustment policy, leaders in Hubei and Wuhan launched their own funding programs. Through an arrangement of matching funds, in June 1979, the provincial Party Committee pulled out 20 million *yuan* from the province's circulating capital, to which the city's Party Committee added another 5 million from funds the city had raised, to serve as "technical measures" (*jicuo*) loans for developing Wuhan's light and textile industries.[35]

In the same year the province and the city put together another 9 million *yuan* to revamp 90 old Wuhan enterprises, in the expectation that the better outfitted plants could yield an additional

Priority for Light Industry 135

16.5 million *yuan* in income "for the state," meaning the central government. The improved plants were also to provide jobs for nearly 5,000 unemployed workers.[36] Around the same time the provincial government laid out 90 million *yuan* to be used as loans to renovate textile equipment in provincially owned firms.[37]

In 1980, the province and unspecified "concerned departments" offered 130 million *yuan* in loans to 123 provincial light and textile enterprises.[38] In addition, in 1980 and 1981 Hubei arranged 261 special project (*zhuanxiang*) loans worth 264.8 million *yuan*; in 1981 the province handed out 286 "technical measures" loans, which called for a capital outlay of just over 74 million *yuan*.[39]

Acting on its own, the city followed up on these cues. In the first year and a half after readjustment had begun, the Wuhan branch of the People's Bank presented 400 light and textile enterprises in the city with medium- and short-term loans totaling 74.29 million *yuan*. This money, doled out as investment funds under the state plan's regimen, was earmarked by the city to be spent on the procurement and installation of equipment and facilities.[40] According to management officials from the city's textile bureau, that branch of industry received a full 40 percent of the entire loan capital disbursed in the city over the years 1980–84. These men, confusing in discussion the concepts of "loan" and "investment," reported that they saw their new "investment" jump from 39 million in 1979 to 65 million just two short years later.[41]

The massive shift in investment appears in sharp relief when calculated in percentages. If loans and investment are combined under the label "investment" (as local bureaucrats grouped them in conversation), and then if pre-1980 allocations are compared with the loans that formed the bulk of funding thereafter, heavy's share of industrial investment on a national basis fell from about 90 percent in the period 1966 to 1975 to 80 percent at the height of readjustment in 1981. The shift in funding can be seen in the data on the investment figures in capital construction for light and heavy industry shown in Tables 12 and 13.

A Hubei journal reported that between 1978 and 1981, the respective shares of light and heavy industry in total productive investment went from 3.8 percent to 12.5 percent for light and

TABLE 12
Capital Construction Investment by Industrial Sector
(Yuan 1 billion)

Year	Light industry	Heavy industry	Year	Light industry	Heavy industry
1978	2.93	24.39	1981	4.34	17.26
1979	3.06	22.63	1982	4.65	21.42
1980	5.09	22.47	1983	3.88	24.35

SOURCE: Guojia tongjiju bian 1985: 72.

TABLE 13
Investment in Capital Construction by Industrial Sector
as Percent of Total Investment

Year	Light industry	Heavy industry	Year	Light industry	Heavy industry
1953–57	6.4%	36.1%	1978	5.8%	48.7%
1958–62	6.4	54.0	1979	5.9	43.2
1963–65	3.9	45.9	1980	9.1	40.2
1966–70	4.4	51.1	1981	9.8	39.0
1971–75	5.8	49.6	1982	8.4	38.5
1976–80	6.7	45.9	1983	6.5	41.0
1981–85	6.9	38.5			

SOURCE: State Statistical Bureau 1986: 375.

from 64.7 percent down to 49.2 percent for heavy.[42] The changes in relative proportions between the sectors in Wuhan city were similarly impressive. Mayor Li Renzhi announced in the autumn of 1979 that already that year light and textile's investment as a percent of total local investment had leaped from 1978's 11.3 up to 17.3.[43]

These various bits of data suggest that these so-called loans were really earmarked grants pegged to ensure central policy implementation, and that localities were living by the line on sectoral development that had been promulgated in Beijing. Together such data weaken the notions that at this stage banks and decentralization were the vehicles on which readjustment rode to its realization. The next question is how the actual enforcement took place, that is, how the central government managed to make the bank branches in the localities behave as it chose in that era of seemingly rampant reforming and decentralization.

Enforcement: procedures and relationships. Implementation of readjustment relied on tested behavioral habits of verticalism and local corporatism. Interviews with municipal officials in Wuhan and articles in the city press revealed the continuing presence of vertical domination both in the mode of distributing the investment funding suddenly called "loans" after 1980 and in the decisions made about their use. To the extent that the city authorities had any decision-making leverage, they could exercise it effectively only in a corporate fashion. These principles held whether monies were donated freely or whether they had to be obtained via supplication.

The ongoing clout of the upper levels—most immediately the province but beyond that in Beijing ministries and commissions[44] —was evident most fundamentally in the rhetoric officials used when talking about policy enforcement. According to officials at the Wuhan Municipal Economic Commission (MEC), handing out the six priorities to sectors and firms in the city involved following the strictures of *pingheng*, or balance.

This notion of balance, used in preparing the national plan for decades in China, immediately exposed the conceptual and procedural continuities between readjustment, a product of the supposedly market-prone reform era on the one hand, and the relationships out of which the command economy had long been constructed on the other. Planners at the central government level performed this balancing act in the case of readjustment by deploying outlays of money so that they would go to light rather than heavy industry through "control by plan," according to interviewees.

More evidence of this continuity of vertical power carried over from the past comes from informants from the bank, who spoke of their "loaning according to plan." These men were in no sense bankers as the term is usually understood, however. They were made to operate within parameters set by the fixed amount of loan capital they received from their superior levels in the state banking hierarchy.* Although there was leeway to overstep this

---

*Wuhan MEC officials explained (May 23, 1984) that "the center gives a set amount of capital to Hubei for capital construction, and then the province gives the Wuhan branch its share." In allocating loans for circulating capital, according to city bank informants (November 15, 1984), the center considers the nationwide financial and materials supply situation and reaches a "central balance" in determining how much of the total each area will obtain.

limit,[45] that predetermined figure formed a rough and working boundary that guided the sums allotted among regions nationally as well as the proportions to be granted to the various departments within a given city.

From 1979 to 1982, local bank officials disbursed loans according to one clear, centrally designated guideline: they were to use the capital to increase the quantity of light industrial products turned out in the city. As a result, the amount the light industrial departments (including the electronics trade) of Wuhan received shot up from just over half of the city's loan capital (51.97 percent) in 1978 to over two-thirds of it (67.84 percent) five years later.*

Wuhan's loans for manufacturing daily-use industrial products were also subject to provincial authorities' balancing of funds among the several industrial cities within the province. As grant monies passed through Hubei's hands, decision makers at that level balanced Wuhan's allocation with those for other, smaller cities that provincial planners deemed either more worthy, more promising, or more needy.[46] Here again the city was caught in a vertical power hierarchy that restricted its officials' initiative.

Yet another kind of loan that limited local authority came from funds that also flowed downward from higher-level organs but were outside the usual banking channels. Sometimes industrial ministries in Beijing donated money directly to the individual sector for which they were responsible.[47] A July 1979 disbursal of 16 million *yuan* (still termed a loan) from the Ministry of Textiles to the city's textile bureau fell in this category.[48] These loans account for some of the loan capital that a bureau manages more or less on its own, which it in turn then "balances" among its subordinate enterprises.[49]

That this final link in the vertical chain, the textile bureau itself, operated through procedures of vertical control within its own local system in other ways as well is evident in its level-by-level arrangement for awarding funds to the firms in the city. At the start of readjustment, once the province and the city party com-

---

*Bank officials explained that the reason the light industrial firms got so much relatively was that the loans that this municipal branch controlled went only to city-owned enterprises, many of which were light industrial firms. The big heavy industrial plants at that time were either provincially or centrally owned. See Wong 1986a for a discussion of ownership in state-run enterprises at the various administrative levels and its complicated relationship with funding.

mittees began to set aside capital for developing Wuhan's light and textile sectors, the city's textile bureau, its subordinate companies (which stand between the bureau and the firms), and every enterprise that received a loan each established its own little "loan leadership group." The bureau's own loan group met as often as once a week to decide how to allocate money among its subordinate firms.[50]

Donation. Once these vertically organized monies reached the locality via donations, city offices mounted a corporatelike mobilization of resources and cooperative efforts as their matching exchange for the central funds. The body that commanded that urban corporation was clearly the Municipal Planning Commission. But the Municipal Economic Commission, formerly the junior partner in this work, saw its authority enhanced in these years when it was placed in charge of the readjustment. This apportionment of tasks followed from the usual division of labor between these bodies: whereas the MPC's role has always been to oversee the playing out of the entire city plan, the MEC has special responsibility for industry.

This corporate leadership always has had some capacity to enforce consensus in the city. But its ability to do so was greatly enhanced in the case of the readjustment's donations from above and the vast new sums suddenly available for light industry. Municipal departments that might have haggled over limited finances in ordinary circumstances energetically joined ranks in support of key-point projects that had been chosen by upper-level bureaucrats. One such instance occurred when Hubei province approved 40 light and textile renovation projects, blessing them with a total of 44 million *yuan* in loans. At that point the city branch of the People's Bank coordinated all the relevant offices to adopt measures to guarantee that the loans served their intended purposes.[51]

Another example was a set of 61 loan projects funded by a pot of provincial-cum-city capital. Once the firms housing these projects were designated as recipients of money, local officials guaranteed that they also were awarded the requisite raw and building materials, machinery, and electricity to execute the job and ensured that the workers in the local supply and capital construction departments accorded them special support.[52] By the end of

1979, 70 percent of these projects had reportedly already gone into production, a remarkable achievement in this usually maddeningly sluggish approval- and agreement-seeking urban bureaucracy.[53]

The No. Five Textile Factory was one of these showcase efforts. Chosen as a key point of the city textile system, it was presented with modern spinning equipment. An array of local departments quickly responded to the donation by "turning on the green light" for the project. The offices involved included the bank and those in charge of financial affairs, urban construction, building materials, materials supply, metallurgy, and transportation. A set of other factories was also corralled into cooperation, including the Wuhan Smelting Factory, the Wuhan Forging Factory, and the Wuhan Blower Factory.[54] Among the more remarkable benefits that were conferred on a key point was the urban construction office's acceleration of its typically interminable approval process. As a result, for this one case assent required a mere 30 days.

A local firm's attaining key-point designation thus could lead to a marshaling of intracity collaboration that was the hallmark of the local corporate strategy, once that strategy was activated by a cost-sharing bargain with its donor, a ministry or commission within the central government, or a provincial-level office.

Supplication. Upper-level decisions about the amounts of funding within which city bureaucrats—whether bank branch operators, MPC officials, or industrial bureau leaders—had to operate formed the more welcome side of the vertical relationship that defined the work of these bureaucrats. The flip side of donation, which I call supplication, involved another dynamic, one that was far more limiting. Whereas donation was automatic, supplication was cumbersome, frustrating, and unpredictable.

At a June 1979 meeting of the city's industry and transport sectors, Mayor Li Renzhi issued a telling order to the managers in attendance, which illuminates the groveling subordination required by the supplication relationship under which they suffered: "Get rid of losses in operations," he threatened. But this was not to be done for the sake of running an efficient, productive urban economy. Rather, he admonished, it was because "otherwise next year the state won't subsidize, and the banks won't give us loans." One can question whether his words were accurate, given the socialist economy's propensity to subsidize loss. Still, the stance of supplication that city leaders and the firms under their care had to adopt is clear in the mayor's prodding of enterprise managers.[55]

For the individual, undistinguished firm—and even for bureaus desirous of particular allotments not offered them by fiat—the means for obtaining financing were fraught with hassles and uncertainty. An illustrative contrast is afforded by the treatment accorded to the same local textile factory at two different times. The cadres in the loom workshop of the Wuhan No. Four Textile Factory had once hopefully drawn up an extension project that was delayed for want of funds and materials for eight long years. Once the firm became a key point in the readjustment program, targeted to produce chemical fiber needed on the market, however, this project was showered with all the resources it needed in one giant windfall.[56]

But even key-point status did not automatically result in a ready response to every entreaty. That same No. Four factory had accumulated 400 million *yuan* in foreign exchange; besides, it had already won MPC approval of its request for a U.S.$20,000 loan to import two sets of combing machines. Still, this application was delayed while the provincial-level foreign trade bureau hesitated over whether to assent. "The enterprise hasn't much power; the managing bureau and the company [beneath it] also haven't much power; [but] the *tiaotiao* of the upper levels in charge are many. Without their nod, one can't do anything,"[57] the local paper lamented in relating this tale.

The process of seeking funds was actually even more complicated than this article indicates. For, according to Textile Bureau informants, the Hubei Foreign Trade Bureau had first to allocate an allotment of foreign exchange to the Wuhan Foreign Trade Bureau. Next, a group of decision makers from several city offices determined how to distribute these funds to the various city industrial bureaus.

Only then could the money be "balanced" and handed over to a particular applicant, though even then there was no guarantee.[58] This process, however, was limited by the relatively paltry sums over which the city itself had control. During the readjustment era, the city could authorize joint venture projects if only up to U.S.$5,000 was entailed, and even the province's approval power stopped at 3 million.

Voluminous accounts decrying excessive local capital construction have filled the pages of the Chinese press since the late 1970's. Notwithstanding these critiques, municipal officials still felt hampered by regulations checking their ability to get control over loan capital for this purpose. In this period Wuhan could draw loans for new capital construction involving solely domestic purchases that amounted to less than 500,000 *yuan*. In this sphere Hubei's far greater range (up to 10 million) aggravated Wuhan's sense of being restrained.[59]

And in the case of technical transformation grants, which entailed renovating old machinery, a local industrial bureau could allocate funds on its own only if under 300,000 *yuan* were needed. For middle-sized projects (up to 1 million *yuan*), the MEC became the arbiter. Work costing up to 10 million *yuan* was dependent on provincial deliberations;[60] beyond that, it was out of local hands altogether.

For ordinary proposals, when upper levels had not designated a key point or otherwise specified the recipient, the process of petitioning for financing could often be absurdly lengthy and tiresome. The firm requiring funds had to traverse two distinct channels of appeal, both mandatory—one involving its functional superior, its bureau, and one through the local bank branch.[61]

The enterprise's first line of attack was to present its case to the local representatives of its functional hierarchy, its own managing bureau. Here it essentially entered a plea to have the project approved in principle. The bureau had some discretion in balancing this request against those from other local firms. For larger-scale projects, though, the bureau was subject to vertical controls, compelled to report to its superiors for endorsement.[62]

But the bureau was limited in another way as well. This verticalism was supplemented by local corporatism because each request also had to be considered by a set of representatives of local offices: individuals from the MPC, the MEC, the city's Finance Bureau, and the local bank branch.[63] If it was a demand

Priority for Light Industry 143

for technical transformation,* the MEC had more authority;† for capital construction, the MPC took charge.⁶⁴ For both these sorts of loans the funding came from the Construction Bank, so the decision makers in that body took a role in the discussion as well. Within this group of bureaucrats, the MEC was responsible for reporting weekly to the mayor on concrete issues and had also to inform its own *tiaotiao* leadership, the State Economic Commission in Beijing, on the overall course economic development was taking in Wuhan.⁶⁵

Besides this functional channel, the firm also had to place an appeal for the money with the local bank. The bank's assessment, though, rested not on its independent judgment but on the outcome of this joint city collaborative decision, as well as on concurrence from its own superior branch if the request was a large one. Whereas the first channel entailed a minute and specialized appraisal by the factory's functional superiors, the bank was to make a more overall assessment, weighing the project's general feasibility and the standing of the proposal in relation to other requests.‡

But the municipal bank branch did not act independently; it mainly filled the role of agent of this corporate urban elite.⁶⁶ In principle, it was up to the MPC, the MEC, and the bank branch to decide how to allocate the loan capital granted by the provincial plan for the city each year.⁶⁷ But by the early 1980's the bank was still, as it had for years, filling a computational, ledger-

---

*Technical transformation referred to plant expansion (of up to 30 percent of the original area) or servicing or revamping of old equipment in the original factory, buying some new equipment, or building a new workshop. Capital construction meant the erection of wholly new buildings and outfitting with a whole new set of technology. Both sorts of loans were to be repaid at the rate of 0.042 percent per month (People's Bank interview, November 15, 1984).

†The MEC's authority covered only the enterprises under city ownership; the affairs of the provincially owned (of which there were 86 out of a total of some 4,000 enterprises in Wuhan as of May 28, 1984, according to the MPC) and centrally owned (of which there were 79 at that time) firms were governed by economic commissions at those levels.

‡Interview at Wuhan Branch of People's Bank, November 15, 1984. The Wuhan First Bureau of Light Industry stated that it used roughly the same procedure regarding decisions on importing: the factory would give its suggestion to the bureau, which took it to the MEC. Then the MEC and the bureau together presented the request to the bank (interview at Wuhan First Bureau of Light Industry, November 17, 1984).

keeping function and therefore in a less than coequal position. For instance, once the MEC elected to approve a project requiring technical transformation loans, the Construction Bank entered the deliberations to place a *yuan* figure on the size of the loan.[68] Moreover, when the local bank branch made any independent decisions, it had to report to its *kuaikuai* (local) leadership in the city government, in particular to the MEC.*

Two comments of local bureaucrats brought to life the subservient position the bank occupied. Bank officials explained the sequence in which decisions were taken. First, the industrial bureau (in conjunction with its upper level and the corporate city elite) approved loans for the purchase of equipment. Only then was the bank called upon to give approval. "In the majority of the cases, the two agree," they admitted. Since the bank played a secondary role, that "agreement" must have amounted in effect to a rubber stamp. A manager at a city textile firm was even more explicit: "If the bureau assents, the enterprise then applies to the bank, which of course will approve once the bureau [and its superior and the city corporate elite] has."[69]

Thus supplication was considerably more complicated than donation. First, in distinction from the quick cooperation that automatically granted monies elicited among local actors, any request for funds had to be subjected to a cumbersome consultative process among municipal organs, which invariably entailed negotiation over the use to which limited capital could be put. And even once agreement was reached within the city economic bureaucracy's decision-making councils, the supplication was still hostage to verticalism. That is, the plea was yet subject to a nod from the upper levels, which held greater authority. The requirement of obtaining acquiescence for loans from the vertical, formal bureaucratic channels into which each local body was enmeshed continued to obstruct wholly decentralized investment decision making in the early 1980's. Vertical controls, then,

*Interview at Wuhan branch of People's Bank, November 15, 1984. According to this interview, the People's Bank in Wuhan had charge only of the circulating capital loans, set at 0.06 percent per month. These funds were to be used for buying extra raw materials if the original capital given the firm proved inadequate, and such loans were called *chao ding'e daikuan* (loans exceeding the quota). In handling these, the bank worked directly with the requesting firm and merely kept the responsible functional bureau informed.

were a problem for local leaders whose moves they hemmed in. But these controls clearly did make possible the application and enforcement of central policy in the city.*

The increase in the quantity of funds under local control and the shift to using bank loans to organize investment during the readjustment period did not cut off the central government's ability to ensure that the program progressed as its authors had intended. The amount of the loans in this period and, to a large extent, their destination—for the light and textile trades and even for particular key-point plants and projects—were based on planned decisions taken higher up the vertical hierarchy.

In addition, whether funds reached the city in the form of a donation from above or whether municipal officials attempted, through a complicated supplication process, to push enterprise demands up the bureaucracy, local decision makers had only the most limited authority. Many of the local projects financed from these funds ultimately required that superiors in functional hierarchies outside and above the city initiate or at least approve of them.

Nor did loans for technical transformation or capital construction result from independent decisions by local bankers. Even when approval came from the locality, it issued not from bankers but from a localistic corporate consultation among various municipal bureaus and commissions and from the balancing of local monies between potential recipients. In this local corporation, the bank was simply an agent. Thus readjustment worked in large part because local corporations' use of centrally sent monies was tied vertically to central leaders' objectives.[70]

Electricity

After funding, the delivery of electricity was the next most successful among the six priorities.[71] It was relatively easier to control the direction in which electrical power flowed and its final destination than it was to keep track of raw materials. Unlike raw materials, electrical power does not come in small, discrete por-

---

*There has been much reporting about the proliferation of unauthorized capital construction on the local level since the early 1980's. But if cities had had sufficient funds to do everything they wished to do, they would not have had to have recourse to these cumbersome procedures.

tions that can be bandied or bartered; nor can it be converted to unintended uses under cover, because, since the electricity used in a given city comes from only one source, the regional grid, it is much simpler to monitor its disposal.[72]

According to the press, however, some electrical power did flow in undirected paths. The regional electrical power grids are initially centrally donated to the localities, but once they have been constructed, the switches that control the direction of their currents are necessarily close to the point of destination and far from the donors in Beijing.[73] Therefore, there is scope for some diversion and thus for deviation from central-level intentions.

Immediately on the commencement of readjustment, the State Economic Commission ordered the planning and economic commissions, along with the electrical power departments in the localities, to set norms for the usage of electricity so as to guarantee the power supply needed by light and textile firms. The relevant directive also decreed that at fixed periods provinces and departments must inspect the enforcement of this guarantee and report back to the commission as frequently as every ten days.[74]

The reaction in Hubei seems to have been instantaneous. There, in the past, the press related, "No matter how serious the power supply shortage, the steel industry would always get sufficient power. . . . Whenever a proposal to reduce the power supply was made, it always affected [negatively] the light and textile industries and the households." But once the readjustment policy was announced, the iron and steel firms "made some concessions" so that "the imbalance in the distribution of energy [began] to take a turn for the better."[75] By early July 1979, according to the media, six major Hubei cotton mills that had been operating only three or four days a week in the first quarter of the year were running at full capacity six days each week because of increases in power allocations.[76]

Over the first nine months of the year, power consumption for all of the province's industry (except at the Wuhan Iron and Steel Plant [Wugang]'s 1.7-meter rolling mill), went down 8.3 percent from the usage in 1978. But in the light and textile trades the use was up by 52.7 percent. The upshot was that production in the firms in these sectors changed from a state of half-stagnation to one in which all the facilities were working.[77]

In Wuhan the local paper urged that priority be given to supplying light and textile factories. It warned that the special line belonging to these firms must be reserved for their use and that it could not (as in the past) be "casually shut off." Other users that had been unofficially drawing on that line were at once to be switched to other lines.[78]

In interviews several years later, factory officials and bureau leaders in the city verified these press reports. A manager at a large heavy industrial plant said that a limit had been clamped on its electricity allocation in 1980 and 1981; and a manager at a key-point textile plant confirmed that firms like his were the beneficiaries. This manager told how at that time his plant suddenly obtained electrical power that had previously gone to the machine-building industry. He recalled that electricity had been the most critical of all the six priorities in improving his own firm's work, even more crucial than new funding.[79]

City Textile Bureau officials also corroborated what journalists had written. They recalled that at the most strained times before 1979 electricity had been available for the light and textile factories only two or three days a week because the emphasis in supplying electricity within the city in those days was on provisioning large, centrally owned, provincially managed heavy industrial plants, such as Wugang, that were situated in Wuhan. But with the onset of readjustment, heavy industry had no choice but to cede (*ranglu*), and textile firms finally could operate at their full capacity. In sum, reports from these various sources substantiate the notion that diversion was more difficult and verticalism more effective in the case of this resource than it was with other inputs.

Raw Materials

Both Chinese and foreign commentators have emphasized the increasing slippage of centralized control over the distribution of raw materials in the reform era. Wong shows how in the Cultural Revolution period, especially from 1970 to 1978, more and more supplies were handed down to local governments to allocate.[80] By 1978, she reports, half or more of the quantities of several vital materials available nationwide were being allocated by local governments.[81]

In the next few years this situation was exaggerated by the process of economic reform. In 1979 a reform of the planning system reduced the 211 materials once under central government allocation to 64, and management over the remainder was decentralized to subcentral levels. And even materials on that list of 64 could thereafter be sold independently by firms that had delivered their requisite quota to the state. By early 1983, at the end of the readjustment, some 20 to 30 percent of the total materials traded at the provincial levels were being bought and sold by the firms on their own. At this point in the cities and at prefectural levels 30 to 40 percent of the sales of supplies were being arranged outside the state planning process.[82]

This increase in the amount of materials under local control resulted in problems in getting the supplies to the light-industrial sector enterprises in these years. About eight months after localities had been apprised of the new policies designed to favor this branch, the *Workers' Daily* complained, "It's been nearly a year since readjustment began, and the policy has not been conscientiously and resolutely implemented." As evidence, the paper stated that light industry was "facing shortages of raw materials, fuel, [and] electricity."[83] Several months later, the *People's Daily* sounded a more urgent note on the same theme:

At present there are still some localities where no arrangements have been made in accordance with the "six-priorities" policy and where some of the necessary conditions such as supply of electricity and fuel are still lacking. How can light industry be encouraged under such conditions? There are also signs in some localities of pushing light industry aside; in other localities the planned allocation of materials to light industry has been used widely for other projects. This is definitely not permissible. Resolute action should be taken so that similar practices do not occur again.[84]

But even though the paper spoke of the six priorities in general, it singled out for particular emphasis the issue of raw materials. As this editorial stressed, "To tap all the resources for raw materials is the foundation for quickening the tempo in developing light industry."[85] At around the same time the *Workers' Daily* warned about the importance of guaranteeing the six priorities, emphasizing "especially the supply of raw materials."[86]

And yet statistics from the period show that some compliance must have occurred. In Hubei, which was particularly commended in the press for its compliance,[87] by the end of 1980 the textile trade had increased its stock of raw materials by 5,400 tons with the assistance of the central and provincial governments.[88] More dramatically, between 1978 and 1981, the percentage of the national supply of lumber going to the light and textile firms shot up from 17.9 to 32.7.[89]

Diversion. The *People's Daily* editorial quoted above made the point that some raw materials meant for light industry were instead being "used widely for other projects." Diverted raw materials flowed along three different courses. One of these was dominated by heavy industrial plants and by those in the management bureaus that controlled those plants. By the end of the readjustment era, as heavy industry revived around mid-1982, talk of heavy industrial plants "squeezing out" light industry began to appear frequently in the press.[90]

But even during the heyday of the policy, the dynamics of the readjustment policy forced heavy industrial enterprises to fend for themselves in ways that deprived the light-sector plants of some of their officially allocated supplies. In 1980, when the central plan sharply cut back the investment and allocations for heavy industry across the board, a "precipitous decline in machinery demand" followed, as production ground nearly to a halt in many plants. Most machinery and some raw materials were no longer centrally distributed.[91]

As a result, firms with raw materials to market were free for the first time to put these products up for sale. Many of these materials found their way into the construction projects that authorities in the localities were busy erecting, as they made use of the rapidly multiplying extrabudgetary funds they were amassing. These funds were composed in part of new bank loans and of monies accruing to local governments from the right now granted them to retain profits from locally owned plants. These new construction projects threatened the growth of light industry by drawing upon tense raw material and energy supplies.[92]

Another strategy that many heavy industrial firms devised to cope with their plight under the readjustment policy has received less attention from scholars. Management at several of the machine-building plants in Wuhan expanded their prior practice of using barter to fill shortfalls in the plan.[93] At this juncture, enterprises no longer simply engaged in exchanges of materials to meet gaps in their supply allocations as they commonly had in the past. Now metallurgy firms traded with machinery makers, offering the intermediate goods they turned out for finished products and tools they themselves needed.

As one manager described the situation, "Before [the reform period], the materials supply department acted as the intermediary; afterward [after 1979], we dealt directly." His valve works swapped its products and their parts for pig iron, coke, and steel from the Wuhan Iron and Steel Works (Wugang), and from steel factories in other cities. Some larger machinery manufacturers also set up temporary industrial combines with smaller concerns, in which all the associated firms shared their painfully meager supplies.[94] Thus some portion of the diverted raw materials went into traffic between the now abandoned heavy industrial firms, anxious to hold onto their accustomed line of business.

Other materials flowed off into a second channel of diversion on their way down the vertical hierarchy before they ever reached the city. Some of the supplies intended for urban-based light industrial plants got stuck at the provincial levels, as they always had, before being filtered down to this traditionally weaker sector. As the *People's Daily* editorial from spring 1980 cited earlier pointed out, "Most of the raw materials and resources needed by light industry have to be supplied by the provinces, municipalities and regions."[95]

But light industry had long been owned at the municipal government level.[96] For decades that had meant that as materials flowed down the hierarchy to firms in this sector, choice items supposedly destined for them had already been grabbed by those with greater clout at higher levels: "The supply of materials was cut at every level . . . [which was] unfavorable to the light industrial enterprises, most of which were under the jurisdiction of the local authorities,"[97] noted cadres of the Ministry of Light Industry in late 1979, as they reflected bitterly on the past.[98] The temptation for those at administrative levels above the city to siphon off supplies must have been even stronger after 1980, when new revenue-sharing designs granted to the provinces part of the profits from the firms they themselves managed.[99]

This greater than ever incentive for provincial leaders to hoard materials to feed their own firms deprived cities such as Wuhan in at least two important ways. First, as Wuhan MEC officials explained, despite decentralizing reforms throughout the readjustment period, all city-run factories still had to wait for Hubei offices to approve the distribution of their raw materials.[100]

Second, such mammoth plants located within the city as Wugang that were provincially managed continued to rely directly on the province for their supplies.[101] Because of the barter activity in which Wugang participated, it is possible to imagine a network of trading between raw materials supply offices in the provincial government and the larger heavy industrial firms situated in, but not owned by, Wuhan.* Such exchanges would clearly have shortchanged locally owned light industrial enterprises in need of the supplies in question.

And in addition to this skimming off by the upper levels, there was yet one more diversionary path along which supplies for planned light industry illicitly traveled. Managers at small plants at administrative echelons below the city—in counties, brigades, and townships—could now use materials found in their own little regions. New incentives favored these firms, including two- to three-year tax holidays for newly established collective enterprises,[102] many of which were set up at these lower administrative levels with investment from organizations and groups based there, rather than with state funds.

These measures were added to the advantages that came to these plants as a result of their geographical proximity to sources of raw materials no longer tightly controlled by the central government. Furthermore, these small plants could now purchase equipment and supplies that once were allocated only to state-sector firms.[103] The outcome of these several advantages was that crude country workshops were unintentionally encouraged to monopolize for themselves those materials they found close at hand.[104] This then deprived the better-fitted enterprises that cen-

---

*In the fall of 1984, about 50 heavy industrial plants were decentralized from the central and provincial levels to city-level ownership in Wuhan.

tral planners preferred to see as the recipients of these materials. According to economist Ma Hong, 69 percent of the newly built enterprises in 1980 were in the textile and light industrial trades. Most of these were small enterprises competing with the large ones for raw materials and supplies and for fuel and power.[105]

Thus, during the readjustment period raw material supplies that failed to reach their intended target in the urban light industrial sector went astray along one of three principal paths. Either they entered the channels of heavy industrial production through barter or sale, often making their way into illicit construction projects; or they were diverted by actors in the vertical chain at administrative levels both above and below the city level.

Compliance. Despite diversion of raw materials at various administrative levels and to heavy industrial plants, there was a good measure of compliance. If there had not been, the policy of readjustment could never have succeeded. Just as in the case of loans, local corporatism and verticalism were the behavioral modes that guaranteed implementation. Light industrialists benefited because the bureaucracy undergirding the state plan—the same bureaucracy that for years had ministered to metallurgists and machinery producers—continued to operate. The only difference was that the national state plan was now favoring a new set of industries.

Local compliance with central direction was rooted in the welltested habit local officials had developed over the years of rallying the *kuai*, the geographical "lump" of territory for which they had charge, to satisfy orders from above to fulfill and overfulfill the plan. Other, related considerations at the *kuai* (in this case the urban) level were to develop the capabilities of the city while meeting local needs.

The chief commander in ensuring that these obligations were met was the MPC, which was responsible for seeing that its urban *kuai* realized its own plan as one chunk in the larger nationwide plan.[106] Accordingly, in this period the MPC chose to champion the readjustment policy and to oversee its local realization.

Already in August 1979, just a few months after the policy was announced, the chairman of the general office of the city's planning commission authored an article in the local paper laying out eight important measures the city was to enforce so as to lend priority to the growth of light industry. The first of his eight demands was for an increase in the proportion of investment going to the light industrial trades. He also pressed the electricity, fuel, raw materials, and transport departments to satisfy the light and textile firms' needs first, squeezing out other trades' demands if necessary. And he suggested pulling out from other departments some enterprises whose production conditions and facilities were rather good but whose products were not marketable and converting them to the manufacture of light and textile products or to the provision of technical services for those trades.[107]

In response, management in several of the municipal industrial bureaus quickly shifted the output of certain factories under the city's direct control. For instance, in the summer of 1979 output in firms supervised by the city's Fuel and Chemicals Bureau was switched to chemical products needed by the light and textile trades. One factory stopped manufacturing gluside, its main product, of which stocks had long piled up; management in another thought of ways to turn out caustic soda, a staple for many light industrial plants. Officials at a third, upon learning of the printing and dyeing trade's urgent demand for a chemical that would resist salt corrosion, refitted equipment that had been disassembled for many years. Pesticide was replaced by dispersed dyes, according to the press accounts.[108]

But there was also a problem of supplies not directly available within the city's own environs. To cite one case, even after readjustment began, sometimes the local plan did not provide enough coal for the city's textile factories. In such cases the MPC sought to secure from elsewhere the necessary raw materials and then to balance their distribution across the city in an effort to ensure that the six priorities took effect.[109]

Sometimes it was necessary to barter local textiles with Shanxi province for coal, or to purchase coal at negotiated prices from Shanxi in exchange for textiles, since Shanxi abounds in coal but houses no textile production. Another route involved offering technology to Sichuan province, which, like Shanxi, has coal, but lacked textile production technology that Wuhan could supply.

Under the MPC an economic-technology cooperation office (*jingji jishu xiecuo bangongshi*) was specifically charged with organizing this barter business.[110]

Even as barter with other regions became more and more common as the 1980's progressed, efforts to secure scarce supplies through the old planning channels also continued.[111] During this time the State Economic Commission, along with other related departments under the State Council, held monthly adjustment meetings to "arrange" the light industrial market on a national scale. It was still possible at that time to handle problems of the allocation of raw materials from Beijing.[112]

Additionally, enterprises in need continued to solicit assistance from their direct vertical superior, their own management bureaus. If the bureau could not satisfy the need by itself, the firm (presumably through the intervention of its bureau) then applied further up the hierarchy, ultimately to the ministry in the capital. Officials at the administrative level at which the supplies were held would carry out a balance to determine whether the request could be met. Once the request was fulfilled, the supplying office had to give its *tiao* leadership (the bureaucratic superior in its functional hierarchy) a report that finally reached the ministry. It also had to notify its *kuai* (regional) leadership, the planning commission at its own level.[113] Thus for finding scarce supplies both verticalism and local corporatism came into play.

In essence, granting new monies for trades forgotten before and conferring sudden key-point status on firms in light industry initiated a bargain between urban planning bureaucrats and the center. This was essentially a deal made on behalf of the redirection of local developmental efforts in Wuhan. Evidently, municipal planners were not tied to any old accustomed alliance with the heavy industrial plants and bureaus. Instead they were obliged to honor what amounted to rewritten cost-sharing arrangements with higher-echelon offices. This set of conditions motivated local bureaucrats to mobilize materials available at home, either directly for the use of or for barter in the service of a changed recipient.

It was more difficult to ensure the delivery of raw materials in accord with central planners' objectives than it was to pass down funds or direct the flow of electrical power. Compared with these other inputs, it was more onerous for the central-level offices to monitor the deliveries of materials, and more and more of them came under local control in this period. Furthermore, once beyond the reach of central officials, they were the input easiest to barter with impunity.

Still, sufficient stocks of needed supplies did reach their destination during the early 1980's. They did so largely because the vertical hierarchies of the bureaucracy could still rely on time-worn habits of compliance among local planners. It was also possible because these planners could depend on the support of other local bureaucracies when cooperation really counted. When faced with a choice between satisfying their vertical superiors or holding tight to past alliances with local heavy industrial departments, these planners opted to rally the corporate *kuai* to uphold a bargain with the top. For it was the central government level which was, after all, still the ultimate purveyor of stocks and funds.

Thus the readjustment did not work because decentralization and market reforms gave powers and an expanded purse to local-level actors. Rather, its realization came about through the activation of the very behavioral patterns often criticized for preventing national, centrally set policy from being properly enforced at the base. Reliance on vertical, bureaucratic command structures and a pattern of operating through a consensus among municipal organs could, when energized by appropriate incentives, be efficacious in executing national plans; these habits did not invariably spell stalemate and stasis; nor did they need to breed rebellious autonomy.

OUTCOMES

Positive Outcomes

The positive results of local compliance are evident statistically.[114] Between 1979 and 1982 the Chinese government effected a radical shift in the comparative rates of growth of heavy and light industry, in their respective output values relative to each other, and in the proportion of national gross industrial output value each represented. The growth indexes of the major

TABLE 14
Gross Output Value of Industry by Sector
(Yuan 1 billion)

Year	Light industry	Heavy industry	Year	Light industry	Heavy industry
1949	10.3	3.7	1978	175.3	231.4
1952	22.5	12.4	1979	195.8	252.5
1957	38.7	31.7	1980	230.9	258.8
1960	54.7	109.0	1981	263.7	248.3
1965	72.3	67.9	1982	276.6	274.0
1971	102.0	135.5	1983	295.4	313.4
1975	137.6	174.8			

SOURCE: State Statistical Bureau 1986: 31.
NOTE: Figures are given at current prices.

branches of industry in each of the two sectors also underwent impressive change.

From 1978 to 1982, the average annual increase in the output value of light was 11.8 percent, while that of heavy was only 3.3.[115] This may be contrasted with the period between 1953 and 1978, when light's rate of growth had averaged 9.1 percent to heavy's 13.6.[116] Light's output value shot up from 175.3 billion *yuan* in 1978 to 276.6 billion, while heavy's increased only from 231.4 billion to 274 billion. So, whereas light accounted for 43.1 percent of gross industrial output value in 1978 and had climbed up to 50.2 percent by 1982, heavy had dropped from 56.9 percent to less than half the total at the end of the period (see Table 14).

In individual trades, textiles grew faster in these years than metallurgy or machine building did. Though the index of the metallurgical industry's output value stood in 1982 at 2,705.8 percent of its 1952 value, and the machine-building trade's index by 1982 had soared to 5,907.7 over its 1952 level, the index for textiles' expansion over that period had merely reached 931.4. But indexes for the three branches for 1982 as a percent of their 1978 output look quite different, at 119.7, 120.3, and 166.3, respectively (see Table 15).

This quantitative rise in light industry's output almost immediately fulfilled the hopes of those who had supported it for its potential effect on the state's coffers and for its ability to provide foreign exchange. In the first half of 1980, the profits that this sector turned over to the state on a national basis increased by

TABLE 15
Indexes of Output Value by Branch, 1952, 1978, 1982

Year	Machine building	Metallurgy	Textiles
1952	100	100	100
1982	5,907.7	2,705.8	931.4
1978	100	100	100
1982	120.3	119.7	166.3

SOURCE: State Statistical Bureau 1983: 16, 20, 218.

1.9 billion *yuan* as compared with the same period in 1979, and the readjustment policy received the credit.[117] In Wuhan, 1980 profits from the textile sector increased by 42 percent over 1979; those from the city's first light industrial system went up by just over 50 percent.[118] Nationally, China's exports of manufactured goods jumped from U.S.$3.6 billion in 1978 to U.S.$12.7 billion five years later.[119]

The profile of Wuhan's economy underwent notable changes in both textile and light industrial production, thanks to readjustment. In the textile trade, the output of chemical fibers, of which there had been very little in the city before, expanded 3.4-fold between 1978 and 1981. By the end of the period, a million meters a year of both fine and coarse-weave wool came off the city's looms, which had produced none of either before.[120] In 1980 alone, the city's textile system introduced more than 3,000 new colors and varieties into its wares,[121] and the output value in wool, hemp, and silk went from 1978's 20 million *yuan* to 86 million by the end of 1980.[122] In one key-point factory, exports had accounted for only 10 percent of production in 1978, but by the end of readjustment they represented as much as 20 percent.[123]

The story was much the same for the new output in light industry. Nationwide, by the end of 1980, the production of televisions, radios, cameras, sewing machines, tape recorders, and watches had increased by about a third over their 1979 figures.[124] Clothes washers, drink powders, and fans all "had been a blank" in Wuhan when readjustment got under way; by 1982, they were being turned out in profusion, with washing machines in particular even appearing in fancy new colors and models.[125]

Negative Outcomes

But this success had a negative face as well. Reports of what the authorities termed "blind development" made their way into the press within less than a year of the program's initiation and reappeared persistently. This overproduction was occurring despite repeated warnings from the State Council to cease the construction of factories and workshops for the manufacture of popular consumer goods.[126]

The reason for this surplus was that many light and textile firms, grabbing an unexpected and golden opportunity, behaved as heavy sector plants had done in the past, when they were the beneficiaries of donation.[127] Suddenly consumer goods firms, using their new-found funds and materials, busied themselves in duplicating and stockpiling, setting up independent, vertically integrated systems, and essaying to corner local markets. Men from one of the light industrial bureaus in Wuhan had to admit that the city's stores had become overstocked with bikes, watches, and fans by 1984. By that point a decision had to be reached to provide special incentives only for name-brand products.[128]

Other manifestations of this production drive were wasteful in different ways. An untold number of newly endowed textile firms, reportedly "only seeking high output and output value," ignored the health of their staff and workers, arbitrarily adding shifts and setting up new work sites.[129] One broadcast spoke of "some light industrial enterprises" that were "seek[ing] financial aid to expand production capacities and set up their own systems."[130]

An important objective was to achieve self-sufficiency within their own little region.[131] The Wuhan press boasted of a dye factory that managed to achieve a local monopoly so that not just printing and dyeing plants at home but even those in neighboring municipalities had stopped relying on supplies from outside provinces.[132]

This pattern matches the experience of privileged French and Japanese firms and sectors during the early years of industrial policy in those countries.[133] In all three cases, the newly endowed used the favors they received to go their own way, often resulting

Priority for Light Industry 159

in overinvestment in those sectors as a result of new incentives. Alternatively, some competed among themselves for a monopoly share of the preferred markets or for even more of the favors suddenly available to their trades.

In France, some industries failed to carry out the specific investment programs of the state after getting help, but instead developed according to their own dictates once provided with the wherewithal to do so. At the same time, newly nationalized firms engaged in expansionist tendencies. And "pent-up demand" induced investment in a plethora of small firms using antiquated techniques once a sector had been targeted for priority development.[134]

In Japan there was excess capacity in the steel industry in the early 1960's and again in the 1980's as "a negative by-product of industrial policy," in the words of one analyst.[135] And although overinvestment was encouraged in Japan as a means of realizing the ideal of economic growth, the resultant overheating of the economy made inflation a recurrent problem in the early postwar period. The government became "frustrated by excessive competition and preemptive investment" in those industries it aimed to foster.[136]

As pointed out in Chapter 5, this excess production aroused a variety of negative reactions among decision makers. One of these was the opposition that began to surface in central-level policy councils to further investment in the light sector. "Some," for example, as early as mid-1981, were claiming that "light industry's growth speed has already surpassed heavy's, so we've just about readjusted."[137]

Once it was clear that products were piling up and a problem of slack sales had set in, critics began to argue that the six priorities had become unnecessary.[138] Champions of the recipients countered by pointing to low quality, insufficient varieties, and inadequate marketing as the sources of the difficulties in sales. These problems, they claimed without much success, only justified yet more favors and funds.[139]

An early sign of a loss of sympathy for light industry's pleas appeared in the State Council's November 1981 decision to cut the price of polyester cotton because of the glut occasioned in the preceding few years by the speedy development of chemical fibers. On the eve of the readjustment, such garments had been in seriously short supply.[140] But in Wuhan, to cite just one case, by late 1981 more than 70 million meters of chemical fiber products had accumulated. At that point the local bureau acted to limit their output, a move the State Council was to take a year later.[141]

The national media soon drew attention to the need to select for products of higher quality to meet the more sophisticated consumer demand once wage and price reforms had lifted purchasing power in city and rural areas alike.[142] Another move in the same direction occurred when the State Council began to deny the six priorities to makers of ordinary cloth and clothing. In Wuhan, where the problem turned out to be particularly pronounced, at first the complacent new beneficiaries had trouble recognizing the nature of their plight: "The factories didn't believe that there was no market for their products," a local banking official later explained.[143]

But city bureaucrats knew better: the six priorities had fed "too much undifferentiated production,"* according to men from the Wuhan MPC, and the local press warned of the city's products' "weak competitive ability" on several occasions in 1981.[144] When the "masses" rejected local products, central planners allocated goods from Shanghai to the city, and unwanted locally made goods were left to be dumped into warehouses. Here we see an interesting and concrete example of the mix of planned measures and market signals that were still governing the production of light industrial products even by the end of the readjustment period.

Another such example is provided in interviews that revealed that at this point the central government reduced Wuhan's investment for textiles proportionately more than Shanghai's, deciding by 1982 to finance and provide materials only for well-made products.[145] At the same time the Ministry of Textiles announced that the Wuhan textile trade should direct attention to making its products more marketable.[146]

Beginning in the spring of 1981 and continuing into 1982, city

---

*This was the judgment of MPC officials on November 13, 1984; even the Textile Bureau's representatives said (November 14, 1984) that "there are too many things, partly as a result of the six priorities and readjustment."

Priority for Light Industry   161

offices mobilized a variety of efforts to upgrade local consumer goods.[147] One strategy was to transfer scientific and technical specialists to work in the light and textile trades; another was to dispatch technical support teams from the large, central plants in the city to help out key-point light-sector enterprises. Yet a third method was to turn local research institutes to the service of the firms in this trade, while attaching scientific research organs to light industrial factories. Fourth, managers and engineers were sent off to Shanghai to try to discover the secrets of the techniques that spurred that city's industrial success.*

But apparently all these measures were not effective enough. For the final verdict, as told by the men from the MPC in late 1984, was that light industry's growth speed fell in 1983 in Wuhan because "we can't produce high-class goods that meet needs."[148] What had begun as a planning project—the injection of massive centrally allocated inputs into the consumer goods sector—overshot its mark, and finally it succumbed to the forces of the market. Another issue here was the nationwide shift back to reviving heavy industry detailed in the last chapter. In the words of the municipal Textile Bureau's cadres in late 1984, "Our days aren't so good now [as during readjustment] because of competition . . . and heavy industry's days have improved."[149]

Wuhan's light and textile trades fell into decline, and their priority status vanished by the end of 1982 for two reasons: because of their inferior products (as recognized both by central government planners and investors and by local consumers) and because of the recovery of heavy industry. But both of these factors constituted proof that readjustment had achieved its primary objective, the rapid (maybe too rapid) expansion of the consumer goods sector.

As local officials recognized in the aftermath—if not in the midst—of the policy's execution, the central government's bestowal of favors in the readjustment had encouraged an extraordinary and rather reckless flourishing of consumer goods, and low-grade output was the result. Thus it seemed to top-level decision makers at the end of the process that no further im-

---

*Management at one textile factory in Wuhan noted that though representatives from Shanghai firms were helpful in Wuhan in 1979 and 1980, by 1984 personnel there tended more and more to keep secrets about technical issues.

provement could take place in this or any branch of Chinese industry until the heavy industrial trades received the materials, the technology, and the imports for manufacturing more specialized and modernized equipment.

The shift away from light industry, then, was the logical outcome of the original turn toward it, given the dynamics of donation. Both decisions had issued from the chambers of the political elite in Beijing, who, aided by the bureaucratic behaviors of verticalism and localism, remained capable in the end of manipulating the consequences of these decisions, despite decentralization. The ultimate defeat of the overly strong push toward light industry was at once the emblem of its success.

SEVEN

Abandoning Heavy Industry
Insulation and Forms of Resistance

BESIDES PICKING WINNERS, industrial policy entails abandoning the losers. While some industries or sectors are favored by a new deployment of resources, others are more or less left out, their wonted share of state favors and funds cut off or at least cut back, and their survival dependent on their own resources and exertions as they are forced to face the open market. Writers on French and Japanese industrial policy from the late 1940's note how this happened to certain sectors in those countries then.[1]

In the case of the Chinese economic readjustment, the heavy industrial sector, for nearly three decades the spoiled child of the planned, state-owned economy, suffered a severe shock when the state reduced its inputs sometimes by as much as 90 percent for some firms during 1980 and 1981. In 1979, as readjustment was just getting started, incomplete statistics showed, for example, that the machine-building trade's plan represented 86 percent of that year's total output value in that trade; in 1980 it had dropped to only 54 percent. By 1981, a mere 20 percent of its output was provided for by the plan.[2] In 1979 in Wuhan, the metallurgical sector got an allocation from the state for capital construction of only one-third of the volume of work that that trade had completed in 1978.[3]

Removing heavy industrial firms from the state plan addressed the second malfunction listed in Chapter 3 which Chinese economists after 1978 identified in their critiques of the Stalinist economic system. This was the undue emphasis on high output targets and speedy growth, and the authoritative Stalinist-style state plan lay at the root of these problems.

Literature on policy changes that disadvantage what a scholar of France labeled "corporatist clients"[4] points to the difficulties of depriving groups that were long the recipients of state largesse. A study of French corporatism found that it was nearly impossible to disentangle the knot that bound the major farmers' union to the state:

> An established corporatist client, having benefited for years from subsidies and other forms of state support, is likely to possess formidable organizational means of resisting change. Even if a new government were willing and politically able to terminate immediately all the forms of state support which had traditionally flowed to a privileged interest group, it could only hope to weaken that group over a period of years . . . in the short run, the erstwhile client would continue to manifest a degree of state-enhanced organizational strength derived from the benefits delivered under the former regime.[5]

Speaking of the same phenomenon, a student of the Soviet system has written about how this principle operates in that country:

> Political resources can be taken away from a program that has lost priority, but can't be taken away *quickly* [author's emphasis]. In the meantime, while a previously high priority program is being scaled down, a declining agency can use the resources remaining to it to fight a rearguard action. . . . In sum, an institution that once had high priority manages to retain some of its influence for a time.[6]

The same line of reasoning informs Mancur Olson's thoughts about the impact of what he calls "special interest organizations and collusions" or "distributional coalitions" in his work on economic development in Britain. His principal point is that such groups "slow down a society's capacity to adopt new technologies and to reallocate resources in response to changing conditions and thereby reduce the rate of economic growth."[7]

And Lester Thurow, in commenting on declining industries in the United States, remarks that "in a dying industry, everyone is out to protect what they have."[8] Speaking of these same industries, again in the American context, Robert Reich notes that they tend to wield vastly greater clout than emerging industries. Their size and age and the dependence of entire regions upon them have helped them to form well-established political connections, which afford them the possibility of blocking change in periods of economic contraction.⁹

The long-coddled heavy industrial firms in the Chinese political economy in the early 1980's, cut loose from the provisioning central plan and its supplies and funding, were temporarily thrust into a depression.¹⁰ Therefore, it might be expected that they would have behaved like corporatist clients who were hanging on and would have mounted the opposition shown by high-clout dying industries in other countries whose positions were being undermined.

The main question this chapter poses is, Given heavy industry's original special status and its superior assets within the old planning system, how did its factories react to the cutbacks, and in what ways did the state bureaucracy handle whatever resistance these enterprises mounted? How, that is, did the Chinese state manage to shield the readjustment policy sufficiently during its implementation that no significant recalcitrance occurred?

Even though resistance from losers seems common and natural, several specialists on industrial policy have stressed—as Chapter 1 specified—that insulation against opposition is crucial for pushing through programs of major economic restructuring.¹¹ One, presenting findings from his research on the French situation, maintains that "an elite wishing to direct or even influence the course of industrialization must . . . insulate itself from or repress the political reaction to dislocations inevitably provoked by industrialization."¹² Thus the makers of industrial policy must be able to proceed largely unhindered in their effort to shift and reorder old priorities and the relationships growing from them. To what extent was this done in China?

Most simply put, the same patterns of verticalism-cum-paternalism by which urban industrial bureaus passed new benefits to the light industrial firms also helped the heavy-sector plants that were in dire straits and saw them through the crisis. As the *People's Daily* enjoined in early 1981, "If enterprises try and feel there is no way to exist, help them."¹³ And in the words of an official at the central Ministry of Machine Building, "*guanting bingzhuan* [close, suspend, merge, convert] was an outlet for failing enterprises, a care-taking [*zhaogu*] method."¹⁴ Partly the bureaus employed this behavioral pattern in the customary ways that they had done under the regime of the state plan in China in the past, with financial and material aid.

But the picture was complicated in this era by the simultaneous introduction of the economic reform program, which devolved funds and decisions about their use to firms and lower echelons in the state administrative bureaucracy. By legitimizing an unplanned use of the slack already present in the economy, the leadership's removal of the planned economy's benefits uncovered a second sphere for the operation of economic life, one theretofore held in reserve, as it were, a kind of safety valve.

This provision of an alternative channel for the now disadvantaged heavy plants to use, to which they could resort for satisfying needs that the state was temporarily unwilling to fill, must have acted to deflect or quell potential opposition. Indeed, this channel operated as a form of co-optation. Bureaus aided their firms, gathering economic intelligence for them and arranging connections in the markets they penetrated. These protective aspects of verticalism enabled the firms to continue accumulating wealth for the state, always a crucial consideration for political elites in China but a particular concern in this era of perceived crisis.[15]

Though management bureaus wished to ensure that their firms would create revenue, they also worried about possible social instability that their workers and staff might cause in this time of cutbacks. This double mission of the bureaus—to collect funds and prevent labor unrest—mirrored the goals of top state leaders in this period on a national scale. It sometimes led bureau leaders to collude with firms in contravening readjustment, either by going on as before in their production of the heavy industrial goods they best knew how to turn out, or in allowing them to wait passively, doing nothing, in the hope that the policy would be only temporary. In such cases, a collaboration existed between firm and bureau, in which the enterprise got protection and preservation in exchange for the quiescence of its workers, its continuing provision of revenue, or both.

THE READJUSTMENT PROGRAM FOR LOCAL-LEVEL HEAVY INDUSTRIAL FIRMS

At the local level, the readjustment program was charged with reducing the amount of production that was purely within the sphere of heavy industry and increasing what was done both for and by enterprises in the light and textile trades. Through these means the shift in proportions between the two major sectors for which the reallocation of resources on a national scale was being undertaken would be realized. The last chapter considered how this process affected the recipients; this one examines the reactions of the deprived.

This effort had several facets, one of which was an effort to switch the "service orientation" of heavy industrial factories. Instead of producing machinery and raw materials for themselves, they were to turn out equipment, components, raw materials, parts, and technology for the light and textile firms. In addition, where the production processes and technologies permitted, plants were expected to shift one of their production lines to the output of consumer products, or at least to add a subsidiary line in this area to their primary one.

Only 1.3 percent of the machine-building system's total output value nationally had gone into the production of technical equipment for the light and textile sectors and for daily-use electronic products in 1979. But by 1981, the proportion had gone up to 8.4 percent.[16] By the end of that year, the machine-building industry was using somewhere between 15 and 30 percent of its manufacturing capacity for turning out durable consumer products.[17]

The program was also to "reduce the scale of capital construction." This was to involve not just cutting back on the central government's funding for major construction projects, but also entailed putting a further squeeze on the machine-building industry in particular because the metallurgy, chemical, petroleum, coal, and electrical power departments temporarily had less need for large-scale sets of equipment.[18] And yet one more dimension was to deal with the long-standing issue of enterprises that were suffering losses.[19]

These various sorts of transformation were encapsulated, as

they had been in the early 1960's recovery from the Great Leap Forward, in the slogan *guanting bingzhuan*. As Wuhan Mayor Li Zhi announced at a session of the city's People's Congress in early 1981, both the goal of realigning proportional relations among the light and heavy sectors and the aim of curtailing capital construction called for such measures.[20]

Ideally, following the dictates of the slogan would mean that one of four things would happen to targeted plants in the heavy industrial sector: redundant and inefficient firms would be closed down or their work would be at least temporarily suspended; alternatively, their workers, equipment, materials, and working space would either be merged into light industrial plants or, when possible, switched to the manufacturing of consumer goods. All of these measures were, of course, in line with the central elite's program of generating revenue by relying on the quick turnover of funds that light industrial products could provide.

Mainly out of concern for social stability, however, that four-pronged label was soon collapsed into two main thrusts. This happened when policy makers and local implementing officials—who were responsible for providing jobs for their populace—concluded that merging (usually of heavy with light firms) and converting (changing the product line, generally from heavy industrial machinery to daily-use consumer products) worked out far more successfully than did attempts to close or even suspend ongoing projects and existing plant. By the end of the first year of readjustment, more than 3,000 state-owned enterprises, or about 3.6 percent of the total, had undergone some form of *guanting bingzhuan* nationwide.[21] In Hubei province, after three years, 1,951 enterprises had gone through that process.[22]

Resistance to readjustment can be defined with respect to these various programs and objectives. It would have consisted of continuing to engage in heavy industrial production, expanding rather than curtailing the scale of capital construction, and refusing to merge and convert enterprises. In resorting to these practices, some firms made little change in their wonted activities.

Apart from these modes of obstinate persistence, some heavy

industrial firms covertly opposed the policy's aims. Covert activity was possible because of the central leadership's promotion of economic reform. The reform program's fiscal decentralization allowed enterprises and local entities to retain some of their profits and loosened the restrictions on the provision of bank credit. According to one estimate, monies outside state-sanctioned budgets that had fallen under the control of the local governments, local economic departments, and enterprises were amounting to more than 50 billion *yuan* a year, or one-half of state budget revenue by mid-1982.[23] And the continuing weakness of the banks in this era meant that local economic commissions and industrial bureaus could avoid cutbacks by demanding bank loans.[24]

Clearly, new systems and measures placed significantly expanded levels of funding in the hands of localities, industrial bureaus, and firms, while slackening the controls over how they were used. As Naughton, writing in this period, pointed out, "The[se] enterprises' ability to continue producing is directly related to the collapse of central government control over investment."[25]

For some central-level politicians, the behaviors that reform encouraged were not necessarily always in conflict with the aims of readjustment. True, as noted in Chapters 4 and 5, throughout 1980 policy debates flared over whether to emphasize the decentralizing reform program or to stress instead readjustment, with its reliance on a modicum of direction from the central government.[26] Nonetheless, Zhao Ziyang, for one, made the argument that readjustment could serve the purposes of reform.

In early 1980, while still the party boss in Sichuan province, later to become premier, Zhao made this claim in an article on economic reform. He reasoned that, as factories' production plans from the state shrank and as the inputs to fulfill these plans were drastically reduced, firms had no choice but to "study [and, he implied, strive to meet] market demand."[27]

As demand fell in response to cutbacks in capital construction of more than 10 billion *yuan*, the supply of machine-building products far surpassed demand. Meanwhile, the old state distribution system ceased to play its customary role of allocating materials and procuring output. The legitimation for unplanned trading that reform granted gave or, as one commentary put it, "forced" enterprises "to find a way out" to survive.[28]

That way was through experimenting with what the Chinese label "market (as opposed to plan) regulation." Nationally, by 1982 approximately half the output of the production of enterprises under what was then the First Ministry of Machine Building was being exchanged through marketing, according to an official count.[29] In Hubei province by 1982 some individual machine-building enterprises were forced to rely on the market for a full 90 percent of their tasks.[30] Reportedly, in 1979, 37 percent of the output value of Wuhan's machine-building industry was involved in marketing activity; by 1980 the proportion had jumped up to 47.[31]

As Wong points out, "freeing large numbers of machinery and electrical products from state allocation [also] facilitated the shift from heavy industry to increased consumer-goods production," as local governments put their new monies into the purchase of producer and investment goods now available in the market,[32] which they then turned to light industrial use. But for a certain proportion of heavy industrial firms, the opportunity, even the imperative, to find markets and work outside the confines of the state plan's dictates could clash with the call to serve light industry. For the staff in some plants found it easier to locate buyers and cut deals with their previous plan partners within the heavy industrial system by continuing with their old lines of production. And some managers and local leaders chose to draw on new channels for investment to expand extant plant and engage in capital construction.[33] To the extent that such activities went on, the central purpose of readjustment was undermined.

Thus firms in opposition chose two principal means of action which obstructed the shift to light industry. Following James Scott's formulation, each was a product of the then "existing forms of labor control." He holds that each such mode of control "generates its own distinctive forms of quiet resistance and 'counterappropriation.'"[34]

Either enterprises resisted the policy of switching to light industrial production by remaining essentially immobile,[35] or else they did so by depending on their old buyers "in the market" for some portion of their orders. Either way, two crucial elements of their opposition stand out: often in both cases, the adaptation involved was eased by verticalism—protection and paternalism from management bureaus. Moreover, both alternatives served to co-opt or pacify potential overt opposition to the readjustment program, as firms that might otherwise have caused disturbances found themselves sheltered from the shocks of change. Here then was the secret of the program's insulation.

DIE-HARD RESISTANCE

According to one Western economist's analysis of the behavior of Chinese firms during and immediately following the readjustment, what I call die-hard resistance is the common initial response that enterprises typically adopt to weak markets. He labels such a response neglect and disbelief, which occur when the firm has not yet recognized that market conditions have changed. The next step, still encompassed by my term "diehardness," is what this economist terms despair and passive dependency, which occur once the enterprise realizes the new situation. In that next phase the firm sees no means of coping by itself and so relies for help from its superiors to stay afloat.[36]

But in fact, according to the press, such reactions continued for some firms throughout the entire several-year period of the program. In at least some places the root was more than economic. Political factors and the continuing support of superiors at different levels were likely contributing elements.

For instance, the attitude at first of Wuhan's party first secretary and mayor Li Renzhi must have communicated ambivalence toward the policy to those in the industrial firms of the city. In announcing the newly publicized policy of readjustment in Wuhan, Li phrased its content in a way far more favorable to the continued growth of heavy industry than pro-readjustment forces would have intended: "After the heavy industrial and defense departments have finished their own task, they should also utilize their excess production ability and *leftover bits and pieces of material*, plus their own accumulated stocks, to produce marketable daily-use industrial products" (emphasis added).[37]

Throughout the year 1979, Li repeatedly focused his public speeches at municipal meetings more on the production side of the simultaneous campaign to "increase production and economize," stressing overall—and sometimes even specifically heavy—industrial growth rather than readjustment. At a city Party enlarged Standing Committee meeting in July, Mayor Li took advantage of the famous 1978 Third Plenum's switch to socialist modernization to encourage the city forcefully to promote both industrial and agricultural production in this period of supposed retrenchment, making no special reference to cutbacks in heavy industry or to readjustment's priority for light.

Moreover, he emphasized once again the speed of growth and the rapid economic recovery the city had seen since 1976. These remarks closely matched the tone of Hua Guofeng's words at the recently concluded Second Session of the Fifth National People's Congress, where Hua evinced his continued support for heavy industry.[38] True, Li did admit that industry's internal proportional relations would have to be reorganized and that supplies of the various requisites for production should be guaranteed for the light and textile industries.

Nonetheless, he continued to ask only that the heavy and defense departments use their "surplus ability" on behalf of these industries. None of this could have seemed much of a threat to the heavy sector, for Li also proclaimed that the other industries (besides light and textile) would "get a corresponding development" during the three years of readjustment.

Even as late as the end of September 1979, when Li praised progressive units and labor models on the occasion of the thirtieth anniversary celebration of the founding of the People's Republic, he discussed only the Third Plenum, but not readjustment, and continued to speak of the movement to increase production. His interest was especially centered on the city's results in completing state plans for output.

But Li's tactics were eventuallly turned around. It seems that he received a reprimand for his inattention to national policy at a provincial party three-level cadre meeting either at the end of 1979 or the beginning of 1980. At a January city Party enlarged Standing Committee meeting, he transmitted the "spirit" of the national planning conference (where the six priorities for light industry had been enunciated) and the instructions of this provincial meeting. He said that Hubei provincial party secretary

Chen Pixian had been "very realistic,"[39] and he admitted that the current policy [of readjustment] "fits our city's situation."[40]

He went on to promise, "We'll continue with the eight-character policy (the shorthand term for the policy of readjustment, reform, consolidation, and raising standards). This time, finally, Li urged that "light and textile industries should go full steam ahead" and that "local heavy industrial departments should mostly produce things needed by agriculture, light industry, and on the market." Even then, however, he failed to mention the six priorities for light industry, even though they had only a few days before been published by Xinhua in the national media.[41] Such at best muted advocacy for this policy as it got under way must have signaled to its target firms in the city that they need not respond actively.

In addition to the mayor's attitude, press materials from Wuhan indicate other relevant political factors at work. The range of affected actors there displayed a set of differential interests in dealing with the program. These actors were the city planning and economic commissions; the various industrial management bureaus, in particular machine building and metallurgy; and the staff and workers of targeted firms.

Each local actor involved in implementing the readjustment policy had a different objective, and their separate motives contributed to the tensions simmering in the atmosphere surrounding this policy.[42] We have seen in the last chapter that a chief official from the city planning commission wrote in the local newspaper on behalf of guaranteeing the six priorities for light industry as early as August.[43]

The Municipal Economic Commission, the principal city bureaucracy responsible for the readjustment, was ultimately answerable to the State Economic Commission in Beijing. Its job was to ensure realization of the prime task of the moment, which then was to favor light industry, even though that meant abandoning its customary clients, the heavy industrial bureaus and their firms.

Heavy industrial bureaus, however, were caught in a more complicated context. Their role is best understood as that of middlemen. For they at once continued to be responsible for the survival and health of the firms under their control but still had to push these plants to fit their production to the new policy. These were, unfortunately, two chores whose outcomes by no means always or easily coincided. Different bureaus reacted differently, although a sympathetic drive to see their firms through the difficulties was common to all.

For the most part, open requests for redress were directed at the national level, and their fate was reported in Chapter 5. But according to the press, reaction was more commonly covert. Many of the firms went on as before, refusing to undertake the production shifts demanded of them. And a sizable number waited passively for the policy to change, sometimes doing absolutely nothing in the interim. There were also reports of sabotage of dismantled operations, as firms in need scrounged for spare parts, scrap raw materials, and idle equipment.

Making Demands

Probably because of the heavy industrial sector's longstanding favored position in the Chinese industrial bureaucracy—evident in the level of investment its branches received, the wage scale of its workers and managers, and the rank of its cadres[44]—its spokespersons felt justified in voicing claims when policy turned against them. It is worth repeating, however, that this favored position did not enable spokespersons for these branches to prevent the 1979 decision against their interests.

The major forums at which they voiced their claims were the Third and Fourth Sessions of the Fifth National People's Congress, held in September 1980 and December 1981, respectively.[45] There representatives of the provinces in which heavy industry was prominent forthrightly put forward their plaints. Some pleaded for investment and work. Others asked for guarantees that their output would not fall any further, alluding to a "state of mental depression and helplessness" among heavy-sector firms.

Yet others demanded that their own sector be given a chance for development, and some suggested a national program to advance the interests of the machine-building industry, coupling that request with special urgent cries for large plants employing thousands of workers each. And people from one of the affected

Abandoning Heavy Industry   175

provinces begged for a reinstatement of unified, centralized distribution of key raw materials, in short, the old planning system, which had always served heavy industry well in the past.[46] But these representations fell on deaf ears until the policy-making elite was prepared to shift course.

Occasionally the media carried proposals that reflected the views of the heavy sector which were aimed at changing the behavior of lower levels of government. Some heavy industrial enterprises reportedly "insist[ed] that the state purchase whatever they had produced, thinking that their status would be lowered if they were to shift to producing light industrial goods that were needed on the market."[47] A *People's Daily* editorial that appeared soon after the policy was first enunciated enjoined against reducing investment in every trade by the same percentage and against treating all projects as the same. This injunction indicated that opponents of the reallocations going on were attempting—but without any luck—to fight for their spheres.[48]

And in Wuhan, as presumably in other cities too, the new mayor, Li Zhi, had to warn his listeners in a government work report of March 1981 that "thinking of increasing production only by relying on capital construction, *demanding investment*, adding equipment is divorced from real possibility"[49] (emphasis added). Thus he revealed that such petitions were still being presented locally well into the readjustment era.

These various published accounts of vocal supplications show that there was such a form of opposition in China then. But the two more indirect modes of resistance described below ultimately had more impact in that they contributed to the negative indicators that eventually brought central politicians around.

Going on as Before

The most audacious of the two more indirect modes that heavy industrial firms adopted in obstructing the policy of promoting light industry was simply to continue producing their old products as before. Losers in France and Japan were similarly stubborn. MITI's efforts to reduce capacity in cottonweaving in the early 1950's met with obstacles. Agreements signed were kept with the greatest difficulty, such that "it was often necessary to seal the participants' machines to ensure that they weren't used against the agreements."[50] Similarly, in France, "the suggestion to shut down was ignored by some of the smaller producers."[51]

As officials at the Beijing Ministry of Machine Building understood the situation, such enterprises failed to follow orders out of laziness or because they found the instructions too much trouble or too difficult.[52] The press sometimes presented cases that illustrated this explanation. For instance, one representative military factory at first gloated over its large plant and relatively sophisticated equipment and excused itself from complying with commands by charging that processing parts in small batches was, indeed, "too much trouble, not worth it."[53]

The Wuhan Machine Tools Factory, whose story was also typical, was not affected by the new policy, at least at first. In 1980 the plant achieved its highest level of output value ever. It was not until the next year that the place began to "go hungry" for work. But until that happened, its personnel boasted openly that "readjustment or no readjustment, our factory won't have to worry about food to eat."[54] Like any enterprise whose products belonged to the heavy sector, this plant had only to wait for customers to take away whatever its workers turned out for nearly three decades.* The constant surge of capital construction over those years, along with the automatic procurement arrangements of the planned economy, had always guaranteed that all their products would be purchased. Therefore, when capital construction was cut back, they were at a loss as to how to cope.[55]

Thus the customary primacy of heavy industry in socialist China led many connected with this sector to cast a jaundiced eye toward the idea of switching their service orientation or reducing their level of productive activity. A common manifestation was to view compliance as being "without long-term vision," or, at best, as "an expedient to get over the present difficulties." People holding these views planned to "preserve strength" to wait for what they considered the inevitable future redevelopment of their branch.[56]

Others could not set aside their pride. As the papers put it,

---

*Bureaucrats from the Wuhan City Machine Building Bureau described their memories of pre-reform days in such seemingly nostalgic tones on November 13, 1984.

they wanted only to "sing the main role," not to play "supporting actor." Confident that their products were merely selling slowly for the moment, they banked on "turning around the situation when their time comes in the future."[57] Similarly, the long-ingrained notion that heavy industry's products were more important to socialist economic development than were light's nurtured a sense that converting one's plant's output would be "putting great materials to petty use" (*dacai xiaoyong*).

Such opinions—and the concomitant behavior—were the object of journalistic criticism in 1980 and 1981. But by 1984, when heavy industry had already long since revived, managers of firms that had acted on these views felt free to announce that their behavior in those years had been fully justified. Asked about whether his plant had "served light and textiles" during the readjustment, one manager of a large valve works replied almost scornfully: "Light and textiles don't need our products much . . . the Bureau suggested that we produce mechanical equipment for light and textiles and repair their parts and fittings. But our products and facilities are large and specialized. We can't make those things for them. Others converted. . . . Our things can't suit them."[58]

Standing behind the resistant firms that were struggling to stay afloat in a changing environment by doing what they could do best were the bureau leaders. These cadres nursed a genuine empathy for the plight of the staff and workers in these firms. More than pure empathy was at work, though. Such bureaucrats calculated that they could ultimately best fulfill their own role as regulator and revenue collector by ensuring that the heavy plants under their charge continued to fill their special place in society and in the economy.

Officials at the Wuhan City Planning Commission admitted in retrospect that the machinery makers had been in serious straits when state-led demand and imports undercut the call for most of their principal products. Not only was new construction officially scaled down, especially after the deficits of 1979 and 1980, but automobiles from abroad began to find a Chinese market around this time.

And all this was taking place just when the peasants, released from communal organization after 1979, no longer needed the larger agricultural machinery that had been one of the most important items manufactured by this branch. As their confreres the metallurgists (who, as we will see, did much better in Wuhan), explained the situation, "There was no way out for them [the machine builders] then; their products had no sales outlet." The machinery bureau leaders lamented their fate several years after the fact, still, it seemed, smarting with a sense of having been slighted: "At first we wouldn't accept it. Our old products couldn't be sold then. The city party told us to serve textiles and light, but there were problems with getting good market information, and we weren't clear just what to produce. The city government decided that we should switch production . . . but this couldn't be done in a day."[59]

Thus concrete conditions provided a foundation for a fairly prevalent view among heavy industry workers that their inclination to disobey was reasonable. Some bureaucrats actually incited their subordinate firms to struggle to hold onto their own niche, rather than having to suffer the dislocations of a conversion: "Leading comrades call for resolutely resisting," revealed the press. "A few areas and departments and units try to 'firmly resist,' taking no action and going their own way," another piece announced.[60]

Some bureau officials even went so far as to prevent their enterprises from converting or merging with other firms, slandering their legitimate behavior as "hotheaded transgressions." Instead, they instructed the units to "lie low," waiting for a big development later on, while they "gnashed their teeth and dodged the 'readjustment wind.'"[61]

Where did the bureaus and firms find the wherewithal to continue producing in their usual way in the face of state cutbacks? Firms in opposition had a few illicit tactics at their disposal as they "carried on surreptitiously" and "left the orientation unaltered and held out while heavy's tasks were not too overwhelming," verbally agreeing and supporting readjustment but in fact proceeding as they wished.[62]

The most common solution resonated with the ideas in quotations from John Keeler and Thane Gustafson on corporatist clients that appear at the beginning of this chapter: "Some heavy industrial projects that ought to stop building or projects that should postpone construction hold on tightly and won't let go. . . . They use the personnel, material and financial power in their own hands to oppose readjustment."[63] And why was it that they continued to have access to resources despite the central level's cutbacks? Naughton's and Walder's analyses of the unintended consequences of economic reform at the local and enterprise levels outlined above provide a major part of the answer. They show that those dedicated to sticking to tried lines of production could use retained funds and personal and intrabureaucratic connections to turn the new reform policies to advantage.

Several other tactics helped the resistant firms find funding or materials to support their intransigence. Some initially resorted to spare tasks to tide themselves over, although the payoffs for this effort turned out to be short term.[64] There were also barter arrangements for materials between heavy industrial plants.[65] Others had the nerve to forage and salvage among the equipment and debris of dismantled projects, alerting the *People's Daily* to print editorials about the need to keep special guard over discontinued projects and to warn against encroaching on the state's property by privately dividing up the materials that had been used in such abandoned construction.[66]

Many of the firms that acted out this first indirect mode of opposition exhibited the pride they possessed as the previously privileged. Others, though, were simply strapped by their intractable technology from effecting a rapid transformation in accord with state dictates. That many managed to hold fast must be attributed in most cases to support or even pressure from their supervisory departments, which shared their wish to continue earning revenue from their wonted productive activities. Upper-level assistance along with the resources this aid helped them to acquire combined to make their quiet and covert refusal even more potent than the pleas of the open protesters.

Passive Waiting

The other form of quiet obstinacy went under the label of *dingzhe buban*, meaning waiting and not acting. Rather than doggedly persisting in forbidden forms of production, the workers and staff in some firms just hung around. Here too, the attitude of the bureau in charge played a role. Sometimes hesitation grew out of what the press termed "leftist thought": seeing readjustment as a passive measure, as "blowing a cold wind" or "throwing cold water" on socialist construction.[67] But more frequently, inaction stemmed from confusion, from a sense of being at a loss. Wuhan Machine-Building Bureau officials told me: "Many factories didn't know what to do, so they just took a wait-and-see attitude (*guanwang*) and waited around. They put their materials into the warehouses unused. The majority were like this. They didn't refuse, but just didn't know what to do."[68]

Managers in these firms fell into passivity, becoming dispirited. They slackened their leadership, and their workers' attendance dropped off.[69] They were supported by the city Machine-Building Bureau, whose officials did not understand how to readjust at first and simply bided their time.[70] The papers spoke of those who "used readjustment as an excuse to downgrade the importance of those production assignments still sent them. . . . In the name of opposing over-ambitious targets, some even refuse to take up production chores that could be fulfilled."[71]

Those who felt the situation was too complicated for them to master looked to others for a formula, waited for their leaders to present a draft plan, or relied on the upper levels for instruction in a proper method.[72] Some who were even less resourceful stood about hoping for a fluke or waited for their turn to be closed, converted, or merged.[73]

Two factors were primarily responsible for this passive obstruction. First, there were signals from Beijing that social stability must be preserved at any cost. In the interest of insulating the state against antagonisms turned disruptive, top leaders underlined the seriousness of arranging some labor or other activity for workers affected by the readjustment of their plants.

At the time of the policy's institution, Li Xiannian warned of the need to continue issuing wages as before, while organizing workers to study or transferring them to other similar factories, to light industrial firms, or to the service sector. Additionally, at this time Li, and another 20 months later Deng Xiaoping, stressed the role of political indoctrination in the interest of preserving stability.[74] Moreover, throughout the period of the readjustment, continuing injunctions in the press reminded local bureaucracies, whether leading departments and enterprises or labor departments, to take care of the workers displaced by *guanting bingzhuan*.

When no specific work could be found for them, such caretaking was to include giving them training and periodic classes in political, cultural, business, technical, and management matters. It could also involve having them apply themselves to equipment maintenance, building repairs, gardening, roadbuilding, and urban sanitation work, in short, "giv[ing] everyone something to do,"[75] in the hope of blunting the restiveness of enforced idleness.

In Wuhan, of 158 factories that were the object of this program, only 6 were closed either permanently or temporarily, and the Municipal Economic Commission admitted that this was because of the city's continuing need to provide for the livelihood of workers, employed or not.[76] A similar ratio held nationwide: Ministry of Machine Building officials estimated after the policy had ended that less than 5 percent of the factories targeted for alterations were actually either shut down or suspended.[77] Sporadic incidents of discontent occurred here and there,[78] but by and large workers' reactions were carefully restrained by watchful authorities.

In spite of these efforts at caretaking, there were disgruntled workers, engineers, and management personnel in the factories that were forced to convert and merge. This discontent points to the second factor that accounted for passive resistance: the hopelessness of protest against arbitrary and irrational conversions, at least for substantial periods.

A few years after the fact, when heavy industry's perquisites had been reinstated and some of these plants were permitted to return to their original line of production, the newspapers began to reveal the upheaval that had attended some of this restructuring. One report spoke of errors made in the readjustment by management departments which had "blindly decided that machine-building factories convert to light industrial products." Boiler factories were making bicycles, and tractor plants were producing sewing machines—or trying to. In many such cases, the product structures of the two types of output were not interlinked and the technologies involved were insufficiently related, so that the original equipment could not be used and technical strengths were not brought into play. The sad effect was that millions of *yuan* went to waste before the central authorities were ready to confront the losses. Surveying the worst of the cases, a commentator writing in 1984 bemoaned, "What's done can't be undone, what's been disassembled has been disassembled, what's been sold is sold, and those thinking of reconverting find it too late to repent."[79]

In one grotesquely drawn-out case, an enamel factory in Shenyang was coerced by "a city committee for managing industry" (presumably the City Economic Commission). This committee, overzealous in its effort to enforce the readjustment policy, changed the provincial First Light Industry Bureau's September 1980 draft design for a partial conversion of this factory. The bureau's design had called for expanding a paint workshop and adding a bicycle parts workshop. But instead, six months later, the committee commanded that the entire enamel factory cease production and its site be used for making the bicycle parts.

The order compelled the plant to tear down more than 3,000 meters of buildings and to demolish a large amount of specialized equipment, altogether netting over 4 million *yuan* in losses. Factory representatives spent more than two years "running about between Beijing and Shenyang" and compiled 56 reports to send to the city party and government committees seeking restitution. But no relief had been granted even as late as the end of 1983, when a letter recounting the plant's plight appeared in the *People's Daily*.[80]

A similar incident took place in Wuhan, again a result of excessive enthusiasm by city-level commissions. In October 1980 a boiler factory was made to shift a portion of its personnel and equipment to a larger boiler plant, and the bulk of the staff was turned over to the First Bureau of Light Industry to employ in electroplating bicycles.[81] For the new electroplaters, everything went awry. Their technology did not fit with that used in making bikes. Also, only unskilled workers, who did not adequately understand their new task, were put in charge. Finally, the area where the electroplating was to be done turned out to have polluted water, and the job could not be accomplished.

The startling result was that virtually nothing was produced for two full years. It was not until October 1982 that the City Economic Commission agreed to return the factory to its original function. By then thousands of *yuan* had been lost; workers had become disaffected because of the inconvenience of the move and because they felt their training was being wasted; and managers were frustrated by the burden of having had to transport and reinstall their own equipment into poorer, unsuitable quarters.

And yet, as one interviewee put it, "Nothing can be done if the city government has sent an order." Throughout the period, the Machine-Building Bureau disagreed (had *yijian*) with the conversion because the factory had previously been a profit-earning one. Nevertheless, as an informant related the tale, the bureau "just obeys; it's a lower level, it won't oppose. It could have raised objections, but that would have depended on their being accepted. Since the factory's staff was upset, of course the Bureau supported them. As for the workers, Chinese workers cannot do other than obey (*buhui butinghua*)."

Here as in Shenyang, the City Economic Commission, responding to central government stipulations that, as a respondent explained, "the principal task was light industry," persisted in its decision despite the bureau's remonstrances. This situation continued until the commission chose to recognize that the costs of cleaning up the water pollution outweighed any possible benefit. It was only when the commission saw this financial proof that its officials were finally willing to acknowledge the factory's dissatisfactions. Concern with resource gain and loss motivated change here (but not in Shenyang). But this did not occur until a window for policy reversal had opened in Beijing, undoing the special promotion of light industry in the period from late 1981 to early 1982.

Thus one logical outcome of verticalism was passive waiting, a practice that included the paternalistic treatment of workers in this period of transition and also the authoritarianism of the local bureaucracy set out to enforce the state's policy.[82] As the state tried to insulate itself and to effect its new program for resource generation, covert opposition drained resources and ultimately stymied the policy. The cumulative effect of such resistance must have helped to bring about a policy switch.

In sum, as Scott has pointed out, repression created its own mode of resistance, one that was most often covert or passive. Heavy industrial firms across the nation, laboring under sometimes impractical commands from local economic commissions, obviously had a cause in common. But firms long schooled in habits of unitism and of vertical dependence on bureaucratic superiors molded a mode of opposition that mirrored these traits rather than choosing one based on horizontal cooperation among themselves.

DEALING ON THE MARKET

Insulation against resistance need not be confined to reducing or eliminating channels of appeal; in the People's Republic, effective channels of this sort never existed. In other cases of industrial transformation, politico-economic systems have found different means of achieving this same end, more by co-optation than by repression. T. J. Pempel, for instance, writing in the late 1970's, spoke of the "ultimate success of small and medium-sized firms" in Japan derived from their linkage to the success of the huge enterprises, the industrial leaders. This tie, he claims, "reduces the likelihood that individual firms left out of the first order benefits will organize to oppose [the] distribution collectively."[83]

This issue is discussed from a slightly different angle in Kent E. Calder's book on the "crisis and compensation dynamic" in Japan. He contends that the conservative majority in the form of the Liberal Democratic party has handled political crises by buying influence and support from threatened or frustrated groups. It has accomplished this time and again by compensating such groups for losses caused them by the processes of economic modernization.[84]

Other variants of this theme are offered by John Zysman and Suzanne Berger, each of whom points to the protective treatment accorded what Zysman terms "the politically delicate traditional sectors" in France.[85] Berger maintains that traditional groups, in this case the smaller firms, are permitted to persist and adapt in the face of larger-scale industrial change because they serve crucial functions of social stability for political elites.

Specifically, Berger explains, French elites have valued the firms' role in providing employment for a significant portion of the working force that might otherwise have turned militant in the face of increases in unemployment nationwide as modernization progressed. She cites a range of solutions to which policy makers have resorted to "stave off mass discontent" in this context, including financial incentives to industry to keep workers on at least part time, state funds to pay the wages of young workers who would otherwise be without jobs, loans, tax credits, and aid to keep dying industries alive.[86]

In China during the readjustment, the coterminous program of market reforms played these same roles of insulating the readjustment policy by co-opting the personnel in some firms. Without the new "market" to act as a safety valve, the more assertive enterprises might otherwise have mounted a more aggressive resistance. With this market they found an outlet for their energy.

But this was not a market in the usual sense, for its operations were skewed when they were crucially mediated by the structures and networks formed by the state plan over the years. Certainly there was widespread publicity given firms that, allegedly on their own, ran ads, sent out sales personnel, and, as a result of market investigations, switched their production lines and improved the quality or increased the varieties of their products to meet market demand.[87] But in fact the state plan and the relationships it had created over decades provided much of the scaffolding on which that maneuvering was built.

In some instances, individual firms were able to respond to incentives designed specifically for them. Wuhan's Iron and Steel Company, for example, was named one of some 400 "experimental points" nationwide in the early stage of the readjustment program. It was allowed to substitute tax payments for the previous submission of all its profits to the central treasury.

Since this reform policy let the company retain some of its profits for the first time, its management chose to produce more sheet metal than before. Sheet metal, unlike other varieties of steel, could be used in consumer goods whose profit rates were high, such as bicycles, tin cans, and cars.[88] Another representative case was the Nanfang Electrical Machinery Factory in Wuhan, which received a low-interest loan at 0.022 percent per month for costs associated with manufacturing a second consumer-oriented product, washing machines, in 1982.[89]

But explicitly market incentives were not usually the driving force of change. Many of the press and journalistic reports of these new seeming market activities and all of my interviews at Wuhan machine-building plants contained elements of at least one of three ways in which the old state plan and its vertical arrangements facilitated the transition to marketlike behavior during the early 1980's.

First, bureaucratic superiors supplied their firms with "help" with marketing. Second, "contacts" (*guanxi*), formed by linkages that grew out of state planning long before the market reforms occurred, smoothed the way. And third, special relationships spawned deals that were essential for the survival of entire sectors, without which no amount of markets would have been sufficient at that stage.

Help

Bureaus, city governments, and even ministries took it as their duty to furnish the firms with economic intelligence by investigating and forecasting supply-demand conditions locally and nationally.[90] Officials staffing these offices knew that they were responsible for the economic success of the enterprises under their charge, and, though it was a long-established truth, the State Council still reminded them of this duty from time to time.[91]

Economic journals in that period were filled with reports from cities claiming that their local machine-building trade had successfully navigated the readjustment's cutbacks. Invariably, bureaus in those spots had taken a role in providing market intelligence.[92] As a manager at one Wuhan firm freely admitted, "The Bureau's economic intelligence is greater than our own."[93]

After the bureaus had done the research on demand conditions, they went on to set up barter arrangements for supplying the necessary raw materials. This job was one they had performed throughout the period of planned management whenever there were gaps and misconnections in the supply work done by the planning apparatus. But the work expanded tremendously during the readjustment when allocations for heavy industry were reduced.

Sometimes the firms were able to find their own connections. But often enough the bureau's years of experience in forging swaps with other cities and other bureaucracies stood the now relatively deprived enterprises in good stead. In Wuhan, local corporatism came into play when the city's party and government together set up a team composed of authorities from the Municipal Planning Commission (MPC), the local materials supply department, and the municipal commerce bureau to regulate the distribution of scarce materials and look for new sources of supplies.[94]

The Zhejiang provincial leadership created a small group and an office headed by a vice governor. Their function was to coordinate the distribution of materials. These leaders also organized a sales and marketing network created from organs at the provincial, district, and municipal levels to link buyers and sellers and locate materials.[95]

Once production had been oriented toward demand and the necessary inputs were procured, bureaus and even higher levels in the bureaucracy then would help firms find sales outlets. Even as late as mid-1985, some six years after the market reforms had been well under way, bureaucrats at the central-level Ministry of Machine Building continued to subscribe to the belief that, as one explained, "We want the customers and producers to get together [*jianmian*]. . . . If they can't, we introduce them. They still need help. . . . China's too big. . . . People can't know about everything."[96]

One Wuhan valve-manufacturing firm that was proud of its success during the readjustment admitted that its bureau had suggested where it could most profitably establish a sales outlet. This same factory attributed its survival in part to an exchange relationship it forged with the Wuhan Iron and Steel Company (Wugang), initiated at meetings held in Wuhan and in Beijing that were arranged for the sale of valves by the First Ministry of Machine Building. According to the terms of the arrangement, Wugang traded coke, finished steel, and pig iron, which the valve works then processed. In addition to the more formal meetings, "the bureau sometimes set up liaisons that led to this barter," related firm officials.[97]

Bureaus and city governments also assisted machine-building factories in reducing the level of output of their previous principal products and either converting the bulk of their output to a consumer-oriented product or adding a second production line.

In Wuhan, the party and government analyzed the city's industrial foundation and the supply and demand situation and then picked 23 consumer items for development (including shoes, sheets, printed cloth, leather products, and baby carts, in addition to the usual popular products such as sewing machines, watches, and fans). The offices in charge then organized some 40 machine-building factories to produce these commodities.[98] Sometimes the city was able to convert the buildings, technical skills, and equipment of enterprises suffering losses to the manufacture of these more marketable items.[99]

One article made reference to a city "plan" for plant conversion;[100] another spoke of the provincial party's collaboration with economic and planning commissions at that level, and with the financial bureau and bank branch, to adopt special incentives to support enterprises that switched to serving the light and textile trades.[101] With the firms' bureaucratic superiors arranging so much of their exchange behavior, many enterprises shortchanged by cutbacks that might otherwise have been inclined to oppose the orders to readjustment must have been eased into compliance.

Contacts

Dealer firms, whose initial response to the shock of cutbacks was to attempt to adjust and adapt to their changed environment rather than to protest, resist, or fall passive, often began by drawing on old connections to carry themselves through. They naturally had nowhere to turn for this help but to the relationships that their obligations to the planned economy had long since created for them.

The resort to taking on sundry miscellaneous orders as a transitional remedy was apparently common.[102] One example was a general-purpose machinery factory in Lanzhou, which performed odd jobs for buyers with which it had *guanxi*, using the work to stay afloat.[103] In Qingdao, a forging machinery plant faced its fate at first by seeking help from contacts in the state materials supply administration. But the orders it received through this source were soon canceled when demand dropped off.[104]

A manager in a Wuhan valve plant, talking about how his plant found work on its own, told of users coming to survey his stock and of his posting ads and sending out samples. But he disclosed that the majority of these users were people acquainted with his firm, "friendship units" (*youyi danwei*) from the time of the planned economy. "We knew where the money came from when they bought our things before, even though there was a middleman [the materials supply department]," he explained.[105] Similarly, when Wuhan's No. Two Machine Tools Plant, fitting itself into the market reforms, began to send out sales and purchase personnel, it "mainly depended on units with which it had *guanxi*."[106]

Another of this same factory's activities illustrates yet another contact built on bonds created by the plan which served the purposes of readjustment. When the drilling and boring lathes that were the plant's main products no longer brought in all the income the firm required, its leaders turned to a second line, packaging machinery for glass and food products. In marketing this item, staff managed to establish a liaison with the provincial First Bureau of Light Industry. That bureau introduced the tools plant to customers because bureau officials knew from their own work which light industrial factories needed the machinery.

Thus initial reliance on old connections for disposing of firms' regular products eventually gave way to ventures with new commodities. Both interview and press materials indicate that the marketing networks for at least some of these grew out of vertically arranged, plan-fashioned links.

Special Deals

In Wuhan the city Metallurgy Bureau increased its output value each year from 1979 to 1984 despite the "fierce slap" it received from the readjustment.[107] Newspaper accounts credit its success mainly to its firms' interviews with customers, changes its leadership made in the quality and specifications of its products and its staff's design of new products to serve light and textiles. But the real answer lay in a special arrangement the bureau chief was able to devise with city officials, an agreement that had to be approved by decision makers at the provincial level.[108]

This plan, called *chao-e fen-cheng*,[109] began in 1980 and governed

TABLE 16
Sources of Investment in Wuhan City Metallurgy Bureau, 1979–1982
(Yuan 1 million)

1. State (central-level) investment:	
a. For technical transformation	2.15
b. For special projects (*zhuanxiang*)	.70
2. Local government investment	1.58
3. Bank loans	18.40
4. Straight state investment (*bokuan*)	6.11
5. Ministry of Metallurgy loans for technical transformation (loaned at interest rate at which the ministry borrowed it from the People's Bank)	4.80
6. Enterprise's own funds:	
a. From depreciation	20.00
b. From *chao-e fen-cheng*	30.00
TOTAL	83.74

SOURCE: Interview at the Wuhan City Bureau of Metallurgy, Nov. 16, 1984.

the handling of the bureau's finances for three years. It stipulated that as long as the bureau turned over 9 million *yuan* of profits to the state per year, it could keep the bulk of the rest. The remaining portion went to municipal accounts in the form of a "locality adjustment tax" (*difang tiaojishui*). By the end of the three-year term, the bureau had collected a total of 30 million *yuan*, which amounted to 36 percent of its total funding sources for the period beginning in 1979 and ending in 1982 (see Table 16). In the words of one of the bureau's leaders, "Without the profit retention program, we would have had no way to go on."[110]

The inside details of this deal are murky. Such "responsibility systems" began to proliferate in the early 1980's, but in 1980 they were rare. The bureau officials boasted in late 1984 that "four years ago we did today's thing," implying that they received special treatment when their own responsibility system first appeared. Such a plan had been proposed not only by the Metallurgy Bureau chief in Wuhan but also by the head of the city's Machine-Building Bureau. Only the former, however, was granted his request. Why was metallurgy favored?

One clue lies in the relative flexibility with which that sector—as opposed to machine building—was able to respond to the new priorities during the readjustment. Unlike machine building, it was able quickly to adapt its technology so that it could continue to generate resources in the changed economic environment. Local leaders at a July 1981 Wuhan municipal party meeting contrasted the two branches and specifically chastised the machine-building branch for not readjusting well and, as a result, "falling behind." By contrast, they described metallurgy as having "tightly grasped readjustment work, and quickly converted its service orientation." Consequently, "its situation, despite many problems, was much better than expected."[111]

Although lathes, cars, and tractors accumulated as unsold stock, metallurgists could meet the demand to favor light industry and the people's livelihood simply by changing the specifications of their products. They shifted their thick planks of metal to thin ones; turned out steel wire, less weighty belts, and clubs that could be used in producing consumer goods and building materials; and made water and gas pipes for dwellings in a time of surging housing construction.

This information suggests that among other elements that may have gone into the favoritism of metallurgy was an economic calculation by city—and then by provincial—decision makers that significantly boosted the metallurgy sector's chances for survival and success in this climate of cutbacks. Because of its ability to adapt to state-set developmental priorities, the bureau managed to carve out a special profit-sharing plan set up by vertical connections. A bureau chief, working with city officials, obtained the approval of the province for in effect bestowing a huge pot of added state investment (if under a new label). That extra funding then served as an incentive for this bureau and its firms to continue to meet these priorities. The "market" provided the arena, but the modes of entering and excelling in it were timeworn.

All told, heavy industrial firms' dealing on the market in the early 1980's was mediated by bureaucratic arrangements and support from vertical superiors. To the extent that heavy-sector factories used the new incentives to continue turning out old products, the help, contacts, and special deals spawned by verticalism amounted to one of Scott's "forms of labor control" that create their own opposition.[112]

CONCLUSION

This chapter took a micro view of the policy change examined in Chapter 5, which showed how opposition to the readjustment voiced in policy councils in Beijing found a hearing only when political elites were finally faced with truly dire financial results. Closer examination of the resistance that occurred at the local level provides a basis for understanding why the policy created so much economic loss. It suggests the negative situations and attitudes in the cities that the 1981–82 restoration of funding for heavy industry was meant to turn around as politicians attempted to ensure revenue generation for the state.

And yet the policy was able to reach its immediate goal of servicing and bolstering light industry despite recalcitrance on the part of some heavy industrial firms. In the relationships between the bureaus and firms that pushed the readjustment along, die-hard resistance could occur without massively disrupting the social peace on which the regime counted. In losing firms the factory officials were permitted and even encouraged to wait out the policy, and programs were designed to keep disgruntled workers at bay. These means of protecting against disaster provided by vertical arrangements reduced the massive and disruptive discontent that could have occurred. Moreover, such support from superiors helped to prevent firms from forming horizontal combinations with peers in defiance of the policy.

At the same time, a policy of cutbacks for heavy industry that could have been extremely unpopular was insulated because of the simultaneous program of market reform. This loosening of the old state plan offered an escape valve for the abandoned enterprises, even as the firms that made that escape were guided by their vertical supervisors. The new market freedoms thus worked to co-opt the resistance of at least the more enterprising firms in the affected trades. According to one Chinese commentator, the annual average output value in the machinery industry in the period 1976–78 was 33.4 billion *yuan*, but in 1980–81, in the midst of the readjustment, it rose to 34.8 billion. "If we had not persevered in reform during the readjustment," this account concluded, "it would have been impossible to obtain this kind of results."[113]

Both responses on the part of firms dependent on a bureaucratic benevolence informed by state goals of resource accumulation and social stability shielded the program long enough to make it work and, one might conclude, turned crisis to normalcy.

Connections, patterns of paternalistic assistance, and networks that the management bureaus had created over three decades protected the resisters, the die-hards, even as these same behavioral patterns guided the dealers through the unfamiliar maze of the incipient market.

EIGHT

Rationalization
The Limits of Verticalism and Unitism

THUS FAR I have examined the dynamics of reallocation from heavy to light industry, the part of industrial policy that the Japanese call "industrial structure policy."[1] But there is another dimension of industrial policy, which the Japanese label "industrial rationalization policy." This second dimension of industrial policy encompasses the adoption of new techniques of production, investment in new equipment and facilities, and quality control. But more to the purposes of this book, it also entails the remodeling of entire industries. The aim is first to ensure that all the enterprises within a trade can compete fairly or that they can cooperate in cartel-like arrangements of mutual assistance. Second, it seeks to rationalize the industrial structure as a whole so as to meet international competitive standards. It "means state policy at the micro level, state intrusion into the detailed operations of individual enterprises with measures intended to improve those operations (or, on occasion, to abolish the enterprise)."[2] This chapter considers how local, urban economies in China handled this second component of industrial policy during the readjustment.

In China in this era, industrial rationalization became an explicit goal. According to a spring 1981 statement in Wuhan's newspaper, "Readjustment is not just aimed at forcing down capital construction; it includes readjusting the economic, industrial, product, and organizational structures and rationalizing them."[3] At this same time, Yuan Baohua, then minister in charge of the State Economic Commission, listed eight components of the economic readjustment program at a national work conference on industry and communications. One of these, he said, was to link the reorganization of the industrial structure and the formation of "joint enterprises"—essentially, rationalization—with *guanting bingzhuan*, referring to the principal procedures for the readjustment (closing down enterprises, suspending their operations, amalgamating them, or switching them to other lines of production).[4]

In the main, the rationalization effort in China emphasized mergers* among firms to redistribute productive factors in a more judicious fashion than the previous setup had done. Its other objectives were to enhance the degree of specialization among individual firms, expand and better use productive capacity, orient production toward market demand, and fit and reequip existing technology to the task of modernization.

These objectives were given shape in a set of State Council regulations on forming *lianheti* (combinations) promulgated in July 1980.[5] The document states that these bodies were to help put material and financial powers then under local and enterprise control into the service of the state's construction effort and to set up conditions for more specialized cooperation among firms. At the same time, by bringing together potential competitors, these combines were to eliminate contention between inefficient resource-devouring small firms on the one hand and larger, more productive plants on the other, thereby cutting out duplicative ventures and blind development.

Doing all this properly would have dealt with the third element in the Chinese critique of the Stalinist industrial system noted in Chapter 3: that system's creation of a dual vertical and horizontal control structure which the Chinese call *tiaotiao kuaikuai*. This term, as spelled out more fully in that earlier chapter, refers to the prereform system's tendency to slice the economy into ver-

---

*Here and throughout this chapter I am loosely using the English word "merger" as one of the translations of the Chinese word *lianhe*, more properly translated as combination, association, or union. The Chinese word with the meaning closest to merger, *jianbing*, entails a thorough amalgamation of all the assets of the firms in question and the creation of a new independent accounting unit. But the political and organizational problems that arose in attempting to form the far looser "combinations" were similar in character to those that came up in forcing mergers in France and Japan, as will be shown below. Moreover, the catchphrase for the readjustment, *guanting bingzhuan*, does use the word *bing*, indicating that a merger of sorts was intended.

tical and horizontal command frameworks. Among its other effects, these power arrangements threw individual units back on their own self-protective devices and thus curtailed rational cooperation and specialization throughout the economy as a whole.

The reorganization that rationalization was supposed to achieve was part of the response to the industrial crisis discussed in Chapter 3, for certainly one of its chief aims was to position the total national economy better for competitive success internationally. In an unplanned market economy in danger, this job is generally the work not of the state but of large business enterprises that "internalize crisis management" by reassigning labor or by effecting mergers.[6]

But even among the market systems, there is a difference between industrial cultures that emphasize a "private" concept of the self-sufficiency of the firm and those that stress a "public" conception of the enterprise, according to a characterization by Kenneth Dyson.[7] It is only in the latter, of which he cites France as an example, that the state is "expected to exhibit interest in the welfare of its citizens by direct and detailed intervention in industrial affairs." This second type of culture fosters what Dyson labels an "organized capitalism," which he sees as being symbolized by the cartel. Among the capitalist economies, both French and Japanese governments have encouraged the formation of cartels, along with mergers, for purposes of rationalization.[8]

That a similar concept was present in the Chinese case* is evident in many discussions of the policy of state-directed mergers during this time.[9] "Combination" (*lianhe*)[10] among firms was justified as a way to help enterprises to develop that were languishing "without enough to eat" (*chibubao*), that is, enterprises lacking work assignments. Arguments promoting this policy viewed assisting firms in trouble as a state responsibility as well as a

---

*In France and Japan, there is yet another form of preserving firms in trouble. Within the private sector in both these market societies, self-organization through industrial associations serves to reduce risk. These bodies promote an equilibrium among their members as they carry out protective and regulatory functions. In effect, they supplement the market in shifting resources from stronger to weaker products and firms within a given trade.

means of "help[ing] make the economic structure more rational."[11]

Officials at the Ministry of Machine Building thought of the procedures used in readjustment in just this light: "Merging is a method for ensuring *pingheng* [balance]," they explained. For them this referred to situations when one enterprise was suffering losses and the other was not, or when one had a market for its goods and the other was failing to find an outlet.[12] Unfortunately, readjustment's attempt to undo the *tiaotiao kuaikuai* ties that made up the prereform industrial economy became entangled in its nets.

This chapter begins by looking at the roots of the problems that rationalization sought to address and its corresponding purposes. It goes on to consider procedures used in implementation. The argument then offers an explanation for the failure of mergers by focusing on the role the systemic behavioral traits of verticalism and unitism often played in thwarting these purposes. These same traits that were beneficial to attaining the other, macro aspects of readjustment—priority for light industry and abandoning while protecting heavy industry—acted as obstructive forces when the more micro-oriented rationalization was the goal. The concluding section will ask to what extent the aims of rationalization were actually achieved and show the reasons why they frequently were not.

ROOTS OF THE PROBLEM

The issues that rationalization was supposed to address sprang from several sources. Some of these could be traced back for decades; others cropped up as offshoots of the readjustment. The older roots lay in the management structure by "strips" (*tiao*) and "chunks" (*kuai*) outlined in Chapter 3 and in the haphazard growth pattern industry had followed over time. But the readjustment introduced new problems, increasing slack in the economy by reducing state demand for the products of many plants and aggravating unemployment.

A Chinese economist offers the following explanation of the problem posed by the *tiao* and *kuai*, which he translates as "lines" and "blocks." " 'Lines,' " he says, refer to the enterprises from higher levels down to the grass roots, whereas "blocks" refer to several enterprises on the same level bound together. The lines [strips] and blocks [chunks] are all trying to be independent firms with their own systems, which results not only in the overlapped construction of various enterprises but also in a situation of "big and complete" or "small and complete" in quite a few enterprises.... It is against this background that, in recent years, many corporations have sprung up and developed.[13]

It was hoped that through combining firms rationalization would break through the boundaries of verticalism and unitism that these strips and chunks had formed over decades.

Favoritism for the heavy industrial sector and gratis allocation of investment and inputs to its firms, coupled with a philosophy of development over the years that had enshrined high output and growth of any sort, had long made expansion in the basic industries all too easy. Then the Cultural Revolution spawned the birth of additional new plant, when the unhinging of the planning apparatus in those years erased administrative controls that had previously monitored excesses. At the same time, advocacy of regional self-sufficiency granted local governments the right to manage key resources.[14]

Over the decade 1971 to 1980 the number of industrial enterprises almost doubled, increasing from 195,000 to more than 377,000.[15] But the national economy was unable adequately to sustain all of these firms. Many of them operated under capacity or could not go into operation at all, plagued by insufficient supplies of raw and semifinished materials and energy. Slack productive capacity characterized a great deal of the machine-building trade in particular, as equipment lay idle and the labor force was plagued by disguised unemployment: "three people eating five people's rice," as the Chinese put it figuratively.[16]

Another effect of these conditions was the turnout of a large amount of low-quality products by nonspecialized, comprehensive firms operating at a loss. These "big—or small—but complete" outfits could only dump unwanted output that did not fulfill market demand into the trucks of hapless procuring agents. For there had been no check on such backward plants that operated inefficiently, wasting resources.

But even though readjustment was meant to solve this problem of untrammeled growth by reducing the investment and supplies for heavy industry, it brought new problems in its wake. For as planned industrial construction projects were canceled, funds allocated for buying machinery and equipment over the years 1980 and 1981 fell about 30 percent nationwide compared with the period between 1976 and 1978. Consequently, a new surge of slack and idleness ensued.[17] When the number of production tasks assigned to firms in this sector was reduced, "many units had more people than work," as Deng Xiaoping told a party conference in December 1980.[18]

For long-standing reasons, then, as well as because of repercussions from new policy, too much capacity was being ill-used or going unused because its malcoordinated management made no provision for specialization or a cooperative division of labor. Many firms dissipated scarce inputs, and the resulting output failed to mesh with the market, and much labor was either underemployed or irrationally deployed.

PURPOSES, MEANS, AND STATE GOALS

Purposes

Rationalization was meant to solve these problems. One of the main aims was to promote specialization within and among firms so that their respective comparative advantages could come into play.[19] This would then "tap the potential" of existing equipment stock so that the productive capacity of old machinery could be more fully employed.[20] A third objective was to change the nature of what was produced, with scarce, name-brand, high-quality, trendy goods having definite competitive ability (on both domestic and foreign markets) replacing the overstocked, out-of-date, low-class merchandise of the prereadjustment era.[21]

Specialization. The first of these purposes was to be served when city-level bureaucrats rearranged assets among their local firms in the interest of achieving greater specialization. A few examples will illustrate the methods they used. In one case, the Wuhan Second Bureau of Light Industry merged the operations of 26 factories suffering from insufficient demand, including a rope and a comb-producing firm. The new union enabled each to go on producing in accord with its own technology and skills, but the two factories were urged to turn their abilities to manufacturing shoes, brushes, and other items actually in demand.[22]

In another case, relevant city departments created the Wuhan Motor Vehicle Company out of two comprehensive car assembly plants, the old products of one of which were selling poorly, the other of which was turning out newer vehicles but was unable to keep up with demand. Since each had been trying to produce a full line of cars, the equipment and the technical strength of neither were being properly put to use. The merger reorganized the entire production effort of the two into specialized smaller plants, so that more varieties of cars could be created. The various plants concentrated, respectively, on assemblage, body work, equipment, and motors.[23]

A third example was the Wuhan Industrial Boiler General Factory, set up in the second half of 1978. This company combined nine factories, of which four made boilers and five manufactured accessory parts. Their linkage permitted the output of specialized models, which had not been possible before, when a lack of a division of labor had kept both technical standards and quality low. In the process, as tasks were reassigned, the firms exchanged some equipment, and some of their staff members switched work sites.[24]

Tapping potential. An illustrative case of tapping potential, the second goal of rationalization, was provided by the district-managed collective Jianghan Casting Factory in Wuhan. This little plant was merged with the Wuhan Weighing Apparatus General Factory in early 1979. Before they were joined, the casting plant relied on its own efforts to make some small-scale casts, but its products were of poor quality and its costs high. Once it became simply a casting workshop for the larger factory, its production ability was expanded as it turned its efforts to manufacturing standard casts according to specifications.[25]

Upgrading products. Rationalization's aim to upgrade products to meet demand was mediated by vertical ties. Hubei provincial officials investigated a set of products' long- and short-term markets, the availability of the resources necessary for the production of these items, and the relevant equipment holdings and technical capacities of a set of factories, and then rearranged those firms into 155 new units. Of these 155, 107 belonged to the light and textile trades.[26]

Another effort to meet demand by upgrading products occurred when the Wuhan city party and government organs analyzed the city's industrial foundation and then scrutinized the fit between extant supplies and the demand for key products in the local market. Officials in these organs then selected 23 specific products for special emphasis and readjusted the city's industrial structure accordingly, merging and converting firms to increase the proportion of superior name-brand products; products in short supply; and goods for export, such as textiles, leather products, and medicines, while upgrading the quality of local furniture and jeeps to serve a more discriminating buyer.

Means: Balance and Technological Upgrading

The central principle for serving these purposes was balancing (*pingheng*) to create mergers or combinations (*lianhe*). Each combination was to bring together firms that boasted adequate space, facilities, skilled personnel, capital, and markets and those short of these assets. The idea was that the firms so linked could then share tasks according to a more rational division of labor than either could have done on its own.

The other way of reaching these ends was to rearrange technology, partly through reallocating existing technology to new jobs so as better to match up tasks and tools with capabilities and market demands, and partly by technological upgrading and importing. This chapter will concentrate on the first of these two methods, balancing through merging, which carried more explicit organizational and political implications.

Balancing. The essence of the policy of balancing was to connect two kinds of "eaters": those without enough (work, job orders) to fill their stomachs (*chibubao*), and those that could not finish everything on their plates (*chibuliao,* those plants that had more orders than they could handle). The bottom line was to "utilize long-line [surplus] production ability to produce short-line [in scarce supply] products."[27]

As one set of authors explained, "Some enterprises in difficulty without salable products or technical equipment only have buildings and labor power . . . only through *lianhe* can they develop production."[28] As a *People's Daily* editorial of early 1981 advised, this meant finding a way to use the surplus production capacity—buildings, sites, equipment, and labor power—in the machine-building, defense, and metallurgy enterprises that had been idled because of the readjustment.[29] That slack capacity went primarily to replenish the light industrial sector.[30]

In Wuhan, a factory producing clothing for distribution to factory workers had been housed in a spacious site with many workers and good equipment, but the tasks assigned it left it "hungry." The city's Second Bureau of Light Industry and its subordinate company for clothing, shoes, and hats merged this plant with another one whose down export garments were in great demand. This second enterprise had been struggling in crowded buildings with insufficient numbers of workers and inferior facilities. After the merger, the factory-worker clothing producers received some short-term training, and the workers from both plants concentrated on clothing for export.[31]

The city Textile Bureau contracted with a district-level government so that its Wuhan Woolen Cloth Factory could get the use of a brigade factory under commune management within that district. The urban factory's sites were scattered around the city, and the brigade had excess land and buildings that could house surplus equipment. The purpose of the contract was to promote the development of the city's woolen industry, which had been a serious weak spot in the Wuhan textile trade before readjustment.[32]

Technological upgrading. Rationalization also aimed at more than this simple shifting around of resources. According to an article in the Wuhan journal *Social Science Trends*, "One purpose of *lianhe* is to change the backward technological situation."[33] As the readjustment period progressed, this dimension became more prominent. In spring 1981, a spate of articles began to appear in the local paper telling how the city party's organizational department and the city Personnel Bureau together selected a batch of technical workers to aid the light and textile firms.[34]

At the same time, the Municipal Economic Commission held a work conference for technical support teams from large factories. These cadres were then dispatched to key-point light industrial enterprises to improve the production of light industrial goods. More than 100 engineering and technical personnel, management cadres, and experienced workers left some dozen or so firms in the heavy industrial sector—even including the major, then centrally owned Wuhan Heavy-Duty Machine Tool Factory and the Wuhan Materials Production Research Institute—and turned their attention and skills to the manufacture of bicycles, sewing machines, fans, and baby carts.[35]

In early 1982, the State Council issued a directive urging that staff in idle heavy industrial firms be put to work on the technical transformation of existing enterprises. The intent was to have the machine-building sector begin to produce new technology to renovate and replace what had been in use for decades. The statement made clear that this approach would entail research and new attention to scientific technique. Technical transformation also was to involve drawing on foreign capital and importing progressive technology and crucial equipment that could not yet be manufactured in China.[36]

Thus rationalization was to reach its goals in part by mergers, through their more balanced sharing of the factors of production among have and have-not firms. But a genuine effort at modernization and enhanced competitiveness, as in the Japanese case, would ultimately have to involve the adoption of new production techniques and investment in new equipment and facilities.

Linkage to Larger State Goals: Stability and Savings

The entire program was constantly informed by the persistent twin state goals that have echoed throughout this study: first, to ensure popular satisfaction ("stability and unity," in Chinese parlance), in this case by solving the unemployment problem; and second, to lead to an increase in state investment funds, in this instance simply through efficiency-induced savings.

Stability. When Li Xiannian first unveiled the readjustment program, he made clear that "in this readjustment, we must *guanting bingzhuan* [close, suspend, merge, convert] a batch of capital construction projects, but the personnel can't be reduced; we still must arrange the employment of a large amount of labor power."[37] This determination to engage displaced labor reflected a lesson learned in the early 1960's. Injunctions to care for affected staff often were accompanied by references to that earlier readjustment, when "we stopped and suspended more than 800 large and middle-sized construction projects, closed, suspended, merged and converted nearly 60,000 industrial enterprises, and retrenched 20 million staff and workers."[38] Presumably, that time a resultant restiveness among those laid off had made the elite uneasy. Mishandling in that earlier era may well have been a factor in the discontent in the cities that soon fueled excesses among the masses during the Cultural Revolution.

As earlier chapters have shown, top leaders suggested an assortment of methods for handling the problem. Mergers were one prominent way.[39] But putting workers into new lines of employment in the mergers meant that they needed new skills. Nationally, the government took the responsibility for training and retraining seriously: by the end of 1981, more than 7,600 labor service companies had been established throughout the country, one-third by central-level labor agencies and enterprises and two-thirds by local labor offices and firms.[40] Hubei, like other localities, picked up the charge, announcing at one of its provincial people's congresses, "When enterprises are consolidated, they can design training and study classes for the surplus personnel, or they can create labor service companies to rationalize support work for the enterprise."[41]

At the urban level, there is the case of the Shashi Municipal Machine-Building Industrial Bureau. That office organized 19 of its 24 enterprises to form a set of companies (among them, one for machine tools, one for metallurgy, one for valves, and one for diesel engines). This rearrangement not only solved the problem of "hunger" for work in the city's machine-building trade but was considered to be "beneficial to social stability and unity and stable economic development" as well.[42] Apparently leaders realized that a more rational division of labor could better deploy otherwise idled workers.

For the individual firm, new attached workshops not only served to rationalize production operations but also created job openings for the children of staff and workers. One example among many was the Wuhan Flannel Factory, which in one year's time arranged work for 187 youths and created the capability of producing its own hypochlorous acid, which it formerly had had to purchase.[43] In these various ways, rationalization as carried out in China pacified those who in other modes of disinvestment would surely have suffered unemployment.

Saving state funds. Rationalization was designed to save state investment funds as well. Near the end of the policy's life, the need for foreign technology began to be apparent, and it would be expensive. But those in charge of rationalization found many means of attaining structural transformation that were cheap or even free. In advocating plant conversions, one writer explained in *Red Flag*: "For a heavy industrial enterprise to shift to producing consumer goods, it must pay certain incidental expenses; at least it must acquire new equipment. But this is still more economical than to start a new light industrial enterprise."[44] Following this logic, the Wuhan Machine Tools Factory used its own technology and equipment to meet the needs of the light and textile trades by producing parts for sewing machines and bicycles and by making fittings for textile machinery. This activity was lauded for not requiring much new investment.[45]

Combinations were similarly valuable because creating new companies from old, smaller firms to develop salable key-point products did not require extra investment, adding new equipment, or hiring more labor. Instead, the products could be manufactured simply by shifting around productive factors until they found their optimal point of usage.[46] The Wuhan paper praised the *lianhe* approach because it could guarantee that industrial development would proceed at a certain speed with little or no investment.[47]

When rationalization worked as it ideally was meant to do, individual enterprises could express their own comparative advantage and small groups of them could cooperate in a more specialized manner. Productive capacity was expanded by drawing on the potential of existing stock; and production was reoriented to fit market demand. This was carried out by balancing assets, advantages, and sales much in the manner of a cartel or an industrial association in managed market settings and by reallocating and upgrading technology. All the while displaced labor was to be pacified and state investment economized.

PROCEDURES

The legislation authorizing the formation of combinations placed responsibility for them in the lap of the immediate superiors of the units composing each of them, in typically bureaucratic, verticalist fashion: "Various levels of government should strengthen leadership over economic combinations," it decreed. This State Council decision also charged the management departments of combining firms (that is, the bureaus responsible for them) with handling any problems that arose in carrying out the contract and with resolving any quarrels connected with these unions.[48]

Despite references to the importance of mutual benefit and voluntary cooperation among the firms involved, "it was not enough to rely on the voluntary efforts of the enterprises," the official party journal concluded about a year after this directive was issued. "It is also necessary," it instructed, "to step up administrative intervention and strike an overall balance."[49]

Accordingly, for the most part, one or another part of the planning hierarchy, and not the firms themselves, initiated these mergers. In the vast majority of cases, it was clear that a push for concentrating resources and generating income at each administrative level motivated the formation of these new associations. Sometimes the State Council took the lead: a March 1981 meeting of the council's Office for the Reform of the Management System, together with the State Economic Commission, combined firms from several redundant trades to retrench the heavy capital investment going into haphazardly organized, inadequately specialized, and technologically backward firms in the same sector.[50]

In another instance the State Economic Commission and the State Machine-Building Commission collaborated to assist the Ministry of Light Industry and Shanghai and Tianjin municipalities in setting up cooperative production of the popular Phoenix, Forever, and Flying Pigeon bicycles. Maximizing the output of these well-selling brands would certainly be a money-making venture for the state.[51]

Provincial governments oversaw a similar procedure within their own regions. By early 1981, Hubei province had allegedly already closed or merged some 400 enterprises in an effort to turn the dismantled technical capacity, buildings, and equipment to the production of light industrial items needed on the market. Within two years, Hubei had organized as many as 142 combinations, companies, and general factories, reorganizing a total of 1,184 firms.[52]

In early 1981 this provincial government authorized its subordinate Wuhan city government to make out its own plan for organizing *lianhe*. Still, the province remained ultimately in control, decreeing that the city must refer any problems upward. And even after delegating this authority to the city, Hubei held a meeting to research how to "help Wuhan out."[53]

The city economic administration used its power in an endeavor to concentrate local resources on the development of particular key-point light industrial and textile products. By the end of 1981, it had set up 30 companies, 24 general factories, and 55 economic associations, with the aim of putting 32 name-brand and, of course, revenue-generating products on the market.[54]

When more than one industrial "system" (*xitong*, roughly, a trade) was involved, only the city economic and planning commissions (MEC and MPC) were competent to arrange cross-departmental mergers. For such ventures would necessarily affect the total allocation of materials within the overall urban plan and could easily incite conflicts that no one bureau would be able to settle on its own.[55] Cross-trade mergers were also helpful in redeploying labor idled by the readjustment and so in contributing to social peace in the city.

One such instance involved a match between the machine-building and textile sectors. Six or seven small machinery concerns stuck with unsalable products were linked to plants in the textile industry and another half dozen went over to light industry. The machine builders converted their own production and underwent training in their new homes.[56] In textiles some one to two thousand people were involved; in light industry there were as many as three to four thousand.

Textile officials generally appreciated this opportunity to win jurisdiction over new enterprises. The workers from heavy industry earned their pay from the new profits the light industrial factories were able to amass because they set up new workshops and produced more after taking in extra personnel. And in many instances the work processes entailed required the workers to do something only marginally different from their previous jobs. Moreover, the recipient firms could save investment and time as they expanded their production, got control over new equipment, and added to their labor forces.

But there were drawbacks as well. Some old workers were unable to master new skills; others simply did not want to be doing light industry. And yet these older workers, some of whom became a drain on enterprise resources, still had to be paid, even though they were unable to perform as well in light industry as they had in heavy.[57] Nonetheless, from the perspective of those in the city economic administration, a major problem had been addressed, at least for the moment. These officials could take comfort in having placated inactive workers at least to some extent and placing them in a money-making venture.

Individual industrial bureaus at both provincial and municipal levels were given the right to initiate mergers that involved only the firms under their command. For instance, in Hubei, the first light industrial system composed seven *lianheti* from among its various subordinate firms at the provincial and the city levels. Bureaus hoped thereby to reduce the amount of "long-line," unpopular products for which they were accountable because production of such goods was fruitlessly tying up their capital. They hoped their new mergers could enable their charges to augment the proportion of "short-line" items in their output, thereby driving up sales and bringing in new income.[58]

Most of the combinations reported in the media involved firms in the same city within the same trade and under the same industrial management bureau.[59] Generally what happened was that a bureau—textiles, light industry, or machine building—chose to unite a few enterprises whose capabilities or facilities could be fitted to the production of some commodity considered highly salable. One case was the combining of a cloth factory that produced window screens, a new dye plant, and a belt-weaving firm, which together set up a woolen production line. Reportedly, this one merger raised the city's woolen production capacity a startling tenfold.[60]

Sometimes, according to the press, the impetus came from individual factories. In late 1980 the Wuhan city government decided to merge several machine-building factories into a comprehensive bicycle factory. After its decision had been made, several factories subordinate to the city Machine-Building Bureau whose products were uncompetitive and which had been suffering from insufficient tasks and economic losses, petitioned to join this *lianhe*. This petition apparently had little impact on the final outcome. After "many negotiations" between officials of the city machinery bureau, the city's First Light Industrial Bureau, and the new general factory, an association was brought about. The machinery factories selected—a bike fittings plant, a motor vehicles spare parts plant, and an agricultural tools fittings enterprise—were ones with advantages to offer such as good locales, technical strength, and useful equipment.[61] This suggestive article sheds light on the interest of faltering firms in submitting their operations to the care of larger, stronger units.[62] But it also shows the conflict of interest between such firms and management bureaus interested in using the combinations to increase their own capital.

Press accounts suggest that most associations were formed through administrative channels and not by the firms themselves. Consequently, administrative concerns usually motivated this initiative at various levels in the bureaucracy. In general, either earning income for the locality or the region or better arranging its labor power were the chief motivating factors for the offices in charge.

THE FAILURE OF MERGERS
Responsibility, Interests, and the State Plan

The very strengths of the Chinese bureaucracy for effecting allocation and reallocation—with the dependence of these processes on insulation for decision making—became serious sticking points when the finesse and fine-tuning of merging were needed. Vertical chains of command (verticalism) were sufficiently adept at deploying and redistributing resources and at placating petitioners; and the isolation of individual units (unitism) usually confined the expression of the dissatisfactions of those in abandoned work units to discrete instances of passive resistance. These systemic properties enabled the prioritizing and abandonment dimensions of readjustment to proceed in the general direction intended.

But rationalization required at least a partial dismantling of these hierarchical bureaucracies. It also demanded breaking through the atomization of the *tiaotiao kuaikuai* framework to build new modes of production based on specialization and division of labor. Thus for this aspect of readjustment vertically oriented and unitistic behavioral patterns became obstacles, not facilitating factors.[63]

The heart of the problem lay in the special understanding of responsibility that has historically integrated the Chinese economy and continued to do so in the socialist bureaucracy.[64] According to this concept, officials at each level in the bureaucracy are accountable to authorities at the level just above them for the completion of assigned tasks and are also in charge of the behavior of all the units under their jurisdiction.

The notion of verticalism contains a sense of paternalistic caring for subordinates. It also entails the burden of ensuring that not just each lower-echelon entity but the group of them as a whole performs as expected. When this obligation is added to the interest that those at each administrative level take in accumulating wealth for their echelon, an incongruence of goals may readily develop between the various levels in the administrative hierarchy and, in turn, between the management bureau and individual firms under its supervision.[65]

The introduction of a nationwide state economic plan in the early 1950's exacerbated this traditional sense of responsibility and burden, even as the "socialization" of national assets that quickly followed it focused requests for finances on one economic center. At that point the goal of constructing a modernizing economy according to Soviet precedent led Chinese leaders to carve up the industrial system into branches, sectors, trades, and departments. In the process, a division of interest defined both by functional and geographic spheres resulted in a mesh of self-aggrandizing and self-protective hierarchies and pockets of control labeled *tiaotiao kuaikuai*.

The rationalization of the early 1980's was affected by the often insuperable difficulties in bringing together for cooperation entities subordinate to different strips (or functional bureaucratic chains of command) or lumps (geographical areas). For such combinations invariably instigated clashes—or perceived clashes—of rights, powers, and advantage among and between the units involved (deriving from unitism) and sometimes between units and their managing superiors (upsetting verticalism).

This fractious play of interests was expressed after 1949 in a series of financial and material systems that further defined the bureaucratic web and served to enforce the duties of the occupant of each niche within it. Formally and legally* each enterprise, urban managerial bureau, city, province, and central ministry had to orient its work around the fulfillment of a particular and specific annual economic plan for production and revenue generation.

Since most enterprises were the responsibility first of a bureau and then of a city (or province), they had to submit to the orders imposed on them in the interests of these more powerful higher-echelon agencies. And each such agency was jealous of keeping command over every asset and decision that it could to fulfill its own responsibility.

As one analyst expressed the problem:

Obstacles toward developing specialized production are very great under the present management system. The allocation system for materials and products, finances, prices, and taxes are all arranged according to the *tiaotiao kuaikuai* management system. This is not beneficial to breaking district and trade boundaries and organizing the specialized large-batch production of parts.[66]

Taxes, Profits, and the "Four Unchanges"

Related to these clashes sparked by the efforts to combine firms, unitism produced two key sticking points that frequently stymied the creation of mergers: one associated with tax assessment, the other with profit division. Because of the demands of

---

*It is well known that each responsible unit and level had to become adept at arranging informal and semilegal exchanges and subterfuges for meeting the formal and legal targets assigned to it. But the main point here is that economic and bureaucratic behavior were defined by and oriented around what was legally and formally expected, even if achieving these expectations meant using extra, unofficially obtained resources.

the *tiaotiao kuaikuai* network, enterprises working in cooperation had to pay duplicate taxes, one set to each of the bureaucratic hierarchies affiliated with the merger.[67] Alternatively, taxes would be collected once each from firms representing the various stages of a production process, as well as being assessed on the final product. These double assessments inhibited the formation of unions among the producers of accessory parts and the assemblers of finished products.

To deal with this problem, the State Council instituted a value-added tax (VAT) in mid-1981 to encourage specialized cooperation among firms.[68] Its regulations stipulated that the manufacturer of each component would pay a tax to the factory that assembled the final product, which, in paying its own tax, could deduct all the taxes paid at intermediary stages. In Wuhan the VAT was tried out first in the machinery and agricultural tools trades because the products of both of them involved many parts. After successful experimentation with those two trades, the tax was expanded in 1982 to bicycles, sewing machines, and fans, all of which were key consumer items being promoted during the readjustment years.[69]

The division of profits was handled in different ways, depending on which combination was involved. *Lianhe* came in two principal forms: those that were "loose" (*songsan*), simply entailing cooperation in sales, purchasing supplies, and exporting; and those that were tight (*jimi*), involving integrated accounting procedures and linked by the nature of the parts they produced and the production processes that marked their work.[70]

According to a Chinese economist writing in the mid-1980's, closely integrated enterprises were to leave a portion of their profits in the hands of the company as a fund for technical transformation. This capital would then serve as the source of the investment that the company would make in the subordinate enterprises. The loose combinations were to negotiate contracts for profit sharing, in which the component firms generally drew profits according to the proportion of overall investment their initial assets represented.[71]

In Wuhan, one example was a merger between a district-level hemp-spinning enterprise and the city Textile Bureau. According to the agreement signed, the factory used its fixed assets in printing and dyeing equipment as its investment base, and the bureau then put up capital equivalent to the value of the equipment.

Thereafter, the funding necessary for expanded reproduction was to be contributed by both sides, with profit calculated according to the investment proportion of each. Apparently even this simple agreement was not easily reached, for the press refers to "necessary consultation" between the two parties before the money needed to assemble new equipment and expand the factory's buildings could be assessed. Ultimately, the bureau was compelled to appeal to the provincial Textile Bureau for financial assistance.[72]

Because of such nearly intractable obstacles, policy designers came to believe that the best way to resolve the clashes of economic interest occasioned by combinations was to leave the economic rights and powers of all the relevant units unchanged in creating any given *lianhe*. This belief was soon coined into an injunction under the slogan "the four unchanges." The four things to be left unaltered were the ownership system and property relations (of the concerned enterprises as a whole), ownership of facilities and equipment, the profit and taxation systems, and the wage systems of workers and staff.[73] This formulation amounted to honoring the sensitivities long since established by the state planning system because it joined firms without touching the extant financial, income division, and distribution systems or the relationships of authority and possession that attended them.

The hope behind this scheme was that maximum cooperation would more likely be obtained if old interests and networks remained undisturbed. Indeed, this was frequently borne out when local authorities assented to mergers only after being promised that they would suffer no loss of profits, assets, or equipment from the enterprises they gave over to such associations.[74]

At the outset in 1980, it was agreed that it would not be possible casually to shift these various relationships.[75] In the course of forming combinations, though, offices with greater clout must have attempted to commandeer the assets of the weaker, resulting in friction destructive to the program. For more than a year later, after many associations had been undertaken, commentaries still were urging, "Whatever associations transcend trades, departments, and districts should be organized loosely in the near term to preserve flexibility and the relative autonomy of the units."[76]

As one source explaining the logic behind this procedure put it, "Each enterprise's original material, technical, and management foundation is different, and the origin of their personnel is different, so there are a lot of complicated problems. We should use different forms [for different *lianhe*]." The discussion went on to suggest that financial power ought not to be "excessively concentrated," at least at first, and that the various enterprises' fixed assets and circulating funds should stay relatively independent, kept separate in accounting even if used jointly during production.[77]

Here, then, was a paradox at the very heart of the policy. A choice was made to rely for compliance on the same mechanism that was bound to keep the rationalization program from working: letting bureaucratic authorities retain their powers over their subordinate firms in the hope that they would then acquiesce in the new arrangements. But their continued rights over these enterprises often obstructed genuine unification. Indeed, the effort at rationalization exposed the fissures and divided interests among levels in very stark terms.

CLASHES CONNECTED WITH VERTICALISM AND UNITISM

Verticalism

The opposition of economic interests created by bureaucratic responsibility and finite funding from one source found concrete expression in a number of case stories told by the press. These stories show that the effort at rationalization revealed cracks in the verticalism which worked so well in achieving other ends. For verticalistic behaviors instigated a battle for resource accumulation throughout the economic system, with those in command at each level wanting to accumulate or save resources for their own level.

City governments sometimes had the power to resist the commands of newly created specialized companies formed at a superprovincial level. A five-province Central South company for motor vehicles had tried to "detach the backbone force from the Wuhan truck trade and [had] thrown out the part that was left." As a result, the company "met local resistance."[78] Obviously the local government fought to hold onto assets that had once accrued to itself. This case certainly suggests that the only associations that could have a chance of working had to be ones that did not essay to wrench assets from their owners, at least not without compensating side payments.

Another press release featured a conflict between Sichuan province and a city under its jurisdiction. Sichuan had tried to organize a bearings company because provincial officials determined that the production of bearings was irrationally scattered throughout the province. This scattering, they reasoned, had led to duplicated efforts, many of which relied on backward technology, causing losses. The new provincial-level company was to counter many of these problems by organizing specialized cooperation on the principle of division of labor.

At first, provincial leaders had thought of transferring authority over locally (city) managed bearings factories to the provincial-level officials, with all the business of all of them—personnel, financial, materials, supplies, production, and sales matters—handled jointly at that level. But according to a writer in the *People's Daily*, "because its [the company's] interests were contradictory to those of the locality, the obstacles were very great." Though the project got under way in early 1978, as late as the end of 1979 it had not yet been put into practice. Ultimately, the only way to obtain cooperation was to establish a union between the province and the localities, with shares and thus profits calculated according to the net worth of the assets that any participating factory contributed.[79] In this case of conflict, in which the city owned assets, the city's customary submissiveness to vertical authority could not be activated.

Another battle between cities and the authorities holding power over them occurred in Shenyang, where a "certain tractor factory" had built a 30,000-plus-meter building around the time of the readjustment. But at that time there was no market for agricultural machinery, and the project had to be dismantled. The Municipal Planning Commission then wanted to use the building to expand its wool production capacity. But, according to a journal article, that was impossible because of "ownership limitations." Here the fight was between the city and a functional bureaucracy: presumably the machine-building bureaucracy at higher levels refused the city's claim to take over the facility.[80]

There was also discord between factories and their management departments (the bureaus) and between factories and the companies set up between the bureaus and the firms to manage factories in the same line of production. Managers at a diesel factory that had been transferred from being directly subordinate to the city machine-building bureau to being subordinate to the bureau's tractor company felt more constrained under the company's jurisdiction than it had before.

In 1979, though the factory should have been able to retain 783,000 *yuan* in profits (it was a key point for experiment in the enterprise autonomy program), the company gave it only 530,000. The company "snatched away" the rest in the name of a slogan that held that "the big factory should take care of the small factory." Seeing its own economic interest as distinct from that of this factory subordinate to it, the company limited the factory's right to select its own equipment. The purpose behind this restriction was to force the firm to purchase a similar product, but at eight times the cost, from another firm within that same company.[81] In another instance dissatisfied units withdrew from companies when the companies took over for joint use the production development funds that had belonged to the individual units.[82]

And yet when the staff in some factories, "having nothing [no production tasks] to do," wanted to reorganize their firms and form unions, their upper-level leadership departments sometimes worked to prevent their doing so. The management bureaus considered the enterprises their "accessory parts" and did not want them taken out of their grasp.[83] This is another case of a disjuncture of economic interest, or goal incongruence, between an organ with responsibilities of supervision and the units it is to manage.

At first glance the local industrial bureau appears to serve functions similar to those served by a cartel or by an industrial (or trade) association in capitalist contexts. All these bodies represent a sectoral interest and amalgamate a number of same-sector firms. All also are to rationalize productive activities among the firms within their jurisdiction and have the capacity to redistribute assets and material supplies. The cartel may take advantage of economies of scale in production and divide up market shares in sales in ways that take the assets and capacities of all individual enterprises in a trade into account as a unit. And the industrial association can coordinate intraindustry adjustment in times of slowdown and recession, acting to reduce risk and shifting resources within that industry from uncompetitive products and producers to competitive ones.[84]

But in China the bureau could not function as an instrument of interest aggregation selflessly serving its subordinate units.[85] For the bureau-to-firm link, though at times a paternalistic and protective one, at crucial moments did not express a shared interest but rather bonded interests in combat. This was the situation when that link became worn down by the separate responsibility and thus the separate economic interest at each level in the bureaucracy. Because each bureau had to answer above its head for a block of lower-level units, its interest was to control the whole set of assets involved in a way that benefited the block as a unit. This process often brought pronounced disadvantages to individual units, rupturing the smooth flow of vertical order and obedience.

Unitism

Just as the sectoral hierarchies and their vertical relationships could be useful for transferring resources but dysfunctional when rationalization was at stake, so unitism had a double edge as well. The atomization of individual plants helped stave off organized, active resistance and so facilitated shifts of resources. But the same proclivity toward insularity made firms try to husband their own resources and to shut themselves off from what might seem to their staff to be potentially costly cooperation with other units. This behavioral pattern obstructed specialization, micro fine-tuning, and mergers, because it drove each separate unit to essay to be "small [or large] yet complete."

In Japan and France, where firms are also characterized by unitism, writers have noted "stubborn resistance to outright mergers." Among Japanese firms, rivalries between directors and officers, lifetime commitments to the labor force, differing wage scales, and beliefs that the two concerns, once merged, would fare less well together than apart all get in the way. Most interfirm agreements there tend to be short-lived, with "evasion and sabotage common, especially from smaller firms eager to grow."[86] One scholar made the point that the "group structure" that marks Japanese businesses "has a crucial external weakness of not permitting cooperation between groups."[87] Another speaks of the "concern of each [firm] about losing its identity" and of status considerations.[88]

Unitism also sparked opposition to the principle of joint investment in modern facilities in France at the end of the war. There, according to John Sheahan, "Pent-up demand . . . did encourage investment, but when left alone it took the form of a multiplication of small firms and a repetition of outmoded techniques," as each separate economic unit strove to perpetuate its own place in the old economic structure.[89] But at least in France and Japan cartels and trade associations could foster cooperative activity in ways that the Chinese bureaus, with their separate administrative interests, could not do.

Many items in the local Chinese press brought the qualms and concerns of the bureaus to life. Some referred to certain comrades in charge of enterprises being "full of anxiety" about the measures being taken in converting their firms' production lines and in forming *lianhe*. Most often mentioned were fears of a firm's being "eaten up" if it was weak, or of having to "cut out a piece of flesh to supplement other people" if it was doing well.[90] When mergers did take place, disgruntled personnel apparently never fully adapted, leading a journalist to comment that in such cases, "the factory joins but the personnel don't, or the people join but their hearts don't connect" (*chang he ren buhe; ren he xin buhe*).[91]

Firms, like the bureaus, were jealous of anything they controlled: "At the mention of raw materials and products, some enterprises immediately think of having sole control over them."[92] Others concentrated on their precious equipment: "Some comrades think, 'Our factory's repair equipment represents several decades of blood collected up; it's managed with ease and it's conveniently used. We can do a thousand things without calling on anyone for help and sleep without worries.'"

Such people allegedly also feared onerous problems because "the parts' varieties are complicated, various factories' models are different."[93]

But the contention was not always directly over material interests. Often it was more about rights and powers. As the magazine *Economic Management* explained, "The problems are usually reflected in powers and interests, such as under whose leadership the merger will occur, who will have power over supplies, production, and sales, how to allocate profits, and how to price parts internally within the merger."[94]

From press accounts it would appear that the most sensitive combinations were those between large and small firms and between state-owned and collectively owned ones. The bigger enterprises were said to "think that small enterprises profit at other people's expense," while some small enterprises felt that *lianhe* amounted to "taking care of the large plants and squeezing the small."[95] Similarly, another article warned that two situations in particular should be avoided: those in which a large factory "eats" a small one and those in which a state enterprise "eats" a collective, or those in которых, to care for (*zhaogu*) firms in difficulty the big factory is made to carry (the burden of) the small one or the state firm must carry the collective.[96]

The local Wuhan paper offered one story of a state-collective merger in the Wuhan textile trade in which the young workers from the two plants were said to be victims of "thought problems." Laborers in the collectively owned plant, conscious of their inferior status, worried about being the target of discrimination and feared that they would be unable to keep up with the more experienced staff from the state-owned firm who were using more sophisticated techniques. Meanwhile, those in the state factory felt "stained" from association with these young people from the less prestigious collective sector.[97]

In all these cases, personnel in firms of all sorts grew apprehensive about erasing the boundaries that they felt had previously protected them from exploitation by other enterprises. The anguish existed regardless of whether the potential partner firm was more successful than their own or less so, bigger or smaller, with better or worse assets, and more or less prestigious. Behind all these anxieties was a deep-seated attachment to the encapsulation among units that had been customary in China for decades.

CONCLUSION

Unlike the two other components of readjustment, prioritizing resources for the benefit of light industry and abandonment of heavy industrial firms, rationalization was not well served either by vertical chains of command and allocation or by the atomization of enterprises. These traits created organizational rigidity because they both reflected and furthered a structure of interests that impeded the specialization that was absolutely essential for rationalization.

Thus rationalization required a fine-tuning that was stymied by the system, with its clearly delineated boundaries and borders and with each supervisory organ and management level charged with a responsibility that spawned repetitive conflicts of interest at every point of contact. The success of the readjustment, then, cannot be judged as a whole, for its separate dimensions were severally served by the Chinese economic system and its behavioral correlates.

The main problem with rationalization was that the mergers on which it depended had to be grafted on an intractable economic system that, in its mode of defining interest, had long estranged the very units the designers of rationalization hoped to bring together. The habits and the forces that expressed those interests proved difficult to adapt to the attempt at economic combination.

Conclusion
Cross-Systemic Implications of the Chinese Case

THIS STORY OF CHINA'S effort at effecting industrial policy demonstrates first that theory developed in the study of one policy type—industrial restructuring—in advanced capitalist countries can illuminate the case of socialist China as well. In this regard it parts from the bulk of comparative social science research which typically confines its analysis simply to groups of capitalist states or to groups of socialist states.

The episode as related in the preceding pages, though, offers more than a transferal of theory from the capitalist to the socialist world. In particular, this study brackets system-specific influences such as party systems and markets and urges giving special consideration to traditions of state-societal relations in understanding policy choice and performance. It asserts that under similar historical and economic circumstances, states with like traditions may succeed in selecting and enforcing essentially the same policy in its largest outlines. Furthermore, given similarities in tradition and timing and in centralized resource control, insights from the experiences that otherwise seemingly disparate states have had in managing the same policy will apply across systems.

Industrial policy, in short, has structural regularities that transcend ownership systems, mode of production, institutions, and political forms, if certain societal traits are present and if a specific conjuncture of historical forces and economic capabilities exists. These regularities find expression in the manner in which concerned parties fight for their interests, defend their privileges, and resist encroachments. In this light, findings from research on economic restructuring in both France and Japan, where the notion of industrial policy was first attempted, have proven relevant to the interpretation that has been advanced in this volume.

In submitting this argument, the book eschews the frequently counterposed terms "structure" and "culture." Instead, its framework is built around an assumption that embedded in any societal order there exist historically rooted, customary modes of interaction between states (personified as political elites) and their publics that do not necessarily continuously obtain in identical formats over time. Still, such modes, even if variously available in different periods, may at certain interludes—especially, as delineated in this study, at times of crisis—be used, capitalized on, and even amplified.

These modes of interaction entail practices and behaviors that may, but need not, be labeled "culture." Whatever they are entitled, their familiarity at both elite and mass levels tends to constrain politicians in their choice of structures and institutions so that they design or adapt some structures over others to cope with new events. The structures (or, one might say, the institutions), once installed, often bear uncanny resemblances to what some may call cultural patterns that existed in that society in the past. Such structures in turn shape behavior, often in ways that at once borrow from and reinforce old patterns.

It is true, of course, that institutions structure behavior, as the "new institutionalists" insist. But any truly operative institutions do not arise de novo in a given society at a particular moment. Instead, leaders pick certain structures and not others. This study shows that the structural patterns Chinese leaders selected—and relied on—to execute their economic readjustment had historical roots, which can be connected to the modes of interaction that occurred during the readjustment process and to its behavioral outcomes.

I have identified pervasive bureaucracy as the chief pattern that accounted for industrial restructuring in China in the late 1970's and early 1980's. This was a bureaucracy which, as of 1979 was yet bolstered by its upper reaches' control over the bulk of societal resources, by a century of state-initiated industrialization, and by a legitimating ideology that justified such state action. Behaviorally, it was a bureaucracy underpinned societally by vertically oriented authority relations, with responsibility taken from above and obedience from below, and it was insulated against concerted action from social forces through an organization of society into insular units unaccustomed to—and prevented from engagement in—horizontal collaboration.

These elements enabled an elite—politicians fixated on a form of economic growth that would at once garner resources for the state while ensuring social stability—to push through a basically divisive policy with minimal reaction from the losers.

If my broader comparative claims are sustained, it should be possible to show that other countries that successfully adopted industrial policy at a minimum shared similar societal patterns, even if they are different from China in many other important respects. These other countries also ought to have restructured their economies during a crisis at a time when a significant portion of their national resources was concentrated in the central government leaders' hands. Moreover, other states that tried but failed to launch industrial policy should lack some or all of these conditions.

To examine this claim, I have undertaken exploratory examinations of the French and Japanese cases in the period just following World War II. For these are the two states that have had the most exemplary experiences with industrial policy, and this was the period when each instituted its own successful economic structural transformations. Parallels between the execution of industrial policy in these countries and that in China suggest the potential utility of drawing comparisons outside the usual systemic models. Briefer material on Britain, Italy, and Germany in the postwar period, where ventures in industrial policy failed or where such policy was attempted but not under the aegis of the central government (as it was in China, France, and Japan), should strengthen the argument.

FRANCE AND JAPAN

Although they were essentially capitalist systems using markets to direct the flow of commodities and capital, and despite their democratic politics, France and Japan in the late 1940's exhibited in very gross terms the features I have associated with the Chinese case in 1979. Each began its industrial policy at a time of unusually enhanced state power; each experienced crises at that point, if of a disparate magnitude and a dissimilar nature from the one in China; each of these states then managed to concentrate resources in the national capital; and each could draw upon traditions of state-societal relations that underpinned bureaucracy and that permitted political insulation for the leadership.

Crisis Perception

Literature about France and Japan in the immediate postwar period draws attention to the same four elements that together composed the Chinese crisis syndrome of the late 1970's: a backward and imbalanced industrial structure, a new relationship with the international economy, a leadership switch, and a national consensus over economic growth as the overriding priority. Granted, the relative emphasis among the four factors varied in degree in the three cases, and the severity with which the individual factors expressed themselves was also different in each place. But the presence of a similar conjunction of elements in all these countries at the time when their leaders adopted industrial policy suggests that our understanding of the choice and conduct of that policy may be connected to these factors.

For all three countries, the threat was economic, though far more so for France and Japan than for China. Still, in the eyes of the political elite then in place in each nation, this economic threat came from what that elite suddenly was prepared to acknowledge as a backward and imbalanced industrial structure. Also like China, joined to this admission was a commitment to a new relationship with the international economy. As in the case of China in 1979, France for decades and Japan during the war had been estranged from that market, to different degrees and for disparate reasons, at the time their politicians decided to readjust.

As new leaders emerged in France and Japan, a decision was reached to build up their often obsolete and war-shaken economies first to join and then to compete with the rest of the industrialized world. For both, a heightened interaction with the world economy was vastly facilitated by the reevaluation of old economic strategies that political shifts made possible. Political factors were more centrally salient for the Chinese than for the French and Japanese. Still, in large structural terms a common opportunity beckoned as successor elites in all three places engineered a new-found national consensus over economic growth.

Just before readjustment was undertaken, both the French and Japanese economies were suffering under retarded development and a serious lack of international competitiveness. Their situations were mightily exacerbated, of course, because each was emerging from a major and devastating war. For their leaders, this scenario spelled a threat of massive, if varying, proportions.

Bottlenecks, capital shortage, and stagnation defined the macro dimension of the economic crisis in the two countries. Japan's dire economic straits—GNP in 1947 standing at only slightly more than half the 1937 level, the index of real income per head at 54.9 in that year as against 100 in 1934–36, 40 percent of the capital stock destroyed—were largely war-related.[1] The crisis was also manifested in the war-induced dreadful daily living conditions for the people, who suffered from severe food shortages, inflation, and unemployment.[2]

In France, some of the causes predated the war. For most of the century and a half preceding the war economic growth had been slow. Besides, France had not recovered from the Depression of the 1930's when the war began. On top of this already weak foundation, France had to contend with the ravages and demolition wrought by the war. Nearly one and a half million people had perished; the value of the capital equipment destroyed amounted to an alarming double of the GNP of 1938. Acute raw material shortages, depleted inventories, and capital scarcity drove industrial production down to a mere 20 percent of the 1938 level.[3]

At the micro level, both countries had traditions of unitism in their typical management practices not unlike those in China. This meant that there was in both countries a prevalence of more or less self-sufficient firms unconcerned with specialization or larger-scale cooperation.

With regard to the international economy, both of these countries, like China in 1979, experienced what could be termed a "catch-up crisis." It quickly became clear that only by restructuring could they become full-fledged participants in the world market. Japan's recent period of near autarky had kept the nation largely ignorant of developments in international technology not just during the war but also throughout the preceding period of military preparation.[4] For France the war followed a long-term separation from the world market because it had remained a self-contained agrarian economy into the twentieth century.[5] But wartime isolation contributed toward keeping France detached from technical advances abroad.[6]

Both France and Japan also smarted under a sense of having been ostracized from the international community as a result of their respective roles during the war. The feeling of being pariahs that both experienced heightened their isolation even as it made them anxious to assuage wounded pride. As their time of isolation came to a close, both France and Japan received a crucial boost from U.S. aid. Nonetheless, politicians in both countries became obsessed with a "quest for rank" and an "urge to catch up"[7] that in its intensity matched China's in 1979.

Besides the presence of this economic sense of threat, an element of opportunity was attached to the experience of crisis in France and Japan, as in China. Changes in leadership enabled newly installed politicians to attempt something novel. For the big business elites that had managed economic policy in the recent past in France and Japan were at least temporarily ostracized, having been associated with militarists, military defeat, and collaboration with the enemy.

For both, the economic bureaucracy and its officials provided continuity. In Japan, the Supreme Commander for the Allied Powers (SCAP) was forced to rely on the preexisting economic bureaucracy because this was the only segment of the presurrender government it had left untouched. Also, Japanese private industry had no way to recover on its own without the funds, raw materials, and energy sources that were being disbursed through the state. Thus management of the economy became largely the preserve of this officialdom.[8]

When private sector assets in France were nationalized, the state bureaucracy, placed in charge of these resources, saw its power expand. Other factors that contributed to the new clout enjoyed by the civil service included the lack of stable political leadership, weak parties, and a newly enlarged definition of the state's role in the economy.[9]

The new sense of consensus in France derived explicitly from a widespread feeling of economic crisis. Some maintain that the war's destruction actually had a "purging effect" (perhaps in some ways parallel to the effect of the Cultural Revolution), leading to a change of values that released energy for economic advance. This shift came about as dissatisfaction with all that had gone before produced a universal attitude favoring economic expansion.[10]

In Japan, there was a "new conservative hegemony" by early 1949 that went beyond party label; in the first half of the 1950's the Socialists shared the goals of their usual rivals, the conservatives, for economic independence, full employment, and modernization. Indeed, the economic plans of the left opposition at that time were little different from those of the government.[11]

In their designs for reducing the role of the market, Japanese and French policy makers benefited from a diminished public faith in market mechanisms in their countries and a consequent willingness to experiment with national economic planning. In Japan this distrust of capitalism had begun with the Depression and the ascendancy of the militarists in the early 1930's; in France, at the same time, a commonly entertained belief had held that the capitalist system then in force was wasting resources, causing demoralization, and crushing the economically defenseless.[12]

By war's end, the experience of the intervening decade had reinforced a predilection for national economic planning and nationalization of key industries and credit in both countries.[13] These prewar biases positioned these peoples well for the institution of state-led growth, a form of economic management for which their own histories had prepared the way.

Resource Concentration

The most immediate enabling factor for both France and Japan in their adoption of industrial policy was the sudden accumulation of national wealth in state-owned or dominated institutions.

In Japan, the way was cleared for policy changes, at least at first, by the discrediting and weakening of the old economic and financial elite, which occurred in the context of a generalized reaction against the prewar rightist system[14] and under the aegis and with the encouragement of the U.S. occupation. In this climate, the government was able to benefit from the divestiture of the *zaibatsu* capital groups (the control networks of the holding companies were dismantled; most of the directors of big business were replaced).

U.S. aid to the government obviously enhanced the Japanese state's power over national financial assets. Still, it was Prime Minister Yoshida Shigeru who worked out the plan for stimulating industrial production, who defined economic reconstruction as the outstanding national goal, and who pushed through a program of priority production that was at the heart of the country's industrial policy.[15]

In France too there was an attitude of antagonism toward big business just after the war, especially manifested in a wish to lay sanctions on those in the business world who had collaborated with the enemy. Nationalization of their holdings was used as a means of cashiering these capitalists, just as China's socialist transformation dispossessed those merchants and industrialists still left in the country after the flight of the Kuomintang at the end of the Chinese civil war.

For both France and Japan the period surrounding the end of the war marked a peak in the level of state control over the economy, one never matched before or since. Indeed, it has been said that the role of the state in France was suddenly doubled at this time as compared with what it had been under the Third Republic. Some have put the turning point at 1944, when new nationalizations and a commitment among policy makers to modernization, management, and planning arose, sparked by the need for centralized allocation of the dangerously scarce resources of the nation.[16]

New funds in the hands of the leaders of the French state paved the way for the central government to direct the national economy.[17] The nationalization of major credit institutions put the state in a position to provide two-thirds of all investment financing directly from public funds or through state-owned credit institutions between 1946 and 1949.[18] In addition, in the late 1940's the state had access to Marshall Plan monies which its politicians and bureaucrats used to fund projects of their choice.[19] During their short stint in power just after the war, the communists and socialists supported these programs of nationalization and the installation of a planning system.

In Japan, the intensification of government also began during the war, with the growth of the role of the bureaucracy, especially once political parties were dissolved by the militarists in 1940. Just after the war, SCAP eliminated the military at the same time it dismantled the *zaibatsu*, thereby throwing command over the economy fully into the lap of the administration.[20] Interestingly, here too the socialists enjoyed a brief period of political control, and, as in France they worked for an intensification of state control.

Dissolving these giant "industrial empires"[21] involved shifting their securities to the Ministry of Finance, which, in Japan as in France, gave the state the wherewithal for dominating the economy.[22] By collecting large amounts of *zaibatsu* stock and stock in outside companies held by nationalized companies, the government came into control of from one-third to one-half of paid-up capital in all Japanese companies.[23] State power over key banks also played a role.[24]

Thus both France and Japan began their industrial policy at a point when the state possessed the wherewithal to control and channel public investment funds, even though they were not socialist states.[25] The main distinction in the case of China was one of degree and extent of control, since essentially the entire Chinese economy fell under state ownership after 1956.

State-Society Relations: Bureaucratic Underpinnings

In France and Japan, as in China, state involvement in the economy had an important historical precedent. Industrialization first got its start under government initiation in all three countries. The roots of French state intervention can be traced to Colbert's selective stimulation and subsidies in the seventeenth century and to the protective mercantilism of that same era. From this foundation grew up two traditions of state involvement in the economy, one paternalistic, the other entrepreneurial.[26]

After industrialization was initiated, the state in France later took on the job of financier, initiator, and promoter of industrialization. The centers of the modern French economy developed from state concessions through the extension of state capital, guarantees, and subsidies and in state corporations and monopolies.[27] The traditional practice, vastly intensified after the war, was for the government to promote those industries deemed crucial to the state. This function was accepted by French business classes, and its long history honed the skills and set the precedent for economic management at the government level that was entailed in postwar planning and industrial policy.[28]

In Japan, beginning decisively in the Meiji period, the government embarked on an economic policy that would later lead to modern industrial policy.[29] Though for its first decade in power the new regime served as the founder and owner of modern industry, this venture became too expensive to continue. In 1880 its leaders began to sell off the enterprises on favorable terms to the private sector. Thus was initiated a partnership of government-business collaboration that continued with government bailouts and support to industry in the recession and Depression of the interwar years. Indeed, such a partnership has gone on, if in varied forms, to the present.[30]

As in France, the Japanese tradition was one of government participation oriented toward nourishment, for growth and help, more than toward control so that business came to expect intervention in a common quest for national development.[31] Thus both Japan and France were fully prepared for guidance by the government following the war.[32]

France and Japan share with China an ideological heritage that stresses the organic nature of the state, a view of the national whole as a sort of superfamily. In both the Japanese and Chinese languages the written symbol for country contains the word for family as one of its two characters; in France, too, various family metaphors have been used to express the notion of the overall general interest. For instance, in the French political lexicon there are references to the state as the head of the household, the state sheltering its children, and the state as a community living like a family.[33] A conception of a single general interest represented by

Conclusion 231

the state harks back to the *ancien régime* and Louis XIV.[34] Political virtue in France historically was to reside in patriotic commitment; other forms of interest were, as in China, viewed as illegitimate.[35]

This background in belief proved useful in launching industrial policy in France after the war. For many of those in charge of the conduct of economic policy agreed that the purpose of economic progress should be to reconstruct French power and not to enrich individuals. With the creation of the *économie concertée* in the Monnet Plan, a shared responsibility for economic growth joined bureaucrat with businessman. Even so prosaic a document as the national plan appeared to those connected with it as a manifestation of a Rousseauian general will.[36] In the words of three analysts, a "statist ideology motivated the action" after 1945.[37]

Authors writing on Japan have pointed to a similar syndrome. Here, too, statism had its underpinnings in a vision described by the term *kokutai* that saw the entire nation as one family, headed by the emperor.[38] The notion of *wa*, meaning harmony, customarily served as the appropriate model for integrating the society and the nation. In this country as well, the government has been driven by a sense of duty to promote growth in the national interest, and company managers link the success of their own firms to the larger well-being of the Japanese nation.[39] Following the war, there appeared among the populace what seemed to be a "national mobilization of a united people for economic goals."[40]

In addition to centralized resource control after the war, a history of statist involvement in industrialization, and similar legitimating ideologies, a bureaucratic tradition is also strong in France and Japan as it is in China. Japan has been categorized as "a highly bureaucratized society";[41] French authority patterns have been found to resemble those in China.[42] These bureaucratic heritages were if anything bolstered in both countries in the period when industrial policy first took shape.

In France a strong bureaucracy had commanded policy under the Third Republic (1871–1940). But the pattern can be traced much further back in time: a well-developed administrative system was present in Napoleon's designs. Some see a significant degree of centralization present in the French state even before the Revolution[43] in an autonomous state bureaucracy instituted to serve French kings and reinforced by Napoleon.[44]

A tradition of executive supremacy in Japan could be traced back to the seventh century A.D. In more recent times, samurai ex-warriors turned into a "service nobility" playing a bureaucratic role during the Tokugawa peace of the seventeenth through mid-nineteenth centuries.[45] Strong administration certainly had its modern incarnation after the Meiji Restoration, when the statist constitution of 1889 at least initially placed no limits on central state power. And with parliament weak, the agency of that power was the strong bureaucracy. Moreover, the interwar and World War II years saw a gross enhancement of state power, as the militarists in command ran an increasingly absolutist state.[46]

In the immediate postwar period, bureaucratic power grew because of the ineffectiveness of political forces, in both France and Japan, but in different ways. Especially in the period under review, neither the French parliament nor the Japanese Diet played an economic role of any consequence.

The Fourth French Republic (1946–58) saw weak parties and shifting coalitions, which, continuously embattled over their mutual alliances, deadlocked parliament. Deals among weak parties resulted in the formation of 23 different cabinets in a period of only twelve years. Such instability and ineffectiveness deprived the legislature of any role in the design of the national plan—as one observer put it, gaining influence in parliament was useful mainly for obstructing, not for making, policy.[47] The outcome of this near impotence was that power devolved to the bureaucracy and its ministries.[48]

In Japan, similarly, the early postwar Diet was too weak to serve even as a channel for the views of minority groups. Instead, it acted as more of a "sounding board" or "national forum" to legitimate the work of the executive branch. At that time (and indeed thereafter as well) it had next to no weight in the process of hammering out the national budget.[49]

As a consequence, here too legislating fell to the executive branch and in particular to the great ministries. The policy process thus became one in which executive and legislative powers were fused. This was and remains a process in which, especially after the creation of the Liberal Democratic party (LDP) in 1955, the dominant party has been closely bound to the administration. After the war up to 1955, with the exception of only one brief period, the LDP's "conservative forebears" played the same role.[50]

But whereas in France parliamentary instability handed power to the administrative agencies,[51] in Japan political stability did not strengthen the role of political forces in policy. Rather, that stability simply permitted the bureaucrats to work in a climate of certainty, for the most part without unexpected disruptions.[52]

Thus, in France and Japan, as in China at the moment of economic restructuring, historical legacies of a state that had taken an interventionist role in the process of industrialization and a belief system that legitimated that intervention worked together to heighten the role of the bureaucracy at a time when massive quantities of material resources had come under state control.

State-Society Relations: Political Insulation

In both Japan and France long-standing behavioral patterns on the part of the populace shored up bureaucratic rule as they did in China. In those places, too, small, exclusive social units have habitually drawn boundaries around themselves that sharply constricted their connections with others. Accordingly, in these societies unitism facilitated the state's effort to penetrate society. In both of these countries the self-enclosed family unit has served as a model[53] that influences both the orientation of the firm and the parochialism of the locality.

In France, the traditional autonomy of administrative units is called *cloisonnement*;[54] John C. Campbell (following Robert Cole) points to its basis in *uchi* in Japan, the sense of being "inside together" which informs the strong commitment to groups there. As in China, this bias has often limited the inclination of unrelated collectives to combine in opposition.

Both French and Japanese firms, like those in China, have typically been functionally comprehensive, which has kept them largely self-reliant. What the French speak of as "polyvalency" the Japanese refer to as the "one-set service." In all these cases, the same bias toward diminishing risk through internal diversification is evident.[55] Nakane makes the very interesting point that the hostility between unconnected groups that is part of unitism in Japan reduces the power of society against the state, which then facilitates the vertical transmission of governmental commands while obstructing horizontal unions joined in confrontation against the state.[56]

Historically in France and Japan tight bonds to locality reinforced the tendency of small work units to encyst. Though apparently this local exclusivity is not so prevalent today, Japanese scholarly treatment of local administration and regional politics still puts much emphasis on localism.[57] In their volume *Politics in Japan*, Bradley Richardson and Scott Flanagan explicitly link localism to what I call unitism and maintain that "trust of the proximate has strengthened local, community-based organizations,"[58] which they relate to modes of political expression: "The strongest expression of a citizen's participation in politics often takes the form of a citizens' movement organized around a single local community. . . . In contrast to this strong expression of localistic interests, other kinds of interests that cut across communities . . . are not as likely to engender citizen participation."[59]

The seminal discussion of French localism in politics is Kesselman's study of consensus in the commune; others refer to this proclivity in the organization of pressure groups and in the small firms that typified French industry throughout most of the period of French industrialization.[60] Because of this generalized atomization of society, horizontal groupings with political aims have been fragile historically in France and Japan as well as in China. In France, for instance, intermediary associations were viewed as detracting from a Rousseauian general will.[61] Throughout French society there coursed "a long-standing distrust of corps intermédiaires."[62] Even though such bodies existed, their memberships were unimpressive, their actions unstable, and their bases localized. In addition, the unit-boundedness discussed above meant that even within broader associations, individual component units retained a separateness that rendered truly effective combination not totally nonexistent but rare.[63]

The Japanese attachment to small groups made it very difficult historically to form and maintain voluntary groupings.[64] In more recent times, though interest groups have existed, there is no legacy of a theory of pluralism to legitimate their activities.[65] Richardson and Flanagan state:

> While the trust of the proximate has strengthened local, community-based organizations in Japan, the distrust of the distant and unfamiliar has impeded horizontal mobilization of socio-economic strata and interests.... This village consciousness has weakened the strength and effectiveness of nationally organized interests and peak associations, such as labor federations, consumer interests, and environmental groups.... There may be outbreaks of violence by unions, students, or other radical groups, but these rarely touch the mass of society and often do not even stir to action other groups with similar interests.[66]

Both France and Japan, it is true, have been subject on occasion to what have been called "surge movements," protests sparked by dissatisfied splinter groups.[67] Labor unions, probably the most significant horizontal grouping for the purpose of this study, existed in both countries after the turn of the century. But their organizational weakness, their co-optation by paternalistic management, and their systematic exclusion from policy making by the political elite deprived them of any real power or even influence.[68] Strikes did occur in both countries in the late 1940's, the period of interest here. They were, however, short-lived and unpopular, costing the communists in both places loss of a role in politics, at least in part because of these communist parties' association with the strikes.[69]

Industrial paternalism has been a prominent feature of the verticalism that has marked economic organization in both French and Japanese firms historically.[70] Beyond the firm, paternalism finds larger expression in vertical chains of command in these societies generally. Commentators on both France and Japan link social solidarity along vertical lines to the feudal past of these countries and see it as an important source of the discipline that has been behind industrial change there.[71] Confucianism's emphasis on obedience and on dependence on authority has influenced Japan as well as China.[72] This verticalism, like unitism, grows out of the paternalistic family patterns characteristic of these three societies. Writers on all three have taken note of the premium people in these cultures put on security over other values; and it must be security that disposes its seekers to submit to superiors.[73]

Along the same lines, as in China, French and Japanese political patterns echo this reliance on and cultivation of superiors. In each country, lower-level administrations and their officials, as well as managers in work units, must appeal above for much of their capital, on matters concerning personnel, and for approval of their decisions.[74] Thus in Japan, the *ringi* procedure for endorsing documents at each level up the hierarchy is omnipresent,[75] in a manner reminiscent of China's ubiquitous pressures for *pizhun* alluded to in Chapter 2.

In Japan and France, then, just as in China, strengthened states after World War II built upon particular traditions in their historical repertoire. In doing so they were able to rely for their empowerment in part on weakly organized societies made up of collectivities that were enclosed horizontally but porous to influences flowing from above. This quick review of the immediate postwar climate in France and Japan and of salient features in the historical interaction of society and state in these countries points to broad commonalities between them and China at the time that each introduced its program of economic restructuring from the national government.

This study intentionally sets aside for the purpose of analysis the many systemic diversities that exist among these countries. But the presence in three countries where such restructuring took place of several generically similar key factors—crisis conditions, centralized concentration of resources, a strong and coherent bureaucratic apparatus, and a weakly organized society— each of which would obviously have a strong bearing on the capability of a central government to reorient industrial activity, must buttress my claim for the centrality of these factors, both in the Chinese case and generally. At a minimum the existence of these features in all three places creates a strong case for listing them as necessary if not sufficient conditions for the selection and execution of industrial policy.

ITALY, BRITAIN, AND GERMANY

The case for the significance of this syndrome of four traits for industrial readjustment is strengthened by considering three other countries where governments at one time or another attempted economic restructuring but in which the effort failed. To make this point in the most parsimonious way, I will operationalize these traits by picking out the dimensions of them that are both must salient and most relevant for the study of industrial policy.

Thus I ask if their projects of restructuring were taken during a *crisis* by considering whether they were begun following a time of economic disaster and whether new elites had just replaced previous elites who had been discredited. Second, I inquire into whether the bulk of national *resources* and capital were *concentrated* in the coffers of the central government at the moment of trying to engineer a transformation.

For the third trait, I look at the nature of *bureaucracy* in the country in the period when the attempt was undertaken. And for the fourth, I ask not about all forms of horizontal, voluntary associations but, in particular, whether a robust *trade union structure* allowed labor to speak for itself in policy councils. We will find that for Italy, Britain, and Germany hardly any of these conditions were satisfied.

In the discussion the reference point(s) for each country is the particular time(s) in the postwar period when the government in each made an attempt to carry out planning and an industrial policy. These periods are the following: for Britain, the early and mid-1960's and the early 1970's; for Italy, also the 1960's; and for Germany, several different junctures, including the immediate postwar period, the early 1960's, and the early 1970's.[76]

Crisis Perception

Italy took up the issue of industrial restructuring and attempted its planning not in the immediate aftermath of war but in the early 1960's. The aim of the program was principally to deal with regional disparities and to correct sectoral imbalances that had become manifest after a period of high growth, not one in which stagnation had signaled crisis to politicians. As it happened, these readjustments did not occur. One reason was that the same business elites who had benefited from the development of the 1950's were still powerful enough to block any significant structural change. Indeed, the right wing of the Christian Democratic party, the Liberals, and the peak business confederation, Confindustria, were in strong opposition and found support for their stance even within the Ministry of Industry and Commerce, whose bureaucrats agreed that state controls should remain limited.

In Germany after the war, official policy actually favored a reduction in the power of the state in the economy, in a renunciation of Nazi strategies. True, there was a program in the 1950's that worked to refurbish the basic industries, but no comprehensive government plan organized this effort. All that was called for at that point was reconstruction on the foundations of a preexisting industrial structure. Thus one can say that the sense of generalized economic crisis that spurred activity in France and Japan was missing, even though targets for recovery were announced by the government so that the basic industries, along with exports and housing, received tax benefits, subsidies, and cheap loans.

Britain also let the late 1940's and 1950's go by without the state restructuring industrial organization or behavior. Although the late 1940's would have been an appropriate time for engaging in reassessment and restructuring, opposition from both trade unions and business associations prevented any such move. As distinct from France, British business organizations and their leaders were still sufficiently powerful in this period effectively to prevent the execution of the National Economic Development Act of 1947.

Later, planning was introduced in 1961 in the midst of a financial crisis, set off by speculation against the sterling, but not in the spirit of an urgent response to economic failure. Another notable difference from the French and Japanese cases was the British proclivity truly to seek consensus from all the major concerned parties, labor included. The outcome was that industrial policy ultimately had little if any impact on the overall structure of industry. Similarly, Harold Wilson's 1964 creations—a Department of Economic Affairs and a National Plan—remained essentially stillborn. National monies, to the extent that they were applied to planned growth, were largely used nonselectively in both the early 1960's and the 1970's to fund undifferentiated subsidy programs or for regional aid, instead of in the service of a major state-led program of industrial reorganization.

Thus in none of these three countries were plans to engage in industrial policy accompanied by the amalgam of conditions that presented themselves to newly ensconced Chinese, French, or Japanese elites. In none of these cases was a brand new national mood, joined to a sense of significant economic danger, forged by altered elites.

Resource Concentration

In Italy the state played a role in economic direction mainly through cooperation between the central bank, state enterprises, concerned business groups, and party factions. In general, the disbursements that issued from this union did not contribute to any coherent state control. As one analyst observed, "extensive state activities" took place in Italy, "but they were insignificant as adjuncts of a national policy."[77] True, the central bank's control over the flow of Italian credit and investment funding enabled it to provide large amounts of investment funds to public firms. But these firms then went on to use their capital in part to patronize the dominant party rather than to shape or even to participate in a broad national policy.

The German state concerned itself more with matters of overall policy, but for a different reason was not the central source of development finance. Instead, commercial banks took charge of the industries in which they had an interest, organized large cartels, and mapped out long-term projections to which they compelled individual firms to conform. The usual pattern was for the bank in question to intervene between the state's Reconstruction Loan Corporation (an investment bank with public funds at its disposal) and any given firm requesting an investment loan. Even the publicly owned banks escaped much supervision from the federal authorities.

In short, the German public authorities and the banks worked together to carry out the national recovery programs of the 1950's. Schemes were later introduced to rationalize individual sectors (such as for steel in 1962–63 and 1971–74), but they were engineered almost entirely by three large banks and not by the state.

Among these three countries British firms were the least prone to solicit assistance from the state or even from the banks. There enterprises are far more inclined to finance their activities through internally generated funds and equity, following old traditions that grew up with the small businesses of Britain's early industrialization. In addition, financial capital is separated from the state much more than it is in any of the other countries under consideration, and the state essentially lacks any means of controlling the direction of private investment. British banks were never nationalized as they were elsewhere, nor is the Bank of England tied to the government.

The governments of Italy, Germany, and England, then, for disparate reasons and to varying degrees, lacked the power over crucial resources that allowed the Chinese, French, and Japanese states to initiate industrial shifts.

Bureaucracy

None of the three countries under examination here enjoyed the prominent, powerful state bureaucracy deeply engaged in purposeful economic management that is found in France or Japan. The Italian administration for nearly a century had been characterized by decentralization and malcoordination when industrial policy was considered. Its fragmentation and complexity have rendered it unable not only to direct a unified state program but even to execute legislative decisions faithfully. When industrial policy was attempted, the bureaucracy was not fit to administer it so the various plans were handed to separate state corporations to manage. Related to this ineffectiveness, members of the Italian state bureaucracy have not been perceived by the public as possessing integrity or as worthy of trust.

In Germany the problem was not so much weakness in the bureaucracy but that the bureaucracy was in many ways irrelevant. For the heavy role played by separate banks placed their officers in the position of administrators of economic planning, thereby sidestepping the official administration.

British bureaucracy is not inherently weak, incoherent, or irrelevant, but it has been hostage to a tradition of self-restraint in government and to long-held attitudes that militate against state economic intervention and guidance. It has been termed, paradoxically, "powerful but immobilist."[78] Thus, in line with public expectations that civil servants' powers must be minimal, when economic development committees were created in the experiment with planning of the early 1960's, representatives from the government departments sat in the bargaining sessions simply as junior partners. This is in distinct contrast to French civil servants, who held dominant seats on the modernization commissions composed to thrash out the details of the French plan.

Instead of essaying to impose a plan, the British state used its public servants to consult with and to persuade delegates from the business and labor worlds in a pattern that has been labeled "toothless tripartism."[79] The generalist training of British bureaucrats also distinguishes them from the technically prepared officials who staff the offices in the French and Japanese administrative apparatuses.[80]

Thus we find that the condition of an activist, responsible, and capable bureaucracy, which proved so crucial in France, Japan, and, in different ways, in China, has been missing or rendered more or less irrelevant to restructuring efforts in Italy, Germany, and Britain.

Labor

The exclusion of labor from the policy-setting arena and the consequent ability of the directors of economic reconstruction to proceed, insulated from any significant pressures from the most adversely affected groups, was another factor that united the successful cases. But only Italian policy makers among the three abortive cases kept the trade unions from participating in and at times interfering with the process of potential industrial change.

The German state since the war has treated labor with more respect. This better treatment appears in the legalistic guarantees given to workers in their collective bargaining negotiations, in official enforcement of the outcomes of these negotiations, and in a "tacit tripartism" that characterizes wage settlements.[81] Furthermore, the centralization that marks German unions means that, unlike in Britain, agreements reached between the politicians and the workers are more binding because they can generally be enforced.

British unions were notoriously potent in the period when planning was attempted in Britain, in the 1960's and 1970's. That nation's historical respect for the voluntary association of individuals shored up the position of the trade unions in this period. As a consequence, they were powerful enough at that time to stymie any tampering with the industrial structure, which, they suspected, might somehow threaten their industrial relations system. Indeed, the unions often acted as veto groups whenever industrial policy was on the agenda. The bureaucracy's habit of seeking consensus and compromise on industrial as on other policy heightened the power of the private sector of which workers were still a prominent component in the days before Margaret Thatcher. This was an important reason for the failure of industrial restructuring in Britain.

This brief exercise in comparison yields simple but stark conclusions: in countries where new elites encountered crisis of a sort that made them place economic recovery and reorientation at the top of their agendas; where these elites had somehow come into the control of the bulk of national funds; where bureaucracies are competent and perceived as the natural arbiters of economic strategy; and where groups in opposition are excluded from the deliberations, industrial policy has proceeded, and structural change has occurred.

Where some or all of these conditions were missing, this kind of policy has not been realized though the intention to realize it might have been present. My more thorough treatment of France and Japan situates these factors in longer-term traditions of state-societal interaction. But even a more cursory review that underlines their absence in other places can suggest the centrality of this set of factors.

THE QUESTION OF TIMING

An important question that arises from this research concerns the relationship between this syndrome of facilitating conditions—especially those pertaining to long-standing traditions of state-societal interactions—and their time-boundedness. Just because there have been historical traditions in the nature of the bond between state and society, traditions that in recognizable configurations have reappeared in different eras, we cannot conclude that what was possible for one regime to accomplish can, simply on the basis of these traditions, necessarily be achieved by all Chinese regimes, or by all French or all Japanese regimes at all junctures. What, then, is the linkage between tradition and circumstance?

In the case of China, when the communist leaders took control of the country in 1949, they built upon and amplified Chinese traditions that were useful to their own purposes. Thus they massively strengthened the old bureaucratic controls over society through a much more thorough penetration by the party of social nodes and networks than any past regime had accomplished; they enhanced state involvement in the economy to a degree never attempted by past regimes; and, using the modern modes of communication at their disposal, they propagated an organic, all-encompassing ideology justifying the role of the state and the collectivity perhaps along the lines of what previous rulers may have dreamed of but far beyond what they were equipped to realize.

Moreover, in the group-based social order these new elites fashioned, severe restrictions on both geographical mobility and autonomous political activity checked the formation of horizontal bonds between units and among members of different units to a far greater degree than any historical arrangements had managed to do. By the same token, that multifaceted dependency, which encapsulated work and residential units prompted in the populace, trained citizens to look upward for security, support, and succor, but tutored them not to dare to reach outward beyond their units. All of these behavioral patterns had historical analogues, but the precedents from which they derived were sharply exaggerated under the communist regime after 1949.

As of 1979, despite the ravages of the Cultural Revolution, the greatly diminished faith in the party and its belief system that that disaster had wrought, and the consequent diminution of the party's ability to command and control Chinese society, at least the core of the old party order still remained and could be refurbished. At that time it was yet possible for party politicians to use their bureaucracy as a tool of rule and still within their power to exercise significant, if by no means complete, direction over the flow of national resources and so to shape economic policy. For their part, the overwhelming mass of the people remained largely locked within their units at that point, responsive (if cynically so) to their group leaders' regulations, fearful of overtly expressing dissatisfactions, and certain to be quickly quelled if they did.

In the years that immediately followed, however, the elite consensus on economic growth as the overriding priority did not simply give birth to "economic readjustment," the plan to shift resources from heavy to light industry. It also disposed most of the political elite to agree on a strategy of development that has gone by the title "economic reform." This approach was premised on the notion that decentralizing financial and material resources and economic decision-making powers to lower levels of administration and to families and enterprises would stimulate higher levels of productivity than a centralized, more comprehensively planned control of resources could do.

The corollary of this decision was that many materials and products now found their transfers not through administrative fiat decreed in Beijing but in the marketplace. At the same time, a far greater amount of funds for investment than before made their way into lower-level bureaucrats' hands. Localities and firms in possession of materials began to hoard them for local gain, and economic agents in charge of scarce supplies speculated in them.

Accordingly, it became more and more difficult to maintain resource concentration at the center and so to ensure the allocation of assets for state-designated sectoral priorities or even for so-called key-point construction projects. Under these conditions, vertical patterns of ensuring implementation faltered, as heightened clashes of economic interest among levels replaced what were formerly more often fatherly liaisons.

Once these old linkages loosened, political insulation could no longer be guaranteed. The decentralization of controls over portions of what was once the central budget (as projects funded from "extrabudgetary" monies accumulated at lower administrative levels sprung up) and the momentum of marketization that accompanied this decentralization combined to melt the freeze in which prices had been locked for decades, going far beyond what central policy makers had intended. As inflation mounted, the unitism that paternalism within the firm had fostered began to crack apart, and managers were no longer in a position to provide the security on which their flock of employees customarily had counted.

Political passivity among workers accordingly gave way to protest as the political economy undergirding the behavioral orientations of the later 1970's and early 1980's shifted.[82] Thus, we can say that the inclinations toward verticalism and unitism that were strong enough in the early 1980's to effect the readjustment had been nurtured by the old state planning system; indeed, they had supported the realization of the plan's dictates. Once the controls of the plan contracted, so did the efficacy of these inclinations.

Thus the "reform"'s decentralization precipitously unraveled the already more vulnerable central authority that had just, somewhat precariously, reestablished itself in the wake of the Cultural Revolution. In short, in the service of a changed economic ideology, in the early and mid-1980's the state gave away much of the economic power that it had just begun to recoup after 1976.[83]

The outcome was that the conditions that had shored up state power and made the readjustment of 1979 possible all began to totter uncertainly. As a loosened state plan permitted quasi-market forces beyond the reach of the central organs to gather force, the interlocked sinews binding the bureaucracy together began to disintegrate into separate, often corrupt, deals and bargains.

Central policy—and, by extension, the state's effort to play a directing role in the economy—became less able to call forth a sure response from below.[84] When this occurred, ideological pronouncements sounded as a sham. At the basic levels, alternative economic opportunities for individuals appeared and gained a measure of legitimacy, with the result that in the factories and in the villages, the old work units lost at least some of their ability to bind individuals vertically and, consequently, to check their formation of horizontal associations.

Growth as the overriding priority, then, not only forged a consensus that ushered in the readjustment. By promoting a decentralization of financial power in the reforms, it also drastically undermined the regime's capacity to draw upon the very traditions of central power and its underpinning which had made the readjustment possible in the first place.

For industrial policy, the implications have been stark. As Chinese critics analyzing their own system lamented in late 1989: "The reasons we have not been able to change the structure of industry in all this time are as follows: 1) Regulation by planning is no longer as effective as it was 30 years ago. Targets mapped out in the state plans sometimes fell through because financial resources of the central government were exhausted."[85]

Crisis conditions in various forms may reemerge. Portions of the elite in the central government may even be able to coalesce for a time around one definition and one solution. But without the substantial concentration of national resources they and their predecessors enjoyed in the late 1970's, the tasks of reactivating responsiveness in the bureaucracy and of insulating their policies against resistance have proven—and should continue to prove—more formidable and prohibitive as time goes on.

REFINEMENTS TO THEORY SUGGESTED BY THE CHINESE CASE

This concluding chapter began with a claim that this study does more than simply apply comparative political economic theory on industrial policy to the Chinese case. First, it emphasizes the historical roots of what I call necessary behavioral patterns, patterns that combined with crisis and resource concentration in the Chinese and several other cases to make industrial policy possible.

More broadly, it has shown that states of certain types have a dynamic that supersedes the economic system: at critical moments these states, whether capitalist or socialist, can effect similar policies. For these reasons, this research encourages the observer to think in terms of history and of comparisons based on large economic problems and their solutions. The problems in question are, clearly, ones confronted across the systemic spectrum, and so they beg for analyses that rest on factors more general than type of economic system.[86]

Each of the empirical chapters added specific examples. The chapters on crisis and consensus (3 and 4) made explicit the double-edged nature of crisis by analyzing separately the economic threat but also the political opportunity that came together in China in 1979 (and also, as this chapter has shown, in France and Japan just after the war). It also underlined the centrality of perception because in the Chinese case the conditions then defined as crisis derived from long-term systemic difficulties which had existed for decades. They had been recognized far earlier by some observers but had never previously been so dramatically labeled by the leadership as a whole, and thus could never before be addressed.

The lesson here is the mutual interdependence of consensus and crisis. What was required first was that the leadership configuration be radically altered so that a consensus could be forged. Most crucially, elite turnover occasioned by the death of Mao Zedong in 1976 permitted the new elite to admit openly that the economic structure had to be reordered. Once Mao's death allowed for a freer airing of views, it became evident that there was significant agreement among the elite on the need to confront serious economic problems. Conversely, consensus or at least near consensus was necessary before the situation could be categorized as a crisis. Leadership switch, in providing political opportunity, then, is a crucial component of crisis, broadly understood.

Thus it is not just, as Gourevitch discovered, that "economic crisis leads to policy debate and political controversy."[87] Economic crisis can also produce policy consensus, whereas broad consensus on political style and overall strategy can further the awareness and promote the admission of economic crisis.

The fifth chapter, on policy making, challenged a widely held view about the political economy of socialist systems. This view holds that the planning at the foundation of Stalinist economies and the special dependence of these systems on heavy industry render them too rigid to be able to undergo more than the very minor and incremental alterations in allocations that individual bilateral bargains can engender. Even if the switch from priority treatment of heavy to light industry was relatively limited in time, this study has shown, this episode does illustrate the possibilities for change in alliance patterns at central and local levels in one socialist state.

It has also exposed the ultimately passive stance of pleaders of any sort under communism (as well as under capitalism) at times of crisis, economic restructuring, and redistribution. Lobbying is not an adequate concept for describing the role of interests at such points. Communist systems, then, like some democracies, are open to major shifts under particular conditions, and at such times power is not monopolized by any one interest, even one that was privileged in the past. Its possession is instead determined by the leadership.

The chapters on implementation also offer new insights into the processes that attend industrial policy. Chapter 6 demonstrates the mutual reinforcement that can take place between verticalism and unitism and the potential for change that these two behavioral patterns that often seem to block change can in fact provide. Where incentive structures encourage local elites to fulfill any commands—even new and altered commands—from superiors, hierarchies of power can act as the mechanism for transformation. For instance, when a significant quantity of resources remains under the control of those at higher administrative levels, normally conflictual bureaucracies within localities coveting these resources are often inclined to cooperate to meet new demands, through joint cost sharing and coordinated supplication.

Chapter 7, on the reactions of the abandoned sector, its coping strategies, and central-level policy makers' attempts to contain opposition and preserve social stability, argues that those whom Keeler, writing about France, called corporatist clients need not necessarily fatally obstruct policy. Instead, that chapter presents material indicating how a responsive yet paternalistic bureaucracy can cushion change and provide sufficient insulation against resistance that unpopular policies can proceed apace. The habits that shore up bureaucratic practices, however—verticalism and unitism—do have their limits. The eighth chapter exposes their weakness in handling the finer dimensions of industrial policy, where micro rationalizations must replace the simpler macro action of reallocation.

Taken as a whole, this volume on China's brief but successful economic readjustment of 1979 to 1982 suggests the value of comparing across systems. The body of the study is structured around concepts derived from literature on capitalist systems, and it demonstrates that this literature can indeed offer fresh insights to the student of a socialist society. But the Chinese case yields findings that refine some of the truisms in the broader literature as well.

Institutions typically tied to specific systems cannot by themselves wholly account for the achievements and pitfalls encountered in selecting and executing industrial policy. Instead, broader patterns of state-social interactions and circumstances of timing can stretch across systemic boundaries. Once we see this, it becomes clear that recognition of these patterns and circumstances can throw light on crucial conditions that states usually not paired together for analysis may share.

Reference Matter

Abbreviations

The following journals and newspapers appear in the notes and in the bibliography. Most of the newspaper titles appear only in the notes; the bibliography lists just the citations for journal-length articles. I have noted the place of publication for publications issued abroad. The titles of journals listed only once or a few times are not abbreviated in the notes or in the bibliography.

AS	*Asian Survey*	JJGL	*Jingji guanli* (Economic Management), Beijing
BR	*Beijing Review*		
CBR	*China Business Review*	MC	*Modern China*
CD	*China Daily*	POC	*Problems of Communism*
CJRB	*Changjiang ribao* (Yangtze Daily), Wuhan	PR	*Peking Review*
		RMRB	*Renmin ribao* (People's Daily), Beijing
CQ	*China Quarterly*		
FBIS	Foreign Broadcast Information Service, *Daily Report: China*	SCB	*Zhongguo Renmin Gongheguo Guowuyuan gongbao* (State Council Bulletin of the People's Republic of China), Beijing
GMRB	*Guangming ribao* (Bright Daily), Beijing		
		SHKX	*Shehui kexue* (Social Science), Shanghai
GRRB	*Gongren ribao* (Workers' Daily), Beijing		
		SKDT	*Shehui kexue dongtai* (Social Science Trends), Wuhan
HCXX	*Hubei Caijing Xueyuan xuebao* (Journal of the Hubei Finance and Trade Institute), Wuhan		
		XHYK	*Xinhua yuekan* (New China Monthly), Beijing
HQ	*Hong Qi* (Red Flag), Beijing	ZM	*Zheng Ming* (Contend), Hong Kong
I&S	*Issues & Studies*, Taipei		

Notes

Chapter One

1. See Brodsgaard: 38–41 for an exposition of this strategy of growth and its theoretical foundation.
2. Ma and Sun: 1; and Zhou Shulian: 29.
3. N.a. 1982e: 40.
4. State Statistical Bureau 1986: 34.
5. Lardy 1984b: 5.
6. N.a. 1983: 41.
7. Field: 750.
8. Kueh: 439.
9. This is from an article by Li Yue in *RMRB*, May 30, 1988, p. 5, translated in *FBIS*, June 14, 1988, p. 33.
10. *RMRB*, May 25 and 30, 1979. Later, the term "the six priorities" came into use. The Jan. 8, 1980, issue of *RMRB* published the State Economic Commission's command to allocate these to light, textile, and handicraft firms. The six priorities were listed then as: (1) raw materials, fuel, electrical power; (2) measures focused on tapping potential, reform, and transformation; (3) capital construction; (4) loans; (5) foreign exchange and rights to import technology; and (6) transportation. See *RMRB*, Aug. 19, 1985, p. 2, for a slightly different listing of these priorities.
11. This is published in Tidrick and Chen: 1, 2. The book is the outcome of a study conducted jointly by researchers from the World Bank and from the Institute of Economics of the Chinese Academy of Social Sciences.
12. Johnson 1986: 200, 201.
13. Johnson 1988: 110 also makes the point that "industrial policy is by definition distorting of the allocative efficiency that is theoretically available from an unfettered market."
14. Fong: 295, note 2.
15. Zysman 1977: 12.
16. See Johnson 1987: 145.

17. Japan Economic Institute of America: 3–4.
18. Komiya: 208.
19. Sandholtz: 112.
20. This is in Deyo. The following discussion and quotations are found on pp. 230–32.
21. See, for example, Rueschemeyer and Evans: 51.
22. This is in sympathy with the approach Charles Tilly takes on p. 47, where he speaks of his edited volume's "emphasis on mechanisms," which, he explains, "draws attention away from the forms of states . . . toward the implications of alternative public policies."
23. Dyson and Wilks is one example; another is Barfield and Schambra; Katzenstein 1978a is also in this category; the individual chapters in Evans, Rueschemeyer, and Skocpol also look at same-system states in tandem when they undertake concrete comparisons, as do Brada and Montias on Czechoslovakia, Hungary, and Poland. These are only a few recent examples.
24. Thurow: 7, 15, 81–82, 212.
25. Brada and Montias: 384, 389.
26. Nove 1983: 95.
27. Skocpol: 12.
28. See note 20.
29. Skocpol: 12.
30. Katzenstein 1978c: 14–17.
31. See Lindblom: 7 and 11 for the two quotations and for his statement of purpose.
32. See pp. 18–19.
33. Zysman 1977: 16.
34. On the Soviet Union, see Conquest, Nove 1969, Hanson, and Linden. For Poland, see Montias, and Gamarnikow. On Hungary, see Robinson. For Czechoslovakia, Jancar.
35. For only a few works in the vast body of literature on this subject, see Bornstein, Brus, Schroeder, Brada and Montias, and Comisso and Tyson.
36. This argument is elaborated in Connor: 309–10.
37. Deyo: 230.
38. Poznanski: 280.
39. For a treatment of typical tactics used, see Schroeder.
40. Bornstein: 108.
41. See the table in Hanson: 93, which shows the investment for Industrial Group B (consumer goods) simply shifting between 5 and 6 percent of total investment over the years 1937 and 1964, despite the publicized and debated reform platforms and budgetary alterations. Even under Malenkov, who was deposed as premier in 1955, explicitly for his focus on consumption and neglect of heavy industry, plans in-

volved very little actual reduction in capital goods production, according to Conquest: 27, 251. And Montias: 65 says that political turmoil in Poland during the period of his study resulted in annual changes in the levels of gross investments so that no consistent application of policy was possible.

Chapter Two

1. Gourevitch: 17, 19.
2. See Wilks and Dyson: 1 and 4–6; and Dyson: 28.
3. Gourevitch: 22.
4. See Ma 1983: 20, 22, 24.
5. See Ma 1982: 3–4.
6. See Reynolds 1984 and Harding 1984.
7. My concepts of "orientations" and "historical repertoire of behaviors" resonate with the treatment of political culture in Richardson and Flanagan. On p. 163, they state: "Culture conditions behavior by providing certain resources that may be drawn upon as a new problem emerges and by setting certain limits on what kinds of solutions to the problem will be compatible with social sensibilities and expectations. As the environment changes, new institutions and practices are called forth to meet new needs. Such institutions and practices represent true innovations that do not duplicate traditional practices but rather emerge as an amalgam of traditional elements adjusted to modern structural requirements and situational exigencies."
8. The best source on this is Zhongguo Shehui Kexue Yuan.
9. In a recent essay, Naughton points to what he considers to be central planners' weak control over investment resources by the end of the 1970's. But even while noting this, he admits that, "before reforms, financial control over one-third of investment had been decentralized, and only two-thirds of investment was disbursed directly through the government budget." Obviously, though, much can be done by top leaders capable of commanding even only this still sizable proportion of national finances. See Naughton 1989: 5.
10. My *Chinese Business Under Socialism*: 132 summarizes this form of partnership and contains references to key works of scholarship that outline it in more detail. See also Rowe 1984b, which describes the changing relationship between public and private sectors in Hankow in the late nineteenth century, when officials shifted from interference and exaction to consultation and nourishment of commercial activity.
11. On the operation of the salt monopoly, see P. T. Ho.
12. Rawski: 67–68, in assessing the development of factory industry

after 1895, judges that, "despite the blunders that bedevil all efforts to master radically new technologies, the outcome of officially sponsored industrialization projects appears modestly successful." He points out that foreign merchants and the Chinese mercantile community also played a role in a process joined by modernizing officials within China's central and provincial governments. Rowe 1989: 185 describes the activism of Viceroy Zhang Zhidong after arriving at his post as head of the provinces of Hunan and Hubei after 1889. Rowe states that "a new age of radically expanded direct state initiative began."

13. See Feuerwerker: 9–30. Rowe 1984a discusses one key region's experiences during this period, under the leadership of Governor-General Zhang Zhidong, one of the most important of the official self-strengthening bureaucrats. As Feuerwerker emphasizes, this system was essentially a regional one and was tightly bound to provincial bureaucrats' direction.

14. See Coble.

15. See Nathan: 49; and Munro. The Munro quotation is from an early draft of Chapter 5 of this manuscript; the concept is developed in the book's fifth chapter.

16. For the specifically fiscal operations of the imperial bureaucracy, see Zelin. This book illustrates well the tight interechelon relationships that made the bureaucracy run.

17. Meyer: 325–26; and Hough 1977: Chapter 2, especially p. 68.

18. The original study setting out the hierarchy of administrative and party power in China is Barnett 1967.

19. The major statement documenting the more informal dimensions of this system is Lieberthal and Oksenberg 1988. These traits are spelled out in Chapter 4.

20. See Burns; and H. Y. Lee.

21. Johnson 1982: 44, 315 notes that a crucial function of the Japanese political system is to "fend off the numerous interest groups in society which if catered to would distort the priorities of the developmental state." Zysman 1978: 265 states that "an elite wishing to direct . . . the course of industrialization . . . must insulate itself from or repress the political reaction to dislocations inevitably provoked by industrialization."

22. Li Xiannian, introducing the policy of economic readjustment in a central work conference on Apr. 5, 1979, spoke of the idle urban labor force totaling some 2.3 million workers: "If this is not handled appropriately, something could be triggered at any moment that would seriously influence social stability." He argued for a labor-intensive growth

strategy because labor power that is not "arranged" would only lead to new difficulties. This speech is in Zhonggong Zhongyang Wenxian Yanjiu Shi 1982. See 1: 115, 123. I return to this speech in Chapter 5.

23. As in note 7, I am using a concept of cultural orientations sympathetic with the treatment of political culture in Richardson and Flanagan: 163, in which they state that culture provides resources that can be drawn upon when new problems emerge and that it sets limits on acceptable solutions.

24. Munro shows the influence of the image of the family in Chinese thought. Ch'u details how the family and its organization have been at the foundation of much of the Chinese legal tradition. And Dittmer 1987: 54 calls the "unit" that organizes Chinese society today "the functional substitute for the extended family."

25. The best treatment of this concept and its practical operation in China is Henderson and Cohen.

26. See Cheng: 148–50, 154. 27. L. T. White: 156–57.
28. Chesneaux: 118. 29. See Rowe 1984b: 330–34.
30. Shue: Chapter 4.
31. I have dealt with the present problem extensively in 1984b. A more concise version was published in Solinger 1987.
32. Nakane: 102.
33. Morse: 21.
34. Strand: 154.
35. This point comes from the work in progress of Elizabeth Perry.
36. See Esherick.
37. Naquin and Rawski: 16.
38. Henderson and Cohen: 36n.
39. Walder describes how the communist regime's "network of political organization . . . makes worker resistance and even informal coordination of action difficult." See Walder: 95.
40. From a report by Yan Jiaqi, director of the Political Science Institute of the Chinese Academy of Social Sciences, given to the Beijing Theoretical Workers' Conference and translated in *FBIS*, May 20, 1988, p. 16.
41. Walder 1983: 60.
42. See note 32 above.
43. Walder 1986: 248 speaks explicitly of enterprise paternalism.
44. Henderson and Cohen: 140.
45. Strand: 148. 46. Hershatter: 139.
47. Johnson 1982: 146. 48. See Wylie: 221.
49. Writing on Japan, Passin connects paternalism to repression. See Passin: 102.

50. Dittmer 1987: 55–56 writes of the security functions of the Chinese unit.
51. In many hours of interviewing Chinese economic bureaucrats I frequently encountered references to this process.
52. Pitts: 276–77.
53. Hoffmann 1974: 133–34.
54. This term was coined by Kornai.
55. Beginning in 1985, the Chinese began to experiment with the concept of bankruptcy and in late 1986 passed a bankruptcy law which went into effect on Nov. 1, 1988. But only a tiny handful of firms really "went bankrupt," as I explain in Solinger 1989.
56. For instance, see Liu: 10, which says that the centralized management system of the first three decades of socialist rule made the enterprises "wait, rely, and demand."
57. Ibid., p. 8.
58. On this, there are references in Ehrmann 1957: 379, 429; Kesselman: 113–14; and Zysman 1977: 64, 65, all on France. For Japan, Johnson 1982 discusses protection by cartels and governmental elimination of risk for firms in trouble.
59. Zysman 1977: 3, 198.
60. See Anchordoguy: 4–5.
61. See Calder.
62. On these points, see Hoffmann 1963: 99; Kaplan: 20, 32; Shonfield: 129; and McArthur and Scott: 245, 250.

Chapter Three

1. Premier Zhou Enlai introduced the notion of a "four modernizations" program first in 1964 and then again at the Fourth National People's Congress in 1975. But the program was more or less shelved until Mao died in late 1976, after which it steadily picked up momentum. The program's four prongs were industry, agriculture, science and technology, and the military.
2. Simon: 43.
3. This document was one of three on economic development prepared under Deng's aegis at this time, all of which were labeled "poisonous weeds" by the Gang of Four. This one is "Some Questions on Accelerating the Development of Industry," and it is translated along with the other two in Chi: 201–95.
4. The Maoist concept of "self-reliance" is explicated in Feeney: 267–68.
5. Hua's government work report is in PR, no. 10 (1978), pp. 7–40. The sole mention of foreign trade is in one paragraph on p. 24.

6. This work report is in *BR*, no. 27 (1979), pp. 5–31; the section on foreign trade is on p. 18.

7. Xue 1981: 77. This period is discussed in Lieberthal and Oksenberg 1986: Chapter 5; C. J. Lee: 47–53; Cumings 1984: 242; Feeney: 269–71; and Kokubun.

8. Several analysts have pointed to the running down of oil deposits as crucial to the developing financial crisis at that point. Perkins 1986: 50–51 speaks of a growing energy shortage, noting that petroleum output, which had grown at an average annual rate of 20 percent a year between 1962 and 1978, grew only 2 percent in 1979 and fell in 1980. "The immediate solution to this growing energy shortage," he concludes, "was to shift emphasis to sectors that made less use of energy, notably consumer goods." Cumings 1984: 242 credits the peaking of oil production by the end of 1978 as an important factor in what he calls the "critical shift" to the market strategy at that time. And Ishikawa: 12 explains the discontinuation of imported plant projects after 1978 as owing to the large amounts of energy they needed.

9. Two-way trade doubled from U.S.$14.7 billion in 1977 to U.S.$29.3 billion in 1979. Foreign currency reserves dropped to less than U.S.$500 million. See Feeney: 269.

10. See Zhonggong Zhongyang Wenxian Yanjiu Shi: 173. Chen also mentioned, however, one potential difficulty of a portion of this approach, i.e., that the United States, Europe, and Japan had protectionist policies that could limit their imports of China's textiles.

11. The relevant points were well made by two of my students in their papers. Browne wrote, "Once [China] decided to open up to the world economy, [it] was vulnerable to competition and in the early years of [its] second industrialization . . . [its leaders] knew that their industrial sector would need help to compete." And Melnick stated: "The most essential awakening factor which spurred [China's] industrial policy was the arrival of international forces. . . . Circumstances forced [it] to examine [its] role in the international economy as a direct reflection of domestic structures."

12. The author was Zhang Peiji, then deputy director and vice chairman of China's International Trade Research Institute of the Ministry of Foreign Trade. See. p. 118.

13. For instance, Ma 1982: 3–4, which mentions China's economic backwardness in comparison with the developed world. *RMRB*, in its editorial of Feb. 20, 1979, blames China's "lack of international competitiveness" on the Gang of Four, which, roughly speaking, really referred to foreign trade in Mao's day. Gu Mu, one of the top leaders most con-

sistently supportive of China's open-door policy, wrote in 1985 that China had "missed a golden opportunity" during the Cultural Revolution when the world was witnessing rapid economic and technological development and other less-developed nations were drawing on foreign funds and technology to boost their economies (in *FBIS*, Oct. 10, 1985, p. K1).

14. This was a major shift in perspective. Not only had Mao stressed the importance of self-reliant development from the late 1950's onward, but the outside world had been viewed as more of an obstacle to growth than a potential source of aid. For instance, in Ma 1983: 19, he referred to imperialism's blockades and provocations and to threats and sabotage from the Soviet Union. Among other things, he noted, these outside influences forced the country to spend more on national defense, and so proportionately less on development, than might otherwise have been possible and desirable.

15. From *RMRB*, Feb. 5, 1988, p. 2, as translated in *FBIS*, Feb. 19, 1988, p. 18.

16. Perkins 1988: 622.

17. Chong: 25.

18. Huang: 98.

19. By that point the decision makers had access to such statistics as the following, which no doubt influenced their thinking: for each *yuan* spent on light and textile industry, the state receives 52 cents in profits and taxes, whereas for each *yuan* put into heavy industry, the return is only 6 cents. This is in *RMRB*, May 30, 1979, translated in *FBIS*, June 4, 1979.

20. Ma 1982: 8–9. Ma states that from 1958 to 1978 the speed of economic development (considering agriculture and industry together) dropped from an average rate of 14.6 percent per annum during the period 1949 to 1957 to 7.6 percent and that over the same period the national income's average annual speed of increase dropped from 12.7 percent to 5.4 percent. But Ma 1983: 19 also stated that industrial growth had increased at an average annual rate of 12.9 percent over the 32 years from 1949 to 1981, faster than that in the economically developed countries. This paradox highlights the perceptual and definitional dimension of the concept of crisis noted at the outset of the last chapter.

21. Ma 1983: 41.

22. These statements come from, respectively, Field: 743 and Yeh: 691. Field mentions work stoppages, shortages of raw materials, and disruptions of transport as causes of this serious impact.

23. One such analysis is in Dernberger: 146.

24. Ma and Sun: 1; and Zhou Shulian: 29. An unexplained discrepancy in the data is that *BR*, no. 29 (1985), p. 15, states that heavy industry accounted for 56.9 percent in 1978, not 57.3 percent.

25. *RMRB*, Oct. 25, 1979.

26. Liu: 196–97.

27. This is from a report Xue Muqiao made to the Central Party School. See Xue 1982b: 4.

28. In Chapter 1 of my book *Chinese Business Under Socialism*, I trace the ideological foundations in Marxism for this attitude toward the market and the market's perceived connection with capitalism, profit seeking, and the creation of income differentials.

29. *CD*, Sept. 10, 1984, and Ma 1982: 8.

30. Ma 1982: 32.

31. Ma 1983: 36.

32. This point is noted in *FBIS*, Dec. 5, 1979, p. L7; in Ma 1983: 67; and in Donnithorne: 12.

33. Song Jiwen 1981a: 12; and *RMRB*, Mar. 29, 1979. For the Shanghai material, see Shanghai Economic Forum Secretarial Group: 80. For Hubei, see *FBIS*, Nov. 28, 1979, p. P7.

34. Sun: 28.

35. Shanghai Economic Forum Group: 81.

36. Commentator 1980: 4.

37. Tang and Ma: 630. In addition, Wong 1986a: 589 explains that, during the Cultural Revolution, through sizable agricultural procurements the state left at lower levels very little of the raw materials needed for local light industrial production. At the same time, the state permitted local-level development of the "five small industries," all of which were in the heavy industrial sector. These policies maintained a pattern in which heavy industry dominated in investment within each individual province.

38. *GRRB*, Nov. 12, 1979. For taxation rates in some light industrial trades, see Wong 1985: 270. Watches, for example, were taxed at the rate of 61.1 percent, bicycles at 39.8 percent, and cotton textiles at 32.3 percent, while farm tools were taxed at 3.1 percent and iron ore mining at only 1.6 percent.

39. Lardy 1984a: 849.

40. Lin Zili: 92. Lin notes on the same page that a similar problem existed within the textile trade, which did not have enough cotton to occupy the machinery. See also Ma 1983: 37–38.

41. Hubei Province Statistical Bureau Comprehensive Office: 24. The exact proportion given for fixed assets in metallurgy and machine building was 65.1 percent of the total.

42. This information comes from Premier Zhao Ziyang's report on the Sixth Five-Year Plan, delivered in Dec. 1982 and translated in *FBIS*, Dec. 14, 1982, p. K21. See also Ma 1982: 13 and Ma 1983: 34.

43. Liu: 209. Liu made the same point a year earlier, in *RMRB*, Apr. 13, 1979, p. 3, where he noted (as translated in *FBIS*, Apr. 30, 1979, p. 5) that "shortages of power, coal, raw and semifinished materials in recent years have caused many enterprises to operate at less than full capacity and factory hands and machinery to lie idle." Also see Editorial Board: 3.

44. Ma 1983: 45.

45. Ibid. 24–26.

46. Xue 1981: 78.

47. These points are made in Ma 1983: 37; Qiu and Huang: 329–32; and Yan 1980b: 34.

48. This analysis is in *RMRB*, Oct. 9, 1981, translated in *FBIS*, Oct. 19, 1981, p. K9. For a more concrete discussion, see Yan 1980b: 35, which describes the machine-building industry as having "three smalls": the proportion of high-precision processing equipment, the amount of high-efficiency automatic equipment, and the amount of forging and pressing equipment.

49. Lin Zili: 88–89.

50. Qiu and Huang: 326.

51. Xue 1982a: 23. Other interesting analyses of this phenomenon are in *RMRB*, May 18, 1980; and Sun and Qin.

52. Qiu and Huang: 319.

53. "Dangdai Zhongguo" Cong Shu Bianji Weiyuanhui 1984: 298.

54. Wu: 8.

55. *FBIS*, May 29, 1979, p. L6.

56. Qiu and Huang: 326–27.

57. Zhou: 38.

58. The city's gross value of industrial output ranked fourth among the cities of China in the early 1980's.

59. Rowe: 1984a.

60. See Li and Wang.

61. This comes from Naughton and Solinger, esp. pp. 1–11, which were written by Naughton.

62. In *CJRB*, June 1, 1979, pp. 1, 2.

63. Jin 1983b: 7. Hubei's light industry in 1978 represented 45.8 percent of the gross value of industrial output. This figure is in Wang Zhengxing: 37. Of course, there were provinces such as Heilongjiang and Liaoning, where the proportion of heavy industry was much greater than in Hubei. In Liaoning, light industry accounted for only 26.7 per-

cent of gross value of industrial output (GVIO) in 1978 (*CD*, May 22, 1985, p. 3), and in Heilongjiang it represented 29.3 percent in that year (Yang Yichen: 5). But the Northeast was an exceptional case. In Guangdong, a province much more similar in economic structure to Hubei, light industry accounted for 58.6 percent of GVIO in 1978 (P. N. S. Lee: 18).

64. *CJRB*, Jan. 3, 1981, p. 1.
65. These points are made in Jin 1983b: 7; and in *CJRB*, Mar. 31, 1981, p. 1, and Apr. 14, 1981, p. 4.
66. *CJRB*, July 4, 1979, p. 1.
67. Lu and Huang: 31.
68. *CJRB*, Aug. 3, 1982, p. 4.
69. *CJRB*, July 12, 1979, p. 4 (except where otherwise indicated, most of the analysis on the textile trade immediately following is from this source).
70. *FBIS*, June 12, 1979, p. P4.
71. *CJRB*, June 17, 1979, p. 1.
72. Interview with officials from the city Textile Bureau, Nov. 14, 1984. In interviews in Nov. 1984 at individual plants, management personnel at the No. One Textile Mill in the city reported shutdowns because of electricity shortage of twenty hours per week before 1979; the No. Two Mill experienced stoppages one-third of the time.
73. Xu and Yan: 12; and *CJRB*, Aug. 19, 1979, p. 2.
74. Jiang: 24.
75. *CJRB*, June 15, 1980, p. 1.
76. *CJRB*, Sept. 4, 1979, p. 2; Dec. 7, 1979, p. 1; and Apr. 2, 1981, p. 2.
77. Xu et al.: 9–11.
78. For Wuhan, the figure is from *CJRB*, July 12, 1979, p. 4; the national figure is from *FBIS*, June 4, 1979, p. L5, a translation of an article in *RMRB*, May 30, 1979.
79. Interview with the city's Foreign Trade Committee, Nov. 14, 1984. The same figure is in *CJRB*, Sept. 4, 1979, p.2. *CJRB*, July 12, 1979, p. 4, states, however, that in 1964 textiles represented 76 percent of the total purchases for foreign trade and that by 1977 that figure had declined to 41 percent.
80. N.a. 1982b: 42.
81. Hubei Province Statistical Bureau Comprehensive Office: 26.
82. *CJRB*, Aug. 8, 1979, p. 2.
83. *CJRB*, Dec. 18, 1980, p. 1, and Dec. 7, 1979, p. 1. This was true nationally as well; see Lardy 1984a: 849.
84. The figure 4,000 is given for Wuhan in the Shanghai paper *Shijie*

jingji daobao [World Economic Report], May 28, 1984; a year earlier another source (Jin 1983a: 59) claimed that 5,157 varieties of machine-building products were produced in Hubei in 1983.

85. Ye: 19.
86. Hubei Province Statistical Bureau Comprehensive Office: 26. This figure may be compared with the 54.6 percent of machine tools in use nationally in 1977. See Zhou: 38.
87. See *CJRB*, Nov. 11, 1984, and an article on the Wuhan Machine Tools Factory in *CJRB*, Feb. 29, 1980, p. 1.
88. *CJRB*, Nov. 8, 1979, p. 2.
89. *CJRB*, Nov. 24, 1979, p. 1.
90. Jin 1983b: 7.

Chapter Four

1. As Bachman: 308 notes, Deng revealed at a late 1980 Party Central Work Conference that Chen had been in charge of financial and economic affairs since the Dec. 1978 Third Plenum of the Eleventh Party Central Committee and that it was he who had proposed the policy of readjustment.
2. Hao and Duan 2: 699.
3. Li's speech at this meeting is in Zhonggong Zhongyang Wenxian Yanjiu Shi bian 1: 111.
4. This is from a speech Xue delivered to a discussion on theoretical questions in the national economy's comprehensive balance, entitled "Readjust the National Economy, Do Comprehensive Balance Well." See Xue 1981: 77.
5. Barnett 1986: 2.
6. See Ma 1983: 45, 48–49.
7. This argument is made in *RMRB*, Feb. 20, 1979 (an editorial). Apparently it needed repeating more than once. Another appearance, among many, of the same justifications, is in *RMRB*, May 25, 1979.
8. As some publicists held, workers were also consumers, who, once their material needs were better met, would be stimulated to work harder for the cause of modernization (*GMRB*, May 20, 1979).
9. The unemployment problem in the late 1970's is summarized in G. White 1987: 369–70. He refers to pressure from job seekers and their families, when during the Cultural Revolution rusticated youths swarmed back into the big cities. This pressure was expressed in petitions, protest marches, attacks on government offices, and occasional violence as well as acts of delinquency in the years 1978–80. Riskin: 265 cites estimates for 1979 of at least 10 million urban unemployed, representing about 9.5 percent of the urban nonagricultural labor force of 104

million at that time. Zuo: 73 refers to "several ten's of millions of unemployed" in 1980. Walder 1984: 36 notes that 43 percent of those given jobs in 1980 were assigned to collective enterprises. Such firms were almost invariably a part of the light industrial sector.

10. Dong: 99.
11. This is from a translation of a *HQ* article which appeared in *FBIS*, May 15, 1979, pp. 8–9.
12. *RMRB*, June 26, 1979.
13. As quoted in C. J. Lee: 58. Gu made this remark in Nov. 1980.
14. This was the Third Plenum of the Eleventh Central Committee, which reversed the Mao-era concentration on class struggle and shifted the focus of the party's work to socialist modernization.
15. See text in *PR*, no. 52 (1978), pp. 11–12 and 13.
16. These arguments appear, among other places, in Li's Apr. 1979 speech in Zhonggong Zhongyang Wenxian Yanjiu Shi bian: 119; in *FBIS*, Feb. 26, 1979; in Special Correspondent: 4; and in an article dated Apr. 1979 in Liu: 7–8.
17. Fang: 622.
18. See C. C. Lin for careful documentation of this effort.
19. Ibid.: 4.
20. Schurmann: 203–4, 360.
21. Translated in MacFarquhar, Cheek, and Wu. See pp. 185, 186, 187.
22. Yang and Li: 203. Thanks to Thomas P. Bernstein for bringing this article to my attention.
23. As summarized in Ho and Huenemann: 3–4.
24. Chen's approach at the time of the Eighth Party Congress, in the Great Leap era, and in the early 1960's can be found in the documents collected in Lardy and Lieberthal. Chinese publications containing Chen's published speeches are cited in Bachman: 298.
25. The speech to this effect is in Mao 1974, 2: 258–59. Thanks to Thomas P. Bernstein for bringing this to my attention.
26. Lieberthal: 330–31.
27. Xue 1986. In these years Mao removed himself from the conduct of daily affairs, an absence whose outcomes he bitterly resented, as the diatribes from the Cultural Revolution make evident.
28. Naughton 1987: 4. On p. 19 he cites "overall figures" which show that in the Third Five-Year Plan, 52.7 percent of national investment went to Third Front projects.
29. See C. C. Lin: 27; Brodsgaard: 38–43; and Nove and Nuti: 13, plus their chapters 1 and 6.
30. See Commentator 1981a: 89; and Ma 1983: 85.

31. I use this term to refer to those who favored readjusting the economy in the 1978–81 period in Solinger 1982.

32. Mao's authority was still so great in the early period after his death that the new policy of readjustment, when first introduced, was justified by references to statements he had once made in favor of "comprehensive balance" and to his recognition of the need at times for switches in economic line (in *RMRB*, Jan. 12, 1979); for rectifying the proportions of investment going to agriculture, heavy and light industry, respectively (*RMRB*, Mar. 29, 1979); and in support of the idea that agriculture and light industry must be strengthened in order to develop heavy industry (*RMRB*, June 3, 1979).

33. This speech is in Mao 1977: 267–88. The part on sectoral proportions is on pp. 268–69.

34. These quotations of Mao's are collected in C. C. Lin: 28.

35. This comes from the intellectual newspaper *GMRB*, Jan. 3, 1980, translated in *FBIS*, Jan. 24, 1980, p. L18.

36. These various phrases and comments come from *RMRB,* Jan. 29, 1981, translated in *FBIS,* Feb. 17, 1981, P. L10; Liu: 178, 213; and Zuo: 41.

37. See Bunce.

38. Ibid.: 141, 159.

39. See Harding 1986: 50, in which he makes the point, summarizing a body of literature on communist successions, that there are two distinct types of successions. In the first, relative stability has not necessarily entailed policy changes; in the second, into which he says China after Mao fits, more protracted struggles and purges have led to more drastic changes in policy. But successions have involved more bitter conflict and disunity at other times and places than in post-1976 China. See, for example, Conquest on the immediate post-Stalin period and Robinson on the early and mid-1950's in Hungary. In those cases it was more difficult to reach a consensus solid enough to undertake significant and lasting initiatives.

40. Tsou: 148–49.

41. This process is spelled out in Dittmer 1982: 33–35.

42. Neither was the consensus total in either France or Japan at the time they reoriented their industrial structures. Ashford describes the intentional exclusion from power of the more extreme political parties of the left and right in France in 1951. See Ashford 1982: 32; and Pempel 1982: 55.

43. See note 4, above.

44. See Cumings 1984: 238–39, where he lays out three different

models of political economy. In his categorization, political economy I, "accumulation in command," reigned from 1976 to 1978 but was overtaken by political economy III, "the market in command," in 1978. See also Solinger 1982.

45. Chang notes that this faction had as its ally the "Whateverist Faction" of Wu De, Chen Xilian, Wang Dongxing, and Ji Dengkui. See Chang.

46. C. J. Lee: 47. On the role of the Petroleum Faction at this time, see Ju: 10, which states that the Petroleum Faction controlled the economy from 1976 to 1978. C. J. Lee: 52 also notes that it was "widely assumed that members of the Petroleum Group with Hua Guofeng's support" were the "chief advocates" of the Ten-Year Economic Development Plan worked out during 1977 and presented in Feb. 1978 at the First Session of the Fifth National People's Congress. This plan featured high growth rates, extensive foreign plant purchases, and investments in heavy industrial construction. Lieberthal and Oksenberg 1986: Chapter 5 discuss the activities of this group in this period. See esp. pp. 190–92 and 204–7. Another good study of the politics of this period is Kokubun.

47. Xue 1981: 78; C. J. Lee: 47.

48. Hao and Duan: 700.

49. Lieberthal and Oksenberg 1986: 204; and C. J. Lee: 46. See Cumings 1984: 243 for a list of the other factors he counts as responsible for the critique.

50. C. J. Lee: 47.

51. Cited in C. J. Lee: 50.

52. One instance when leaders in charge felt proud appeared in *RMRB*, Oct. 25, 1977, in an article quoting Yu Qiuli as stating that from June 1977 the monthly gross value of output had exceeded the highest average in the past. Yajima: 42 noted contradictions in the media so that sometimes excellent production results were cited during that period and at other times production was presented as still being in a state of stagnation.

53. As quoted in the translation of Deng's speech to the Dec. 1980 Party Central Work Conference. See Teng.

54. See Xue 1981. 55. In Hao and Duan: 700.
56. Ma 1982: 6. 57. Xue 1981: 81.

58. See Solinger 1982: 1250–52; and C. J. Lee: 50. Hua's speech is in *BR*, no. 27 (1979), pp. 5–31, and these quotations are on pp. 11 and 12; Yu's speech is in *BR*, no. 29 (1979), pp. 7–16, and his words on the prior two years are on p. 7.

Chapter Five

1. With regard to the "lobbying" interpretation of allocatory politics, Shirk has written of the process of policy formation and change as an outcome of influence peddling by coalitions, or as a "contest between . . . industrial ministries." See Shirk 1985: 195–221, esp. p. 197, where she presents her concept of the "Communist coalition"; and also Shirk 1983: 24, where she speaks of a contest between heavy and light industrial ministries in which the machine-building trade enjoyed proportionate advantages. The bargaining model is presented in Lampton 1987a and Lieberthal and Oksenberg 1986.
2. Lampton 1987a: 16.
3. These quotations come from Lampton 1987b: 14 and 18.
4. Lieberthal and Oksenberg 1986: 139.
5. See Shirk 1985: 197 and 204–7.
6. The zero-sum dimension to this two-party conflict is one it shares with industrial policy, a policy entailing disinvestment in Western polities and in Japan. As Reich, probably the primary publicist of such policy in the American setting, has explained: "A political theory of economics would predict that the process of economic change necessarily imposes losses on some people and confers gains on others." See Reich: 29.
7. For a discussion on the general features of redistributive politics in the U.S. context, see Ripley and Franklin, esp. chapter 6; Lowi, Hayes, and T. A. Smith.
8. Hayes: 153 says, "Redistributive programs will be enacted only when the electoral costs normally associated with choice among conflicting interests can somehow be discounted"; Rueschemeyer and Evans: 65–66 argue: "Some insulation from direct control [by the dominant class] would seem more critical to state interventions aimed at redistribution than to interventions aimed at promoting accumulation." Even though these authors are discussing redistribution in vastly different environments from the Chinese one, their writings on this subject share the notion of decision makers needing autonomy when major shifts in benefits are being undertaken.
9. Ripley and Franklin: 156, 179, 180, 183.
10. Kingdon.
11. On the concept of "policy window," see Kingdon: 204. He defines this term as "an opportunity to push pet proposals or one's conceptions of problems." He states that these windows "are opened either by the appearance of compelling problems or by happenings" in what he calls "the political stream." He defines "political stream," ibid., pp. 18, 21, 93, 152–54, and 170.

12. This argument was made repeatedly in 1979. One place to find it is in *RMRB*, May 25, 1979, p. 3, translated in *FBIS*, June 21, 1979, pp. L18–21. Page L19 notes the importance of the light and textile trades for developing foreign trade, for supplying the basic necessities of people's lives, and as an important source of revenue.

13. Guojia Tongjiju bian 1985b: 72.

14. Ma and Sun, 2: 745.

15. On the degree and extent to which that economy was really "planned" (as compared with other socialist states) see Naughton 1989: 6; and Granick.

16. According to *BR*, no. 47 (1984), p. 20, only 38,000 tractors were sold to individuals throughout China in 1980, but 380,000 of them found a market in 1981 and a million did so in 1982.

17. The reference here is to France and Japan in the aftermath of World War II; see my Conclusion for further analysis of similarities.

18. Lieberthal and Oksenberg 1986: 204. Leung: 10–12 noted that the economists of the Ministry of Finance were the initial authors of readjustment. They undertook research and surveys of the economic situation in late 1978 and early 1979 and won the support of Chen Yun and Li Xiannian.

19. Fang: 614, 615 cites Chen's and Deng's statements and mentions the light industry meeting. Ibid., p. 624, states that the plan was revised in mid-May 1979. Light industry was to grow by 8.3 percent in this revision and heavy by only 7.6 percent.

20. For instance, two members of the Petroleum Faction, chairman of the State Economic Commission Kang Shi'en and chairman of the State Planning Commission Yu Qiuli, in May both argued for the promotion of the coal industry, placing it in a position of primary importance. For Kang, see *FBIS*, May 23, 1979, p. L4. Kang spoke at a meeting of the State Economic Commission on readjustment, where he placed the increase of coal, oil, electricity, and transport as the number one priority, followed by undertaking special measures for the promotion of light industry as number two; Yu called for a "rather large increase in coal production" in *GRRB*, May 23, 1979. Also, it is intriguing that, though the plan's revision began (or maybe even was completed; it is not clear from the original source [note 19]) in mid-May, at the Second Session of the Fifth National People's Congress, held in June that year, Premier Hua Guofeng had called for only light industry and textile production to grow over the following three years "in pace with or slightly faster than heavy" and had said that the output of major light and textile industry products should increase just "as domestic purchasing power rises." For this speech, see *BR*, no. 27 (1979).

21. "Dangdai Zhongguo" Cong Shu Bianji Weiyuanhui, 1: 248. This source simply notes that the "state plan determined that. . . ." But because it includes reference to the year 1979, we may assume that the plan in question is the revised plan for 1979 which issued from Chen Yun's January advice.

22. *RMRB*, Dec. 7, 1979.

23. *RMRB*, July 9, 1980. The article also notes that in the first half of 1980 light industry grew by 24.2 percent over the same period in 1979, while heavy grew by only 6 percent.

24. G. White 1987: 616, 618, 619. According to Jie: 216, as of 1980, enterprises in the collective ownership system represented the majority of light industrial system enterprises, and their output value accounted for over half of the total output value of light industrial sector firms.

25. The various quotations from Li's speech appear in Zhonggong Zhongyang Wenxian Yanjiu Shi bian, 1: 146, 132, 115, and 123. The centrality of the concern over unemployment and the possible instability it could induce was cited by several economic theorists in this period. For instance, see Lin Zili: 91 and 96, who warns, "We must lower the accumulation rate or there will be unrest." Ma Hong, writing the next year (Ma 1982: 18), opined that, "if we mechanized all the departments there would be a problem in arranging labor power."

26. Zhonggong Zhongyang Wenxian Yanjiu Shi bian: 144.

27. Chen Yun, "Readjust the National Economy, Persevere in Development According to Proportions," March 21, 1979, ibid.: 76.

28. Ma: 6.

29. *RMRB*, Feb. 20, 1979.

30. *RMRB*, Apr. 6, 1979, p. 3, in *FBIS*, Apr. 19, 1979, pp. L6–8.

31. *RMRB*, Mar. 24, 1979, in *FBIS*, Mar. 27, 1979, pp. L10–14.

32. Liu: 169, 173. Liu speaks here of "disagreement about the rate of accumulation," a point that also comes across in *RMRB*, Nov. 23, 1979, in *FBIS*, Nov. 28, p. L12. That article states, "It is feared that cutting down accumulation and curtailing capital construction will make it impossible to expand reproduction." And *RMRB*, May 1, 1979, p. 3, in *FBIS*, May 25, p. L11, quotes "some" who try to make the case that agriculture and light industry are backward chiefly because rolled steel, timber, cement, agricultural machinery, chemical fertilizer, fuel, motive power, and light industrial equipment are in short supply. They insist that it is necessary to develop heavy industry further to strengthen reinforcements for agriculture and light industry.

33. *GRRB*, Nov. 10, 1979.

34. Yan 1980b: 34.

35. *FBIS*, Apr. 4, 1979, pp. L5–7.

36. Kingdon: 17–18, 96–119, 156, 204.
37. *Summary of World Broadcasts: FE*, no. 6410 (May 2, 1980).
38. Guojia Tongjijubian 1985a: 309. These figures are calculated according to 1970 constant prices.
39. State Statistical Bureau 1983: 513.
40. See Solinger 1982: 1255–59.
41. Yao's speech is in *BR*, no. 38 (1980), pp. 30–43. In light of Leung's finding about the coalition soon to be formed (note 51 below), Yao's concern here for the plight of some key trades within the heavy industrial sector is interesting.
42. Guojia Tongjiju 1987: 633 shows that in 1978 subsidies "to stabilize the people's livelihood" amounted to 5.56 billion *yuan* in 1978 but quickly climbed to 13.60 as the reforms began in 1979 and then to 17.86 in 1980. In 1981, the last year of the readjustment, they had reached nearly four times the 1978 figure, standing by then at 21.77 billion *yuan*. Obviously, this put special pressure on industry to yield returns to the state budget. I appreciate Tom Bernstein's drawing this to my attention.
43. C. J. Lee: 59 lists the outstanding problems as of the end of 1980 as follows: government budget deficits amounted to about 10 percent of the total budget; 35 billion *yuan* was in circulation as against only 27 billion the year before; the inflation rate in the urban areas had reached 15 percent; and the number of unemployed persons had climbed to 10 million (however, Li Xiannian had already admitted to a figure of 20 million unemployed in 1979 so it is unclear just what Lee's total refers to—it seems unlikely that half the state's employment problem had been solved in just one year's time); and major construction materials were in scarce supply.
44. Leung: 16–22 documents the role of the Ministry of Finance and its economists at this point.
45. Premier Zhao Ziyang admitted this in his work report to the Fourth Session of the Fifth NPC, held in Dec. 1981. The report is in *FBIS*, Dec. 16, 1981, K1–35. Part of the new data must have been that in Aug. 1980 profit deliveries to the state budget were 17 percent below what they had been in the same month the previous year (on this, Naughton 1983b: 14). Naughton notes that from June 1980, profit remittances to the state began to fall below the previous year's figures in each month (1985b: 231).
46. See Byrd 1983: 27, 55, 66–67; and Naughton 1983b: 15. According to *FBIS*, Dec. 14, 1989, p. 27, a "sluggish market for the means of production was brought about by reducing investment amounting to 16 billion *yuan*." The piece, as translated from the Hong Kong paper *Ta*

Kung Pao (Nov. 30, 1989, p. 2), does not state whether this reduction was just that for the means of production or if it was an overall reduction.

47. *FBIS*, Apr. 20, 1981, p. K18; Xue 1982b; and Xue 1982c: 93–94.

48. Xue 1982b: 5. The article does not account for the discrepancy between Xue's different figures for the drop in overall growth rate in the first half of the year as presented on pp. 4 (1.7 percent, as given in Table 11) and 5 (3.75, here), respectively.

49. Xue 1981.

50. Xue 1982b: 4 and 6.

51. Leung: 22 speaks of a coalition that formed at the end of 1980 and persisted in its support of readjustment (and, it seems, of new funding for heavy industry), consisting of the State Planning Commission (since summer 1980 under Yao Yilin, whose ties with readjustment champion Chen Yun had long been very close), the State Economic Commission (newly placed under the charge of Zhang Jingfu, who had a history of connections with the financial system), the Ministry of Finance, the People's Bank, and the Construction Bank. He says that this team was able to obstruct reform plans until the end of 1982.

52. According to *FBIS*, Dec. 14, 1989, p. 27, "the disagreeable situation was brought to an end by increasing the loans for purchasing short-term equipment for the textile and light industries, thereby augmenting the money supply for purchasing the means of production."

53. Xue 1982c: 93–95.

54. Such reports about Wuhan and Hubei appeared in *CJRB*, Oct. 20, 1981, p. 1, which noted that in September Hubei's heavy industry had registered an 11.79 percent increase over August; on Nov. 5, 1981, p. 1, the paper announced that in Wuhan October was the first month of the turnaround; and on Nov. 8, p. 4, the paper carried a Xinhua report saying that nationwide there had been an improvement in heavy's growth for the first time in October.

55. N.a. 1982c: 13, 15.

56. *FBIS*, May 15, 1981, p. K14.

57. This information is reported in G. White 1982: 624 and 626. His citations come from *Peking Daily,* Mar. 6, 1981, which reported more unemployed in 1981 than in 1980, partly because of the readjustment; Agence France Presse, Apr. 22, 1981, in *FBIS*, Apr. 23, 1981; and *The Times* of London, May 8, 1981.

58. Naughton 1983b: 15 notes that in September 1981 heavy industry received new investment, and plans for its expansion were revised upward.

59. *RMRB*, Oct. 16, 1981, p. 5, in *FBIS*, Oct. 29, 1981, pp. K9–13.
60. Zhong Yi, "Comments on the Economic Situation in the First Half of 1981," *JJGL*, translated in *FBIS*, Nov. 13, 1981, p. K9.
61. *FBIS*, Dec. 14, 1982, p. K15.
62. Wang Yongzhen: 16–18, 15.
63. *RMRB*, Feb. 27, 1982.
64. Xue 1982c: 94.
65. Zhang Rodan: 23 and *FBIS*, Nov. 17, 1981, p. K5.
66. N.a. 1982c: 12.
67. "Dangdai Zhongguo" Cong Shu Bianji Weiyuanhui 1985: 248–49 gives three examples of this. It states that Zhao raised the issue of consumer goods in February, April, and November 1981; the April occasion was in a speech to a State Council plenary meeting in which he presented a nine-point proposal on tactics. There he suggested increasing the production of consumer goods and reorienting the output mix of enterprises in the heavy industrial sector. See Solinger 1982: 1262.
68. Commentator 1981b: 4.
69. Commentator 1981a: 88–90.
70. Zhao's work report to the Fourth Session of the Fifth NPC is in *FBIS*, Dec. 16, 1981, pp. K1–35.
71. Such arguments appeared in *RMRB*, Oct. 16, 1981; in *FBIS*, Oct. 28, 1981, pp. K9–12; and in an undated *RMRB* editorial in *FBIS*, Nov. 24, 1981, p. K4.
72. Translated in *FBIS*, Sept. 15, 1981, pp. K16–19.
73. *CJRB*, Nov. 17, 1981, p. 4.
74. *FBIS*, Jan. 7, 1982, p. K14 (from the Dec. 1981 issue of *HQ*), claimed that the goals of further readjustment set in December 1980 had been attained; *FBIS*, Jan. 25, 1982, p. K15, stated that in the three years from 1979 through 1981 light industry had created jobs for 2.5 million more people and that its output value in 1981 was 32 percent above that in 1978; *FBIS*, Aug. 19, 1982, p. K8, noted that light industry had grown by 48.1 percent from 1979 to 1981, that "the three major sectors are showing coordinated growth now," and that "this was one of the major aims of the economic readjustment." The Aug. 9, 1982, *FBIS*, on p. K7, reported: "Practice has proved that the long-backward agriculture and light industry have caught up with heavy industry, which has laid a solid foundation for a sounder development of heavy industry." And the Aug. 10, 1982, issue, p. K16, recounted: "The growth of these two sectors [light industry and agriculture] has provided a more solid base for heavy industrial growth . . . agriculture has provided more raw materials for light industry which, in turn, has turned out more profit for undertaking capital construction." Then, at the time of the Twelfth Party

Congress, Wang Renzhi: 69 stated: "Since 1979 we have carried out the direction of readjusting the national economy, and the seriously maladjusted condition of proportional relations among agriculture and light and heavy industry has had a great change." "This aspect of readjustment's task," he judged, "has already been basically done."

75. As Gottschaung: 8 put it, certain of the areas of policy emphasis during the readjustment were difficult to fulfill because they tended to work at cross-purposes to each other. Thus, "eliminating wasteful investment projects and reducing the number of inefficient firms in the heavy industrial sector, and the goal of easing bottlenecks in transportation, energy, and building materials could only be achieved by new investment and increased output of a number of heavy industrial goods, such as steel, coal, rolling stock and cement."

76. Zhongyang Renmin Guangbo Diantai Lilun Zhengzhibu Jingjizu: 19 states that in 1980 the textile trade, with its 20 billion *yuan* worth of fixed assets, had realized 15.8 billion *yuan* worth of profits and taxes; by comparison, the machine-building industry had given the state profits worth only 3 billion *yuan* in 1981 (although, of course, this was a year in which it did very badly). This figure on the machine-building trade is in *FBIS*, Aug. 13, 1982, p. K9.

77. See *FBIS*, Oct. 28, 1981, pp. K1–2, a translation of *RMRB*'s Oct. 17 editorial.

78. *FBIS*, Feb. 8, 1982, p. K5 (an *RMRB* editorial of Feb. 3).

79. *BR*, no. 29 (1985), p. 16.

80. See Xue Muqiao in *RMRB*, June 3, 1983, p. 5; and Ye: 17.

81. See Yuan: 3, where he states: "Industry's modernization should mainly begin with the existing enterprises, [so that] limited capital and goods should be used preferentially in the technical transformation of the existing enterprises."

82. See Gao.

83. *FBIS*, Feb. 17, 1982, p. K12, states that such quotas "will certainly be higher in 1982 than in 1981"; *CD*, Dec. 7, 1984, p. 2, says, "Following the expansion of the construction scale, mandatory targets expanded in the machine-building industry's production plan." The Wuhan Bureau of Machine Building confirmed that its own recovery in 1982 came from new demands to renovate equipment (interview on Nov. 13, 1984); and officials in a large valve works in Wuhan spoke of its tasks increasing by 1983 after their serious drop in 1980 and 1981 (interview on Nov. 30, 1984).

84. *FBIS*, June 18, 1982, p. K4.

85. Interview at the Ministry of Machine Building, May 22, 1985.

Chapter Six

1. The best discussions of these issues are Naughton 1985b and Wong 1985.
2. Wong 1985: 268.
3. Wong 1986a: 594.
4. Kornai 1: 218–19. Kornai 1: 233 and 2: 555 admits that it is possible to "break out of [this] comfortable rigidity" by "putting out the fire." But his interest is in what he sees as the larger persistent, structural condition of shortage and its behavioral concomitants and not in the less typical transfer of resources among sectors. For his purposes such transfer is relatively insignificant because it does nothing to alter the systemic condition of overall shortage.
5. See, for example, Walder 1986b: 631; and Wong 1986b: 377.
6. Lampton 1987a: 12; and Lieberthal and Oksenberg 1986: 123; see also Lampton 1987c.
7. An example is the Third Front program of the mid-1960's, which shifted much heavy industrial development to remote western sections of the country. This was, as Naughton phrased it, "a classic manifestation of the ability of a centrally planned system to mobilize vast quantities of resources for industrial development and dispose of those resources according to the preferences of central planners *relatively unconstrained by economic considerations*" (emphasis added). This is from Naughton 1987: 17.
8. For instance, an old classic on this theme is Schroeder.
9. Johnson 1982: 146 cites a former vice minister of that body on this point.
10. See Wylie: 221.
11. DeWitt: 244.
12. Dower: 360.
13. Kesselman: 91; and Tarrow: 151.
14. This point is made repeatedly in the material about France and Japan in Katzenstein 1978a. See also Katzenstein 1978b: 327 and 335. On p. 335 he stresses that for both Japan and France "a policy of sectoral transformation . . . has relied primarily on the allocation of state-controlled investment funds."
15. Nakane: 134.
16. See Kesselman.
17. Nakane: 102.
18. *RMRB*, Jan. 8, 1980.
19. See also Naughton 1985b: 229, where a table indicates the percentage of total fixed investment under local control over the years 1977 through 1982. These are the percentages: 1977, 40%; 1978, 34%; 1979, 35%; 1980, 49%; 1981, 58%; and 1982, 63%. His point is that, as local

governments had more funds under their control—because of profits and taxes accruing to them with new financial decentralization measures after 1980 and with more flexible policies on bank lending in the localities—they had increasing ability to direct the flow of investment on their own. The result was that they chose to channel money into the profitable light industrial sector. The new role for banks is discussed in Byrd 1983.

20. See Naughton 1985a: 25 and 28–29. For a chart showing the tax and profit rates for various commodities at this time, see Wong 1985: 270. Light industrial products such as watches, bicycles, and cotton textiles had much higher rates in both categories than, for instance, chemical fertilizers, farm tools, and farm machinery. On p. 273, she lists several light industrial products that have very high tax rates. The important point that Wong makes in this article is that, for locally owned enterprises in this period, taxes and profits were indistinguishable to local governments because taxes were paid to them and profits also accrued to them from the enterprises they owned. In Wuhan officials from the Municipal Planning Commission revealed that the city's investment in light industry went from constituting 18.71 percent of investment in 1979 to 33.16 percent three years later (interview, Nov. 13, 1984). See Table 7.

21. *RMRB*, Mar. 31, 1980; also Qing; and *CJRB*, Jan. 4, 1981. See also circulars published in *RMRB*, May 25, 1979, and Dec. 7, 1979 (the latter was a circular sent by the State Economic Commission); *XHYK*, no. 6 (1979), p. 169 (also an SEC circular).

22. See Byrd 1983: 43–44.

23. *CJRB*, June 15, 1979, pp. 1, 4.

24. See Hough 1969, which repeatedly makes the same point about party officials in the localities in the 1960's in the Soviet Union. See pp. 26, 195, 226, and 255. Naughton also advances this argument in 1985b: 237.

25. This finding comes from a binational survey of industrial firms in China conducted in the early 1980's, as reported in Reynolds 1987: 5. This study's findings are only seemingly in conflict with those in Wong 1985b: 267 (table), which shows that localities controlled almost 50 percent of the total output of coal and steel by 1982, 43 percent of lumber, and 75 percent of cement. In fact, some local supplies are planned by local governments and allocated by them; thus local control does not by any means necessarily amount to marketization.

26. Kornai discusses the process of obtaining investment in a command economy. On p. 195, for instance, he says, "Obtaining investment is a complicated campaign which necessitates clever maneuvering." This

characterization continued to hold true for China in this time. As late as 1987 a commentary in a Chinese paper noted that "funds are still appropriated in a planned way" (translated in *FBIS*, Dec. 7, 1987, p. 35).

27. For another, different treatment of the concept of bargaining among administrative levels in the Chinese political economy, see Lieberthal and Oksenberg 1986: 119, 139–40, and their chapter 7.

28. For instance, see Cohen: 21, which states that the plan buys the cooperation of private firms, and p. 67, which speaks of the use of incentives to bribe business. Bauchet: 229–30 says that the French steel industry promised to fulfill the objectives of the plan in return for various advantages in loans and prices. Magaziner and Hout: 41 say that firms vary in the rate and spirit of compliance, but that all firms see MITI's "administrative guidance" as part of the price they must pay for the services of the economic bureaucracy.

29. Zysman 1977: 196.

30. Officials from the First Light Industrial Bureau of Wuhan, for example, told me on Nov. 17, 1984, that their department had seen growth of 62 percent over the years 1979–84 and that this could be attributed to investment and loans. They did not mention any of the other of the six priorities without prompting.

31. *CJRB*, Aug. 5, 1980, p. 1.

32. Fang: 643. This is also reported in Byrd 1983: 60 and in *FBIS*, Jan. 4, 1980, which states that these loans were given to revamp plants and improve equipment, with an eye to increasing exports. The foreign exchange portion is reported in *FBIS*, Jan. 23, 1980, in a broadcast which claimed that "this is the first time the state has favored certain industries in this way." At the end of 1981, the radio proclaimed that in the previous two years the state had "invested" nearly 10 billion *yuan* in light industry and nearly U.S.$10 billion in foreign exchange loans to aid the production of export commodities (*FBIS*, Dec. 30, 1981, p. K6). The curious thing about this report and the figure it gives is that on Jan. 22, 1982, p. K5, *FBIS* stated that the People's Bank had extended 10 billion *yuan* in short- and medium-term loans for 31,000 industrial projects in 1980 and 1981, of which 70 percent had gone to replace equipment or technically update light and textile enterprises. Probably this is the same batch of money, described as "loans" rather than as "investment."

33. *FBIS*, Mar. 25, 1981, p. L19.

34. *FBIS*, Jan. 22, 1982, p. K5.

35. *CJRB*, Sept. 14, 1979, p. 1.

36. Xu and Yan: 10.

37. *CJRB*, Mar. 16, 1980, p. 1.

38. *FBIS*, Mar. 24, 1981, p. P5.

39. *CJRB*, Feb. 4, 1982, p. 1.
40. *FBIS*, June 23, 1981, p. P8.
41. Information provided in interviews on May 26, 1984, and Nov. 14, 1984. See footnote on page 132 on "investment" and "loans." This confusion underlines the weakness of the banks in this period.
42. N.a. 1982b: 40.
43. *CJRB*, Sept. 23, 1979, p.2.
44. See Lieberthal and Oksenberg 1986: Chapter 3 for a discussion of the organization and duties of the ministries and commissions in the capital.
45. On this point, see Naughton 1986: 57: "The government gives local banks an annual quota for maximum lending in a given year, but in most years this quota is not particularly strict. Banks that make loans above their quota are rarely reprimanded, as long as they can argue that their additional loans were required for legitimate purposes."
46. Interview, Nov. 17, 1984, at the Wuhan First Bureau of Light Industry.
47. These loans are described under the label "loans from grants" (*bo gai dai*) in Walder 1988: 11. Walder states: "If the funding for the project is to come from the budget of the city, or from that of a national ministry, it reaches the bank in the form of a grant earmarked for a specific enterprise. The bank manages the investment for the government, eventually returning all repaid principle to the public coffers, but keeping the interest as a service fee." Though Wuhan officials did not use this term, they appear to be describing the same kind of disbursement.
48. This was probably the case, for the city paper (*CJRB*, May 15, 1980, p. 1) speaks of "the upper level" having "decided to give this bureau a loan."
49. In this case, ibid. says that the bureau developed "cooperation" "in a situation in which some enterprises' technical strength was weak and they lacked materials . . . to guarantee the smooth carrying out of the loan projects." Several times in my interviews reference was made to separate loan capital under the control of the city textile officials. Walder 1988: 21 also describes administrative levies (*jizhong zijin*) that industrial bureaus assess on the retained profits of more successful firms, which the bureau then deposits in a bank, using it as loans or grants to needy enterprises at preferential rates.
50. *CJRB*, Sept. 4, 1979, p. 1.
51. *CJRB*, May 26, 1980, p. 1.
52. For instance, see *CJRB*, Sept. 4, 1979, p. 1, on the assistance provided for the loom workshop extension project of the No. Four Textile Factory.

53. *CJRB*, Jan. 4, 1980, p. 1.
54. *CJRB*, Mar. 26, 1980, p. 2.
55. *CJRB*, June 1, 1979, pp. 1, 3.
56. *CJRB*, Sept. 4, 1979, p. 1. The No. Six Textile Factory in Wuhan experienced a similar situation. In an interview on Nov. 13, 1984, the MPC explained that No. Six became a key point simply by being chosen by the MEC and the Textile Bureau so that the favors it received were the result of superiors' selection, not local application.
57. *CJRB*, Oct. 14, 1980, pp. 1, 2.
58. Interview with Textile Bureau officials, Nov. 14, 1984.
59. Interviews with the MPC, May 28 and Nov. 13, 1984.
60. Interview at the First Bureau of Light Industry, Nov. 17, 1984.
61. This procedure was explained to me in interviews at the MEC on May 23, 1984, the Machine-Building Bureau, May 24, 1984, the Wuhan Wool Spinning Factory, May 26, 1984, the Wuhan branch of the People's Bank, Nov. 15, 1984, and the Wuhan No. Two Textile Factory, Dec. 19, 1984.
62. For a discussion of the various steps a food products factory in Hunan had to follow in its effort to obtain approval for expansion, see Lo: 23–24; p. 23 has a chart tracing the process. According to the article, this chart originally appeared in *Jingji Tsankao* (Economic Reference), July 11, 1985.
63. These four agencies, repeatedly referred to as the validators of any loan in interviews with city economic bureaucrats, were probably the organs that made up the "light and textile *jicuo* [technical measures] loan leadership small group" formed by the city's party and revolutionary committees just after readjustment became policy in mid-1979. According to the press, this group created a citywide loan office at that time. See *CJRB*, Sept. 4, 1979, p. 1. The procedure described in this article is the same as the one reported in the interviews. Walder 1986b: 638–44 discusses what he calls a "local circle of officials" or an "informal management team" that made financial decisions for each enterprise. Although each separate enterprise, according to Walder, had its own such team, the structural pattern of consultative deliberation that he alludes to also occurred repetitively on a citywide basis, each time with delegates from the same set of offices.
64. This information was given by the MEC on May 23, 1984; however, on Nov. 13, 1984, Machine-Building Bureau officials reported that although the MPC was in charge of technical transformation in 1979, by 1982 this was the sphere of the MEC. The power of the MEC grew in the course of economic readjustment, they explained.
65. Interview with MEC officials, Nov. 12, 1984.

66. Walder's analysis in 1988: 10–12 concurs with this assessment of the bank as essentially an agent of other, more powerful city organs.
67. Interview at MPC, Nov. 13, 1984.
68. Interview at MEC, Nov. 12, 1984.
69. Interview at Wuhan Number Two Textile Factory, Dec. 19, 1984.
70. Walder 1988 also uses the metaphor of the Chinese municipality as a corporation, but for purposes somewhat different from mine here.
71. Lewek acknowledges the successful direction of electrical power to light industry in the 1980's. On p. 108, on the success of the readjustment program, he comments, "Thus, in the mid-1980's, the electric power supply in China is being stretched to satisfy not only planned growth in light industry, but also unplanned and phenomenal growth in heavy industry."
72. See Tidrick: 189. He notes that "electricity is a special case [more easily centrally controlled than are other inputs] because it is almost entirely allocated, cannot be stored or traded, and is seldom self-generated."
73. See Weil for some information on the placement and operation of power grids in China as of 1985.
74. This circular appears in *XHYK*, no. 6 (1979), p. 169.
75. *CJRB*, Nov. 19, 1979, pp. 1, 3.
76. *FBIS*, July 6, 1979, pp. P3–4.
77. *CJRB*, Nov. 19, 1979, pp. 1, 3.
78. *CJRB*, June 17, 1979, p. 1.
79. Interviews on Nov. 30, 1984, at the Wuhan Valve Works and on Dec. 19, 1984, at the Wuhan No. Two Textile Factory.
80. Wong 1985: 262.
81. Wong 1986a: 575.
82. Wong 1985: 266–67. Naughton cites "one account" which states that between 1981 and 1983, only 30 to 40 commodities (of the 256 raw materials, energy products, and machinery items officially listed as belonging to Category I, i.e., those balanced by central planners) were allocated by the Bureau of Material Supply. See Naughton 1985a: 6.
83. Translated in *FBIS*, Nov. 13, 1979, p. L18.
84. *RMRB* editorial, Mar. 31, 1980, translated in *FBIS*, Apr. 2, 1980, p. L9.
85. Ibid., p. L10.
86. *GRRB*, Feb. 9, 1980.
87. The Mar. 31, 1980, *RMRB* editorial, translated in *FBIS*, Apr. 2, 1980, p. L12, says: "Since last year the principal responsible comrades in Zhejiang, Hubei and Sichuan provinces and Tianjin Municipality

have personally grasped light industry work, studied principles and policies and adopted effective measures. As a result, light industry has progressed relatively significantly in those places."

88. Nie: 124.

89. "Dangdai Zhongguo" Cong Shu Bianji Weiyuanhui 1985, 1: 250.

90. For instance, see the excerpts from State Economic Commission Chairman Zhang Jingfu's speech.

91. Naughton 1985a: 6.

92. According to Jing: 16, these funds had already risen to 49 percent of the total volume of investment nationally by the end of 1982.

93. This practice was described in interviews at the Wuhan Valve Works, Nov. 30, 1984; at the No. Two Machine Tools Factory, May 27, 1985; and at the Eastern Electrical Equipment factory, May 28, 1985. Certainly it must have been a common adaptation; Wong 1985: 263, 267, 268 comments on this practice.

94. Interview at Wuhan Valve Works, Nov. 30, 1984.

95. Translated in *FBIS*, Apr. 2, 1980, p. L9. Wong 1987: 12 notes that the central government allocated blocks of materials to provinces for their discretionary use.

96. Jie: 215.

97. In Wuhan, as of 1981, light industrial production under the city accounted for 66.8 percent of the total output value of industry (Lu and Huang: 34).

98. In *FBIS*, Dec. 5, 1979, p. L8.

99. Wong 1985: 268.

100. Interview at the MEC, May 23, 1984.

101. Interview with officers from the Wuhan Tax Bureau, Nov. 16, 1984. The tax officials said that 20 percent of Wugang's profits went to the provincial government. Wong states in 1987: 12–13 that some central and provincial departments directly allocated materials such as steel to certain specially designated key-point enterprises that bore the label "direct supply" enterprises, bypassing the city's material supply system.

102. For instance, N.a. 1981: 19–20, says: "Some policies encouraged localities to manage or build small factories, like the remission of or low taxes for commune and brigade industry and the no-interest or low-interest loans. All newly managed factories had three years without taxes." This latter policy applied to the wine, cigarette, small leather and hide, plastics, tin cans, and fan trades.

103. Interview at Wuhan Tax Bureau, Nov. 16, 1984; and Wong 1985: 268.

104. This issue came to a head in the press and in the elite's con-

sciousness in the fall of 1980. For one example, see Commentator 1980: 2. Not only did such plants deprive larger factories of the wherewithal for their own production, but they could compete in prices with the state firms in the large cities for their wages were not set by the state, and they avoided transport costs because, located in the countryside, they were near the source of the materials. This was explained by the Wuhan Textile Bureau on Nov. 14, 1984.

    105. Ma 1983: 76.

    106. Interview with Wuhan Machine-Building Bureau management, Nov. 13, 1984.

    107. *CJRB*, Aug. 24, 1979, p. 2. This man was sent to meet with me when, in 1983, I requested interviews in Wuhan on the subject of the readjustment.

    108. *CJRB*, June 22, 1979, p. 1, and Sept. 23, 1979, pp. 1, 2.

    109. Interview at MEC, Nov. 12, 1984; interview at Textile Bureau, Nov. 14, 1984.

    110. Interview at Textile Bureau, Nov. 14, 1984.

    111. The account that follows, drawn from interviews in Wuhan, is akin to the procedures described by Hough 1969. My sense in comparing Hough's book with the materials from my own interviews, however, is that the *kuaikuai*, or, in this case, the city-level leadership, has somewhat more of a role in China than it does in the Soviet Union. This seems to be the case in its ability to make decisions and arrangements, both in managing funds and in reaching consensual determinations about the balancing of raw materials.

    112. *CJRB*, Feb. 25, 1981, p. 1, and Jan. 12, 1982, p. 1.

    113. Interview at the Machine-Building Bureau, Nov. 13, 1984, and at the No. One Textile factory, Nov. 30, 1984. According to informants from the Machine-Building Bureau, the *tiaotiao*'s accounting was more precise because of ministerial responsibility for balancing supplies on a nationwide basis. In contrast, the *kuaikuai* did not need to take such care or do such detailed planning for every small request, so its calculations tended to be "rougher, cruder."

    114. Western economists have taken note of the success of the program in achieving the goals it set out. See, for instance, Field: 750, who states, "The Chinese have achieved a remarkable change in the composition of output in the past five years," and Naughton, who says that the government "has succeeded in rapidly redirecting investment into the production of consumer goods and into the construction of housing" (1983a: 3).

    115. N.a. 1983: 41.

    116. Li Chengrui: 15.

117. *RMRB*, July 9, 1980.
118. *CJRB*, Jan. 19, 1981, and Jan. 20, 1981, both on p. 1.
119. Cited in *Business Week*, Jan. 14, 1985, p. 54.
120. Interview at Textile Bureau, Nov. 14, 1984.
121. *CJRB*, Jan. 19, 1981, p. 1.
122. *CJRB*, Apr. 2, 1981, p. 2.
123. Interview at Wuhan No. One Textile Factory, May 26, 1984.
124. Zhou Chuan: 7.
125. *CJRB*, Aug. 26, 1982, p. 1.
126. See *FBIS*, May 31, 1980, p. L1, for an early report; May 15, 1981, pp. K16–17, contains a discussion of the continuing problem and mention of this State Council circular against expansion "on the pretext of 'filling gaps.'"
127. See Byrd 1987: 262: "In a highly profitable industry that has been given priority access to investment resources and for which raw material constraints are relatively unimportant, producers (supported by local supervisory agencies) will engage in the expansion response . . . supply will grow rapidly and in a fairly short period it will meet and then surpass demand."
128. Interview with management from the First Bureau of Light Industry, Nov. 17, 1984. Naughton 1985b: 249 notes that before the readjustment Wuhan had only one factory producing electrical fans, but that as soon as one year later there were 23 of them. The same trend held in the production of synthetic fabrics, cigarettes, liquor, and other consumer goods.
129. *GRRB*, Nov. 7, 1979.
130. *FBIS*, May 15, 1981, p. K9.
131. Song 1981b: 4.
132. This was the achievement touted in the Wuhan press of the Wuhan Dyes Factory, which, supported by the readjustment policy, was able to push its wares in the Shashi printing and dyeing trade, which previously had used other provinces' products (*CJRB*, Oct. 11, 1980, p. 1).
133. See Bauchet: 230, where he mentions fights to monopolize the market and overinvestment in France; and Cohen: 99, who states that the plan in France overdeveloped the basic sectors. And just as Wong 1986b: 375 writes that government officials and enterprise managers, accustomed to sellers' markets, were unable to anticipate the effects of growing competition but expected that all additional output could be sold at current prices as it always had been before the reform period, so Bauchet describes a situation in which management failed to adjust properly to the changed market environment in early postwar France.

Bauchet: 230 explains that French firms' overproduction stemmed from their reckoning on the basis of the increased purchasing power and expanding sales predicted in the plan.

134. See Sheahan.
135. Anchordoguy: 14.
136. Yamamura: 69, 85–86; Johnson 1982: 312.
137. Song 1981a: 11.
138. Wang Yongzhen 1983: 12.
139. See Yang Bo.
140. Reported in *CJRB*, Nov. 18, 1981, p. 1.
141. *CJRB*, Mar. 6, 1982, p. 1. *SCB*, no. 18 (1982), p. 783, contains the central-level order to this effect, dated Oct. 1982.
142. For instance, see *RMRB* editorial of Feb. 27, 1982. I discuss this from another angle at the end of Chapter 5.
143. Interview with bank officials, Nov. 15, 1984.
144. *CJRB*, Jan. 3, 1981, p. 1, and Apr. 14, 1981, p. 4.
145. Interview at MPC, Nov. 13, 1984. The market side of the picture is presented in a local journal article which spoke of a "rather large part of the provincial internal market being squeezed out by outside products, noting that because our products can't be sold, our light and textile development speed has begun to slow down" (Jin [of the Hubei Provincial Economic Commission] 1983b: 10).
146. *CJRB*, May 28, 1982, p. 1.
147. Such efforts are reported in *CJRB*, Mar. 21, 1981, p. 1; Apr. 4, 1981, p. 1; May 5, 1981, p. 1; May 6, 1981, p. 2; May 10, 1981, p. 1; Oct. 2, 1981, p. 1; Nov. 25, 1981, p. 1; and Feb 22, 1982, p. 1.
148. Interview at MPC, Nov. 13, 1984.
149. Interview at Textile Bureau, Nov. 14, 1984.

Chapter Seven

1. On France, see Sheahan: 93, where he says that the first, Monnet Plan left the equipment industries to fend for themselves in an environment in which credit, manpower, and necessary imports were nearly impossible to secure without outside help. Kuisel: 233–34 states that public funds and foreign aid were used for increasing the basic sectors, while "all other sectors had to depend on individual savings, company funds, gold and exchange holdings and bank credit." And Cohen: 86 notes that "the rest of the economy [beyond the six basic sectors] was left largely outside of the plan's active attention and out of the government-financed reconstruction program for which the plan was to be the basic framework." On Japan, see Yamamura: 44–49, where he describes MITI's restriction of production for three industries most af-

fected by the U.S. curtailment of procurement orders during the Korean War.

2. Ding: 8. Another source states that in 1981 the First Ministry of Machine Building had quotas under the state plan that amounted to less than one-third of its firms' production capabilities. *FBIS*, June 18, 1982, p. K4, says that in 1981, because of a further readjustment early in the year that called for a shrinkage in the scale of capital construction—and a consequent decline in the numbers of machinery and electrical products demanded—the production task given to the machine-building enterprises dropped to the equivalent of 10 billion *yuan*, which accounted for merely one-fourth of production capacity.

3. *CJRB*, June 24, 1979, p. 1.   4. See Keeler.
5. Ibid.: 243.   6. Gustafson: 146–47.
7. See Olson: 65.   8. Thurow: 81.
9. Reich: 29.

10. According to *CD*, economist Sun Yefang commented in late 1981 that the heavy industrial enterprises had then been idled for two years and were suffering a depression resulting from economic readjustment. See *FBIS*, Dec. 18, 1981, p. K29.

11. See Johnson 1982: 44, 325; and Zysman 1978.
12. Zysman 1977: 265.
13. *RMRB*, Mar. 26, 1981.
14. Interview at the Ministry of Machine Building, May 22, 1985.
15. The strong interest management bureaus take in their firms' ability to generate revenue is discussed in Naughton 1985b: 237–38; and Walder 1986b: 638.
16. Sun: 26, 28.
17. N.a. 1982c: 13.
18. *RMRB*, Apr. 7, 1980.
19. *GMRB*, translated in *FBIS*, Jan. 24, 1980, p. L19, is one instance among many stating that work in enterprises that have been losing money for a long time and are without markets should be halted in the readjustment. But a piece in the Wuhan *CJRB*, Apr. 29, 1981, p. 1, warns against "thinking of utilizing readjustment to throw out difficulties," in reference to those who believe that the purpose of the policy is simply to reorient "factories with inadequate conditions and big problems . . . to throw off burdens." Instead, it maintains, the implementers locally should concentrate on the real goals of readjustment: readjusting the national economic structure, strengthening the light and textile trades, and producing more consumer goods. Doing this properly would mean having heavy industrial enterprises with good equipment and technical conditions genuinely support light and textiles.

20. Li is cited as making this point at the meeting in *CJRB*, Mar. 20, 1981, pp. 2, 3.
21. Byrd 1983: 80.
22. Wang Zhengxing: 37.
23. *RMRB*, Sept. 7, 1982, p. 5, translated in *FBIS*, Sept. 15, 1982, p. K19.
24. See Byrd 1983: 52, 74, 79, and 81. On p. 74 he states, "New decentralized systems of credit management let localities inflate the money supply well beyond what is called for in the plan"; on p. 81, he says, "The diversion of bank loans for working capital to fixed investment is a common form of irregularity."
25. Naughton 1985b: 250.
26. I deal at greater length with this in Solinger 1982, esp. p. 1254.
27. Discussed in Bachman: 315.
28. *FBIS*, Feb. 20, 1985, p. K18; N.a. 1984. This issue is also discussed in Byrd 1987: 264.
29. Ma 1983: 109. Balassa: 14 quoting William Byrd, "The Role and Impact of Markets" (Washington, D.C.: World Bank, 1985, mimeo), pp. 1-2, states that "non-planned machinery sales by firms under the Ministry of Machine Building Industry rose from 13 percent in 1979 to 46 percent in 1980 while non-planned sales of rolled steel increased from 4 percent in 1979 to 19 percent in 1981."
30. N.a. 1982a: 21.
31. Lu and Huang: 32.
32. Wong 1985: 268-69.
33. See Byrd 1983: 74, 124, 127; and Naughton 1985b: 238.
34. Scott: 35.
35. Scott would call such immobilism one of the "ordinary weapons of relatively powerless groups," which include "foot dragging, dissimulation, false compliance, pilfering, feigned ignorance," which "undo or evade threatening state policy." See ibid.: 29, 31.
36. Byrd 1987: 243.
37. *CJRB*, June 1, 1979, pp. 1, 3.
38. *CJRB*, July 4, 1979, pp. 1, 2. For Hua's stance at this meeting, see Chapter 4 of this volume.
39. It seems that Chen was more enthusiastic about readjustment from the start. At a provincial party Standing Committee's enlarged meeting on the Third Plenum and the readjustment held in mid-June, Chen already commanded that special measures should be used to implement priority treatment in the light and textile trades and that "everything possible" should be done to bolster these branches of industry (*CJRB*, June 15, 1979, pp. 1, 4).

40. For accounts of Li's statements at these various meetings, see *CJRB*, June 1, 1979, pp. 1, 3; July 4, 1979, pp. 1, 2; Sept. 23, 1979, pp. 1, 2; and Jan. 11, 1980, p. 1.

41. Li's attitude as deduced from these remarks contrasts sharply with the advocacy of the readjustment within his own province that appears in the words of Guangdong provincial party secretary Xi Zhongxun, as relayed in P.N.S. Lee.

42. The analysis that follows draws mainly on interviews in Wuhan in May 1984, Nov.–Dec. 1984, and May 1985.

43. See Chapter 6, note 107.

44. Shirk 1983.

45. I deal with the opposition voiced by those from provinces where heavy industry is strong in my 1982 article: 1257–59, 1267.

46. For this discussion, see ibid., pp. 1258, 1263, 1264, and 1267.

47. *FBIS*, May 15, 1981, p. K9.

48. *RMRB*, Aug. 22, 1979.

49. *CJRB*, Mar. 20, 1981, pp. 2, 3.

50. Yamamura: 66.

51. Sheahan: 69.

52. Interview at Ministry of Machine Building, May 22, 1985.

53. *CJRB*, Apr. 29, 1981, p. 1, and Jan. 22, 1980, p. 1.

54. *CJRB*, Feb. 5, 1982, p. 1.

55. *CJRB*, Apr. 14, 1981, p. 4.

56. *CJRB*, Mar. 31, 1981, p. 1.

57. *CJRB*, Apr. 8, 1981, p. 1, and Aug. 26, 1981, p. 1.

58. Interview at Wuhan Valve Works on Nov. 30, 1984.

59. Interviews at the City Planning Commission, Nov. 13, 1984, the Metallurgy Bureau, Nov. 16, 1984, and the Machine-Building Bureau, Nov. 13, 1984.

60. *FBIS*, July 17, 1979, p. L2, and Nov. 28, 1979, pp. L13–14 (the second article appeared first in *RMRB*, Nov. 23, 1979).

61. *CJRB*, Dec. 30, 1980, pp. 1, 2.

62. *RMRB* editorials of Aug. 22, 1979, and Nov. 16, 1981 (translated in *FBIS*, Nov. 24, 1981), and *FBIS*, Apr. 20, 1981, p. K19.

63. Qi: 63.

64. *CJRB*, Feb. 5, 1982, p. 1.

65. See Chapter 6, section on diversion of raw materials, and below, on the Wuhan valve plant's arrangements with Wugang.

66. One such editorial appeared on Mar. 3, 1981. See also a decision of the Fifth NPC Standing Committee on this, dated Mar. 16, 1981, in *SCB*, no. 3 (1981), pp. 80–81.

67. *RMRB* editorial, Dec. 2, 1980, in *FBIS*, Dec. 3, 1980, p. L5. Label-

ing this opposition "leftist" is in line with the material in Chapter 4 that discusses the ideological obstacles against investment in light industry in Mao's day.

68. Interview at Wuhan Machine-Building Bureau, May 24, 1985.
69. *FBIS*, May 15, 1981, p. K8.
70. *CJRB*, July 26, 1979, p. 1.
71. *RMRB*, Mar. 9, 1981, in *FBIS*, Mar. 11, 1981, p. L14.
72. *CJRB*, Apr. 5, 1981, p. 1.
73. *RMRB* editorial, Aug. 22, 1979; *FBIS*, May 15, 1981, p. K8.
74. The pertinent sections of Li's speech of Apr. 5, 1979, is in Zhonggong Zhongyang Wenxian Yanjiu Shi 1: 132, 146; Deng's address of Dec. 25, 1980 is in ibid., see p. 635.
75. N.a. 1982a: 21; *FBIS*, Jan. 13, 1981, p. L11; and *RMRB*, Mar. 3, 1981.
76. Interview at MEC, Nov. 12, 1984.
77. Interview at Ministry of Machine Building, May 22, 1985.
78. Strikes are noted in G. White 1982: 624 and 626.
79. Ding: 8. A report on this problem in Wuhan is in Lu and Huang: 33, where they speak of problems of blindness and costs in the more than 50 machine-building plants that had been turned over to light and textiles in 1980 and 1981.
80. *RMRB*, Oct. 17, 1983, p. 2.
81. This story was pieced together from interviews at the Municipal Machine-Building Bureau on Nov. 13, 1984, and May 27, 1985, at the plant in question, with the City Economic Commission on Nov. 12, 1984, and at the First Bureau of Light Industry on Nov. 17, 1984.
82. The link between paternalism and repression has often been drawn. As noted by a scholar writing on French industrial paternalism, "Previous studies of paternalism have focused on the reproduction of labor power and the imposition of social control through persuasion and repression" (Reid: 582). Walder 1986a also makes this point. Passin refers to it in speaking of Japan.
83. Pempel 1978: 175. Also on Japan, see Adams and Ichimura: 310, in which they say that purchasing agents were assigned to buy products of certain depressed industries to reduce the severity of the impact on unemployment in the cotton textiles industry in 1953, when U.S. orders were cut back. Yamamura: 45 tells of the Save the Bankruptcies Policy to protect enterprises severely affected by these cutbacks.
84. See Calder.
85. Zysman 1978: 256; Berger 1980.
86. Other discussions of co-optation in France are in DeWitt: 236, where he writes that layoffs were delayed for political reasons in the

mid-1970's when steel capacity was reduced in France. "The steel industry had no alternative but to obey government measures," he explains, but "it did so knowing in the end that state money would bail it out . . . which it did." Baum: 242 tells of a government fund set up in 1954 for the reconversion of outmoded industrial concerns and a retraining fund for displaced workers. "Various government policies have the effect of providing shelter for the inefficient," he notes on p. 244. McArthur and Scott: 246 say, "In some cases massive state aid was given to hopelessly inefficient manufacturing operations in isolated areas to keep them operating and thereby postpone the inevitable disorders which would accompany their abandonment."

87. This story has been told in detail in Byrd et al.
88. Interview at the Wuhan Municipal Tax Bureau, Nov. 16, 1984.
89. Interview at the factory, May 28, 1985.
90. In July 1979, a newspaper article stated that the Wuhan Machine-Building Bureau "went through the upper levels to understand the machine-building situation in the whole country." See *CJRB*, July 26, 1979, p. 1.
91. *FBIS*, July 28, 1981, p. L9, contains a directive from the State Council to the localities demanding that they help enterprises turn deficits to profits.
92. For instance, N.a. 1980; Jin and Tong; and Sun.
93. Wuhan's No. Two Machine Tools Factory supplied this quotation on May 27, 1985.
94. *CJRB*, Apr. 5, 1981, p. 1.
95. Jin and Tong: 4, 6.
96. Interview at the Ministry of Machine Building, May 22, 1985.
97. This valve plant set up a retail outlet in Chengdu after the bureau informed it that there would be a demand for its products there, according to my interview on Nov. 30, 1984.
98. *CJRB*, Apr. 5, 1981, p. 1.
99. *CJRB*, Aug. 24, 1979, p. 2, and Jan. 22, 1980, p. 1; Jan. 15, 1981, p. 1 has an article about Hubei province doing the same thing.
100. *CJRB*, Feb. 5, 1982, p. 1.
101. *CJRB*, Oct. 20, 1981, p. 1.
102. *CJRB*, Feb. 5, 1982, p. 1, tells how the Wuhan Machine Tools Factory began with spare tasks; Lu and Huang: 36 note the same response by the Wuhan machine-building enterprises generally.
103. Zhu: 42.
104. Byrd et al.: 80.
105. Interview at Wuhan Valve Works, Nov. 30, 1984.
106. Interview at No. Two Machine Tools Plant, May 27, 1985.

107. Material here draws on *CJRB*, Nov. 26, 1979, p. 1; Jan. 4, 1981, p. 1; July 27, 1981, p. 1; and Oct. 31, 1981, p. 1; and from an interview with bureau officials on Nov. 16, 1984.

108. This arrangement is described briefly in *CJRB*, Oct. 31, 1981, p. 1, and also in my interview.

109. This is the label used by bureau officials in my interview with them. In the *CJRB*, Oct. 31, 1981, p. 1, article, the arrangement is referred to as *chao-shou fen-cheng*, which has essentially the same meaning. In both the idea is that profits collected from the bureau by the state treasury beyond a set amount are shared.

110. Interview at Wuhan Bureau of Metallurgy, Nov. 16, 1984.

111. *CJRB*, July 27, 1981, p. 1

112. Scott: 35.

113. "Dangdai Zhongguo" Cong Shu Bianjizu Weiyuanhu 1984: 316.

Chapter Eight

1. For Johnson's discussion of the two concepts that make up the Japanese notion of "industrial policy," see Johnson 1982: 27–28. The first concerns the respective proportions that various branches of the national economy occupy within the total output value of production; within manufacturing, it pertains to the respective shares taken by light and heavy industry. At its kernel lie choices about which industries are to be developed and which converted to other lines of work.

2. Ibid.: 27.

3. *CJRB*, Mar. 25, 1981, p. 1.

4. *FBIS*, Apr. 20, 1981, pp. K16–17.

5. The document was published in *SCB*, no. 8 (1980), pp. 227–29.

6. Wilks and Dyson: 6.

7. See Dyson.

8. As Ehrmann 1957: 382 put it. Cohen: 75 notes that "French planners encouraged mergers to rationalize industrial structure and to spur cooperative growth and modernization." Trezise: 800–801 states that the Japanese government has been reluctant to abandon existing industries. He explains how MITI's cure for troubles with overcapacity and downward pressures on prices in the cotton textile and apparel trades in the 1950's was to encourage the formation of a cartel to restrict output. Also on Japan, Komiya: 213 discusses government organization of what the Japanese call rationalization cartels and the promotion of mergers and specialization.

9. Much has been written on these associations. For the period I have studied, see, for example, Baum: 251–54 and McArthur and Scott: 197–202; on Japan, see Komiya: 211, 213, 222. There is often a fine line be-

tween the private sector's formation of trade associations and government initiatives in these countries, as is noted by Caves with Uekusa: 499. They make the point that MITI uses administrative guidance via trade associations to promote the movement of resources toward certain favored industries. Dore: 19, speaking of a later period, maintains that industry associations are "the principal instrument through which recession cartels can be formally arranged by MITI." Writing on France, Cohen: 70 says that planners often work with trade associations in investment, output modernization, and restructuring programs, and that it is up to the associations to break down government plans for their industry into programs for individual firms.

10. Or combination bodies, *lianheti*.
11. *CJRB*, Oct. 7, 1981, p. 2.
12. Interview at Ministry of Machine Building, on May 22, 1985.
13. Xu: 293–94.
14. Wong 1986b.
15. This figure is in Premier Zhao Ziyang's late 1982 report on the Sixth Five-Year Plan, in *FBIS*, Dec. 14, 1982, p. K21.
16. Yang and Luo: 32; N.a. 1982d: 20; and *CJRB*, July 15, 1979, p. 3.
17. "Dangdai Zhongguo" Cong Shu Bianjizu Weiyuanhui 1984: 316.
18. This speech, entitled "Implement the Readjustment Direction, Guarantee Stability and Unity," is in Zhonggong Zhongyang Wenxian Yanjiu Shi 1: 635.
19. *SCB*, no. 8 (1980), p. 227. According to the State Council directive on combinations printed in this bulletin, *lianhe* was a "new form following the initial management system reform" undertaken to "develop each economic unit's superiority."
20. State Construction Commission Economic Research Office Investigation Group: 23 says that "raising the utilization rate of fixed assets is the basic path for enterprise transformation."
21. Indeed, one of the primary criteria to be used in deciding which enterprises to maintain, which to transform, and which to eliminate was whether their products met market needs [were *duilu*], as Vice Premier Li Xiannian directed at the outset of the program. This is in his speech at the Party Work Conference that launched the readjustment on Apr. 5, 1979, published in Zhonggong Zhongyang Wenxian Yanjiu Shi: 129.
22. *CJRB*, Dec. 18, 1980, p. 1.
23. *CJRB*, Apr. 11, 1982, p. 1.
24. Interview at this general factory, May 29, 1985.
25. *CJRB*, Nov. 8, 1979, p. 2.
26. *CJRB*, Jan. 18, 1981, p. 1.
27. "Dangdai Zhongguo" Cong Shu Bianji Weiyuanhui 1984: 306.

28. Yang and Luo: 32.
29. *RMRB*, Mar. 20, 1981.
30. N.a. 1982a: 19 speaks of taking part of the surplus labor in the machine-building system and converting it to light industrial production and service work.
31. *CJRB*, May 27, 1980, p. 1.
32. *CJRB*, Aug. 12, 1980, p. 1.
33. Bai and Zhang: 24.
34. *CJRB*, Apr. 4, 1981, p. 1.
35. *CJRB*, May 5, 1981, p. 1; Nov. 25, 1981, p. 1; and Feb. 22, 1982, p. 1.
36. "State Council Decision on the Keypoint, Step-wise Technical Transformation of Existing Enterprises," Central Document no. 15, dated January 18, 1982, in *SCB*, no. 3 (1982), pp. 75–80.
37. This is in Li's Apr. 5, 1979, speech published in Zhonggong Zhongyang Wenxian Yanjiu Shi: 132.
38. Yue: 24.
39. N.a. 1982d: 20.
40. Tang and Ma: 636.
41. *CJRB*, Feb. 20, 1982, pp. 1, 2, 4.
42. Yang and Luo: 31–32.
43. *CJRB*, July 29, 1980, p. 1. The prominent Wuhan Heavy-Duty Machine Tools Factory, in creating four branch factories and one company, introduced the principle of specialization into its management and also solved the employment problem of some 700 sons and daughters of the plant's original labor force. See *CJRB*, Feb. 12, 1982, p. 1.
44. This is from a commentator's article in the no. 8 (1981) issue of *HQ*, as translated in *FBIS*, May 15, 1981, p. K10.
45. *CJRB*, Oct. 29, 1981, p. 1.
46. Yang and Luo: 30.
47. *CJRB*, Oct. 7, 1981, p. 2.
48. *SCB*, no. 8 (1980), p. 228.
49. *HQ*, no. 8 (1981), translated in *FBIS*, May 15, 1981, p. K10.
50. *FBIS*, Mar. 13, 1981, pp. L1–2.
51. *CJRB*, Feb. 25, 1981, p. 1.
52. *CJRB*, Jan. 15, 1981, p. 1; and Wang Zhengxing: 37.
53. *CJRB*, Mar. 25 and 26, 1981, p. 1 in both issues.
54. *CJRB*, Mar. 26, 1981, p. 1; and Lu and Huang: 35.
55. Interview at the Wuhan Municipal Machine-Building Bureau, Nov. 13, 1984.
56. Interviews on this merger were at the Wuhan Textile Bureau on Nov. 14, 1984, for textiles and at the First Bureau of Light Industry of Wuhan on Nov. 17, 1984, for light industry.
57. Interview at the Wuhan Textile Bureau, May 26, 1984.
58. Sun: 29.
59. In theory, associations could be formed by nine different sorts of

partners: between productive enterprises and raw material bases; among firms in the same ownership system; between firms transcending functional systems and trades; among concerns managed by different administrative levels; between military and civilian plants; among factories in different districts, provinces, and cities; among firms in different sectors, as among industrial and commercial firms, materials supply units and foreign trade organs; between productive enterprises and scientific research and design institutes; and among production units in industry and agriculture in urban and rural areas (*CJRB*, Nov. 16, 1980, p. 1). Interviews with officials from the Wuhan Textile and First Light Industrial bureaus revealed a difference between the mergers initiated within the two trades. Those from textiles maintained that most of the *lianhe* in their system were between collectively owned enterprises and state-owned ones. Staff from the light industrial department explained that their mergers were usually performed within the same ownership system because workers did not like to combine operations with those from the other ownership system. These interviews were, respectively, on May 26, 1984, and Nov. 17, 1984.

60. *CJRB*, Dec. 30, 1979, p. 1.
61. *CJRB*, Dec. 5, 1980, p. 1.
62. Sometimes bureaus could turn the assets of failing firms to good use. The city machine-building bureau formed what later became an important reform model unit, the Wuhan No. 2 Bicycle Factory, from a union between a car factory, two small machine-building plants, and a bearings and hardware factory. All of these firms had been turning out products without a market or showing serious long-standing losses. Their shift to a new product in demand filled a gap in the city's production base (*CJRB*, Jan. 22, 1980, p. 1).
63. *BR*, no. 20 (1987), p. 4, identified these two traits as problems to be eliminated in economic reform: "The major elements of the structural reform now under way also include overcoming the *isolation of enterprises*, which formerly were *administered vertically* by the departments in charge and by their regions" (emphasis added).
64. Feuerwerker: 23 shows how this same concept permeated the Qing bureaucracy. He refers to "the doctrine of responsibility which permeated the legal and governmental structure of China." "Every official," he explains, "from the emperor down to the lowest local officer was responsible for all happenings within his sphere of competence."
65. Williamson and Ouchi: 5–6 draw on the work of Mayo, Barnard, and Vancil in discussing the concept of goal incongruence: "To the extent that one party can achieve his self-interest only at the expense of the other . . . goal incongruence obtains."

66. *RMRB*, May 12, 1980. Other similar statements are in many places, including *FBIS*, May 15, 1981, p. K9, and Sept. 30, 1981, p. K8; and Wang Shufan: 20.

67. *FBIS*, May 15, 1981, p. K9.

68. The directive is in *SCB*, no. 12 (1981), pp. 369–74, and is entitled "State Council Circular on Grasping This Year's Industry and Communications Production, Strive to Increase Production and Receipts, Guarantee Completing the Plan."

69. Interview at the Wuhan Tax Bureau, Nov. 16, 1984.

70. Wu: 9 mentions three types, the second of which, not relevant for the discussion here, was combinations organized on the basis of specialization of products. Another characterization was presented to me in an interview with the Wuhan Municipal Economic Commission, May 23, 1984. Men from that office told me that "tight" (*jimi*) unions were composed of firms all of which came under one management department and that linked production, marketing, supplies, finance, and personnel under one authority, and that "loose" unions were organized around one product and could be between firms under different departments. Some of those focused on spare parts, as when one factory had a good market but lacked the capacity to meet demand so gave part of its work to another factory, which used the brand name of the first firm. They called a third type *ziyou* (free); these involved associations among firms in different districts, under different departments, in different trades, and under separate ownership systems.

71. Xu: 290.

72. *CJRB*, Aug. 4, 1980, p. 1. There are similar stories on Nov. 8, 1979, p. 2; June 15, 1980, p. 1; and Aug. 12, 1980, p. 1. The operative principle was usually the payment of profits according to the proportion of investment contributed. A slight variant in the June 15, 1980, article is the calculation of profits according to the proportion of total fixed and liquid assets in the union that any given enterprise's premerger fixed and liquid assets represented.

73. The four unchanges were referred to, among many other places, in Bai and Zhang: 26. Their definition as given here was explained in an interview at the Wuhan Textile Bureau, May 26, 1984.

74. Dernberger: 164.

75. *SCB*, no. 8 (1980), pp. 227–28.

76. Bai and Zhang: 24.   77. Ibid.: 26.

78. Lu and Huang: 35.   79. Yan 1980a.

80. State Construction Commission Economic Research Office Investigation Group.

81. Zhuang and Kong: 17.

82. Industrial Economics Research Institute Investigation Group. See also Bai and Zhang: 28 on the disbanding of *lianhe* in Hubei. They say that "*lianhe* are hard to hold together."
83. *RMRB* editorial, Mar. 20, 1981; and *CJRB*, Nov. 28, 1980, p. 2.
84. See Pempel 1978: 160; and Dyson: 32 and 55.
85. In discussing the Japanese industrial associations, Dore: 19 makes the point that these groups are effective in that country because of a "strong sense of membership in 'the industry' as a community." He also refers, on p. 131, to "the general propensity to prefer co-operation to competition, when it can be clearly shown to be in one's long-term interest, [which] often gives these associations considerable power to constrain individual firms in the interests of 'the industry' as a whole. This makes them ideal interlocutors for MITI officials' attempts to impose direction on particular industries."
86. Lockwood: 499, 500. 87. Nakane: 57.
88. Kaplan: 66. 89. Sheahan: 231.
90. References to these complaints are in *RMRB*, Apr. 18, 1985, p. 2; *CJRB*, Nov. 28, 1980, p. 2, and Dec. 30, 1980, pp. 1, 2.
91. Lu and Huang: 35.
92. *RMRB* Commentator's article, May 29, 1980.
93. Wang Shufan: 21.
94. Wu Ming: 9.
95. Industrial Economics Research Institute: 39.
96. Wu: 9.
97. *CJRB*, Apr. 18, 1981, p. 1.

Conclusion

1. See Yamamura: Chapter 2; and Patrick and Rosovsky.
2. Dower: 293. See also Yamamura: Chapter 2.
3. See Baum: 14–17; and Hoffmann 1963: 53.
4. See Caves with Uekusa: 516.
5. Ashford 1982: 147–48.
6. See Sheahan: 78.
7. See Pempel 1982: 47, and Pempel and Tsunekawa: 258 on Japan; and MacRae: 2–3; Hoffmann 1963: 54, 56; and Kuisel: x, 249 on France.
8. See Pempel and Tsunekawa: 258.
9. See Baum: 175–76; and Ehrmann 1961: 535.
10. Kuisel: 278; Seibel: 155 notes that the First, or Monnet, Plan was supported by all social groups. See also Kindleberger.
11. Dower: 314; Fukui: 333.
12. See Johnson 1982: 197; Komiya: 190, 205; and Hane: 241–43, 286 for Japan. For France, see Hoffmann 1963: 30.

Notes to Pages 227–31   297

13. See Kuisel; xi, 249, and 278; and Baum: 175–76, and 181.
14. Muramatsu and Krauss: 6–7.
15. Finn: 55, 151, 210.
16. See Hoffmann 1963: 62; Kuisel: xi, 219; and McArthur and Scott: 78.
17. See Pitts: 270.
18. Sheahan: 32.
19. Zysman 1977: 70.
20. Johnson 1982: 41.
21. Ibid.
22. Yanaga: 38.
23. Noda: 123–25. For a brief discussion of the political connection between the *zaibatsu* and the militarist government during the war, see Pempel and Tsunekawa: 257.
24. Cumings 1987: 58.
25. Katzenstein 1978b highlights the significance for state guidance over foreign economic policy of control over investment funds, esp. on pp. 304, 305, and 335. He also stresses the role of the banking sector, as when, on pp. 315–16, he mentions the "de facto nationalization of the Bank of Japan"; p. 321, where he refers to the "parastatal banks which link the French state to the industrial sector"; and p. 327, where he says that "critical to the success of indirect management was a state-controlled credit market" in Japan.
26. Shonfield: 76–77; Sheahan: 29; and Zysman 1977: 55.
27. Baum: 8, 229; Hayward 1972: 287; and McArthur and Scott: 31.
28. Zysman 1977: 3; Sheahan: 29; DeWitt: 221; and Kuisel: 275.
29. How much weight to give to the state as opposed to the private sector and markets in Japanese economic development is a controversial topic among students of the Japanese economy. Nonetheless, many analysts assign it a continuously prominent role. Samuels 1987: 19 points out that Japanese scholars "have assumed a pervasive state in the economy." "Put simply," Samuels writes, "Japan is the most unambiguous case of state autonomy and strength." To use just one Japanese scholar as an example, Komiya: 224 states, "Since the Meiji Restoration, the Japanese government has been the main driving force in Japan's industrialization and modernization."
30. Johnson 1982: 23, 96; and Kaplan: 38.
31. Ohkawa and Rosovsky: 47; and Magaziner and Hout: 35.
32. See Katzenstein 1978b: 329, where he says that "at least since Colbert's mercantilism, Frenchmen have subscribed to the view that the engine of industrial progress is the state."
33. See Wylie: 211; Pitts: 269; and Suleiman 1974: 24.
34. Hoffmann: 123.
35. Maier: 34.
36. Williams 1964: 447; McArthur and Scott: 79–82; and Shonfield: 130.

37. Cohen, Halim, and Zysman: 110.
38. Magaziner and Hout: 37; Pempel 1982: 24; and Finn: 166.
39. Kaplan: 15, 21, 32, 34; Magaziner and Hout: 36.
40. Johnson 1987: 139.
41. Dore: 27.
42. Zysman 1977: 178–79, quoting Kenneth Jowitt.
43. Hoffmann 1963: 17; Ashford 1982: 13; Macrae: 3; Shonfield: 71; and Suleiman 1978: 225.
44. Zysman 1977: 197.
45. Yanaga: 7; Johnson 1982: 36.
46. Pempel 1982: 298; Komiya: 224; and Ohkawa and Rosovsky: 511.
47. Williams: 369–70.
48. See Ashford 1982: 4; Ehrmann 1957: 218; Hoffmann 1963: 96; Hoffmann 1974: 75; Cohen: 58; Williams: 352.
49. Yanaga: 7, 103; Pempel and Tsunekawa: 247; and Pempel 1982: 62–63.
50. Pempel 1978: 147.
51. Ehrmann 1961: 535.
52. Campbell: 297; Johnson 1982: 49; and Pempel 1982: 36.
53. See Wylie: 218. Landes: 336, 345 discusses this pattern and its basis in the family in France; and Ehrmann 1957: 429 says that the community is seen as an extension of the family. Tarrow: 144 and Kesselman: 156 note the "corporate unit of the commune" and "the commune as family." This is related to Macrae's: 31 characterization of the "strength and isolation of the French family." Nakane: 42–44, points to the same inclination in Japan.
54. Lord: 120.
55. See McArthur and Scott: 33 and Sheahan: 39 on France; Nakane: 99–100 on Japan; and Cheng: 148–50, 154 on China.
56. Nakane: 102.
57. Samuels 1983: 89, 85.
58. Richardson and Flanagan: 175.
59. Ibid.: 194.
60. Kesselman: esp. Introduction; Hoffmann 1963: 11, addressing what he terms the "atomization of French society" in the past, explains that pressure groups were always more effective on a local scale; Berger 1980: 104 writes of the small family firms tied to a locality. In another work (1972: 8), Berger speaks of the "network of social relations which extended no further than the village." And Williams: 6 says that the "small-scale economy bred strong local loyalties."
61. Suleiman 1974: 295.
62. Macrae: 28. See also Hall: 163, 165.

63. Williams: 353, 369; Ashford 1982: 59; Berger 1972: 9; Hoffmann 1963: 11, 15; Kesselman: 153; and Macrae: 32.
64. Nakane: 53, 59–60.
65. Johnson 1982: 49.
66. Richardson and Flanagan: 175.
67. Macrae: 322.
68. See Pempel and Tsunekawa: 254, 261–64 on Japan. They lay particular stress on the incorporation of workers into enterprise unions, which cut the force of any broader organization. Dower: 293, 339 details the "red purge" of the late 1940's, when thousands of activist union members were fired in response to strikes in 1946 and 1947. With regard to France, Ehrmann 1957: 433 notes the "notorious numerical and organizational weakness of the free trade unions" during World War II. Ashford 1982: 41, 57 calls the labor movement weak, owing to ideological divisions and its consequent split into three parts. Williams: 359 notes that the small plants of French industry and internal divisions within the working class usually hampered unions. An instance was the 1947 strikes, in which the violence and intimidation perpetrated by the communist-controlled unions provoked most of the non-communist minority to secede from the communist union, the CGT. Cohen: 130 notes that trade unions, along with consumer groups, small business groups, and parliament, were excluded from the planning process under the Monnet Plan. He discusses the social isolation of labor on pp. 195–98.
69. Finn: 214 on Japan; Hall: 158–59 and Safran: 62 on France.
70. For Japan, see Pempel and Tsunekawa: 254, and De Vos. On France, Ehrmann 1957: 430 also speaks of enterprise paternalism.
71. Hoffmann 1963: 73; Lockwood: 4; and Johnson: 78.
72. See Yanaga: 10, 13. Yanaga describes what he considers the basic relationship in Japanese society, the one linking the *oyabun*, or inferior, to the *kobun*, or superior, a relationship he traces to both feudalism and Confucianism.
73. Nakane: 134 notes the "general tendency of the majority of Japanese to seek security rather than autonomy"; Williams: 3 says that "business families valued security and stability more than risky expansion" in France.
74. For Japan, Samuels 1983: 39–55 treats this subject; for France, see Kesselman: Chapters 4 through 6.
75. Noda: 127–29.
76. The material in this section is drawn from Hall; Shonfield; articles by T. Smith, Pasquino and Pecchini, Fraenkel, Young, Hayward 1974, and Ashford 1981.
77. Shonfield: 178.

78. Hayward 1974: 410.
79. Ibid.: 405.
80. Both France and Japan boast world-famous elitist institutions that train many of their bureaucrats to high specialist standards: these are the Ecole Nationale d'Administration in France and the law faculty of Tokyo University in Japan.
81. This terms comes from Hall: 240.
82. Over six months before the spring demonstrations of 1989, the *New York Times* of Sept. 19, 1988, p. 1, reported 49 industrial strikes in the first half of the year sparked by rising prices and declining living standards.
83. There is a parallel in the growing capacity of private business to finance itself in France and to make arrangements with banks in Japan as economic recovery proceeded in those countries after 1950. This rehabilitation of the private sector in both places—a rehabilitation which their economic readjustments had furthered—lessened the degree of and the need for state economic control in those countries that had been necessary for these readjustments initially.
84. It is true that the central government was able to impose a program of severe economic austerity throughout the nation after September 1988, chiefly by cutting off bank credit. It has been singularly less successful, however, in instituting any "industrial policy" in recent years, despite a sudden fascination with this foreign concept from 1988 onward. For some of the many examples of press articles displaying this effort, see *RMRB*, Dec. 27, 1988, p. 1; Dec. 28, 1988, p. 2; Jan. 23, 1989, p. 1; Mar. 15, 1989, p. 1; Mar. 18, 1989, p. 1 (for the text of a State Council "Decision on the Outlines of the Current Industrial Policy"); Apr. 21, 1989, p. 1; Aug. 15, 1989, p. 5; Dec. 4, 1989, p. 2; and Feb. 6, 1990, p. 1.
85. *FBIS*, Sept. 7, 1989, p. 37.
86. I appreciate the comments of Steven Topik and R. Bin Wong in formulating these conclusions.
87. Gourevitch: 19.

Bibliography

For Chinese books in the list below I have transliterated and then translated the titles. For Chinese articles I have only translated the titles, and I have supplied the journals' titles and the volume and page numbers. Therefore, these items should be easy to locate without the transliterated title of the article itself. For journals that are cited more than once or twice, I have abbreviated the titles here; their full titles can be found in the List of Abbreviations. The full title is given for journals cited only once or twice.

Adams, F. Gerard, and Shinichi Ichimura. 1983. "Industrial Policy in Japan." In F. Gerard Adams and Lawrence R. Klein, eds., *Industrial Policies for Growth and Competitiveness*, pp. 307–23. Lexington, Mass.: D. C. Heath.
Anchordoguy, Marie. 1989. *Computers Inc.: Japan's Challenge to IBM*. Cambridge, Mass.: Harvard University / Council on East Asian Studies.
Ashford, Douglas. 1981. *Politics and Policy in Britain*. Philadelphia: Temple University Press.
———. 1982. *Policy and Politics in France: Living with Uncertainty*. Philadelphia: Temple University Press.
Bachman, David. 1986. "Differing Visions of China's Post-Mao Economy: The Ideas of Chen Yun, Deng Xiaoping, and Zhao Ziyang." *AS* 26, no. 3: 292–321.
Bai, Kangbi, and Zhang Siping. 1982. "Certain Issues That Need to Be Investigated in Hubei Province's Present Industrial Transformation and Association." *SKDT*, no. 4: 23–28.
Balazs, Etienne. 1964. *Chinese Civilization and Bureaucracy: Variations on a Theme*. Translated by H. M. Wright and edited by Arthur F. Wright. New Haven: Yale University Press.
Barfield, Claude E., and William A. Schambra. 1986. *The Politics of Industrial Policy*. Washington, D.C.: American Economic Institute.

Barnett, A. Doak. 1967. *Cadres, Bureaucracy and Political Power in Communist China*. New York: Columbia University Press.
———. 1986. "China's Modernization: Development and Reform in the 1980's." In U.S. Congress, Joint Economic Committee, *China's Economy Looks Toward the Year 2000*. Vol. 1: *The Four Modernizations*, pp. 1–14. Washington, D.C.: U.S. Government Printing Office.
Bauchet, Pierre. 1964. *Economic Planning: The French Experience*. New York: Praeger.
Baum, Warren C. 1958. *The French Economy and the State*. Princeton: Princeton University Press.
Belassa, Bela. 1986. "China's Economic Reforms in a Comparative Perspective." Paper presented at the Arden House Conference on Chinese Economic Reform, Harriman, N.Y., October 9–12.
Berger, Suzanne. 1972. *Peasants Against Politics: Rural Organization in Brittany, 1911–1967*. Cambridge, Mass.: Harvard University Press.
———. 1980. "The Traditional Sector in France and Italy." In Suzanne Berger and Michael J. Piore, eds., *Dualism and Discontinuity in Industrial Societies*, pp. 88–131. Cambridge, Eng.: Cambridge University Press.
Bornstein, Morris. 1977. "Economic Reform in Eastern Europe." In U.S. Congress, Joint Economic Committee, *East European Economies Post-Helsinki*, pp. 102–34. Washington, D.C.: U.S. Government Printing Office.
Brada, Josef C., and John Michael Montias. 1984. "Industrial Policy in Eastern Europe: A Three-Country Comparison." *Journal of Comparative Economics* 8: 377–419.
Brodsgaard, Kjeld Erik. 1983. "Paradigmatic Change, Readjustment and Reform in the Chinese Economy, 1953–1981, Part I." *Modern China* 9, no. 1: 37–83.
Browne, Stuart. Unpublished paper. University of Michigan, 1986.
Brus, Wlodzimierz. 1979. "The East European Reforms: What Happened to Them?" *Soviet Studies* 31, no. 2: 257–67.
Bunce, Valerie. 1981. *Do New Leaders Make a Difference? Executive Succession and Public Policy Under Capitalism and Socialism*. Princeton: Princeton University Press.
Burns, John P. 1987. "China's Nomenklatura System." *POC* 36 (Sept.–Oct.): 36–51.
Byrd, William. 1983. *China's Financial System: The Changing Role of Banks*. Boulder: Westview Press.
———. 1987. "The Role and Impact of Markets." In Gene Tidrick and Chen Jiyuan, eds., *China's Industrial Reform*, pp. 237–75. New York: Oxford University Press.

Byrd, William, et al. 1984. *Recent Chinese Economic Reforms: Studies of Two Industrial Enterprises.* World Bank Staff Working Papers, No. 652. Washington, D.C.: World Bank.

Calder, Kent E. 1988. *Crisis and Compensation: Public Policy and Political Stability in Japan, 1949–1986.* Princeton: Princeton University Press.

Campbell, John Creighton. 1984. "Policy Conflict and Its Resolution Within the Governmental System." In Ellis S. Krauss, Thomas P. Rohlen, and Patricia G. Steinhoff, eds., *Conflict in Japan*, pp. 294–334. Honolulu: University of Hawaii Press.

Caves, Richard E., with the collaboration of Masu Uekusa. 1976. "Industrial Organization." In Hugh Patrick and Henry Rosovsky, eds., *Asia's New Giant: How the Japanese Economy Works*, pp. 461–523. Washington, D.C.: Brookings Institution.

Chang, Parris. 1981. "Chinese Politics: Deng's Turbulent Quest." *POC* 30: 1–21.

Changjiang ribao (Yangtze Daily). Wuhan. 1979–82.

Cheng, Chu-yuan. 1971. *The Machine-Building Industry in Communist China.* Chicago: Aldine.

Chesneaux, Jean. 1968. *The Chinese Labor Movement, 1919–1927.* Stanford: Stanford University Press.

Chi, Hsin. 1977. *The Case of the Gang of Four.* Hong Kong: Cosmos Books.

Chong, Tong. 1982. "Looking at the Reorganization of Our Country's Machine-Building Trade." *HQ*, no. 3: 24–28.

Ch'u T'ung-tsu. 1961. *Law and Society in Traditional China.* Paris: Mouton.

Coble, Parks M., Jr. 1980. *Shanghai Capitalists and the Nationalist Government, 1927–1937.* Cambridge, Mass.: Harvard University Press.

Cohen, Stephen S. 1977. *Modern Capitalist Planning: The French Model.* Updated ed. Berkeley: University of California Press.

Cohen, Stephen S., Serge Halim, and John Zysman. 1986. "Institutions, Politics and Industrial Policy in France." In Claude E. Barfield and William A. Schambra, eds., *The Politics of Industrial Policy*, pp. 106–27. Washington, D.C.: American Economic Institute.

Comisso, Ellen, and Laura D'Andrea Tyson, eds. 1986. *Power, Purpose, and Collective Choice: Economic Strategy in Socialist States.* Ithaca: Cornell University Press.

Commentator. 1980. "Readjustment Is Still Key." *HQ*, no. 22: 2–4.

———. 1981a. "In Readjustment Go on a New Road to Develop the Economy." *HQ*, no. 7 (1981). Reprinted in *XHYB*, no. 4: 88–90.

———. 1981b. "Readjustment Isn't a Withdrawal, but Is Going Forward." *JJGL*, no. 4: 3–4.

Connor, Walter D. 1989. "Soviet Interests and Economic Reform." In Victor Nee and David Stark, eds., *Remaking the Economic Institutions of*

Socialism: China and Eastern Europe, pp. 306–27. Stanford: Stanford University Press.

Conquest, Robert. 1961. *Power and Policy in the U.S.S.R.: The Study of Soviet Dynamics.* London: Macmillan.

Cumings, Bruce. 1984. "The Political Economy of China's Turn Outward." In Samuel S. Kim, ed., *China and the World,* pp. 235–65. Boulder: Westview Press.

———. 1987. "The Origins and Development of the Northeast Asian Political Economy: Industrial Sectors, Product Cycles, and Political Consequences." In Frederic C. Deyo, ed., *The Political Economy of the New Asian Industrialism,* pp. 44–83. Ithaca: Cornell University Press.

"Dangdai Zhongguo" Cong Shu Bianji Weiyuanhui ("Present-day China" Collection Editing Committee). 1984. *Dangdai Zhongguo di jingji tizhi gaige* (Present-day China's economic system reform). Beijing: Chinese Social Science Publishing.

———. 1985. *Dangdai Zhongguo di qing gongye* (Present-day China's light industry). Vol. 1. Beijing: Chinese Social Science Publishing.

De Vos, George A. 1975. "Apprenticeship and Paternalism." In Ezra F. Vogel, ed., *Modern Japanese Organization and Decision-Making,* pp. 210–27. Berkeley: University of California Press.

Dernberger, Robert F. 1984. "The Domestic Economy and the Four Modernizations Program." In U. A. Johnson, G. R. Packard, and A. Wilhelm, Jr., eds., *China Policy for the Next Decade: Report of the Atlantic Council, Committee on China Policy,* pp. 139–79. Boston: Oelgeschlager, Gunn & Hain.

DeWitt, François. 1983. "French Industrial Policy from 1945–1981: An Assessment." In F. Gerard Adams and Lawrence R. Klein, eds., *Industrial Policies for Growth and Competitiveness,* pp. 221–45. Lexington, Mass.: D.C. Heath.

Deyo, Frederic C. 1987. "Coalitions, Institutions, and Linkage Sequencing—Toward a Strategic Capacity Model of East Asian Development." In Frederic C. Deyo, ed., *The Political Economy of the New Asian Industrialism,* pp. 227–47. Ithaca: Cornell University Press.

Ding, Zhangqing. 1984. "Questions and Experience in the Machine-Building Industry's Implementation of Three Forms of Planned Management." *JJGL,* no. 4: 8–10.

Dittmer, Lowell. 1982. "China in 1981: Reform, Readjustment, Rectification." *AS* 22, no. 1: 33–46.

———. 1987. *China's Continuous Revolution: The Post-Liberation Epoch, 1949–1981.* Berkeley: University of California Press.

Dong, Fureng. 1982. "Relationship Between Accumulation and Consumption." In Xu Dixin et al., *China's Search for Economic Growth: The*

Chinese Economy Since 1949, pp. 79–101. Translated by Andrew Watson. Beijing: New World Press.

Donnithorne, Audrey. 1981. *Centre-Provincial Economic Relations in China*. Contemporary China Papers, No. 16. Canberra: Contemporary China Centre, Research School of Pacific Studies, Australia National University.

Dore, Ronald. 1986. *Flexible Rigidities: Industrial Policy and Structural Adjustment in the Japanese Economy, 1970–1980*. Stanford: Stanford University Press.

Dower, J. W. 1979. *Empire and Aftermath: Yoshida Shigeru and the Japanese Experience, 1878–1954*. Cambridge, Mass.: Harvard University Press.

Dyson, Kenneth. 1983. "The Cultural, Ideological and Structural Context." In Kenneth Dyson and Stephen Wilks, eds., *Industrial Crisis: A Comparative Study of the State and Industry*, pp. 26–66. Oxford: Martin Robertson.

Dyson, Kenneth, and Stephen Wilks, eds. 1983. *Industrial Crisis: A Comparative Study of the State and Industry*. Oxford: Martin Robertson.

Editorial Board. 1981. "Make Sure to Grasp Readjustment by All Means." *JJGL*, no. 1: 3–6.

Ehrmann, Henry W. 1957. *Organized Business in France*. Princeton: Princeton University Press.

———. 1961. "French Bureaucracy and Organized Interests." *Administrative Science Quarterly* 5 (Mar.): 534–55.

Esherick, Joseph W. 1987. *The Origins of the Boxer Uprising*. Berkeley: University of California Press.

Evans, Peter B., Dietrich Rueschemeyer, and Theda Skocpol, eds. 1985. *Bringing the State Back In*. Cambridge, Eng.: Cambridge University Press.

Fang, Weizhong, ed. 1984. *Zhonghua renmin gongheguo jingji dashi ji* (Record of major economic events in the People's Republic of China, 1949–80). Beijing: China Social Science Academy.

Feeney, William. 1984. "Chinese Policy in Multilateral Financial Institutions." In Samuel S. Kim, ed., *China and the World: Chinese Foreign Policy in the Post-Mao Era*, pp. 266–92. Boulder: Westview Press.

Feuerwerker, Albert. 1958. *China's Early Industrialization: Sheng Hsuan-huai (1844–1916) and Mandarin Enterprise*. Cambridge, Mass.: Harvard University Press.

Field, Robert Michael. 1984. "Changes in Chinese Industry Since 1978." *CQ*, no. 100: 742–61.

Finn, Richard B. 1991. *From Hiroshima to San Francisco: MacArthur, Yoshida and the Occupation of Japan*. Berkeley: University of California Press.

Fong, Glenn R. 1990. "State Strength, Industry Structure, and Industrial

Policy: American and Japanese Experiences in Microelectronics." *Comparative Politics* 22, no. 3: 273–300.

Foreign Broadcast Information Service: Daily Report, China. 1979–82.

Fraenkel, Gioachino. 1975. "Italian Industrial Policy in the Framework of Economic Planning." In Jack Hayward and Michael Watson, eds., *Planning, Politics and Public Policy: The British, French and Italian Experience*, pp. 128–40. Cambridge, Eng.: Cambridge University Press.

Fukui, Haruhiro. "Economic Planning in Postwar Japan: A Case Study in Policy Making." *AS* 12, no. 4: 327–48.

Gamarnikow, Michael. 1968. *Economic Reforms in Eastern Europe.* Detroit: Wayne State University Press.

Gao, Shangquan. 1982. "Doing Equipment Renovation with Keypoints and Steps Is a Strategic Economic Task." *JJGL*, no. 2: 27–30, 39.

Gottschaung, Thomas. 1984. "Comparative Advantage and Government Policy in the Recent Economic Development of Liaoning Province." Paper presented at the Economic Bureaucracy Workshop held at the East-West Center, Honolulu, Hawaii, July 17–20.

Gourevitch, Peter. 1986. *Politics in Hard Times: Comparative Responses to International Economic Crises.* Ithaca: Cornell University Press.

Granick, David. 1987. "The Industrial Environment in China and the CMEA Countries." In Gene Tidrick and Chen Jiyuan, eds., *China's Industrial Reform*, pp. 103–31. New York: Oxford University Press.

Guojia Tongjiju bian (State Statistical Bureau, ed.). 1985a. *Zhongguo tongji nianjian* (Chinese statistical yearbook) *1985*. Beijing: State Statistical Publishing.

———. 1985b. *Zhongguo tongji zhaiyao* (Chinese statistical abstract) *1985*. Beijing: Chinese Statistical Publishing.

———. 1987. *Zhongguo tongji nianjian 1987* (China statistical yearbook). Beijing: China Statistical Publishing.

Gustafson, Thane. 1981. *Reform in Soviet Politics: Lessons of Recent Policies on Land and Water.* Cambridge, Eng.: Cambridge University Press.

Hall, Peter A. 1986. *Governing the Economy: The Politics of State Intervention in Britain and France.* New York: Oxford University Press.

Hane, Mikiso. 1986. *Modern Japan: A Historical Survey.* Boulder: Westview Press.

Hanson, Philip. 1968. *The Consumer in the Soviet Economy.* London: Macmillan.

Hao, Mengbi, and Duan Jieran, eds. 1984. *Zhongguo Gongchandang liushinian* (60 years of the Chinese Communist Party). Vol. 2. Nanjing: Liberation Army Publishing.

Harding, Harry. 1984. "China's Changing Roles in the Contemporary

World." In Harry Harding, ed., *China's Foreign Relations in the 1980s*, pp. 177–223. New Haven: Yale University Press.
———. 1986. "Political Stability and Succession." In U.S. Congress, Joint Economic Committee, *China's Economy Looks Toward the Year 2000*. Vol. 1: *The Four Modernizations*, pp. 49–71. Washington, D.C.: U.S. Government Printing Office.
Hayes, Michael T. 1978. "The Semi-Sovereign Pressure Groups: A Critique of Current Theory and an Alternative Typology." *Journal of Politics*, no. 40: 134–61.
Hayward, J. E. S. 1972. "State Intervention in France: The Changing Style of Government-Industry Relations." *Political Studies* 20, no. 3: 287–98.
———. 1974. "National Aptitudes for Planning in Britain, France, and Italy." *Government and Opposition* 9, no. 4: 397–410.
Henderson, Gail E., and Myron S. Cohen. 1984. *The Chinese Hospital: A Socialist Work Unit*. New Haven: Yale University Press.
Hershatter, Gail. 1986. *The Workers of Tianjin, 1900–1949*. Stanford: Stanford University Press.
Ho, Ping-ti. 1954. "The Salt Merchants of Yang-chou: A Study of Commercial Capitalism in Eighteenth Century China." *Harvard Journal of Asiatic Studies* 17: 130–68.
Ho, Samuel P. S., and Ralph W. Huenemann. 1984. *China's Open Door Policy: The Quest for Foreign Technology and Capital, a Study of China's Special Trade*. Vancouver: University of British Columbia Press.
Hoffmann, Stanley. 1963. "Paradoxes of the French Political Community." In Stanley Hoffmann, ed., *In Search of France*, pp. 1–117. Cambridge, Mass.: Harvard University Press.
———. 1974. *Decline or Renewal? France Since the 1930s*. New York: Viking Press.
Hough, Jerry. 1969. *Soviet Prefects: The Local Party Organs in Industrial Decision-making*. Cambridge, Mass.: Harvard University Press.
———. 1977. *The Soviet Union and Social Science Theory*. Cambridge, Mass.: Harvard University Press.
Huang, Zhenyu. 1981. "How Should the Shanghai Machine-Building Industry be Readjusted?" *SHKX*, no. 4: 97–100.
Hubei Province Statistical Bureau Comprehensive Office. 1981. "Our Province's Industrial Structure Must Be Readjusted." *SKDT*, no. 28: 24–29.
Industrial Economics Research Institute Investigation Group. 1981. "Accurately Handle the Relationship Between Companies and Factories:

An Investigation of the Changzhou Tractor Company." *JJGL*, no. 2: 37–40, 48.

Ishikawa, Shigeru. 1987. "Sino-Japanese Economic Cooperation." *CQ*, no. 109: 1–21.

Jancar, Barbara Wolfe. 1971. *Czechoslovakia and the Absolute Monopoly of Power*. New York: Praeger.

Japan Economic Institute of America. 1984. *Japan's Industrial Policies*. Washington, D.C.: Japan Economic Institute of America.

Jiang, Chufang. 1980. "An Important Topic in Making the Textile Industry Develop Fast." *JJGL*, no. 1: 24–26.

Jie, Wenzuo. N.d. "The Structure of Light Industry." In Ma Hong and Sun Shangqing, eds., *Zhongguo jingji jiegou wenti yanjiu* (Investigations into questions of China's economic structure), pp. 195–222. Beijing: People's Publishing.

Jin, Hui. 1983a. "An Opinion on Raising the Industrial Economic Results of Hubei Province." *HCXX*, no. 6: 57–63.

———. 1983b. "Analysis of Hubei Province's Industrial Development Speed and Economic Results." *SKDT*, no. 20: 6–12.

Jin, Ji, and Tong Tai. 1981. "How Did Zhejiang Province Keep a Certain Industrial Growth Rate During Readjustment?" *JJGL*, no. 11: 3–6.

Jing, Ping. 1983. "Everyone Should Support Keypoint Construction." *HQ*, no. 8: 16–18.

Johnson, Chalmers. 1982. *MITI and the Japanese Miracle*. Stanford: Stanford University Press.

———. 1986. "The Institutional Foundations of Japanese Industrial Policy." In Claude E. Barfield and William A. Schambra, eds., *The Politics of Industrial Policy*, pp. 187–205. Washington, D.C.: American Economic Institute, 1986.

———. 1987. "Political Institutions and Economic Performance: The Government-Business Relationship in Japan, South Korea, and Taiwan." In Frederic C. Deyo, ed., *The Political Economy of the New Asian Industrialism*, pp. 136–64. Ithaca: Cornell University Press.

———. 1988. "Studies of Japanese Political Economy: A Crisis in Theory." In Japan Foundation, ed., *Japanese Studies in the United States. Part I: History and Present Condition*, pp. 95–113. Ann Arbor: Swenk-Tuttle Press.

Ju, Zhongyi. 1980. "'The New Economic Faction' Overturns the 'Petroleum Faction.'" *Dongxiang* (Trend), no. 24.

Kaplan, Eugene J. 1972. *JAPAN: The Government-Business Relationship*. Washington, D.C.: U.S. Department of Commerce.

Katzenstein, Peter J., ed. 1978a. *Between Power and Plenty: Foreign Eco-*

nomic Policies of Advanced Industrial States. Madison: University of Wisconsin Press.

———. 1978b. "Conclusion." In Peter J. Katzenstein, ed., *Between Power and Plenty: Foreign Economic Policies of Advanced Industrial States,* pp. 295–336. Madison: University of Wisconsin Press.

———. 1978c. "Introduction: Domestic and International Forces and Strategies of Foreign Economic Policy." In Peter J. Katzenstein, ed., *Between Power and Plenty: Foreign Economic Policies of Advanced Industrial States,* pp. 3–22. Madison: University of Wisconsin Press.

Keeler, John T. S. 1985. "Situating France on the Pluralism-Corporatism Continuum: A Critique of and Alternative to the Wilson Perspective." *Comparative Politics* 17, no. 2: 229–49.

Kesselman, Mark. 1967. *The Ambiguous Consensus: A Study of Local Government in France.* New York: Alfred A. Knopf.

Kindleberger, Charles P. 1963. "The Postwar Resurgence of the French Economy." In Stanley Hoffmann, ed., *In Search of France,* pp. 118–58. Cambridge, Mass.: Harvard University Press.

Kingdon, John W. 1984. *Agendas, Alternatives, and Public Policies.* Boston: Little, Brown.

Kokubun, Ryosei. 1986. "The Politics of Foreign Economic Policy-Making in China: The Case of Plant Cancellations with Japan." *CQ,* no. 105: 19–45.

Komiya, Ryutaro. 1975. "Planning in Japan." In Morris Bornstein, ed., *Economic Planning, East and West,* pp. 189–227. Cambridge, Mass.: Ballinger.

Kornai, Janos. 1980. *Economics of Shortage.* 2 vols. Amsterdam: North-Holland.

Kueh, Y. Y. 1989. "The Maoist Legacy and China's New Industrialization Strategy." *CQ,* no. 119: 420–47.

Kuisel, Richard F. 1981. *Capitalism and the State in Modern France.* Cambridge, Eng.: Cambridge University Press.

Lampton, D. Michael. 1987a. "Chinese Politics: The Bargaining Treadmill." *I&S* 23, no. 3: 11–41.

———. 1987b. "Introduction." In D. Michael Lampton, ed., *Policy Implementation in Post-Mao China,* pp. 3–24. Berkeley: University of California Press.

———. 1987c. "Water: Challenge to a Fragmented Political System." In D. Michael Lampton, ed., *Policy Implementation in Post-Mao China,* pp. 157–89. Berkeley: University of California Press.

Landes, David S. 1957. "Observations on France: Economy, Society, and Polity." *World Politics* 9, no. 3: 329–50.

Lardy, Nicholas R. 1984a. "Consumption and Living Standards in China, 1978–1983." *CQ*, no. 100: 849–65.
———. 1984b. "Dilemmas in the Pattern of Resource Allocation, 1978–1984." Paper presented at the conference "To Reform the Chinese Political Order," Harwichport, Mass., June 18–23.
Lardy, Nicholas, and Kenneth Lieberthal, eds. 1983. *Chen Yun's Strategy for China's Development*. White Plains, N.Y.: M. E. Sharpe.
Lee, Chae-jin. 1984. *China and Japan: New Economic Diplomacy*. Stanford: Hoover Institution Press.
Lee, Hong Yung. 1991. *From Revolutionary Cadres to Party Technocrats in Socialist China*. Berkeley: University of California Press.
Lee, Peter N. S. 1984. "The Economic Bureaucracy and Industrial Policy in Guangdong During the Post-Mao Era, 1979–1983." Paper presented at the Economic Bureaucracy Workshop at the East-West Center, Honolulu, Hawaii, 17–20 July.
Leung, Chi-yan. 1986. "The Politics of Economic Readjustment: A Case Study of the Economic Policy-Making Process in China, 1979 to 1982." Ph.D. dissertation prospectus, Hong Kong University, Department of Government.
Lewek, Jim. 1986. "China's Electric Power Industry." In U.S. Congress, Joint Economic Committee, *China's Economy Looks Toward the Year 2000*. Vol. 2: *Economic Openness in Modernizing China*, pp. 104–22. Washington, D.C.: U.S. Government Printing Office.
Li, Chengrui. 1985. "Economic Reform Brings Better Life." *BR*, no. 29: 15–22.
Li, Meijun, and Wang Zhenzhang. 1983. "The Historical Situation of Wuhan's Formation as a Domestic Economic Center." *SKDT*, no. 12: 25–32.
Lieberthal, Kenneth. 1987. "The Great Leap Forward and the Split in the Yenan Leadership." In Roderick MacFarquhar and John King Fairbank, eds., *The Cambridge History of China*. Vol. 14: *The People's Republic, Part I: The Emergence of Revolutionary China, 1949–1965*, pp. 293–359. Cambridge, Eng.: Cambridge University Press.
Lieberthal, Kenneth, and Michel Oksenberg. 1986. *Bureaucratic Politics and Chinese Energy Development*. Washington, D.C.: U.S. Government Printing Office.
———. 1988. *Policy Making in China: Leaders, Structures and Processes*. Princeton: Princeton University Press.
Lin, Cyril Chihren. 1981. "The Reinstatement of Economics in China Today." *CQ*, no. 85: 1–48.
Lin, Zili. 1981. *Jingji tiaozheng he zaishengchan lilun* (The theory of eco-

nomic readjustment and reproduction). Shanghai: People's Publishing.
Lindblom, Charles E. 1977. *Politics and Markets: The World's Political-Economic Systems*. New York: Basic Books.
Linden, Carl A. 1966. *Khrushchev and the Soviet Leadership, 1957–1964*. Baltimore: Johns Hopkins Press.
Liu, Guoguang. 1983. *Lun jingji gaige yu jingji tiaozheng* (On economic reform and economic readjustment). Yangchou: Jiangsu People's Publishing.
Lo, Rujia. 1986. "The Background and Prospects for the Chinese Communists' Political System Reform." *ZM*, no. 108 (Oct.): 23–24.
Lockwood, William W. 1965. "Japan's New Capitalism." In William W. Lockwood, ed., *The State and Economic Enterprise in Japan*, pp. 447–522. Princeton: Princeton University Press.
Lord, Guy. 1973. *The French Budgetary Process*. Berkeley: University of California Press.
Lowi, Theodore J. 1964. "American Business, Public Policy Case Studies, and Political Theory." *World Politics* 16 (July): 677–715.
Lu, Hanlin, and Huang Chengyou. 1982. "Certain Problems in the Readjustment of the Service Orientation of Wuhan's Machine-Building Industry." *Wuhan Daxue Xuebao* (Wuhan University Journal), January, pp. 31–36.
Ma, Hong. 1982. *Jingji jiegou yu jingji quanli* (Economic structure and economic management). Beijing: People's Publishing.
———. 1983. *New Strategy for China's Economy*. Translated by Yang Lin. Beijing: New World Press.
Ma, Hong, and Sun Shangqing, eds. N.d. *Zhongguo jingji jiegou wenti yanjiu* (Investigations into questions of China's economic structure). Beijing: People's Publishing.
MacFarquhar, Roderick, Timothy Cheek, and Eugene Wu, eds. 1989. *The Secret Speeches of Chairman Mao: From the Hundred Flowers to the Great Leap Forward*. Cambridge, Mass.: Council on East Asian Studies / Harvard University.
Macrae, Duncan, Jr. 1967. *Parliament, Parties, and Society in France, 1946–1958*. New York: St. Martin's Press.
Magaziner, Ira C., and Thomas M. Hout. 1980. *Japanese Industrial Policy*. Berkeley: University of California Press.
Maier, Charles S. 1981. "The Determinants of Interest Group Formation." In Suzanne Berger, ed., *Organizing Interests in Western Europe: Pluralism, Corporatism, and the Transformation of Politics*, pp. 27–61. Cambridge, Eng.: Cambridge University Press.

Mao, Zedong. 1974. *Mao Zedong sixiang wansui* (Long live the thought of Mao Zedong). Vol. 2. Taipei: Institute of International Relations.

———. 1977. *Mao Zedong xuanji: Diwuzhuan* (Mao Zedong's selected works: Fifth volume). Beijing: People's Publishing.

McArthur, John H., and Bruce R. Scott. 1969. *Industrial Planning in France*. Boston: Harvard University, Graduate School of Business Administration, Division of Research.

Melnick, Diane. 1986. Unpublished paper. University of Michigan.

Meyer, Alfred G. 1970. "Theories of Convergence." In Chalmers Johnson, ed., *Change in Communist Systems*, pp. 313–41. Stanford: Stanford University Press.

Montias, John Michael. 1962. *Central Planning in Poland*. New Haven: Yale University Press.

Morse, Hosea Ballou. 1909. *The Gilds of China*. London: Longmans, Green.

Munro, Donald. 1988. *Images of Human Nature: A Sung Portrait*. Princeton: Princeton University Press.

Muramatsu, Michio, and Ellis S. Krauss. 1985. "The Ruling Coalition and Its Transformation: Hoshu Honryu and the Development of Postwar Japan's Political Economy." Revised. Paper presented at the Japan Political Economy Committee's Second Conference on the Political Economy of Japan. Honolulu, Hawaii, January 6–11.

N.a. 1980. "Jiangsu Province Local (Municipal) Machine-Building Bureau Directors' Forum Discusses Eight Roads: 'After National Tasks Are Cut Back, What Should the Machine-Building Trade Do?'" *JJGL*, no. 2: 19–20.

———. 1981. "Seriously Solve the Problem of Blindly Building Factories, Blindly Producing in Light Industrial Development." *JJGL*, no. 3: 19–20.

———. 1982a. "Hubei Province Economic Theoretical Workers Link with Reality, Discuss Theoretical Questions About Industrial Transformation and Combinations." *SKDT*, no. 4: 16–23.

———. 1982b. "New Changes in the Proportional Relations Between Accumulation and Consumption in Hubei Province." *SKDT*, no. 18: 39–43.

———. 1982c. "Our National Economic Circles Are Just Investigating New Questions in the National Economy." *Jingji cankao* (Economic reference), no. 20 (1981). Reprinted in *SKDT*, no. 4: 12–16.

———. 1982d. "Readjust the Enterprise Structure, Progressively Solve the Problem of Blind Construction and Duplicated Construction." *JJGL*, no. 1: 20.

———. 1982e. *Zhongguo shehuizhuyi jingji fazhanzhong di wenti* (Ques-

tions in China's socialist economic development). Beijing: Chinese Social Science Publishing.
———. 1983. "Cadre Theoretical Study of Deng Xiaoping's Selected Works: Certain Important Theoretical Points." *HQ*, no. 17: 41.
———. 1984. "Exploring Some Problems in Reforming Our System of Distribution of the Means of Production." *Caimao jingji* (Finance and Trade Economy), no. 12: 22–26.
Nakane, Chie. 1970. *Japanese Society*. Berkeley: University of California Press.
Naquin, Susan, and Evelyn S. Rawski. 1987. *Chinese Society in the Eighteenth Century*. New Haven: Yale University Press.
Nathan, Andrew J. 1985. *Chinese Democracy*. New York: Alfred A. Knopf.
Naughton, Barry. 1983a. "The Decline of Central Control over Investment in Post-Mao China." Eugene, Ore.: University of Oregon, Department of Economics. Manuscript.
———. 1983b. "The Profit Motive." *CBR*, Nov.–Dec., pp. 14–18.
———. 1985a. "American Economists' Study Team to the PRC." Manuscript.
———. 1985b. "False Starts and Second Wind: Financial Reforms in China's Industrial System." In Elizabeth J. Perry and Christine Wong, eds., *The Political Economy of Reform in Post-Mao China*, pp. 223–52. Cambridge, Mass.: Council on East Asian Studies / Harvard University.
———. 1986. "Economy." In John S. Major, ed., *China Briefing, 1985*, pp. 53–65. Boulder: Westview Press.
———. 1987. "The Third Front." Manuscript. This paper later appeared in *CQ*, no. 115: 351–86 (1988).
———. 1989. "Hierarchy and the Bargaining Economy: Government and Enterprise in the Reform Process." In David M. Lampton and Kenneth Lieberthal, eds., "Bureaucratic Behavior in China." Manuscript.
Naughton, Barry, and Dorothy J. Solinger. 1984. "Hubei and Wuhan: Shifting Strategies for Economic Development." Paper presented at the Economic Bureaucracy Workshop held at the East-West Center, Honolulu, Hawaii, July 17–20.
Nie, Changze. 1981. "How the Textile Industry in Hubei Province Is Going Forward in Readjustment." *HCXX*, no. 2: 122–24.
Noda, Kazuo. 1975. "Big Business Organization." In Ezra F. Vogel, ed., *Modern Japanese Organization and Decision-Making*, pp. 115–45. Berkeley: University of California Press.
Nove, Alec. 1969. *An Economic History of the U.S.S.R.* Harmondsworth: Penguin Books.

314 Bibliography

———. 1983. *The Economics of Feasible Socialism*. London: George Allen & Unwin.

Nove, Alec, and D. M. Nuti, eds. 1972. *Socialist Economics: Selected Readings*. Harmondsworth: Penguin Books.

Ohkawa, Kazushi, and Henry Rosovsky. 1965. "A Century of Japanese Economic Growth." In William W. Lockwood, ed., *The State and Economic Enterprise in Japan*, pp. 47–92. Princeton: Princeton University Press.

Olson, Mancur. 1982. *The Rise and Decline of Nations: Economic Growth, Stagflation, and Social Rigidities*. New Haven: Yale University Press.

Pasquino, Gianfranco, and Umberto Pecchini. 1975. "Italy." In Jack Hayward and Michael Watson, eds., *Planning, Politics and Public Policy: The British, French and Italian Experience*, pp. 70–92. Cambridge, Eng.: Cambridge University Press.

Passin, Herbert. 1962. "The Stratigraphy of Protest in Japan." In Morton A. Kaplan, ed., *The Revolution in World Politics*, pp. 92–110. New York: John Wiley and Sons.

Patrick, Hugh, and Henry Rosovsky. 1976. "Japan's Economic Performance: An Overview." In Hugh Patrick and Henry Rosovsky, eds., *Asia's New Giant: How the Japanese Economy Works*, pp. 1–62. Washington, D.C.: Brookings Institution.

Pempel, T. J. 1978. "Japanese Foreign Economic Policy: The Domestic Bases for International Behavior." In Peter J. Katzenstein, ed., *Between Power and Plenty: Foreign Economic Policies of Advanced Industrial States*, pp. 139–90. Madison: University of Wisconsin Press.

———. 1982. *Policy and Politics in Japan*. Philadelphia: Temple University Press.

Pempel, T. J., and Keiichi Tsunekawa. 1979. "Corporatism Without Labor? The Japanese Anomaly." In Philippe C. Schmitter and Gerhard Lehmbruch, eds., *Trends Toward Corporatist Intermediation*, pp. 231–70. Beverly Hills: Sage.

Perkins, Dwight H. 1986. *China: Asia's Next Economic Giant?* Seattle: University of Washington Press.

———. 1988. "Reforming China's Economic System." *Journal of Economic Literature* 26 (June): 601–45.

Perry, Elizabeth J. 1990. "Shanghai on Strike: The Politics of Chinese Labor." Manuscript. Seattle.

Pitts, Jesse R. 1963. "Continuity and Change in Bourgeois France." In Stanley Hoffmann, ed., *In Search of France*, pp. 235–304. Cambridge, Mass.: Harvard University Press.

Poznanski, Kazimierz. 1986. "Economic Adjustment and Political

Forces: Poland Since 1970." In Ellen Comisso and Laura D'Andrea Tyson, eds., *Power, Purpose, and Collective Choice: Economic Strategy in Socialist States,* pp. 279–312. Ithaca: Cornell University Press.

Qi, Chang. 1981. "Readjustment and 'Going Against the Tide.'" *JJGL,* no. 11: 62–63.

Qing, Yan. 1982. "Light Industry's Increase in Economic Readjustment in 1981." *JJGL,* no. 2: 17–20.

Qiu, Jingjin, and Huang Juefei. N.d. "The Structure of the Machine-Building Industry." In Ma Hong and Sun Shangqing, eds., *Zhongguo jingji jiegou wenti yanjiu* (Investigations into questions of Chinese economic structure), pp. 317–45. Beijing: People's Publishing.

Rawski, Thomas G. 1989. *Economic Growth in Prewar China.* Berkeley: University of California Press.

Reich, Robert B. 1983. "Why Democracy Makes Economic Sense." *New Republic,* Dec. 19, pp. 25–31.

Reid, Donald. 1985. "Industrial Paternalism: Discourse and Practice in Nineteenth-Century French Mining and Metallurgy." *Comparative Studies in Society and History* 27, no. 4: 579–607.

Reynolds, Bruce. 1984. "China in the International Economy." In Harry Harding, ed., *China's Foreign Relations in the 1980s,* pp. 71–106. New Haven: Yale University Press.

———. ed. 1987. *Reform in China: Challenges and Choices, a Summary and Analysis of the CESRRI Survey.* Prepared by the Staff of the Chinese Economic System Reform Research Institute. Armonk, N.Y.: M. E. Sharpe.

Richardson, Bradley M., and Scott C. Flanagan. 1984. *Politics in Japan.* Boston: Little, Brown.

Ripley, Randall, and Grace Franklin. 1980. *Congress, the Bureaucracy and Public Policy.* Rev. ed. Homewood, Ill.: Dorsey Press.

Riskin, Carl. 1987. *China's Political Economy: The Quest for Development Since 1949.* New York: Oxford University Press.

Robinson, William F. 1973. *The Pattern of Reform in Hungary: A Political, Economic and Cultural Analysis.* New York: Praeger.

Rowe, William T. 1984a. "Economic Change in the Middle Yangtze Macroregion, 1736–1938." Paper presented at the Conference on Spatial and Temporal Trends and Cycles in the Chinese Economy, 980–1980, Bellagio, Italy, Aug. 1984.

———. 1984b. *Hankow: Commerce and Society in a Chinese City, 1796–1889.* Stanford: Stanford University Press.

———. 1989. *Hankow: Conflict and Community in a Chinese City, 1796–1895.* Stanford: Stanford University Press.

Rueschemeyer, Dietrich, and Peter B. Evans. 1985. "The State and Eco-

nomic Transformation: Toward an Analysis of the Conditions Underlying Effective Intervention." In Peter B. Evans, Dietrich Rueschemeyer, and Theda Skocpol, eds., *Bringing the State Back In*, pp. 44–77. Cambridge, Eng.: Cambridge University Press.
Safran, William. 1985. *The French Polity*. 2d ed. New York: Longmans.
Samuels, Richard J. 1983. *The Politics of Regional Policy in Japan*. Princeton: Princeton University Press.
———. 1987. *The Business of the Japanese State: Energy Markets in Comparative and Historical Perspective*. Ithaca: Cornell University Press.
Sandholtz, Wayne. Forthcoming. *Crisis and Collaboration: Toward a High-Tech Europe*. Berkeley: University of California Press.
Schroeder, Gertrude E. 1971. "Soviet Economic Reform at an Impasse." *POC* 20 (July–Aug.): 36–46.
Schurmann, Franz. 1967. *Ideology and Organization in Communist China*. Berkeley: University of California Press.
Scott, James C. 1985. *Weapons of the Weak: Everyday Forms of Peasant Resistance*. New Haven: Yale University Press.
Seibel, Claude. 1975. "Planning in France." In Morris Bornstein, ed., *Economic Planning, East and West*, pp. 153–84. Cambridge, Mass.: Ballinger.
Shanghai Economic Forum Secretarial Group. 1980. "Several Different Kinds of Opinions About Shanghai's Economic Structure." *SHKX*, no. 1: 80–82.
Sheahan, John. 1963. *Promotion and Control of Industry in Postwar France*. Cambridge, Mass.: Harvard University Press.
Shirk, Susan L. 1983. "Bureaucratic Competition." *CBR*, Nov.–Dec., pp. 24–25.
———. 1985. "The Politics of Industrial Reform." In Elizabeth J. Perry and Christine Wong, eds., *The Political Economy of Reform in Post-Mao China*, pp. 195–221. Cambridge, Mass.: Council on East Asian Studies / Harvard University.
Shonfield, Andrew. 1965. *Modern Capitalism*. London: Oxford University Press.
Shue, Vivienne. 1988. *The Reach of the State: Sketches of the Chinese Body Politic*. Stanford: Stanford University Press.
Simon, Denis Fred. 1987. "The Evolving Role of Foreign Investment and Technology Transfer in China's Modernization Program." In John S. Major. ed., *China Briefing, 1987*, pp. 41–67. Boulder: Westview Press.
Skocpol, Theda. 1985. "Bringing the State Back In: Strategies of Analysis in Current Research." In Peter B. Evans, Dietrich Rueschemeyer, and Theda Skocpol, eds., *Bringing the State Back In*, pp. 2–43. Cambridge, Eng.: Cambridge University Press.

Smith, T. Alexander. 1969. "Toward a Comparative Theory of the Policy-Process." *Comparative Politics* 1 (July): 498–515.
Smith, Trevor. 1975. "Industrial Planning in Britain." In Jack Hayward and Michael Watson, eds., *Planning, Politics and Public Policy: The British, French and Italian Experience*, pp. 111–27. Cambridge, Eng.: Cambridge University Press.
Solinger, Dorothy J. 1982. "The Fifth National People's Congress and the Process of Policymaking: Reform, Readjustment, and the Opposition." *AS* 22, no. 12: 1238–75.
———. 1984a. *Chinese Business Under Socialism*. Berkeley: University of California Press.
———. 1984b. "Reform of the Structure of the Economic System: A Spatial Interpretation." Paper presented at the conference "To Reform the Chinese Political Order," Harwichport, Mass., June 18–23.
———. 1987. "Uncertain Paternalism: Tensions in Recent Regional Restructuring in China." *International Regional Science Review* 11, no. 1: 23–42.
———. 1989. "Capitalist Measures with Chinese Characteristics." *POC* 38 (Jan.–Feb.): 19–33.
Song, Jiwen. 1981a. "On Greatly Increasing the Production of Consumer Products." *HQ*, no. 6: 8–12.
———. 1981b. "Speed Up the Development of Light Industry with Readjustment as the Center." *JJGL*, no. 5: 3–7.
Special Correspondent. 1979. "Do Readjustment Well." *HQ*, no. 5: 2–5.
State Construction Commission Economic Research Office Investigation Group. 1982. "How to Do Transformation Work Well in Industrial Enterprises." *JJGL*, no. 2: 21–24, 49.
State Statistical Bureau. 1983. *Statistical Yearbook of China 1983*. Hong Kong: Economic Information and Agency.
———. 1986. *Statistical Yearbook of China 1986*. Hong Kong: Economic Information and Agency.
Strand, David. 1989. *Rickshaw Beijing: City People and Politics in the 1920s*. Berkeley: University of California Press.
Suleiman, Ezra N. 1974. *Politics, Power, and Bureaucracy in France*. Princeton: Princeton University Press.
———. 1978. *Elites in French Society*. Princeton: Princeton University Press.
Sun, Xiaoliang. 1983. "How the Machine-Building Industry Implements the Direction of Planned Economy as Primary and Market Adjustment as Supplementary." *JJGL*, no. 1: 26–29.
Sun, Xiaoliang, and Qin Zongxu. 1982. "Some Opinions about the Machine-Building Industry's Specialization and Transformation." *JJGL*, no. 3: 26–29.

Tang, Jianzhong, and Laurence J. C. Ma. 1985. "Evolution of Urban Collective Enterprises in China." *CQ*, no. 104: 614–40.
Tarrow, Sidney. 1977. *Between Center and Periphery: Grassroots Politicians in Italy and France*. New Haven: Yale University Press.
Teng, Hsiao-p'ing. 1981. "Speech at a CCP Central Working Conference." Translated in *I&S* 17, no. 7: 101–19.
Thurow, Lester C. 1980. *The Zero-Sum Society: Distribution and the Possibilities for Economic Change*. New York: Basic Books.
Tidrick, Gene. 1987. In Gene Tidrick and Chen Jiyuan, eds., *China's Industrial Reform*, pp. 175–209. New York: Oxford University Press.
Tidrick, Gene, and Chen Jiyuan. 1987. "The Essence of the Industrial Reforms." In Gene Tidrick and Chen Jiyuan, eds., *China's Industrial Reform*, pp. 1–10. New York: Oxford University Press.
Tilly, Charles. 1975. "Reflections on the History of European State-Making." In Charles Tilly, ed., *The Formation of National States in Western Europe*, pp. 3–83. Princeton: Princeton University Press.
Trezise, Philip H., with Yukio Suzuki. 1976. "Politics, Government and Economic Growth in Japan." In Hugh Patrick and Henry Rosovsky, eds., *Asia's New Giant: How the Japanese Economy Works*, pp. 753–812. Washington, D.C.: Brookings Institution.
Tsou, Tang. 1986. *The Cultural Revolution and Post-Mao Reforms: A Historical Perspective*. Chicago: University of Chicago Press.
Walder, Andrew G. 1983. "Organized Dependency and Cultures of Authority in Chinese Industry." *Journal of Asian Studies* 43, no. 1: 51–76.
———. 1984. "The Remaking of the Chinese Working Class, 1949–1981." *MC* 10, no. 1: 3–48.
———. 1986a. *Communist Neo-Traditionalism: Work and Authority in Chinese Industry*. Berkeley: University of California Press.
———. 1986b. "The Informal Dimension of Enterprise Financial Reforms." In U.S. Congress, Joint Economic Committee, *China's Economy Looks Toward the Year 2000*. Vol. 1: *The Four Modernizations*, pp. 630–45. Washington, D.C.: U.S. Government Printing Office.
———. 1988. "Bargaining Relationships in Urban Industrial Bureaucracies." Paper presented at the conference "The Structure of Authority and Bureaucratic Behavior in China," Tucson, Arizona, June 19–24.
Wang, Renzhi. 1982. "Set Down a Foundation, Greet a New Economic Development." *HQ*, no. 18: 67–72.
Wang, Shufan. 1979. "Specialized Cooperation Is Good." *SKDT*, no. 32: 15–22.
Wang, Yongzhen. 1981. "Economic Readjustment and the Speed of Increase." *SHKX*, no. 5: 16–18, 15.

———. 1983. "Continue to Implement the 'Six Priorities' Direction, Guarantee the Protracted Growth of the Light and Textile Industries." *JJGL*, no. 7: 12–14.
Wang, Zhengxing. 1983. "Questions on Hubei Province's Industrial Economic Results." *HCXX*, no. 1: 35–37, 16.
Weil, Martin. 1985. "China's Power Industry." *CBR*, July–Aug., pp. 17–22.
White, Gordon. 1982. "Urban Employment and Labour Allocation Policies in Post-Mao China." *World Development* 10, no. 8: 613–32.
———. 1987. "The Politics of Economic Reform in Chinese Industry: The Introduction of the Labor Contract System." *CQ*, no. 111: 365–89.
White, Lynn T., III. 1989. *Policies of Chaos: The Organizational Causes of Violence in China's Cultural Revolution*. Princeton: Princeton University Press.
Wilks, Stephen, and Kenneth Dyson. 1983. "The Character and Economic Context of Industrial Crises." In Kenneth Dyson and Stephen Wilks, eds., *Industrial Crisis: A Comparative Study of the State and Industry*, pp. 1–25. Oxford: Martin Robertson.
Williams, Philip M. 1964. *Crisis and Compromise: Politics in the Fourth Republic*. Hamden, Conn.: Archon Books.
Williamson, Oliver E., and William G. Ouchi. 1980. "Efficient Boundaries." Paper presented at Conference on the Economy of Organization, Berlin, Summer.
Wong, Christine. 1985. "Material Allocation and Decentralization: Impact of the Local Sector on Industrial Reform." In Elizabeth J. Perry and Christine Wong, eds., *The Political Economy of Reform in Post-Mao China*, pp. 253–78. Cambridge, Mass.: Council on East Asian Studies / Harvard University.
———. 1986a. "Ownership and Control in Chinese Industry: The Maoist Legacy and Prospects for the 1980's." In U.S. Congress, Joint Economic Committee, *China's Economy Looks Toward the Year 2000*. Vol. 1: *The Four Modernizations*, pp. 571–603. Washington, D.C.: U.S. Government Printing Office.
———. 1986b. "The Economics of Shortage and Problems of Reform in Chinese Industry." *Journal of Comparative Economics* 10: 363–87.
———. 1987. "Problems of Regionalization in Post-Mao Reforms." Paper presented at the Third International Congress of Professors of World Peace Academy, Manila, The Philippines, August 24–29.
Wu, Ming. 1981. "Discussing the Reorganization and Transformation of Our National Machine-Building Industry." *JJGL*, no. 6: 7–11.
Wylie, Laurence. 1963. "Social Change at the Grass Roots." In Stanley

Hoffmann, ed., *In Search of France*, pp. 159–234. Cambridge, Mass.: Harvard University Press.
Xu, Jinhua, and Yan Zengtao. 1979. "We Must Stress the Transformation of Old Enterprises." *SKDT*, no. 32: 8–15.
Xu, Lu. 1987. "Industrial Corporations." In Gene Tidrick and Chen Jiyuan, eds., *China's Industrial Reform*, pp. 281–96. New York: Oxford University Press.
Xue, Muqiao. 1981. "Readjust the National Economy, Do Comprehensive Balance Well." *XHYB*, no. 2: 77–83.
———. 1982a. "The System of Economic Management in a Socialist Country." In George C. Wang, ed., *Economic Reform in the PRC*, pp. 21–42. Boulder: Westview Press.
———. 1982b. "Throw off the Present Difficulties, Strive to Make a Basic Good Turn in the National Economy." *SKDT*, no. 4: 2–11.
———. 1982c. *Women guomin jingji di tiaozheng he gaige* (Our national economy's readjustment and reform). Beijing: People's Publishing.
———. 1986. "Put the Orientation Right on the Tortuous Journey, Notes on Reading the 3rd Volume of the 'Selected Works of Chen Yun.'" *HQ*, July 1. Translated in *Summary of World Broadcasts* FE/8326/BII, pp. 6–13.
Yajima, Kinji. 1978. "Communist China's Economic Modernization Program." *I&S* 14, no. 7: 37–52.
Yamamura, Kozo. 1967. *Economic Policy in Postwar Japan*. Berkeley: University of California Press.
Yan, Qiushi. 1980a. "In Readjustment Promote the Specialization of the Machine-Building Industry." *RMRB*, May 12.
———. 1980b. "Renovating Equipment with a Plan Is the Present Urgent Task." *JJGL*, no. 2: 34–36, 31.
Yanaga, Chitoshi. 1968. *Big Business in Japanese Politics*. New Haven: Yale University Press.
Yang, Bo. 1982. "Face the New Situation, New Problems; Light Industry Must Change Its Appearance, Raise the Level." *HQ*, no. 23: 21–24.
Yang, Hui, and Luo Qiang. 1981. "Readjustment Needs Combination, Combination Promotes Readjustment." *HCXX*, no. 4: 29–33.
Yang, Jianbai, and Li Xuezeng. 1980. "The Relations Between Agriculture, Light Industry and Heavy Industry in China." *Social Sciences in China*, no. 2: 182–214.
Yang, Yichen. 1981. "Set Out from Reality, Accurately Do Economic Readjustment Well." *JJGL*, no. 4: 5–8.
Ye, Yuansheng. 1983. "Equipment Renovation Is an Important Path for Realizing Hubei Province's Quadrupling of the Gross Value of Output." *HCXX*, no. 2: 13–20.

Yeh, K. C. 1984. "Macroeconomic Changes in the Chinese Economy During the Readjustment." *CQ*, no. 100: 691–716.
Young, Stephen. 1975. "A Comparison of the Industrial Experiences." In Jack Hayward and Michael Watson, eds., *Planning, Politics and Public Policy: The British, French and Italian Experience*, pp. 141–54. Cambridge, Eng.: Cambridge University Press.
Yuan, Baohua. 1981. "Several Questions About Our Country's Industrial Production Development." *HQ*, no. 18: 2–6.
Yue, Wei. 1983. "The Relationship Between the Whole and the Part in Economic Work." *HQ*, no. 14: 23–27.
Zelin, Madeleine. 1984. *The Magistrate's Tael: Rationalizing Fiscal Reform in Eighteenth-Century Ch'ing China*. Berkeley: University of California Press.
Zhang, Jingfu. 1982. Speech at a national meeting on enterprise consolidation. *XHYK*, no. 7: 75–80.
Zhang, Peiji. 1982. "Development of China's Foreign Trade and Its Prospects." In George C. Wang, ed., *Economic Reform in the PRC*, pp. 115–24. Boulder: Westview Press.
Zhang, Rodan. 1982. "Three Answers, Three Questions: Assessing Zhao Ziyang's Economic Report." *Zheng Ming* (Contend), no. 51: 21–24.
Zhonggong Zhongyang Wenxian Yanjiu Shi bian (Chinese Communist Central Documents Research Office), ed. 1982. *San Zhong Chuanhui yilai* (Since the Third Plenum). Vol. 1. Changchun: Jilin People's Publishing.
Zhongguo Renmin Gongheguo Guowuyuan gongbao (State Council, Bulletin of the People's Republic of China). 1980–83. Beijing.
Zhongguo Shehui Kexue Yuan. Jingji yanjiuso (Chinese Academy of Social Sciences. Economic Research Institute). 1978. *Zhongguo ziben zhuyi gongshangye de shehuizhuyi gaizao* (The socialist transformation of China's capitalist industry and commerce). Beijing: People's Publishing.
Zhongyang Renmin Guangbo Diantai Lilun Zhengzhibu Jingjizu (Central People's Broadcasting Station Theoretical Politics and Law Theoretical Department Economic Group), ed. 1982. *Xuexi jingji jianshe shitiao fangzhen guangbo jiangzuo* (Broadcast lectures on studying ten principles of economic construction). Beijing: Broadcasting Publishing.
Zhou, Chuan. 1981. "Continue to Grasp Readjustment Well." *JJGL*, no. 1: 7–9.
Zhou, Shulian. N.d. "Looking Back on 30 Years of Our Country's Economic Structure." In Ma Hong and Sun Shangqing, eds., *Zhongguo*

jingji jiegou wenti yanjiu (Investigations into problems of China's economic structure), pp. 23–55. Beijing: People's Publishing.
Zhu, Jiahua. 1985. "Explorations into the Operational Strategy of Medium and Small-Scale Enterprises." *JJGL*, no. 2: 41–43.
Zhuang, Qidong, and Kong Keliang. 1980. "The Company Should Not Exploit Subordinate Factories' Autonomy." *JJGL*, no. 9: 17–18.
Zuo, Chuntai. 1981. *Liang li er xing, xunxu xianjin: Dangxian caizheng gongzuozhong di rogan wenti* (Act according to ability, proceed in an orderly way: Certain questions in present financial work). Beijing: Chinese Finance and Economics Publishing.
Zysman, John. 1977. *Political Strategies for Industrial Order*. Berkeley: University of California Press.
———. 1978. "The French State in the International Economy." In Peter J. Katzenstein, ed., *Between Power and Plenty: Foreign Economic Policies of Advanced Industrial States*, pp. 255–93. Madison: University of Wisconsin Press.

Index

In this index an "f" after a number indicates a separate reference on the next page, and an "ff" indicates separate references on the next two pages. A continuous discussion over two or more pages is indicated by a span of page numbers, e.g., "57–59." *Passim* is used for a cluster of references in close but not consecutive sequence. Subentries are listed in page-number order rather than alphabetical order.

Accumulation, 72–82 *passim*, 89–99 *passim*, 106–7, 118, 120; disproportion with consumption, 52, 55; verticalism and, 166
Adams, F. Gerard, 289
Adjusters, 104f, 107
Agenda formation, 88–89, 103, 119
Agriculture, 51–52, 80, 82, 116f, 274; investment in, 54, 74–77 *passim*, 267; reform in, 93–94, 177–78
Alliance formation, 103, 106–7, 120, 131–32
Anhui, 104
Antirightist campaign, 75
Appeasement, 31, 42
Ashford, Douglas, 267, 299
Authoritarianism, 15–25 *passim*, 95–96, 125–26

Bailouts, 42
Balance: philosophy on, 77–78; in six priorities, 137; rationalization and, 201–2
Balazs, Etienne, 34–35
Banking system, 12, 90, 105, 273, 281, 287; and comparative systems, 19–20, 240, 297, 300; and six priorities, 97, 128–45 *passim*, 278f
Bankruptcy, 41, 259
Bargaining, 84–85, 86, 96, 99, 108, 120, 278
Barnett, A. Doak, 71, 257
Barter: in six priorities, 154; in heavy industry, 179, 186
Bauchet, Pierre, 278, 284
Baum, Warren C., 290
Beijing Review, 117
Belief system, legitimating, 34
Berger, Suzanne, 29, 184–85
Bernstein, Thomas, 266, 272
Bicycle production, 206
"Blind development," 158
Bo Yibo, 75
Bornstein, Morris, 24
Brada, Josef, 18
Britain, 236–42
Browne, Stuart, 260
Budget, state, 90, 105–6, 110–11, 119, 168, 272. *See also* Investment; Revenue
Bureaucracy, 12, 86, 222–23, 243–44, 248, 257; insulation of, 11, 15, 26,

30–43, 223; in democracies, 20, 226–33 *passim*, 240–41, 242, 300; in socialism, 22, 24, 125–26; implementation by, 32, 123–62 *passim*; strength of, 34–36; formal, 35; informal, 35; and exports, 50–51; and modes of compliance, 123–62; and heavy industry during readjustment, 177, 184–92 *passim*; and marketing, 186, 244; and rationalization, 208–17 *passim*. See also *Tiaotiao kuaikuai*
Byrd, William, 284, 287

Calder, Kent E., 184
Campbell, John C., 233
Capital accumulation, *see* Accumulation
Capital allocation, *see* Finances
Capital construction, 80f, 105–8 *passim*; in six priorities, 97, 128, 132, 136, 142, 143n, 145, 149; heavy industry and, 167–68, 176. *See also* Investment
Capitalism, 20–23, 262; comparative industrial policies and, 3, 13, 221–28 *passim*, 249; paternalism in, 42; and resource concentration, 95; "organized," 196
Caretaking (*zhaogu*), 41–42, 125, 165, 181
Cartels, 196, 217f, 291f
Caves, Richard E., 292
Central Committee: Eighth, 75; Eleventh, 80
Central government, 2ff, 12f, 31, 54, 69, 84–89 *passim*, 245–46, 276, 297; statism, 32, 33–34; and state-led demand, 92–96; and light-industry priority, 123–45 *passim*, 147, 151–52, 155, 160; and decentralization during readjustment, 134, 136, 151, 155, 162, 169; resistance to readjustment and, 169; rationalization goals, 203–5; comparative industrial policies and, 228–36, 243. *See also* Budget, state; Bureaucracy; Resource allocation; State Council; Verticalism
Chang, Parris, 268
Chao-e fen-cheng, 189–90
Chao-shou fen-cheng, 291
Chemical fibers, 65, 159–60
Chemical industry, 102, 153
Chen Pixian, 129, 173
Chen Xilian, 268
Chen Yun, 70–76 *passim*, 80–81, 97ff, 265, 270f, 273, 287
Ch'u T'ung-tsu, 258
Cloisonnement, in France, 233
Coal: exports, 49; Wuhan and, 64, 153; production slowdown, 104, 106; and capital construction cutback, 108; promotion of, 270
Cohen, Myron S., 40
Cohen, Stephen S., 278, 284f, 291f, 299
Colbert, J. B., 229, 297
Cole, Robert, 233
Combinations, 195–220, 292–95 *passim*; types of, 295. *See also* Mergers
COMECON (Council for Mutual Economic Assistance), 23
Communes, agricultural, 93–94
Communism, 21f, 37, 248, 258. *See also* Communist Party, Chinese
Communist Party, Chinese, 31–36 *passim*; party core groups, 36. *See also* Central government; *entries beginning with* Party
Comparisons, 248–49; in economic systems, 16–25, 246, 267–68; in industrial policy, 223–43
Compliance: modes of, 123–62; as bargain between administrative echelons, 131; in raw materials allocations, 152–55; positive outcomes of, 155–57; negative outcomes of, 158–62; resistance to, 163–93
Confucianism, 15, 34, 40, 235, 299
Congress, U.S., 88
Conquest, Robert, 256, 267

Consensus, 244; crisis and, 27–30, 69, 71, 83, 247; leadership succession and, 28, 30, 69, 71, 78–83, 247, 267; localism/verticalism and, 124f, 127, 131, 139, 155; comparative industrial policies and, 227, 234
Conservers, 104f
Construction, capital, *see* Capital construction
Construction Bank, 143f, 273
Consumer goods, 2, 12, 72, 112–13, 161, 274; shortage in, 54; in Wuhan, 62, 157–61 *passim*; Soviet-style development and, 77; exports, 90; popular purchase of, 90; output, 104, 123n, 157f. *See also* Light industry
Consumption, 52, 55, 69, 74, 105
Co-optation, 41, 166, 185, 289–90
Corporatism, 164f, 248; local, 124–32 *passim*, 137–45 *passim*, 152, 154f, 187, 248
Cotton, 63f, 66n, 262
Crisis, 3f, 11–16 *passim*, 26, 47–74 *passim*, 84, 96, 120, 246–47; Chinese term for, 27; and consensus, 27–30, 69, 71, 83, 247; Tongzhi Restoration and, 33; systemic, 47, 51–60, 80; oil and, 49, 69, 80, 260; perception of, 70–71, 224–27, 237–39, 247; deflationary policy response to, 105–6; comparative industrial policies and, 224–27, 237–39; "catch-up," 226
Cultural Revolution, 2, 27, 39, 47, 52, 55, 69ff, 76, 198, 243, 245; *tiaotiao* in, 59; and Wuhan industry, 61, 67f; and leadership succession, 79, 80–81; and localism, 125; raw materials in, 147, 262; mass excesses during, 204; and world trade, 261; and unemployment, 265; Mao diatribes from, 266
Culture (term), 222
Cumings, Bruce, 260, 267–68
Currency, excess, 105
Czechoslovakia, 18, 23

Dealing, on market, 184–93
Decentralization, 244–46, 256, 287; in reform program, 104–5, 169; in light-industry priority, 128, 134, 136, 151, 155, 162
Demand, state-led, 92–96
Democracies, 3, 13, 17–20, 248; redistribution in, 87–88, 103. *See also* Japan; West
Deng Xiaoping, 1, 69, 79, 97, 259; and world economy, 48; and post-Gang years, 81; and social stability, 180; on readjustment problems, 199; on Chen Yun, 265
Depression: in heavy industry, 94, 165; 1930's, 225, 227
Deyo, Frederic C., 15, 19, 23–24, 31
Dingzhe buban, 179–84
Disinvestment, 17–18, 269
Dittmer, Lowell, 258
Donation, 162; in six priorities funding, 139–40
Dong Furen, 72
Dore, Ronald, 292, 296
Dower, J. W., 299
Dyson, Kenneth, 196

East Asian NICs, 15
Eastern Europe, 18, 23–24
"Economic institutional consolidation," 15, 31
Economic Management, 55, 102, 110, 112, 219
"Economic pragmatism," 24
Economic readjustment: term, 9–11; components, 12, 194–95; basis for, 26, 30; Third Plenum reports and, 73, 265; buildup of support for, 79–83; politics at the top, 84–120; and redistribution, 87; decision for, 96–103; debates over, 99–103, 111–15; outcomes of, 155–62, 245, 274–75; resistance to, 163–93; and heavy industry at local level, 167–71; problems caused by, 197–99; comparative industrial policies and, 223–49;

timing and, 242–46; goals of, 286. *See also* Implementation; Industry
Economy, 2–4, 21–22, 261; capitalist, 13, 20–23, 42, 95; comparative systems of, 16–25, 246, 267–68; Mao's philosophy of development in, 30, 48, 77; statist, 32, 33–34, 229–33; balance in, 77–78, 137, 201–2; interdependent, 92–96, 103, 117–18. *See also* Consumption; Crisis; Employment; Industry; Reforms; Socialism; Soviet-style economies; World markets
Ehrmann, Henry W., 298f
Electricity: shortfalls in, 56, 63–64; in Wuhan, 63–64, 145–47, 264; in six priorities, 97, 128, 133, 145–47, 281
Employment, 2, 72, 98–99. *See also* Unemployment
Energy, 12; shortfalls in, 56, 63–68 *passim*, 116, 260, 263; in six priorities, 97, 128f. *See also* Coal; Electricity; Petroleum
Entrepreneurial state involvement, in economy, 229
Europe, *see* Eastern Europe; Western Europe
Evans, Peter B., 19, 269
Exchange-based mode, of social control, 21–22
Exports, 2, 12, 29, 48–51 *passim*; light industry, 48f, 51, 69, 72; heavy industry, 49, 50–51; textiles, 49, 65; consumer goods, 90

Family: and unitism, 37, 258; farms, 93–94; comparative industrial policies and, 230–31, 233, 298
Federalism, 20
Feedback, for policy change, 88–89, 103–9 *passim*, 119
Fel'dman, G. A., 76
Feudalism, 299
Feuerwerker, Albert, 257, 294
Field, Robert Michael, 261, 283
Finance and Economics Committee, 49

Finances, 2ff, 69, 84–86; industrial, 41; of international market involvements, 48; local government, 124–25, 277, 282; for six priorities, 132–45. *See also* Accumulation; Banking system; Budget, state; Foreign exchange; Investment
"Five small industries," 56, 262
Five-Year Plans: First (1952–57), 29, 61, 72, 74; Third (1966–70), 76, 266; Fourth (1970–75), 90–91; Sixth (1981–85), 117
Flanagan, Scott, 234f, 256, 258
Foreign exchange, 260; for six priorities, 97, 128, 132–45, 278
Four Modernizations, 47, 98–102 *passim*, 259
"Four Unchanges," 213–14
France, 2–5 *passim*, 13, 20f, 222–36 *passim*, 276, 278, 297; insulation in, 36–37, 233–36; verticalism in, 40ff, 126, 235–36; localism in, 127, 234–35, 248; compliance in, 131; negative outcomes in, 158–59, 284–85; losers in, 163, 165, 175–76, 184–85, 289–90; mergers in, 195n, 196, 217–18; rationalization in, 196, 291f; unitism in, 217–18, 225, 233–35, 299; crisis perception in, 224–27; bureaucracy in, 226–33 *passim*, 241, 300; consensus in, 267; banking system in, 297; family in, 298
French Republics: Third (1871–1940), 231–32; Fourth (1946–58), 232

Gang of Four, 48, 79–82 *passim*, 259, 260–61
Germany, 236–42
"Gigantism," 38
Goal incongruence, 210, 294
Gottschaung, Thomas, 275
Gourevitch, Peter, 28, 247
Government, *see* Bureaucracy; Central government; Local government
Great Britain, 19, 164, 236–42
Great Leap Forward, 70, 75–76, 81, 168

Gu Mu, 72–73, 81, 260–61
Guandu shangban, 33
Guangdong, 62, 264
Guanting bingzhuan, 109–10, 165, 168, 181, 195, 203. *See also* Economic readjustment
Guanxi, 39, 186, 188f
Guilds, 38ff
Gustafson, Thane, 178–79

Hankow, 60
Hanson, Philip, 24–25, 255–56
Hanyang, 60
Harding, Harry, 267
Hayes, Michael T., 269
Heavy industry, 1, 4, 12, 23–30 *passim*, 49–60 *passim*, 80–86 *passim*, 117–19, 247; investments in, 5, 9, 29, 53–56, 74–79 *passim*, 84, 90–115 *passim*, 135–36, 149, 190, 262, 267, 273; output, 9–11, 51–54 *passim*, 93n, 104, 106, 156; exports, 49, 50–51; "five small industries" in, 56, 262; Third Front strategy for, 61, 76, 276; in Wuhan, 62–68 *passim*, 138n, 147, 149–50, 163, 170–91 *passim*, 203, 207–8, 273, 275, 289f; revival of (1981), 103–19 *passim*, 134, 149, 161; during light-industry priority, 135–36, 138n, 147, 149–50, 163–93, 289; abandonment of, 163–93, 286; local-level, 167–71; rationalization and, 203, 205. *See also* Machine building; Metallurgy
Heilongjiang, 263–64
Hemp, 65
Henan, 104
Henderson, Gail E., 40
Hershatter, Gail, 40
Hoffmann, Stanley, 41, 298
Hong Kong, 15
Horizontalism, 37–41 *passim*, 58, 184, 192, 223, 234, 243. *See also Tiaotiao kuaikuai*
Hough, Jerry, 35, 283
Hout, Thomas M., 278

Hu Yaobang, 117
Hua Guofeng, 1–2, 48, 82–83, 172, 259, 268, 270
Huang Chengyou, 289
Hubei, 55f, 60–68 *passim*, 133–62 *passim*, 168–73 *passim*; heavy industry in, 56, 62–68 *passim*, 138n, 147, 149–50, 163, 170–91 *passim*, 203, 207–8, 262, 273; light industry in, 62–67 *passim*, 133–62 *passim*, 173, 182–83, 202–3, 207–8, 263; rationalization in, 200–208 *passim*. *See also* Wuhan
Hunan, 64, 280
Hungary, 23, 267

Ichimura, Shinichi, 289
"Ideological" form, of state, 22
Ideology, 243, 245; historical, 34; obstacles of, 76–78; for readjustment, 88, 89–90; comparative industrial policies and, 230–31
Immobility: resistance by, 170, 287. *See also* Passivity
Implementation (policy), 5, 15, 32, 244, 248, 286; bureaucracy and, 32, 123–62 *passim*; enforcement of, 136–39; abandonment of heavy industry, 163–93, 286; resistance to, 163–93; rationalization, 194–220, 248, 291–96
Imports, 2, 29, 50, 81; technology, 2, 29, 48f, 69, 128; six priorities and, 128, 132
Incomes, peasant, 94
Industrial policy, 25, 29, 40, 42; term, 2, 3–4, 11–16 *passim*, 26, 194, 254, 291; "picking winners," 14n, 163; critical features of, 16, 84; historical and belief supports for, 36; abandoning losers, 163; rationalization, 194–220; structure, regularities in, 221–22; compar 223–43. *See also* Economic rea...justment; Implementation
Industry, 1f, 33, 261; output figures,

10, 28, 52–54, 107; conditions for restructuring, 26–43; imbalance acknowledged, 27–28, 49–56 *passim*; firm management, 51n; "five small industries," 56, 262; Wuhan history of, 60–68; investment in, 61–69 *passim*; Third Front strategy for, 61, 76, 276; rationalization in, 194. *See also* Heavy industry; Light industry; Textiles

Inflation, 105, 244–45, 272

Institutions, and structure, 222

Insulation (political), 3, 15–22 *passim*, 36–37, 84, 244, 257; of bureaucracy, 11, 15, 26, 30–43, 223; in France and Japan, 36–37, 233–36; and redistribution, 87, 95; with heavy industry abandonment, 163–93; comparative industrial policies and, 233–36

Intentionality, of industrial policy, 13

Interaction modes, between states and publics, 222; comparative industrial policies and, 229–36. *See also* Bureaucracy; Insulation; Verticalism

Interdependence, in economy, 92–96, 103, 117–18

Interest groups, 18, 84–99 *passim*, 210–11, 257

International economy, *see* World markets

Investment, 12, 74–76, 87, 118f, 132, 244, 256, 266, 276–78, 297; in agriculture, 54, 74–77 *passim*, 267; in industry, 61–69 *passim* (*see also under* Heavy industry; Light industry); in Wuhan/Hubei, 61ff; petitioning for, 84–103 *passim*, 108–11 *passim*, 174; new emphases for (1982), 115–19; rationalization and, 194, 203, 205; saving state funds for, 203, 205. *See also* Disinvestment

Iron, 60–68 *passim*, 118, 150, 185. *See also* Steel

Ishikawa, Shigeru, 260

Italy, 236–42

Japan, 2–5 *passim*, 13–14, 20, 222–36 *passim*, 276, 297; Johnson on, 14n, 21–22, 36–37, 40, 126, 257, 291; insulation in, 36–37, 233–36; unitism in, 38, 217–18, 225, 233–35, 299; verticalism in, 40, 42, 126f, 234, 235–36; Wuhan occupied by, 61; localism in, 127, 234–35; compliance in, 131; negative outcomes in, 158–59; losers in, 163, 175–76, 184; MITI, 175–76, 278, 285–86, 291f, 296; "industrial rationalization policy"/"industrial structure policy" of, 194, 291; mergers in, 195n, 217–18, 291; rationalization in, 196, 291f, 296; crisis perception in, 224–27; bureaucracy in, 226–33 *passim*, 241, 300; consensus in, 267; banking system in, 297; family in, 298

Ji Dengkui, 268

Jiangsu, 62

Jie, Wenzuo, 271

Jilin, 104

Jing, Ping, 282

Johnson, Chalmers, on Japan, 14n, 21–22, 36–37, 40, 126, 257, 291

Kang Shi'en, 270

Katzenstein, Peter, 19f, 297

Keeler, John, 178–79, 248

Kesselman, Mark, 127, 234, 298

"Key-point" (*zhongdian*) projects, 116, 130–31, 139–40, 141, 280

Khrushchev, Nikita, 23

Kingdon, John W., 103, 105, 111, 269

Knitting, 65, 66n

Kokutai, in Japan, 231

Komiya, Ryutaro, 291, 297

Kornai, Janos, 42, 125, 276, 277–78

Kuai, 38, 58, 144, 152, 154f, 283. *See also Tiaotiao kuaikuai*

Kuisel, Richard F., 285

Kuomintang (KMT), 32, 61

Labor force, *see* Workers

Labor service companies, 204

Lampton, D. Michael, 85, 125
Landes, David S., 298
Lanzhou, 188
Lardy, Nicholas, 55
Leadership, 243–44; succession of, 28, 30, 69ff, 78–83, 96, 247, 267; and redistribution, 87–88; comparative industrial policies and, 226. *See also* Central government
Lee, Chae-Jin, 80, 268, 272
Leung, Chi-yan, 270, 272f
Lewek, Jim, 281
Li Renzhi, 61, 63, 136, 140–41, 171–73
Li Xiannian, 80, 81–82, 98f, 288, 292; on crisis, 71; on labor, 98, 180, 203, 257–58, 272; and Ministry of Finance, 270
Li Zhi, 168, 175
Liang Qichao, 34
Lianhe, see Combinations
Liaoning, 104, 263–64
Liberal Democratic party (LDP), Japanese, 233
Lieberthal, Kenneth, 85
Light industry, 2, 4, 12, 28–29, 48–55 *passim*, 71–82 *passim*, 103–16 *passim*, 270–75 *passim*; investment in, 5, 9, 29, 53–55, 62–69 *passim*, 74–75, 77, 84, 90–102 *passim*, 117, 128, 133–45, 153, 159, 267, 277; output, 9–11, 53, 55, 93n, 104, 156f, 263–64, 271, 274; exports, 48f, 51, 69, 72; in Wuhan, 62–67 *passim*, 133–62 *passim*, 173, 182–83, 202–3, 207–8, 277, 282, 284; raw materials for, 66, 128f, 133, 145–55 *passim*, 262; lobbying and, 85–86, 115; agricultural reform and, 94, 177–78; six priorities for, 97, 128–62 *passim*, 173, 278–82 *passim*; priority for, 123–62; heavy industry during priority for, 135–36, 138n, 147, 149–50, 163–93; rationalization and, 202–3; tax rates on, 277
Lin Biao, 81f
Lin, Cyril Chihren, 74
Lin Zili, 262, 271

Lindblom, Charles, 21f
Liu Guoguang, 56, 101, 259, 263, 271
Liu Shaoqi, 75–76
Living standards, 72–73, 82
Loans, bank, 287; for six priorities, 97, 128–45 *passim*, 278f
Lobbying, 84–100 *passim*, 108–9, 111, 115, 120, 248; Shirk on, 85–86, 269. *See also* Petitioning
Local government, 54; finances, 124–25, 277, 282; and light-industry priority, 124–62 *passim*; and heavy industry during readjustment, 167–71; and rationalization, 206–7, 214–15. *See also* Wuhan
Localism, 38; corporate, 124–32 *passim*, 137–45 *passim*, 152, 154f, 187, 248; comparative industrial policies and, 127, 234–35, 248
Lowi, Theodore, 87
Lu, Hanlin, 289
Lumber, for light industry, 66, 149

Ma Hong, 260–61; on imbalance in economy, 51–52, 57; on consensus for readjustment, 82; on debates over readjustment, 99–100; and raw materials supplies, 152; on labor, 271
Machine building, 56f, 102–8 *passim*, 116, 118, 198, 275; outputs, 9, 51, 55, 57, 63, 106, 118–19, 156f, 163, 192; in Wuhan/Hubei, 56, 63–68 *passim*, 170, 177, 180, 185–91 *passim*, 207–8, 262, 265, 275, 289f; *tiaotiao* and, 59–60, 67; agricultural tool-making in, 94; during light-industry priority, 149–50, 167, 169, 177–78, 185, 187–88, 192, 286f; "three smalls" in, 263
Macrae, Duncan, Jr., 298
Magaziner, Ira C., 278
Malenkov, G. M., 23, 255–56
Mao Zedong, 69–77 *passim*, 266; after death of, 1, 71, 76, 79f, 247, 259, 267; development conception of,

30, 48, 77; Gang of Four and, 48; on investment, 74–75, 77, 267; and world markets, 261
Market, 262; economies centered on, 21–22; Chinese and, 170, 184–93, 244; local control and, 277; in France, 284–85
Market-rational states, 22
"Market regulation," 170
Marx, Karl, 76
Marxism, 78, 262
McArthur, John H., 290
Media, *see* Press
Meiji period, 230, 232
Melnick, Diane, 260
Mergers, 195–220, 292–95 *passim*; comparative industrial policies and, 195n, 196, 217–18, 291; failure of, 209–14
Metallurgy, 102, 118; Wuhan/Hubei, 56, 67–68, 150, 189–91, 262; outputs, 156f. *See also* Iron; Steel
Meyer, Alfred G., 35
Ministry of Chemical Industry, 80
Ministry of Finance, 105, 270, 273
Ministry of Light Industry, 97, 150, 206
Ministry of Machine Building, 118; and *tiaotiao kuaikuai*, 59; during readjustment, 165, 170, 176, 181, 187, 286f; and mergers, 197
Ministry of Metallurgy, 80
Ministry of Petroleum, 80
Ministry of Textiles, 138, 160
MITI, 175–76, 278, 285–86, 291f, 296
MITI and the Japanese Miracle (Johnson), 21–22, 126
Modernization, 115–19, 256–57, 266, 275; during Tongzhi Restoration, 33; Four Modernizations, 47, 98–102 *passim*, 259; socialist, 88–89, 116, 172, 266; rationalization and, 195
Monnet Plan, 231, 285, 299
Montias, John, 18, 256
Municipal Economic Commission (MEC), Wuhan, 127n; and six priorities, 137–43 *passim*, 151, 280; and heavy industry abandonment, 173, 181, 183; and rationalization, 202–3, 207f, 295
Municipal Planning Commission (MPC), Wuhan, 277; and six priorities, 129, 139–43 *passim*, 152–54, 160f, 280; and heavy industry abandonment, 173, 177, 187; and rationalization, 207
Munro, Donald, 34, 257f

Nagy, Imre, 23
Nakane, Chie, 38, 40, 127, 234, 298f
Napoleon, 231–32
Nathan, Andrew J., 34
National People's Congress (NPC): 1978, 48, 268; 1979, 82, 172, 270; 1980, 104f, 109n, 174; 1981, 109n, 113, 117, 174; 1975, 259
Nationalist regime (1927–37), 33, 61
Nationalization, 32, 227, 228–29, 240
Naughton, Barry, 132, 179, 284; on investment, 128, 169, 256, 266, 273, 276–77, 283
Neoclassical economists, 14n
Newly industrializing countries (NICs), 13, 14–15
Ninth Plenum, 75
Nove, Alec, 19

Oil, *see* Petroleum
Oksenberg, Michel, 85
Olson, Mancur, 19, 164
"Opening to the world," 47–51
Organizational forms, 16. *See also* Bureaucracy; Central government; Combinations; Society; Unions
Ouchi, William G., 294
Outcomes: positive, 155–57; negative, 158–62
Ownership: state (of national assets), 92–96, 120; of industrial firms, 138n, 143n, 150

Party committees, local, 134
Party Congress: Eighth (1956), 74, 77; Twelfth (1982), 117, 274–75

Party Work Conference (April 1979), 81, 101, 292
Passin, Herbert, 258, 289
Passivity: resistance by, 40, 168–69, 170, 174, 179–84, 287; of petitioners, 84–100 *passim*, 248; workers and, 109, 180–83, 245
Paternalism, 125f, 165, 244–45; authoritarian, 15; and repression, 31, 41f, 183, 258, 289; industrial, 40–42, 125, 171, 183, 235, 289; bureaucratic, 124, 210, 248; comparative industrial policies and, 229, 235–36
Pempel, T. J., 184, 299
People's Bank, 105, 134f, 139, 144n, 273, 278
People's Daily: on heavy industry, 50, 100–101, 117, 175, 182; and social stability, 72; on light industry, 100–101, 117, 148ff; on growth speed, 111; on six priorities, 148ff; and *guanting bingzhuan*, 165; on abandoned construction, 179; and rationalization, 202, 215
Perkins, Dwight H., 50–51, 260
Personalism, 35. *See also Guanxi*
Petitioning, 174–75, 248; for investment, 84–103 *passim*, 108–11 *passim*, 174; for six priorities funds, 140–45; for mergers, 209
Petroleum: Cultural Revolution and, 2; and world markets, 48ff, 69; production slowdown, 49, 69, 80, 104, 106, 260; and capital construction cutback, 108
Petroleum Faction, 50, 80f, 268, 270
"Picking winners," 14n, 163
Pingheng, see Balance
Pitts, Jesse R., 41
Pizhun (approval), 41, 236
"Plan ideological" economies, 21–22
"Plan rational" economies, 21–22
Planning, 21–22; Ten-Year Development, 81, 268; comparative industrial policies and, 227, 231. *See also* Five-Year Plans

Pluralism, 20
Poland, 18, 23f, 109, 256
"Policy windows," 88, 90, 269
Politburo, 80–81
"Political closure," 15–19 *passim*, 23–24. *See also* Insulation
Politics, 4–5, 13–16, 25, 223, 243–44; opportunity in, 3, 70–83, 226; authoritarian, 15–25 *passim*, 95–96; and comparative systems, 16–25, 225, 233; consensus in, 27–30; leadership succession, 28, 30, 69ff, 78–83, 96, 247, 267; ideology, 34; at the top, 84–120. *See also* Central government; Implementation; Insulation
Politics and Markets (Lindblom), 21
Politics in Japan (Richardson and Flanagan), 234
Powerlessness, immobility and, 287
Poznanski, Kazimierz, 24
Preobrazhensky, E. A., 76
Press, 109–11, 268; on light industry, 55, 100–101, 112, 129ff, 137, 146–53 *passim*, 160; on heavy industry, 102, 113–19 *passim*, 171–77 *passim*, 189; on six priorities, 129ff, 137, 146–53 *passim*, 160, 173; on "blind development," 158; on restructuring upheaval, 181–82; on rationalization, 205, 208–9, 219. *See also People's Daily*
Producer goods: Soviet-style development and, 77. *See also* Heavy industry
Profits, 272, 277, 282, 291; heavy industry, 90, 110, 261, 275; rationalization and, 211–16 *passim*, 295; light industry, 261, 275

Qing state, 39, 294
Qingdao, 188
Quality: of industrial products/equipment, 56–57, 62–68 *passim*, 94, 116, 160–61; rationalization and, 194, 200–201

Rail line, Beijing-Guangzhou, 60
"Rational" forms, of state, 22
Rationalization, 194–220, 248, 291–96; problems addressed by, 197–99; goals of, 199–201; means, 201–3; and state goals, 203–5; procedures, 206–9; comparative industrial policies and, 239, 291
Raw materials: exports, 2, 48f; for heavy industry, 56, 149–50, 175, 179, 186–87; for light industry, 66, 128f, 133, 145–55 *passim*, 262; in six priorities, 97, 128f, 133, 145–55 *passim*, 282. *See also* Petroleum
Rawski, Thomas G., 256–57
Readjustment, *see* Economic readjustment
Red Flag, 110, 112, 205
Redistribution, 87–88, 95–96, 103, 119, 269. *See also* Resource allocation
Reformers, 104f
Reforms, 73, 104–5, 125–26, 294; in Soviet-style economies, 23–24; and heavy industry influence, 85–86; agricultural, 93–94, 177–78; and six priorities, 125–26, 148, 155; and heavy industry during readjustment, 166–70 *passim*, 179, 185, 189. *See also* Economic readjustment
Regulatory/market-rational states, 22
Reich, Robert, 164–65, 269
Reid, Donald, 289
Repression: and paternalism, 31, 41f, 183, 258, 289; and resistance, 39, 183–84; of petitioners, 95–96
Research, on textiles, 161
Resistance, 39, 163–93; covert, 40, 168–69, 170, 174, 179–84, 287; die-hard, 171–84, 193; dealers', 184–93
Resource allocation, 11f, 14, 24, 87, 125, 282; redistribution, 87–88, 95–96, 103, 119, 269. *See also* Investment; Raw materials; Resource concentration
Resource concentration, 3f, 12, 19–20, 31, 32–33, 84, 103, 120, 244, 246; and redistribution, 87; and petitioning for resources, 93, 95f, 111, 119; verticalism and, 127; comparative industrial policies and, 227–29, 239–40
Responsibility, 190, 209–11, 294
Restructuring, *see* Economic readjustment
Revenue: central government, 105, 110–11, 119, 168; local government, 124–25, 277, 282. *See also* Profits; Taxation
Richardson, Bradley, 234f, 256, 258
Ringi, in Japan, 236
Riskin, Carl, 265–66
Robinson, William F., 267
Rousseauian general will, in France, 231, 234
Rowe, William T., 256, 257
Rueschemeyer, Dietrich, 269

Samuels, Richard, J., 297
Savings, rationalization and, 203, 205
Scott, Bruce R., 290
Scott, James, 170, 183–84, 191, 287
Self-sufficiency, 58, 158, 198
Shanghai, 51, 54–55, 62–68 *passim*, 160f, 206
Shanxi, 104, 153–54
Shashi, 204
Sheahan, John, 218, 285
Shenyang, 182f, 215–16
Shirk, Susan, 85–86, 269
Shue, Vivienne, 38
Sichuan, 215
Silk, 65
Singapore, 15
Six priorities, 97, 128–32, 254; electricity in, 97, 128, 133, 145–47, 281; loans for, 97, 128–45 *passim*, 278f; in Wuhan, 128–62 *passim*, 173, 278ff
Skimming, raw materials, 150–51
Skocpol, Theda, 19–20
Social control, 21–22, 30–32. *See also* Authoritarianism; Stability, social; Verticalism

Social Science Trends, 202
Socialism, 3, 16–25 *passim*, 52, 84–96 *passim*, 221, 247, 249, 259; bureaucracy in, 22, 24, 125–26; "socialist transformation," 32; and verticalism, 41, 125; redistribution under, 87–88, 95–96, 103; modernization, 88–89, 116, 172, 266; and localism, 125; subsidies under, 141; and heavy industry during readjustment, 176–77
Society, 3ff, 30–32, 243; resistance in, 39f, 163–93, 287; comparative industrial policies and, 229–36. *See also* Consumer goods; Corporatism; Employment; Horizontalism; Localism; Social control; Unitism; Verticalism
Solidarity, in Poland, 109
South Korea, 15
Soviet Union, 23, 24–25, 77, 261, 283
Soviet-style economies, 23–25, 47, 74, 76–77; Stalinist-style, 9, 28, 56–57, 77, 80, 163, 247; in Eastern Europe, 23–24; in Soviet Union, 23, 24–25, 77; in Wuhan, 65
Specialization, rationalization and, 199–200, 293
Stability, social, 70, 84, 256–57; and light industry choice, 71–73; and worker discontent, 98–99, 109–10, 111, 118, 180–83, 204, 265, 271; and heavy industry revival, 109–10, 111; and heavy industry during readjustment, 166, 168, 180–85 *passim*; rationalization and, 203–5. *See also* Resistance; Unemployment
Stalinist-style economy, 9, 28, 56–57, 77, 80, 163, 247
Standard of living, 72–73, 82
State, *see* Central government
State Capital Construction Commission, 80
State Council, 35, 82, 97, 105–8 *passim*, 116–17, 186; "six priorities" label coined by, 128; and six priorities implementation, 133–34, 154, 158f, 254; and rationalization, 195, 203, 206, 212, 292
State Economic Commission, 12, 80, 270, 273; and six priorities, 97, 133–34, 143, 146, 154; and rationalization, 194, 206
State Machine-Building Commission, 206
State Planning Commission, 50, 80, 97, 104, 273
State Planning Conference (1979), 97
Statism, 32, 33–34, 229–33
Statistical Yearbook of China (1983), 90
Steel, 82, 108, 118, 287; in Wuhan, 60–68 *passim*, 150; in France, 290
Strand, David, 40
Strategy-led development, 15–16
Strikes, 235, 299f
Structure (term), 222
Subsidies, 42, 141
Sun Yefang, 286
Supplication: for six priorities funds, 140–45. *See also* Petitioning

Taiwan, 15
"Targeting," 14, 29, 127
Tarrow, Sidney, 298
Taxation, 55, 211–14, 261f, 277
"Technical transformation," 117f
Technology, 55, 117f; imports, 2, 29, 48f, 69, 128; in six priorities, 97, 128, 132, 134, 142–43, 145, 153–54; rationalization and, 194, 201, 202–3; Japanese economic readjustment and, 226
"Ten Great Relations" (Mao), 77
Ten-Year Development Plans, 81, 268
Textiles, 262, 270, 275, 289; outputs, 9, 65, 156ff; exports, 49, 65; investment in, 53–55, 117, 133–45; in Wuhan, 61–65 *passim*, 133–62 *passim*, 202, 207–8, 264, 280, 294; six priorities for, 128–62 *passim*; rationalization in, 202, 207–8, 294
Third Front strategy, 61, 76, 276

Third Plenum, 72f, 80–81, 88, 97, 116, 172, 265f
Thurow, Lester, 17–20 passim, 164
Tiananmen demonstrations (1989), 39
Tianjin, 40, 206
Tiaotiao kuaikuai, 38, 41, 52, 57–60, 283; in Wuhan, 67; and six priorities, 143, 154; rationalization and, 195–98 passim, 210–12
Tilly, Charles, 255
Timber, for light industry, 66, 149
Timing, 242–46
Tokugawa period, 232
Tongzhi Restoration (1862–74), 33
Totalitarianism, 125–26
Tourism, 49
Trade, *see* World markets
Training, for workers, 204
Transport: shortfalls in, 56, 116; Wuhan and, 60; in six priorities, 97, 128f
Trezise, Philip H., 291
Tsou, Tang, 79
Tsunekawa, T. J., 299

Uchi, in Japan, 233
Uekusa, Masu, 292
Unemployment, 69, 109–10, 198, 257–58, 265–66, 272f; light industry priority vs., 72, 80, 98, 271; rationalization and, 203–4, 207
Unions: trade, 39, 235, 241–42, 299. *See also* Combinations
United States, 20, 164–65; trade with, 29, 47; and France, 226; and Japan, 226, 228, 285–86, 289
Unitism, 3, 37–38, 57–58, 124, 184, 243–48 passim, 258; comparative industrial policies and, 38, 217–18, 225, 233–35, 299; and rationalization, 194–220; clashes connected with, 217–20

Value-added tax (VAT), 212
Verticalism, 3, 37–42 passim, 57–58, 223, 243–48 passim; in six priorities implementation, 124–32 passim, 137–45 passim, 152, 154f; heavy industry during readjustment and, 165f, 171, 183f, 191f; and rationalization, 194–220; clashes connected with, 214–17; comparative industrial policies and, 234, 235–36. *See also* Bureaucracy; *Tiaotiao kuaikuai*

Walder, Andrew G., 281; and labor, 40, 266; and resistance, 40, 179, 258; and paternalism, 125, 258, 289; and loans, 279
Wang Dongxing, 268
Wang Renzhi, 275
War, French and Japanese readjustment and, 225–29 passim
West, 5; trade with, 29. *See also* United States; Western Europe
Western Europe: crisis in, 27; trade with, 29; comparative industrial policies and, 236–42. *See also* France
White, Gordon, 265
Williams, Philip M., 298f
Williamson, Oliver E., 294
Wilson, Harold, 238
Wong, Christine, 125, 147, 170, 262, 277, 282, 284
Wool, 65, 66n
Workers, 245, 258, 265; organization of, 39f, 235, 241–42, 299; discontent among, 98–99, 109–10, 111, 118, 180–83, 204, 265, 271; before readjustment, 98–99, 257–58; during readjustment, 109–10, 111, 118, 180–83, 199; comparative industrial policies and, 184–85, 235, 241–42, 289–90; rationalization and, 203–8 passim, 219–20; training for, 204. *See also* Employment; Unemployment
Workers' Daily, 148
World Economic Digest, 113–14
World markets, 2, 28, 29–30, 47–51, 260–61; trade deficits, 49, 69; rationalization and, 194; comparative in-

dustrial policies and, 224–26. *See also* Exports; Imports
World War II, 61
Wu De, 268
Wu, Ming, 295
Wuchang, 60
Wuhan, 5, 35, 60–68, 127; textiles in, 61–65 *passim*, 133–62 *passim*, 202, 207–8, 264, 280, 294; heavy industry in, 62–68 *passim*, 138n, 147, 149–50, 163, 170–91 *passim*, 203, 207–8, 273, 275, 289f; light industry in, 62–67 *passim*, 133–62 *passim*, 173, 182–83, 202–3, 207–8, 277, 282, 284; six priorities in, 128–62 *passim*, 173, 278ff; rationalization in, 194, 199–215 *passim*, 219, 293ff
Wylie, Laurence, 40, 126

Xi Zhongxun, 288
Xinhua, 173
Xue Muqiao, 49, 58, 71, 79–82 *passim*, 106–7, 111–12, 273

Yajima, Kinji, 268
Yamamura, Kozo, 285–86, 289

Yan, Qiushi, 263
Yanaga, Chitoshi, 299
Yangtze, 60
Yao Yilin, 104, 272f
Yoshida Shigeru, 228
Yu Qiuli, 80, 82–83, 268, 270
Yuan Baohua, 194–95, 275

Zelin, Madeleine, 257
Zero-Sum Society (Thurow), 17–18
Zhang Jingfu, 273
Zhang Peiji, 260
Zhang Zhidong, 61, 257
Zhao Ming, 50
Zhao Ziyang, 110, 112–13, 117, 169, 272, 274
Zhaogu, 41–42, 125, 165, 219
Zheijiang, 187
Zhongdian (key-point projects), 116, 130–31, 139–40, 141, 280
Zhou Enlai, 75–76, 259
Zhu Xi, 34
Zuo, Chuntai, 266
Zysman, John, 23, 36–37, 42, 133, 184, 257

Library of Congress Cataloging-in-Publication Data

Solinger, Dorothy J.
  From lathes to looms: China's industrial policy in comparative perspective, 1979–1982 / Dorothy J. Solinger.
    p.   cm.
Includes bibliographical references and index.
ISBN 0-8047-1914-4 (alk. paper):
  1. Industry and state—China.   2. China—Economic policy—1976–   I. Title.
HD3616.C63S65   1991
338.95′009′048—dc20   91-2698
                                                                          CIP

∞ This book is printed on acid-free paper.

DATE DUE

MAR 24 1995	

UPI 261-2505 G   PRINTED IN U.S.A.